INTRACTABLE DISPUTES ABOUT THE NATURAL LAW

Intractable Disputes about the Natural Law | *Alasdair MacIntyre and Critics*

EDITED BY

Lawrence S. Cunningham

UNIVERSITY OF NOTRE DAME PRESS

NOTRE DAME, INDIANA

Sections I–VI of chapter 1 copyright © 2006 by Cambridge University Press
used with permission.

Designed and composed Wendy McMillen, set in 10.6/15 Minion.
Printed in the USA by Sheridan Books, Inc., Ann Arbor, Michigan.

Library of Congress Cataloging-in-Publication Data
Intractable disputes about the natural law : Alasdair MacIntyre and critics /
edited by Lawrence S. Cunningham.
   p.   cm.
  Includes index.
  ISBN-13: 978-0-268-02299-0 (cloth : alk. paper)
  ISBN-10: 0-268-02299-2 (cloth : alk. paper)
  ISBN-13: 978-0-268-02300-3 (pbk. : alk. paper)
  ISBN-10: 0-268-02300-X (pbk. : alk. paper)
  1. Natural law.   2. Law and ethics.   I. Cunningham, Lawrence
K428.I58   2009
340'.112—dc22

2009000208

CONTENTS

Preface   vii

List of Contributors   xiii

CHAPTER 1
Intractable Moral Disagreements   1
  Alasdair MacIntyre

CHAPTER 2
Does the Natural Law Provide a Universally Valid Morality?   53
  Jean Porter

CHAPTER 3
Moral Disagreement and Interreligious Conversation:
The Penitential Pace of Understanding   97
  David A. Clairmont

CHAPTER 4
Prophetic Rhetoric and Moral Disagreement   131
  M. Cathleen Kaveny

CHAPTER 5
After Intractable Moral Disagreement:
The Catholic Roots of an Ethic of Political Reconciliation   167
  Daniel Philpott

CHAPTER 6

Moral Disagreement and the Limits of Reason:
Reflections on MacIntyre and Ratzinger   195
    Gerald McKenny

CHAPTER 7

Ultimate Ends and Incommensurable Lives in Aristotle   227
    Kevin L. Flannery, S.J.

CHAPTER 8

The Foundation of Human Rights and Canon Law   251
    John J. Coughlin, O.F.M.

CHAPTER 9

The Fearful Thoughts of Mortals: Aquinas on Conflict,
Self-Knowledge, and the Virtues of Practical Reasoning   273
    Thomas Hibbs

CHAPTER 10

From Answers to Questions: A Response to the Responses   313
    Alasdair MacIntyre

Index   353

In a letter dated October 13, 2004, Cardinal Josef Ratzinger, then prefect of the Congregation for the Defense of the Faith, wrote to the president-elect of the University of Notre Dame, Father John Jenkins, C.S.C. In that communication Cardinal Ratzinger expressed the Church's concern about the difficulty of finding a "common denominator" for the moral principles held by all people. Recalling the Universal Declaration of Human Rights (1948) as an example of how a broad constituency once could agree on certain fundamental moral principles, the letter said that today there is an "obscuring of natural human rights." It went on to note that the Congregation was well aware of the complexity of the issue on both the theoretical and practical-pastoral levels. The Catholic Church—and here the letter quotes directly from Pope John Paul II's Apostolic Letter *Novo Millennio Ineunte*—is not attempting to impose its vision based on faith but "defending the values rooted in the very nature of the human person" (#51), a defense which the Church considers an urgent issue for all of humanity.

In light of this concern Cardinal Ratzinger requested that the University of Notre Dame (along with two other Catholic schools in the United States, the Catholic University of America and the Ave Maria Law School) undertake symposia to address themselves to various aspects of this issue. The Congregation asked for a report on plans for such activities before the end of 2005.

The year 2005, of course, brought a radical change in the Catholic Church: John Paul II died after more than twenty-six years as pope. Cardinal Ratzinger was elected to the Chair of Peter on April 19, 2005, six months after his letter was sent to the schools concerned. By that time, Father Jenkins had been inaugurated as the president of the university. Despite these changes, it was Father Jenkins's intention that the invitation given to the university be pursued.

A study committee was formed by Father Jenkins under the aegis of the chairs of the Departments of Philosophy and Theology, with the participation of Alasdair MacIntyre, to discuss the various strategies we might employ to respond to the mandate given in Cardinal Ratzinger's letter to Father Jenkins. Various approaches were discussed. We learned in due course that both the Catholic University and the Ave Maria Law School had made plans to organize symposia. We decided, after much discussion, that a third symposium was not necessary or desirable. Nor did we intend, as the letter intimated that we could, to invite non-Christians to enter into these discussions. We agreed to take a more focused approach.

The distinguished moral philosopher Alasdair MacIntyre, a member of our faculty, generously offered to revise an earlier substantive essay on the foundational problem of moral disagreements concerning natural law. We invited eight scholars to react to McIntyre's essay, either by addressing his work directly or by amplifying his argument along other but cognate paths. We agreed that the essayists should reflect on MacIntyre's essay from different disciplinary perspectives. The contributors to this volume are theologians, philosophers, civil and canon lawyers, and political scientists. All but two of the contributors are from the University of Notre Dame. When the contributors' studies were completed, MacIntyre responded with a closing essay. In that sense, the two essays by MacIntyre are "bookends" for the other contributions. Our decision to invite contributors who are not only philosophers but also thinkers from a variety of disciplines was based on the conviction that a subject of such seriousness ought to have a variety of perspectives represented.

Each contributor to this volume recognizes that many highly competent scholars in the Anglophone world have been engaged, in a serious fashion, with issues concerning the natural law. Scholars as well known as Germain Grisez, John Finnis, and Timothy George, among others, have contributed to this discussion over the years in a variety of scholarly forums. The writers in this volume are not unaware of the work of those and other scholars but have decided that we would engage directly the thinking of Alasdair MacIntyre so that the end product of the research presented here would be a tightly organized symposium not *viva voce* but in the form of a learned exchange after the model of Cardinal John Henry Newman's observation that the university is the place where "mind clashes with mind."

While the letter to Father Jenkins consistently expresses the concerns of the Congregation and the studies that the Congregation had undertaken in its own right, anyone remotely familiar with the public writings and speeches of then–Cardinal Ratzinger will recognize that the foundational moral imperatives of the natural law have been among his own consistent concerns before he issued this letter. A volume of Cardinal Ratzinger's essays and public speeches published in English under the title *Values in a Time of Upheaval* (New York: Crossroad, 2006) turns time and again to the fundamental moral underpinnings of modern politics, the nature of the state, the moral agreements possible in a pluralistic society, and the relationship of conscience and peace, as well as the identity and intellectual foundations of modern Europe. To Cardinal Ratzinger, as he insists in the preface to that little volume, these are foundational issues: "What are in fact the foundations on which we live? What supports our societies and holds them together? How do states discern their moral bases and, consequently, also the forces that motivate them to moral conduct—forces without which a state cannot exist?" These fundamental issues were also the subject of the famous exchange during this period between himself and the self-confessed atheist and Marxist, Jürgen Habermas, at the Bavarian Academy of Sciences, with a focus on the Christian roots of Europe. Their intellectual exchange was later published under the title *The Dialectics of Secularization* (San Francisco: Ignatius, 2007).

Cardinal Ratzinger was, and, as pope, is, fully aware that the foundational underpinnings of morality are not easily understood in contemporary society. He has said publicly that the concept of the natural law still echoes faintly in declarations on human rights (a subject he addressed in a speech to the United Nations in 2008), but it is today, for many, in his words, a "blunt instrument." In an important speech delivered at Subiaco, Italy, in 2005, the birthplace of Benedictine monasticism, the then-cardinal issued a challenge to secular thinkers. He noted that in the period of the Enlightenment thinkers attempted to articulate fundamental moral rights *etsi Deus non daretur* (as if God did not exist). That Enlightenment project brought forth certain principles, a few of which we find echoed in our own founding documents, but ultimately has not been successful or persuasive to many today. That challenge for contemporary thinkers is still in force, but Ratzinger is skeptical of its chances for success. In a sense, what Ratzinger is asking for both in his letter to us and to the world at large is the following: Can a persuasive case for a foundational morality be made *etsi Deus daretur*? And, of course, persuasive to whom? It is that challenge which is taken up in this book.

The very complex issues embedded in discussions about "natural rights" and "natural law" in the context of Catholic thinking become clear in the essays in this volume. The exchanges that took place between MacIntyre and his interlocutors result, not in answers, but in rigorous attempts at clarification. Readers will have to adjudicate just how much clarity has been obtained.

This volume has had a long gestation period, but we think that what appears here is a useful response to the letter's request. We offer it as a contribution to that request. After Josef Ratzinger became pope, his successor as prefect of the Congregation, Cardinal William Levada, was on our campus for a conference we held for American bishops to celebrate and to study the dogmatic constitution on revelation (*Dei Verbum*) forty years after its promulgation. In describing the letter of his predecessor, the cardinal encouraged us to continue in the path we had already begun. This volume, then, is the end result of that encouragement.

This, then, leaves us only the happy duty of expressing our thanks to the many people who have made this work possible. In the first instance, of course, we are grateful that Cardinal Josef Ratzinger had enough confidence in us to suggest we work on this important theme. We are grateful to Cardinal William Levada for encouraging our endeavor. Reverend John Jenkins, C.S.C., provided both moral and material support in bringing the work to fruition. The chairs of Theology (John Cavadini) and Philosophy (Paul Weithman) convoked the initial planning group, along with Alasdair McIntyre, who, as it would turn out, became the pivotal figure in making the project a reality. We wish to thank the anonymous reviewers who considered the manuscript. Finally, Barbara Hanrahan and her capable staff saw our work through to publication.

LAWRENCE S. CUNNINGHAM
John A. O'Brien Professor of Theology

DAVID A. CLAIRMONT, Assistant Professor of Theology, University of Notre Dame

JOHN J. COUGHLIN, O.F.M., Professor of Law, University of Notre Dame

KEVIN L. FLANNERY, S.J., Professor of Philosophy, Pontifical Gregorian University, Rome

THOMAS HIBBS, Dean of the Honors College, Baylor University, Waco, Texas

M. CATHLEEN KAVENY, John. P. Murphy Foundation Professor of Law, University of Notre Dame

ALASDAIR MACINTYRE, John A. O'Brien Senior Research Professor of Philosophy, University of Notre Dame

GERALD MCKENNY, Professor of Theology, University of Notre Dame

DANIEL PHILPOTT, Associate Professor of Political Science, University of Notre Dame

JEAN PORTER, John A. O'Brien Professor of Theology, University of Notre Dame

CHAPTER 1

Intractable Moral
Disagreements

Alasdair MacIntyre

Reading through what I have written about
moral disagreement—and more generally practical disagreement—
during the past thirty years, I find that an overall view of what such
disagreement is, and of how far it can or cannot be resolved, does
emerge, but it is one that I have never stated systematically in a single
piece of writing. This lacuna I now seek to fill. I do so in order to address a question that is of particular importance to Roman Catholics,
although not only to them.

The Catechism of the Catholic Church speaks of "the natural moral
law" and says of that law that it is "established by reason," that "it is universal in its precepts," and that its authority extends to all human
beings, determining the basis for the fundamental rights and duties
of the human person (par. 1956). Yet, if the precepts of the natural law
are indeed precepts established by reason, we should expect to find

agreement in assenting to them among rational agents. But this is not what we find, at least if we judge the rationality of agents as it is usually judged. Many intelligent, perceptive, and insightful agents either reject what Catholics take to be particular precepts of the natural law or accept them only in some very different version, or, more radically still, reject the very conception of a natural law. And these disagreements seem to be intractable. How can this be? It seems that either the *Catechism*'s account of the natural law must be mistaken or else it is possible for some theses to be rationally vindicated without thereby being able to secure the assent of all rational agents.

For the Catholic Church the problem thus presented is not only a philosophical problem. It is a problem of everyday practice, one arising in all those situations—debates about poverty, about social justice, about war and peace, about abortion and contraception, about capital punishment, and more generally about the common good—in which Catholics appeal to precepts of the natural law in arguing against positions incompatible with the Catholic understanding of human nature and the human condition. This appeal purports to be to standards prescribed by reason, and yet exceedingly often it is impotent in the face of radical moral and political disagreement. It is this practical dimension that gives to the philosophical problem a good deal of its urgency and importance.

The philosophical problem is one arising for *any* philosopher who insists that, if the principles and rules that govern the moral life are to have authority, then they must be justifiable by rational argument. So it is not only with Thomists and other Catholic thinkers, but also with, for example, Kantians and utilitarians. And all these parties are at odds with each other. If what Kantians assert is true, then what utilitarians assert is false, and vice versa. And, if what either asserts is true, then what Thomists assert is false. Yet each contending party claims the authority of reason and each remains unconvinced by the arguments mounted by their opponents and critics. So utilitarians and Kantians need, just as much as Thomists do, to explain how it is possible *both* that they can claim the authority of reason in support of their views *and* yet be unable to convince certain others who are, it seems, not only quite as intelligent, perceptive, and insightful as they are, but also quite as philosophically skillful and informed, yet who remain in radical disagreement.

I shall proceed as follows. First, I will set out Aquinas's claims for the precepts of the natural law as precepts of reason that are universally binding. I will argue, as I already suggested, that, if these claims are true, we should expect to find near-universal agreement among human beings on moral matters. Secondly, we need to examine the impressive evidence that nothing like this extent of agreement is to be found, and I will catalogue a variety of types of disagreement. Thirdly, I will outline and endorse Aquinas's account of what it is to be practically rational and move from that to asking what rationality requires of us in situations in which we confront others who are in radical moral disagreement with us. The answer proposed will be that we will only be able to enquire together with such others in a way that accords with the canons of rationality, if both we and they treat as binding upon us a set of rules that turn out to be just those enjoined by the natural law. How then do failures to arrive at agreement on those precepts occur? They occur, even the most radical of such failures occur, so I shall claim, because of a variety of failures in practical rationality which the earlier arguments now enable us to diagnose. So radical moral disagreements can after all, it may seem so far, be accommodated within the Thomistic account of natural law.

Is this the end of the matter? Not at all. For this account of the genesis of moral disagreement turns out to be itself contentious and not only theoretically. The view of reason and of what reason requires of us that informs it is at odds not only with rival accounts of practical reason advanced by philosophers, but also with views of reason presupposed in a good deal of contemporary everyday discourse. The next step therefore is to spell out one of those rival accounts. The example that I shall use is that of utilitarianism, and the next section of the essay will sketch the history of utilitarianism, as it has developed from Bentham to the present through its encounters with a series of objections to which it has constructed replies that satisfy the requirements of reason, as utilitarians understand them.

How then are we to characterize the practical and especially the moral disagreements between Thomists and utilitarians? Given the different and incompatible standards of practical rationality that each acknowledges, do we here encounter a genuine example of incommensurability? Is this a kind of disagreement that may be irremediably intractable? In the succeeding section of the essay I will argue that the answer to the second of these questions is "No" but that the answer to the third is "Yes," and I will outline a view according to which, even when the protagonists of two or more rival moral traditions do not share enough by way of premises or standards of argument to settle their agreements, one may nonetheless be shown to be rationally superior to its rivals. Finally, I will suggest how an argument might proceed that would at one and the same time show in what ways Thomistic ethics and politics might be rationally superior to utilitarian ethics and politics and yet would remain unacceptable and unconvincing to anyone committed to utilitarianism. That is, I will be trying to show that it is possible to establish that one moral standpoint may be rationally superior to others without securing the assent of highly intelligent, perceptive, and thoughtful adherents of those other points of view.

When we have reached this point, how should we proceed further? The urgent practical question will have become that of how we may most effectively find common ground with at least some of those with whom we are in continuing and irremediable disagreement. It is with a short discussion of possible strategies directed to this end that this essay will conclude.

I

What then are Aquinas's claims concerning the natural law? He argues that the first principles, the fundamental precepts, of that law give expression to the first principle of practical reason: that good is to be done and pursued and evil to be avoided. The goods that we as human beings have it in us to pursue are threefold: the goods of our physical nature, that is, the goods of preserving our lives and health from dangers that threaten our continuing existence; the goods of our animal nature, including the good of sexuality and the goods to be achieved by educating and caring for our children; and the goods that belong to our nature as *rational* animals, the goods of knowledge, both of nature and of God, and the goods of a social life informed by the precepts of reason (*Summa Theologiae* Ia-IIae 94, 2).

There are therefore several distinct precepts of the natural law, each a precept of reason directed to our common good that enjoins the achievement of one or more of these shared human goods or forbids what endangers that achievement. Notable examples are: never take an innocent life or inflict gratuitous harm; respect the property of others; shun ignorance and cultivate understanding; do not lie. To say that these are precepts of reason is to say that to violate them knowingly would be to assert "It is good and best for me here and now to act in such and such a way; but I shall act otherwise." What my actions express, if I knowingly violate the precepts of the natural law, is an incoherence that parallels the incoherence of someone who asserts "It is the case that this is how things are; but I shall believe otherwise." To say of these precepts that they are directed to the common good is to say that the goods that they enjoin are goods for each of us, not *qua* individual, but *qua* member of this family or that household, *qua* participant in the life of this workplace or that political community. And they are therefore goods that we can achieve only in the company of others, including not only those others with whom we share the life of family, household, or workplace, or political community, but also strangers with whom we interact in less structured ways.

Precepts that in this way give expression to the first principle of practical reason Aquinas calls primary precepts of the natural law. They are not derived from any more ultimate precept and therefore are known noninferentially. About them Aquinas makes four assertions: that they are one and the same for everyone, that they are unchanging and unchangeable, that they are known to be what they are by all human beings insofar as they are rational, and that knowledge of them cannot be abolished from the human heart. Each of these needs further explanation and in some cases qualification. The primary precepts of the natural law are indeed one and the same for everyone, but there are also secondary precepts that vary with circumstances. What does Aquinas mean by a secondary precept? Secondary precepts of the natural law (IIa-IIae 92, 4, 5) are those through which primary precepts find application in and to particular circumstances. A primary precept, for example, requires those in political authority to provide whatever may be necessary for the security of their community from external foes. But what is so necessary varies from one set of circumstances to another, depending on the nature of current threats and the level of weapons technology and the resources possessed by this particular community. So the application of a primary precept will often be in and through some set of legally, socially, and culturally ordered institutions which implement that primary precept through secondary injunctions. The primary precepts remain the same in every society and culture, but the socially and culturally embodied forms through which they receive expression do not.

Primary precepts are known and their authority is recognized by human beings in virtue of their rationality. But Aquinas invites us to understand this with two qualifications. One concerns the *amens*, the mentally defective or disordered human being. Such lack the use of their reason *per accidens;* some bodily impediment has prevented the actualization of their rational potentialities. So they are to be accounted rational and respected as rational, even if not aware of precepts of which the normally rational are aware, and they are not culpable for this failure (IIIa, 68, 12; IIa-IIae 46, 2). Another qualification is this: there will in the case of each primary precept be some types of case, relatively rare in occurrence, in which the application of primary precepts to particular situations raises difficult questions. A primary precept of the natural law requires us, for example, not to deprive a legitimate owner of her or his property. But what of the problematic case where "it would be harmful and therefore unreasonable to restore goods held in trust, for example, if they are claimed for the purpose of aggression against one's country" (IIa-IIae 92, 4)? Such difficult cases require a sometimes complex spelling-out of the relevant primary precept through a series of secondary precepts. And how good we are at this task of elucidation and supplementation will vary from individual to individual, depending upon how practically wise each is. So Aquinas's claim is that everyone rational does indeed know what the primary precepts of the natural law are and that they are to be obeyed, but not that everyone knows how to apply them in detail or how to translate them into some set of secondary precepts.

There is of course another way in which our grasp of primary precepts can fail. On particular occasions each of us may and all of us do allow some impulse of desire to blind us to what the primary precepts require here and now. Some strong desire proposes to us a good that is other than and whose achievement is incompatible with that of the particular good that the primary precepts of the natural law require us to acknowledge and to attempt to achieve here and now. Temporarily we allow ourselves to ignore those precepts. Failing to attend to them, we flout them, although it was in our power to attend and obey. Such failures, although endemic in sinful human life, are temporary and involve no tendency generally to deny the authority of the relevant precepts. But what then of more extended and widespread lapses?

Aquinas appeals to evidence provided by Julius Caesar—as it happens, not a reliable witness—for an example of a lapse by a whole culture: "in some reason is perverted by passion, or bad habit, or bad natural disposition; thus formerly theft, although expressly contrary to the natural law, was not considered wrong among the Germans" (Ia-IIae 92, 4). Aquinas does not tell us *how* his explanation of this failure to apprehend a particular precept of the natural law is to be understood, so that the question of how this type of cause could produce this kind of effect remains for the moment unanswered. But Aquinas does take this kind of failure to be exceptional, occurring only "in some few cases." And to note this is also to note what seems on a first reading to be a plain implication of Aquinas's overall account: that agreement in acknowledging what it is that the precepts of the natural law enjoin and prohibit and in according them authority is, if not universal, so widespread that dissent from it can be expected to be an occasional and exceptional phenomenon, always requiring special explanation. But do the facts concerning moral disagreement bear this out? They do not.

II

Consider five types of moral disagreement. The first concerns the inviolability or otherwise of innocent human life. In every culture there is of course some kind of prohibition of homicide. But there have been societies in which infanticide is regarded as a justified means for controlling family size. And Aristotle, considering the ancient Greek practice of exposing unwanted infants, so that they will die, expressed a view that was not just his own when he said that we should not allow deformed infants to grow up (*Politics* vii 1335b 19–21). In our own culture there are many who, although they would condemn the killing of a newly born child, think that a pregnant woman who decides to procure an abortion of the same infant a few months earlier, does no wrong. All these dissent from a precept of the natural law that instructs us that no active intervention intended to terminate an innocent human life is morally permissible.

A second type of moral disagreement is more general, concerning relationships between ends and means. There are those of us who hold that, if some type of action is evil, then no action of that type is morally permissible, whatever predictable beneficial consequences may flow from it. An example is the use of torture on a prisoner, something widely viewed as wrong. Suppose, however, that that prisoner very probably, even if not certainly, possesses information about planned terrorist acts, so that by torturing her or him, it is probable that the deaths of many innocent people can be prevented, and this is our only chance of achieving this good end. May we then torture that prisoner? Those who hold that a means otherwise evil cannot be justified by any end, no matter how good, are committed to answering "No." But the answer "Yes" will be given by those who hold that the goodness of an end always can and sometimes does outweigh what would otherwise be evil in the use of some means. This latter position seems to entail that no type of action is ever morally prohibited as such. For it will always be possible to envisage some set of circumstances, such that in *that* situation the evil of this particular means would be outweighed by the goodness of the end. So there is here the largest of disagreements with all those who, like defenders of a Thomistic account of natural law, or, like Kant, do believe that some types of action are forbidden as such.

A third type of disagreement concerns human sexuality and our intentions in engaging in sexual relations. That sex affords pleasure and sometimes very great pleasure is, I take it, uncontroversial. When Aquinas wishes to give an example of the reasoning of an incontinent human being (Ia-IIae 77, 2), it is the pleasure of fornication that provides him with a premise. The question is: what is the relationship between intending in one's sexual activity to beget, if possible, children for and within a marriage and intending to enjoy the pleasure of that activity? Is the latter intention legitimate when wholly divorced from the former? Here attitudes characteristic of modernity clash with attitudes central to all the great theistic traditions, and it is from different answers given to these questions that the most fundamental disagreements concerning sexuality derive.

A fourth type of disagreement hinges on the place given to certain concepts in our shared moral discourse. An example is the place given to the concepts of honor and loyalty in the lives of seventeenth-

and eighteenth-century aristocrats in Europe and twentieth-century gangsters in Chicago. These of course are not the only cultures in which concepts of honor and loyalty have been at home. But the issue is always whether considerations of honor or of loyalty or of both are or are not held to be overriding in respect of other precepts, justifying in the case of the European aristocrats the avenging of an insult by the infliction of death, perhaps in a duel, and in the case of the Chicago gangsters the assassination of informers who had betrayed their associates.

Fifthly, and in this catalogue finally, there are disagreements that derive from different and incompatible conceptions of justice. Here again just one example must serve to focus our attention. There is a moral tradition concerning economic justice, running from medieval theorists of the just price and the just wage to those modern trade unionists who have demanded "a fair day's wage" in exchange for "a fair day's work." But there are also those who, in the light of what they take to be conclusions of economic theorizing, argue that such expressions as "just wage" and "just price" cannot be given a coherent meaning and that the notion of fairness has application only in relationship to the fulfillment of contracts freely entered into, not to the terms of such contracts. This is of course only one area among a number in which conflicts between rival conceptions of justice are such that the concept of justice appears to be indefinitely contestable.

Each of the contending parties in the conflicts generated by these disagreements characteristically present us with their view as embedded in some more general standpoint. They appeal, that is, to some set of first principles that provides them with what they take to be a justification for their particular moral claims concerning the taking of human life or sexuality or economic justice. Implicitly or explicitly they ground their first principles in some account of human nature and action, and more especially in some account of how the reasons that justify actions are related to the causes of actions, an account whose truth is presupposed by their practical claims. And in the conflicts between these rival points of view appeals to the primary precepts of the natural law seem to take their place as no more than the expression of one more contending standpoint. Furthermore because each of these contending points of view has within it its own standards and mode of justification there appear to be no common, shared standards sufficient to decide between such rival claims. So at a certain point in debate between the adherents of rival views, argument gives out and is replaced by the mere and usually shrill assertion and counterassertion of incompatible first principles.

There are therefore two respects and not just one in which Aquinas's account of the natural law seems questionable when viewed in the light afforded by these facts of moral disagreement. It is not only that, if Aquinas's account is true, we should, so it seems, expect to encounter a much higher degree of uniformity in moral belief and moral judgment than we actually find. It is also that on Aquinas's account the primary precepts of the natural law satisfy the requirements of practical reason and all sets of precepts incompatible with them fail to do so. We should also expect, it may therefore seem, that in rational enquiry and debate the superiority of those precepts would generally become evident without any great difficulty. But this too is not the case. So there is a problem. It appears on the basis of the argument so far that *either* we must revise our assertions about the nature and extent of moral disagreement *or* else we must reject Aquinas's account of the natural law. Are these the only alternatives?

III

We need at this point to make a new beginning by asking to what questions Aquinas's theses about the natural law are an answer. Most obviously they answer the question "*How* is good to be pursued and evil to be avoided?" And that question presupposes a prior answer to the question "What are the goods that are to be pursued and how are we to recognize them?" So we need now to ask how this prior question is to be answered, remarking that characteristically and generally human beings first encounter judgments about goods as small children in situations in which what is for their good is sharply contrasted with what they are about to do or have just done at the immediate prompting of some desire. "Don't eat, drink, do that. It's bad for you." And the same contrast is also central when the young are later initiated into a variety of practices as students or apprentices.

Every one of us initially brings to practices in which we engage motivations grounded in our antecedent desires: we want to please our parents or teachers, we want rewards of income and prestige that excellence or at least competence in this or that activity may bring, we want to present ourselves to others in a favorable light. But what successful initiation into each particular practice requires, whether it is farming or fishing, playing football or chess, participating in a theatre company or a string quartet, house-building or boat-building, is that one should come to recognize the goods internal to that practice and the standards of excellence necessary to achieve those goods. So to achieve those goods our desires have to be redirected and transformed. And in the course of this education of the desires we learn that it is never sufficient to explain or to justify our actions by citing some desire. For the question always arises as to whether it is good for me here and now to act from this desire rather than that and what has to be explained or justified is why I in this particular situation choose or chose to act from this desire rather than that.

We distinguish, that is, between what it is good to do or to achieve and what we currently happen to want. Our reasons for action, if they are good reasons, always involve at least implicit reference to some good or goods to be achieved by acting in this particular way rather than in that. This distinction between goods and objects of desire is one that is primarily embodied in our everyday practice, including our practical discourse, and only secondarily in our theoretical reflections about that practice. And it is at the level of everyday practice that we face the question of what place to give in our lives to the multifarious kinds of good that it is possible for us to achieve. Every individual life does of course already express some answer to this question. Each of us, by living as we do, gives expression, usually implicitly and unreflectively, to some conception of how, with our characteristics in our circumstances and under our constraints, it is best for us to live. That is, we give expression to some conception of what for someone with *these* characteristics in *these* circumstances and under *these* constraints human flourishing is, just by the way in which we assign to some goods a larger place in our lives, to others a smaller place, and to some none at all. What rationality requires is that we ask what good reasons there are for taking the conception of human flourishing that has been embodied in our actions and relationships so far to be the most adequate conception available to us. And is the account of human nature presupposed by that conception true?

Aquinas argued that each of us does in fact pursue some single final end, some single ultimate good (Ia-IIae 1, 5). He makes it clear that this thesis is not incompatible with the fact that each of us does and cannot but pursue multiple ends, multiple goods. But our single final end is revealed in the way in which we organize those goods, in which good or goods it is to which we give the highest place, in what we are prepared to sacrifice for what, in our priorities. We all of us then presuppose in our practice one and the same concept of human flourishing and one and the same concept of an ultimate good towards the achievement of which that practice is directed. But we disagree, as our various conflicting beliefs and modes of life show, about what it is that we take that ultimate end to consist in, about what it is that we take human flourishing to be. So Aquinas catalogues twelve different conceptions of what the human good is, each of which would dictate a different way of life, and eleven of which he takes to be in error (Ia-IIae 2, 1–8; 3, 6; 4, 6–7). It is at this point in his overall argument in the *Summa Theologiae*, long before his discussion of the natural law, that Aquinas takes notice of the facts of fundamental practical disagreement as arising from disagreements about the nature of the ultimate human good.

We each of us then, insofar as we are rational, find ourselves compelled to ask the question of whether the particular conception of our ultimate end that we have hitherto presupposed in our activities is indeed rationally justifiable, when we compare it to alternative conceptions of that end, and to press enquiry into that question systematically. Can we expect such rational enquiry to resolve disagreement? The answer that Aquinas gives is: not necessarily.

In the opening *quaestiones* of the first part of the second part of the *Summa* Aquinas does of course advance what he—and those of us who follow him—take to be compelling philosophical arguments against a range of competing conceptions of the ultimate end of human beings and for a conception in which the imperfect happiness that is the best that can be had in this present life directs us beyond itself towards a conception of a happiness that is possible only beyond this present life in a perfected relationship to God. Did he expect such conclusions to be treated as philosophically unassailable? The answer is "No." Aquinas was well aware that it is of the nature of philosophy that no conclusion is ever treated as unassailable. "Human reason," he wrote, "is very defective in matters concerning God. A sign of this is that philosophers in their researches by natural investigation into human affairs have fallen into many errors and disagreed amongst themselves" (IIa-IIae 2, 4). Continuing disagreement is a permanent condition of philosophy.

Is it then the case that there is no remedy for such disagreement, apart from the gift of faith in divine revelation? This would be a premature conclusion, one that depended on a failure to ask what *practical* rationality requires of us by way of a response to the facts of disagreement. It is the word *practical* that is important here. Fundamental moral disagreements are indeed matter for theoretical, philosophical enquiry, just because in such moral disagreements each contending party presupposes a view of human nature for which *truth* is claimed. And Aquinas follows Aristotle in taking truth to be the aim and end of theoretical enquiry (*Metaphysics* II 993b 20–21; *Commentary on the Metaphysics* II lect. 2, 290). But disagreements concerning the truth of this or that theoretical account of the human end initially come to our attention, not directly but indirectly, at first in the form of practical disagreements, disagreements about how we ought to act here and now. It is in the course of deliberation about what to do here and now that we encounter radical disagreement, and what rationality requires is that we deliberate further with others about how such disagreement should be resolved, including among those others with whom we most deeply disagree. Why so?

IV

It is insufficiently often remarked that deliberation is by its very nature a social activity, that the central deliberative questions are not of the form "What should *I* do here and now?" and "How should *I* live?" but of the form "What should *we* do here and now?" and "How should *we* live?" Of course I always have to decide for myself how to act, but, when my relationships with others are in good order, my conclusions as to how it is best for me to act will often be one of a set of decisions, by others as well as by myself, which give expression to a common mind that we have arrived at together in our shared deliberations. Both Aristotle and Aquinas observe *that* this is so. Both are too brief in their accounts of *why* it should be so. "In important matters we deliberate with others," wrote Aristotle, "not relying on ourselves for certitude" (*Nicomachean Ethics* III 1112b 10–11). Aquinas expands a little further on this remark: "'Council' *[consilium* translating *bouli],*" he says, "means sitting together from the fact that many sit together in order to confer with one another. Now we must take note that in contingent particular cases, in order that anything be known for certain, it is necessary to take several conditions or circumstances into consideration, which it is not easy for a single individual to consider, but which are considered with greater certainty by several, since one takes note of what escapes the notice of another" (Ia-IIae 14, 3).

What Aquinas stresses is the one-sidedness of each individual's point of view and perspective and how that one-sidedness can be overcome by learning how to view this or that particular subject-matter from the standpoints of a number of others. But this remark could have been made just as aptly about theoretical as about practical thinking. Its peculiar importance for practical reflection derives from the relationship between goods and desires. I have already pointed out that we have to learn to distinguish between genuine goods and other objects of desire, but this is not something that is learned once and for all at some early stage in our lives, so that the distinction thereafter becomes easy to make in everyday life. We have to recognize that we always remain liable to suppose that we want this or that because and only because it is good, when in fact what will primarily be satisfied by our obtaining or achieving this or that is our desire for pleasure or power or money or some such.

In the opening *quaestiones* of the first part of the second part of the *Summa,* as I also noticed earlier, Aquinas catalogues a number of misconceptions of our final end. Pleasure, power, and money are all items in this catalogue, and it is important to remember that to take any one of these to have precedence in the hierarchical ordering of our goods is not only to make an intellectual mistake, but also to yield to a practical temptation presented by desire, a temptation that often presents itself in subtle and disguised forms. Indeed, even when the good that we are pursuing is a genuine good, we may be unable to recognize that we are pursuing it not so much because it is good as because its achievement will satisfy our desire for, say, power. This is when we most need the ruthless correction of our judgments by others who can see in us what we cannot see in ourselves, and that is why deliberation not conducted in the company of such others is deliberation on which we would be unwise to rely. We should always therefore treat solitary deliberation as peculiarly liable to error.

Of course others are sometimes a source not of deliberative correction, but of deliberative corruption. We need from others, as they need from us, the exercise of the virtues of objectivity. Lacking that objectivity, others may reinforce our phantasies and collaborate in our misconceptions. So it is not just that deliberation will fail unless it is social, but also that the social relationships in question have to be governed by norms of objectivity. And we can only hope to resolve deliberative disagreements rationally with others who agree with us in respecting certain norms of objectivity. Yet at this point we confront another difficulty.

V

Deliberation, as Aristotle asserted (*Nicomachean Ethics* III 1112b 13–14) and Aquinas repeats (Ia-IIae 14, 2), is about means and not about ends. When we deliberate about what means to adopt in order to achieve some end, we take for granted, for the moment at least, that this particular end should be our end, that it *is* the good to be pursued by me or by us here and now. We may of course pause and ask whether this is indeed so, but, if we do, it will be because we are now considering the achievement of this particular end, this particular good, as a means to some further end, either a means that will be causally effective in producing that end, as traveling across the Atlantic is a means to arriving in Paris, or a means that, as a part of some whole, plays its part in constituting that whole, as moving my pawn is a means to implementing a winning strategy in a game of chess. Debate about means, disagreement about means, always presupposes agreement about the immediate end to which means now have to be chosen. And although, as I have just noted, that immediate end can itself be considered as a means to some further end, and therefore provide subject-matter for deliberation, there is one end that by its very nature can never be a means, namely the ultimate end, that which provides all our practical reasoning with its first premises.

That end, therefore, *that* good can never be subject-matter for deliberation. But, if this is so, what I said earlier must now seem questionable. For I asserted on the one hand that, following Aquinas, I was going to consider moral disagreement as rooted in disagreements about our ultimate end and I proposed to show that such disagreement is to resolved, if at all, through participation in the rational deliberations of everyday practice. But now it emerges that, on Aquinas's view—and I also take that view—practical deliberation is and must be concerned with means and not with ends *qua* ends, and therefore not with our ultimate end. So how is it possible for engagement in deliberation to involve reflection upon our ultimate end, whether in agreement or disagreement?

Here we need to consider what it is to have practical knowledge of our ultimate end. We do not begin, as theoretical enquiry does, with some partly articulated, highly general conception of that end that can be stated in propositional form. It is rather that we begin by discovering a directedness in our particular actions and in our particular deliberations, so that we find ourselves inclined, first by nature, then by habituation acquired through education by others, to move towards certain types of goal, ordered and understood in certain specific ways. A good deal therefore turns on how we are educated into good or bad habits, including the habit of recognizing what it is that has been inadequate in our education so far and finding resources to correct such inadequacy. What should prompt us to undertake such self-questioning is precisely the discovery of disagreement with others as to whether this or that particular judgment or action, choice or project, is or was the best to undertake in this or that particular set of circumstances.

Moral disagreement therefore has a positive function in the moral life, that of stimulating us to reflect upon the sources of our immediate practical disagreements, by identifying the immediate premises from which those disagreements derive, and, if necessary, the further chain of reasoning that led us to argue from these particular premises about this particular situation. Some of our disagreements of course turn out to be relatively superficial, concerning, say, the character of our immediate situation. (This does not mean that they will always be easy to resolve.) Others may derive from rival understandings of this or that particular virtue: we disagree about what courage, say, or justice requires of us. But some of our disagreements, and these the most basic, turn out to derive from rival and conflicting conceptions of the ultimate human good, rival views of the kind of direction in which our lives should proceed and of the place that a variety of goods should have within the overall pattern of our lives. So theoretical disagreements about the nature of the end of human life emerge from immediate practical disagreements in the context of shared deliberation. It is indeed only as they emerge in this way that their practical significance is clear. The practical need to resolve our deliberative disagreements compels us to turn to questions of a theoretical kind, but those questions, although theoretical, now also have practical import. So long as our shared deliberations proceed towards agreed conclusions with only incidental and resolvable disagreements, for so long practice can remain innocent of theory. But when disagreements turn out to be systematic and irresolvable in the context of immediate deliberation, then the identification of their character, let alone any attempt to resolve them, has to involve a resort to theoretical enquiry. Practice itself now requires us to engage with theory.

VI

When we are on particular occasions confronted by so far irresolvable disagreements that arise out of shared practical deliberation, but extend beyond it to questions about the nature of the human good, we always have to face the possibility that shared deliberation with these particular others will no longer be possible. A community that has hitherto been able to participate in joint rational decision making may be fractured by such irresolvable disagreements. It may no longer be possible for its members to arrive through shared practical reasoning at a common mind about how it is best for them to act together. Instead they will have to base their communal decision making either on inherited patterns of authority endowed with nonrational legitimacy or on some implicit or explicit social contract whereby individuals and groups, each trying to maximize their own advantage, arrive at some arrangement about allocations of costs and benefits. In either case it will be inequalities of power that determine the outcomes of decision-making processes. Power rather than practical reason will now have the last word. Is there then any way of avoiding these consequences of radical disagreement? How does practical reason require us to act when we confront the possibility of such consequences and their concomitant evils?

Practical reason requires of us, when we do encounter systematic and apparently irresolvable disagreement with our own point of view, that we do not assume that we are in the right, that it is *our* claims that are well grounded and *our* account of human nature that is true. We have initially no grounds for so judging. It may be that we are in the right or that those who hold the opposing view are in the right or that neither of us is. We need therefore to resort to enquiry as to what the truth about these matters is, in company with those others who hold opposing views. In so doing two crucial truths about the human good immediately become evident.

They are that no account of the human good can be adequate that is not vindicated and sustained by continuing enquiry that takes truth to be its end and good, and that therefore the good of truth must be a constitutive part of the human good. Shared participation in the practice of enquiry presupposes at least this measure of agreement about the human good. The conception of truth that is relevant here is that which Aquinas identified by the expression *adaequatio rei et intellectus* (*De Veritate* I, 1): the adequacy of a mind to a subject-matter about which it enquires and of that subject-matter to that mind.

Truth, that is, is a relationship to be achieved between a particular intellect and some object about which it judges, a relationship that satisfies two conditions: first, that how the thinker conceives of the object has become identical with how that object is and, secondly, that the thinker conceives of the object as she or he does, because and only because that is how the object is. For agents to move towards truth thus understood they will have to discipline themselves, so that they do not project on to the object of their thought their own antecedent thoughts or hopes or fears or needs or purposes, so as to achieve a ruthless and difficult detachment from inertia and wishful thinking and phantasy. And such progress towards truth can be achieved only if three conditions are satisfied.

First, we have to accord to the good of truth a place that does not allow it to be overridden by other goods. I do not of course mean by this that the pursuit of truth always takes precedence over all other types of activity. That would be absurd. There is a time to enquire and a time not to enquire, but instead to catch fish or to sing the blues or whatever. Enquiry has to find its due place, a place that varies with circumstances. I do mean that a more adequate understanding in respect of truth is always to be preferred to a less adequate, no matter how profitable it may be to remain with the less adequate or how painful it may be to exchange it for the more adequate. It is this kind of respect for truth that natural scientists endorse, when they insist that the misrepresentation of data or the ignoring of relevant data may justify the expulsion of an offender from the scientific community.

Secondly, however, for those of us for whom practical disagreement has made it necessary to engage even minimally in theoretical enquiry, enquiry has to find *some* continuing and significant place in our lives. If such enquiry requires of those who engage in it conformity to certain rules, then we will have to make those rules our rules. If the goods of such enquiry cannot be achieved without the acquisition and exercise of certain virtues, then we will have to make those virtues our virtues. Moreover since practical and theoretical rationality both require us to be alive to the dangers of inconsistency—much more needs to be said about this; I shall not say it here—we will have to make sure that the practice of those other rules and virtues which we acknowledge in our lives is consistent with the practice of the rules and virtues of enquiry. So engagement in the ethics of enquiry, without which our response to ongoing disagreements with others about the human good will be less than rational, commits us to agreement with those others, insofar as they and we are both rational, concerning the rules and virtues of enquiry.

Thirdly, we will not however be able to do and be that which we are thereby committed to do and be, unless we have been able to become disinterested, that is, to distance ourselves from those particular material and psychological interests that are always apt to find expression in those partialities and prejudices that are nourished by our desires for pleasure, money, and power. For those partialities and prejudices are apt to distort our thinking and always most effectively so when we ignore or are self-deceived about their influence.

What is necessary in order to counter that influence is a form of intellectual and moral asceticism, both in our thinking and in the ways in which we invite others to assent to our theses and arguments. We need to avoid allowing our own thinking to give expression to our prejudices and to abstain from a rhetoric that is designed to move others, not by the reasons adduced, but by the passions to which the utterance of those reasons gives expression. But, if we are to achieve this kind of disinterestedness our relationship to those with whom we are engaged in shared argumentative enquiry will have to be governed by norms that afford to each participant the best opportunity for considering the rival theses and arguments that have been presented impersonally and impartially. What norms are these?

It is clear first of all that I will be unable to consider and to respond to your arguments impartially and impersonally, if I have good reason to fear present or future harm from you or from others, should I disagree with you. And for us to be able to engage in shared enquiry, so that my arguments and yours contribute to our common end, you too must have good reason to be assured that you are secure from harm or the threat of harm by me. It follows that a precondition of rationality in shared enquiry is mutual commitment to precepts that forbid us to endanger gratuitously each other's life, liberty, or property. And the scope of those precepts must extend to all those from whom we may at any time in our enquiry—and it is a lifelong enquiry—need to learn. So the precepts by which we will be bound, insofar as we are rational, will forbid us ever to take innocent lives, to inflict other kinds of bodily harm on the innocent, and to respect the legitimate property of others. But these are not the only types of precept whose authority must be recognized as a precondition for engagement in rational shared enquiry.

If I am to engage with you in shared rational enquiry, we must both be assured that we can expect the other to speak the truth, as she or he understands it. There must be no deceptive or intentionally misleading speech. And each of us must be able to rely upon commitments made by the others. We must not make promises, unless we have good reason to believe that we will be able to keep them, and, when we have made such promises, they must be treated as binding. And even this is not all. If we are to pursue enquiry within our community through extended periods of time, we will have to make provision for the security of our communal life from both internal and external threats, by assigning authority to some fit individual or individuals to do what is required for its security. But we need go no further than this to recognize that the set of precepts conformity to which is a precondition for shared rational enquiry as to how our practical disagreements are to be resolved have the same content as those precepts that Aquinas identified as the precepts of the natural law. And it is not only in respect of content that the two sets of precepts are one and the same. For the precepts conformity to which is a precondition of reason-informed practical enquiry also share other characteristics that belong to the precepts of the natural law.

First, they are universal in their scope. There is no one with whom I may not find myself in the future a partner in deliberation concerned with some good or goods that we have in common. Therefore there is no one with whom my relationships can be in violation of these precepts. Secondly, those precepts are exceptionless. They state the necessary preconditions for *any* cooperative rational enquiry, and to make an exception to them is *always* going to present some kind of threat to the possibility of such enquiry. Thirdly, they are one and the same for everyone. And, fourthly, just because they are preconditions for rational enquiry we do not acquire our knowledge of them as a result of enquiry. They are not findings or conclusions inferred from some antecedent set of judgments. It is rather the case that in adopting the attitudes of rational enquiry we discover that we have already—implicitly, characteristically, rather than explicitly—had to accord them authority. They cannot but be presupposed and are therefore the necessary starting point for any enquiry that pursues the truth about goods or the good in order to achieve goods or the good. They are in this way first principles for practical reasoning. The precepts conformity to which is required as the precondition for practical enquiry *are* the precepts of the natural law.

Since those precepts as the first principles of practical reasoning cannot be justified by presenting them as conclusions inferred from premises, they cannot be supported by any theoretical argument, including of course the argument of this essay. What theoretical argument can aspire to show is that they *are* so presupposed and that practice which does not presuppose them fails in rationality. And the theoretical argument of this essay is designed to support this conclusion by showing that the facts of moral disagreement do not in fact afford us grounds for rejecting the authority of those precepts, understood as Aquinas understood them.

Let me recapitulate the main heads of that argument. It began by our noting that, when confronted by some immediate disagreement as to what you or I or we should do here and now, reason requires us to ask who is in the right, and the argument then proceeded by our further noting that, if we are to enquire effectively who is in the right, we must do so in the company of others and more especially of those others with whom we are in disagreement. We next remarked that what such deliberative enquiry sometimes discloses is that practical disagreement about what to do here and now derives from some underlying disagreement about the nature of the final end for human beings. So in order to answer questions posed by practice enquiry has to become theoretical and systematic. But it was then argued that it is a condition of the rationality of shared enquiry that the social relationships of those engaged in it should be structured by certain norms, norms that find their expression in the primary precepts of the natural law.

Each stage in the sequence of this argument corresponds to some point at which reason may fail in those sequences of conversation and action that are the sequels to the identification of some fundamental moral disagreement. We may first of all fail to ask who is in the right in our initial disagreement over what is to be done here and now, simply taking it for granted complacently that we are, and deploying our further arguments to support this conclusion. Or we may ask who is in the right, but suppose unthinkingly that the resources that each individual has with herself or himself for answering such questions rationally are adequate and so never pause to consider the social dimensions of deliberative and other enquiry. Or we may recognize those dimensions and yet be so moved by, for example, our desire to triumph in the argumentative debate, that we violate one or more of the preconditions of effective rational enquiry.

Each of these types of failure will be apt not only to perpetuate the initial disagreement, but also to generate further disagreements. What the outcome is on particular occasions will depend in key part on the distribution of power among the particular contending parties. For insofar as the social relationships between those who disagree are not governed by the norms of reason, they will be open to the solicitations of pleasure, money, and power. And of these it is power that will decide the outcomes of social conflicts, although money and pleasure will often act as the agents of power or the masks of power.

Consider all those situations in which to hold one moral view rather than another will be psychologically more comfortable, more pleasing, or will be more acceptable to those who will determine how I am to be financially rewarded, or will render me less dangerous, less of an obstacle to those who have it in their power to determine my future in some nontrivial way. No one can of course allow to herself or himself or to others that his or her present sincere moral judgments are determined not by the good reasons that there are for holding those judgments to be true, but by the influences of pleasure, money, and power. But we recognize easily enough in certain others, both in the present and in the past, and sometimes in our own past selves, that what they now take or what we or they have in the past taken to be excellent reasons for judging such and such to be the good now to be pursued were held to be excellent reasons only because of the unacknowledged persuasions of pleasure, money, or power. The outcome of these nonrational persuasions may be the acquisition or the sustaining of beliefs that involve us in moral disagreement and conflict with others. Or they may instead bind us to others in firm, but nonrational agreement. And whether the outcome is agreement or disagreement will depend on the contingencies of the particular situation. It is disagreement that I have treated in this essay as problematic. But moral and social agreements arrived at only or primarily because of the seductions and threats, the hopes and fears, that are generated by pleasure, money, and power will exhibit failures in practical rationality of a sometimes more dangerous kind than disagreements generated by those same seductions and threats, hopes and fears.

What then am I claiming? I have advanced an argument designed to show that Aquinas's account of the precepts of the natural law, far from being inconsistent with the facts of moral disagreement, provides the best starting-point for the explanation of these facts. It is not accidental that the treatment of the natural law in the *Summa* is immediately preceded by an Augustinian discussion of sins and vices, in which sins are characterized as "transgressions of reason" (Ia-IIae 73, 2) in the context of a complex account of human evil. So the questions that next arise for the reader of Aquinas's text are: In what way are sins transgressions of reason? And what are the precepts of reason that sins transgress? And it is these questions, I believe, that Aquinas proceeds to answer by advancing his account of law in general and of the natural law in particular. Yet now a still further question arises. Is the argument so far in fact adequate to resolve radical moral disagreements? And the answer is certainly "No." Does this mean that the argument fails? To this I also want to say that the answer is "No." But how can both these answers be defended? I begin by considering why, when the argument so far has been fully spelled out, disagreement remains intractable.

VII

Consider someone—or a set of someones—who have been brought up from childhood to believe that it is their duty to promote the happiness of others and whose feelings and dispositions motivate them to act in accordance with this belief. To them it seems *obvious* that it is always better to make two people happy rather than one and three rather than two. And, because they have also been brought up to believe that, except for special reasons that hold for some particular types of case, fair distributions are equal distributions, they also find it *obvious* that in the distribution of happiness everybody should count for one and nobody for more than one. When therefore at some later stage in their lives, they encounter the theory of utilitarianism, they recognize it as a philosophical theory that makes explicit and systematizes their own prephilosophical beliefs. But now they have to ask what kind of utilitarian they are to be.

For utilitarianism names not a single theory, but a tradition of thought which takes as its starting-point Bentham's trenchant declarations, but has undergone many modifications and revisions. Three closely related central theses define that tradition. First, actions are to be judged by their consequences. Secondly, agents are taken to act rightly when, out of the alternative courses of action open to them, they choose that course of action which will predictably result in greater happiness than will any of the alternatives, that course of action which will maximize utility. And, thirdly, there is a standard by which the happiness or utility that will be or has been produced by this action can be compared with the happiness or utility that will be or has been produced by that, so that we can tell whether it is greater, lesser, or the same. How these three theses have been understood has changed considerably during the history of utilitarianism.

So far as the first is concerned, one central issue concerns the place of rules in utilitarian moral theory. When we speak of judging actions by their consequences, should we be thinking of particular actions performed on particular occasions or instead of types of action? Do we ask on each particular occasion which action should I now perform, or do we ask what set of rules should I follow in deciding what to do? If the latter, then it is the consequences of following this rule rather than that that are to be evaluated. And, since it is in practice impossible for individuals to predict and evaluate the consequences of their proposed actions on each occasion on which they are about to act, it is evidently necessary that utilitarians, like the rest of us, should for the most part be guided by rules. Yet, if on some occasion we have had to conclude that, were we now to follow the relevant rule, then our action would be less productive of happiness than it would be, if we broke the rule—even when, in comparing the utility of obeying the rule with that of breaking it, we have allowed fully for the utility that derives from sustaining respect for rules that are generally beneficial—then it is evident that on a utilitarian view we would act wrongly, if we did not break the rule. And, since we can never exclude the possibility of such situations occurring, no rule binds us unconditionally and unqualifiedly.

There are of course many people who from lack of knowledge or for some other reason are bad at predicting the consequences of their actions. And, if such people believe that some rules *are* unconditionally and unqualifiedly binding, then it may be that they will act better from a utilitarian point of view than they would, if they allowed themselves to be open to the possibility of from time to time breaking one of the rules that they normally obey. So it may be from a utilitarian point view good that such people should not be utilitarians. And this is not in the least paradoxical.

So far as the second thesis is concerned, the crucial questions are about the nature of happiness. Bentham took happiness to consist in the presence of pleasure and the absence of pain and he understood both "pleasure" and "pain" as the names of types of sensation, sensations that vary in intensity, duration, and the like. We are thus able, even if only roughly, to estimate the quantities of pleasure and pain that our actions will produce. John Stuart Mill agreed with Bentham that the standard of right action is to be defined with reference to the greatest happiness of the greatest number, but argued that pleasures differ in quality as well as in quantity, distinguishing higher pleasures—those that derive from the exercise of our intellectual and aesthetic powers—from lower pleasures, those that derive from the satisfaction of bodily appetites.

Mill's discriminations at once raised the question of how different types of higher pleasure are to be compared and weighed. And from then on the question of what we are to mean by happiness became inseparable from the question of what standard it is by which we are to estimate happiness as greater or lesser, so as to give determinate meaning to the notion of the greatest happiness of the greatest number. Some argued that priority should always be given to preventing, ending, or alleviating pain rather than to promoting pleasure. More recently some utilitarians have argued that what should be compared are not pleasures and pains, but the satisfaction of preferences. That action is right which maximumizes preference satisfaction. And then there are those for whom some such notion as "greater or lesser quality of life" is to be used in evaluating actions and states of affairs, adding to the wide range of possible formulations of utilitarianism (see on this James Griffin, "Modern Utilitarianism," in *Contemporary Political Theory*, ed. P. Pettit [New York: Macmillan, 1991]).

Yet what we need to focus on are not so much these internal disagreements and the extent to which they have been resolved as the continuing agreements that are basic to utilitarianism. For, no matter how we understand the notion of happiness, and no matter what standards we employ in deciding whether one state of affairs is or is not more satisfactory than another in respect of happiness, it is evident that the maximization of happiness will on occasion require the breaking of what are taken to be otherwise beneficial rules. Two examples will suffice. Taking into account the happiness of every member of the relevant set of individuals, we might well be compelled to conclude that the lives of some elderly people, suffering from various painful and incapacitating ailments, should be terminated, thus not only putting an end to their suffering, but also relieving their children of the burden of looking after them. Or, in the case of those who would find it difficult to go on living worthwhile lives, if they knew certain facts, it might be difficult to avoid the conclusion that we should lie to them about those facts.

Spell out such examples any way that you will, with as many qualifications as you like, and you will find that there are cases, not merely possible, but actual, in which consistent and clearheaded utilitarians will have to approve the intentional killing of the innocent and the intentional utterance of lies. And these are stark instances of the utilitarian rejection not only of conventional moral judgments, but also of precepts of the natural law. Suppose that in the light of such examples we deploy the argument that I advanced earlier, contending that a commitment to the precepts of the natural law is presupposed by genuinely rational deliberation between those engaged in moral enquiry from very different standpoints. How are utilitarians going to reply?

They will have no difficulty in agreeing both on the importance of deliberation with others and on the need for those who participate in such deliberation to be committed to and to be known to be committed to a set of moral principles that enable all the participants in such deliberation to express themselves freely. But they will understand the set of required principles very differently, and they will do so because their reason for engaging in such deliberation will derive from their utilitarian first principle, that which requires them to try to achieve the greatest happiness—no matter how understood—of the greatest number. That is to say, they will be committed to engage in deliberation with others who hold moral views incompatible with their own only insofar as doing so is compatible with their utilitarian aims. Their participation will be qualified and conditional. In the course of such deliberation they may well be prepared on occasion to revise some of their secondary principles, if by so doing they will be able to bring about some overall increase in happiness or welfare. But their unconditional commitment to their first principle will not be open to question.

If it is urged upon them, that a merely conditional and qualified commitment to the precepts necessary for shared deliberation does in fact mean that they are in this respect at least exempting their own first principle from rational scrutiny by others engaging in deliberation with them and that to do so will result in a less than wholehearted commitment by those others, they will be able to make a twofold response. First, they may simply accept these consequences, arguing that nothing worthwhile—worthwhile, that is, in their terms—that might issue from such deliberation will be affected. And, secondly, they may remark that, no matter how firm anyone's initial commitments to shared deliberation, aimed at achieving a practical consensus, may be, it is always possible and often enough the case that there will be a breakdown in the ongoing conversation, and that at that point further deliberation will turn out to be fruitless. Everyone, they may say, will have some point at which they judge that there is nothing to be gained by further deliberation. Everyone's commitment is therefore limited and utilitarians are no different from anyone else.

Here then is a type of moral disagreement that seems to be genuinely intractable, not to be resolved by further reasoning. Does our recognition of this disagreement mean that we should no longer accept the argument about the natural law that I advanced earlier? And how more generally should we respond to that recognition?

VIII

To say that the disagreements between utilitarians on the one hand and Thomists or, more generally, Catholics on the other are not to be resolved by reasoning is ambiguous. It may mean that there are no arguments that can compel agreement between the two contending parties, that there is no way in which one party can evidently defeat the arguments of the other by appeal to some set of standards that both contending parties and neutral observers share. And this is true. But it may also mean that there is no way of showing by means of argument which, if either, is in the right. And this, so I shall argue, is false. What is true is that there is no set of neutral standards, equally available to and recognizable by the protagonists of any party, by appeal to which one view can be shown to be true and the other to be false. Hence it may seem that here there is indeed a case of incommensurability. But such apparent incommensurability does not leave us resourceless.

Begin by spelling out further the nature of the disagreements between the two sides. First, it is both insufficient and misleading to think of such disagreements as constituted merely by two rival and incompatible sets of assertions and denials. Those assertions and denials are answers to questions, questions asked and answered by all human beings, questions always posed and formulated in the idioms and out of the linguistic and conceptual resources of some particular culture. They concern how it is best for us to live, by what standards we should evaluate our lives, and to what norms we should give allegiance in our various activities. But such questions are never answered once and for all. Even the most impressive answers are from time to time scrutinized, criticized, and reformulated, as too are the questions. So out of such processes of criticism and revision, projects of practical enquiry are set on foot, projects that may flourish over extended periods of time, at each stage of which those engaged in the enquiry will both build upon and subject to their own criticism what they have inherited by way of judgments, insights, and arguments from their predecessors, thus setting the scene for successors who can in turn be expected both to build upon and to criticize the present formulations of both questions and answers. A particular practical and moral standpoint, formulated as a set of assertions and denials, always needs to be understood as one moment in the history of an ongoing tradition of philosophical and moral enquiry. So it is with Thomism and so it is with utilitarianism.

Each, that is to say, has a history during which it has confronted a range of objections to its central theses, some from within and some from outside its own tradition, and responded to these by revising its claims. Each has to be evaluated not only in terms of its present theses and arguments, but as an ongoing critical enterprise. When two or more such traditions confront one another as opponents, it is often enough the case, as it is with Thomism and utilitarianism, that each tradition has internal to it its own standards of judgment and that the protagonists of each appeal to their own standards in evaluating the claims and the criticisms of the rival traditions. Each group of partisans then take themselves to have successfully responded to the criticisms of the other and neither finds grounds for treating its own claims as having been put seriously in question, let alone refuted. It is this situation that is apt to lead observers to conclude that here we have a clash of incommensurable standards and values and so an *ultimately* intractable disagreement. If, however, we instead consider the issues not as external observers, but from within the standpoint of each tradition—something that in the case of a tradition that is not our own requires a difficult exercise of the philosophical and moral imagination—some other relevant considerations come into view.

For insofar as each enquiry is a genuinely rational enquiry, those who participate in it are bound to ask—and we who have imaginatively identified with their standpoint, at least for the moment, are also bound to ask—just how successful by their own standards their tradition has been and is at resolving the various issues that have arisen and do arise for it, issues that are problematic by its own standards and in its own terms. And, if they or we were to conclude that there are certain problems that are inescapable for it, they or we would need to ask just what resources this tradition affords for the resolution of those problematic issues. Suppose then that with regard to some particular set of problems they or we were forced to conclude after searching enquiry that this tradition was resourceless in the face of those problems, how then should they and we as rational enquirers proceed? An obvious first step would be to ask what resources other traditions of philosophical and moral enquiry might have, resources both for resolving that particular set of problems and for explaining why, within the constraints imposed by their tradition, those problems are and will remain unsolvable. Were they and we to discover that problems of sufficient gravity—again by their own standards—were insoluble within those constraints, they would have sufficient reason not only for passing a negative verdict on their own tradition, but also for asking whether the other tradition that had provided them with this understanding might not also be able to provide adequate resources for the solution of the problems that had baffled them. The protagonists of such an other tradition, one that claimed to possess the relevant intellectual and moral resources, would be making the claim: "If the central theses that are asserted within *our* tradition are true, then we should expect, given the understanding that we have of your tradition, just those problematic issues to arise for enquirers within your tradition that have in fact arisen and we should also expect that, given our understanding of the resources of and constraints imposed upon enquiry by your tradition, the problems arising from those issues will have to remain insoluble for enquirers within your tradition. So here is some confirmation at least of the *truth* of the central assertions advanced within our tradition. And their truth will be further confirmed insofar as we are able to provide just the kind of understanding of those problems and issues that enables us to solve and to resolve them."

So on occasion one tradition can advance and may perhaps be able to justify a claim to superiority over some rival tradition in respect of both rational justification and truth. To recognize that one thinks and speaks out of a particular tradition of enquiry with its own canons and standards and its own history of intellectual progress is not then to condemn oneself inescapably to some version of relativism. Yet it is also important that the adherents of a particular defeated tradition may in fact fail to recognize when and how their tradition has by its own standards become able to proceed further with problems that are inescapable for it. External observers who are able to identify imaginatively with their standpoint may turn out to be more successful than they themselves are or can be at identifying and diagnosing the nature of their predicament. Indeed the very constraints that disable them in their approaches to those inescapable problems may operate so as to disguise that predicament from them. So they will also be unable to recognize their need for those resources that only a rival tradition had been able to provide.

We can, that is to say, compare two or more incompatible and competing traditions as more or less successful traditions of enquiry. And, if one of those competing traditions were to be able both to make progress in solving its own problems and also to identify and explain the failure of its rivals to solve their problems, then we would under certain conditions have sufficient grounds for asserting its rational superiorty. Yet at the same time the adherents of the defeated tradition or traditions might remain convinced that no such defeat had occurred and be quite unimpressed by the arguments that had convinced others. How so?

IX

An example from the history of the natural sciences is illuminating. In the late fifteenth and early sixteenth century impetus theory, the latest and most sophisticated development of a physical theory starting out from Aristotle's *Physics,* encountered serious difficulties. Impetus theorists had no difficulty in providing explanation of this or that particular set of phenomena, and they could provide equations that enabled them to calculate and predict correctly the movements of this or that type of body. But when they tried to formulate universal lawlike generalizations, expressed in a set of equations that had universal application to moving bodies of all the different kinds that they had observed, all their attempts failed.

Galileo was in his youth, like every other contemporary student of physics, an impetus theorist. It was Galileo's genius to have recognized that physics could progress only by abandoning Aristotle's first principles and by elaborating a theory of a very different kind. So Galileo was able to provide a unified account of the movements of bodies falling from a great height, of the trajectories of cannonballs, and of the rise and fall of tides. Yet the protagonists of a post-Aristotelian physics remained unconvinced. For Galileo had not provided and could not provide a demonstration—as sixteenth-century Aristotelians understood the notion of demonstration—either of the falsity of Aristotelian first principles or of the truth of the first principles of the new physics. What then of the various observations and experiments that were taken to confirm the claims of the new physics? Of each of these the protagonists of impetus theory were able to provide alternative interpretations, even though the ad hoc character of those interpretations made it still more difficult for them to give anything remotely like a unified account of the movement of bodies. So in the University of Paris in the early eighteenth century, when the important debates in France were between Cartesians and Newtonians, there were still Aristotelian defenders of pre-Galilean physics, among them the Irishman, Michael Moore, who became rector of the University in 1701.

Thomas Kuhn used the dispute between impetus theorists and Galileo as an example of the incommensurability of paradigms and, if by the ascription of such incommensurability we mean only that no shared neutral standards can be identified by appeal to which the two rival contending parties could have settled their disagreements, then this is indeed just such a case. Nonetheless the rational superiority of Galileo's, let alone of Newton's physics over the physics of the impetus theorists is plain. And this is not just a matter of the ability of the followers of Galileo and Newton to supply a unified account of the laws of nature of a kind that impetus theorists had been notably unable to supply. It is also that the Newtonian physicist is able to explain why, given that nature is as it is, impetus theory had to fail and to identify precisely the points at which it was bound to fail. So Newton's physics is not only a superior explanation of nature, it also supplies an explanation of the impasse in which impetus theorists had found themselves, something that impetus theorists could not do. They failed in self-understanding as well as in the understanding of nature.

Here then is one case in which a tradition of thought is defeated from a standpoint whose statement and defense becomes the founding moment of another tradition, yet in which many of the adherents of the defeated tradition can find no compelling reason to allow that they have been defeated. In order so to agree they would have had to be able to understand their own theory from an external standpoint, the standpoint of Galileo, or Descartes, or Newton, and so to understand themselves in terms that they were committed to rejecting. This difficult exercise of the intellectual imagination many of them were unable or unwilling to carry through. And as a result they could find no good reason for acknowledging their defeat.

As in the natural sciences, so it can be too in other types of fundamental disagreement, philosophical and moral disagreements among them. It is in this light that I want to reconsider the disagreements between Thomistic Aristotelians and utilitarians. I shall begin by asking what kind of account Thomistic Aristotelians are able to give of utilitarianism, in order to compare a Thomistic Aristotelian understanding of utilitarianism with a utilitarian understanding of utilitarianism.

X

One way in which contemporary utilitarians understand their own positions is by contrasting them with positions upheld by Kant and his followers. For Kant the precepts of the moral law are to be obeyed by rational agents, whatever the consequences. That by lying and only by lying I will be able to save an innocent human life does not, on Kant's view, make it right to lie, no matter how benevolent my motives. For by lying I will violate a maxim that gives expression to a universal law binding on all rational agents, *qua* rational agents. So by lying I wrong not only those to whom I lie, treating them as mere means to the achievement of my ends, and not as agents who are worthy of the respect due to rational agents, but I also wrong myself, failing to respect myself as a rational agent.

For Mill, as for other utilitarians, the rule that prohibits lying binds us unless and until by obeying it I will in fact bring about some significantly less desirable state of affairs than I would by disobeying it. And therefore, if and when I will, for example, by telling a lie save someone's life, without bringing about any further predictable harm, it is not only the case that I may tell that lie, but that I will fail morally, if I do not tell it. Rational obedience to particular moral rules is for utilitarians always a means to an end, that of achieving the greatest possible human happiness. Such moral rules therefore have only a conditional authority. By contrast obedience to moral rules is understood by followers of Kant to be unconditionally required of rational agents.

It is notorious that utilitarians and Kantians have been unable during the past two hundred years to resolve their disagreements. And neither has been able to give an account of why this should be so, of why equally intelligent and perceptive thinkers on either side of this divide should be so deeply convinced of the wrongheadedness of those on the other side. Utilitarians, even if they no longer share Mill's moral standpoint, continue to insist that moral rules are binding only insofar as obedience to them conduces to the achievement of a further end, that of human happiness, and that *therefore* they are, given the contingent circumstances of human life, bound to have exceptions. Kantians, even when they have modified Kant's positions, continue to insist that moral rules are exceptionless maxims binding on rational agents and that *therefore* conformity to them cannot be a means to any further end, including happiness. What they share is the assumption that *either* moral roles are such that to conform to them is to be directed towards the achievement of happiness *or* they are exceptionless prescriptions binding any rational agent *qua* rational agent, but that it is impossible that they should be both. Why do both parties take this assumption to be true?

To this there is a twofold answer. An historical account will tell us how they in fact come to take this assumption for granted. And a conceptual investigation into the ways in which they understand happiness will throw light on why this assumption is a good deal more problematic than they suppose. Begin with the history. There is a long-standing moral and political tradition, whose classic expression in theoretical terms was provided by Aristotle and Aquinas, according to which the precepts of the natural law are *both* binding exceptionlessly on all rational agents as such *and* such that conformity to them directs us towards our supreme good, to achieve which is to perfect our happiness. How is it that those precepts can have both sets of characteristics? Because on the one hand the happiness of rational agents can only be achieved through, and in part consists in, relationships with others that are informed by unconditional obedience to the precepts of the natural law. Whatever might be achieved through violating these precepts, even from benevolent motives, it would not and could not be the happiness of a rational agent. And, on the other hand, rational agents are and cannot but be directed towards the achievement of the kind of happiness that is specifically theirs and, were the precepts of the natural law not to guide them towards this end, it would be quite unclear what the point of conformity to them would be.

When this tradition flourished, as it has done in a number of times and places in a variety of cultural forms, it was embedded in the social practices of those particular times and places and it was sustained by a network of supporting beliefs and by shared habits of mind, feeling, and action. But when in Europe, during the later Middle Ages and the sixteenth and seventeenth centuries, both it and the ways of life that embodied it were challenged by a series of disruptive and transformative events—the rethinking of theology in the Reformation and the Counter-Reformation, the abandonment of teleological modes of thought by the practitioners of the natural sciences, and, much the most important, the remaking of the everyday life of the social and political order—the conceptual scheme that had hitherto been presupposed by moral thought and action was fragmented. Very much the same rules were still by and large accorded authority, but they had now been deprived of and abstracted from the teleological context which had provided them with their rationale. So their status and authority was put in question. And the task confronting moral philosophers from the late seventeenth century onwards was to provide a new and rationally justifiable account of their status and authority.

It was in the course of trying to construct such an account that new kinds of radical and intractable disagreements were engendered, and understandably so. For the philosophers of that age, the philosophers of the Enlightenment, did not recognize that the moral rules which provided them with their subject-matter had both the form and the content that they had only because they were *survivals* from an earlier period and that they are fully intelligible only as survivals. They took themselves to be saying what moral rules were and always had been, as though theirs was a timeless conceptual investigation. But what they were in fact doing was inventing new moralities. And the most important of these new moralities was utilitarianism.

It was not just that utilitarians provided a new justification for moral rules, but that the justification that they provided changed the moral rules themselves. For, as we have already noted, if moral rules are binding only insofar as obedience to them is productive of happiness, then all moral rules have no more than a conditional authority, one dependent on the contingent circumstances in which an agent acts. For the earlier utilitarians therefore everything hinges on the concept of happiness and on the account of it that utilitarians provide. The word *happiness* in English is of course used in a number of different ways, sometimes to translate what Aristotle meant by *eudaimonia*. But utilitarians have used it very differently, as the name of a set of psychological states. Yet they have disagreed among themselves about how those psychological states are to be characterized.

Jeremy Bentham, relying on Hartley's psychology, took it, as I noted earlier, that happiness consists in pleasure and the absence of pain and treated "pleasure" and "pain" as if they were both names of types of sensation, varying in such measurable and therefore comparable properties as number, intensity, and duration. John Stuart Mill, with a more sophisticated psychology, understood that the happiness which gives not just to moral rules, but to human lives their point and purpose must be understood not just in quantitative, but also in qualitative terms. One state of mind may be preferred to another as more worthwhile: "better to be Socrates dissatisfied than a fool satisfied" (*Utilitarianism*, chap. II). And Mill adds that in the course of history our conception of happiness has been transformed. So Mill both asserts that "the multiplication of happiness is . . . the object of virtue," that virtue is a means to happiness (chap. II), but also that virtue has through time come to be loved disinterestedly for its own sake by some, so that for them here now—and Mill clearly includes himself—it "is desired and cherished, not as a means to happiness, but as a part of their happiness" (chap. IV). Some later utilitarians, as I also noted earlier, judging that no conception of happiness, neither Bentham's nor Mill's nor any other, can play the part in their theory that it needs to play, have replaced it with some notion of the satisfaction of the preferences of individuals, so that the maxims of morality are those maxims conformity to which secures the maximization of preference satisfaction.

Yet every one of these characterizations of the end to which conformity to the precepts of morality is to be the means turns out to be open to serious objection. Mill's complex account of happiness itself provides us with sufficient grounds for rejecting Bentham's account. And to both Mill and Bentham such questions need to be put as: How are we to weigh considerations that direct us towards the achievement of pleasures against consideration that direct us towards putting an end to pains and sufferings? And utilitarians need to be able to answer such questions without invoking some principle that is independent of utilitarianism. It is not clear how this is to be done.

Yet, even if we put this kind of difficulty on one side, the question remains of how we are to conceive of happiness. Should we perhaps treat as happy those who identify themselves as happy, who profess to be contented with their lives? One problem with this conception of self-ascribed happiness is that it will classify as happy those who have expectations that are far too low, who have been induced somehow or other not merely to tolerate the deprivations that shape their lives, but no longer to treat those deprivations as negative features of those lives so allowing their desires to be eroded. And there are many such. Lassalle spoke of "the damned wantlessness of the poor." Suppose that we were to respond to this by taking only those to be happy who would still be contented with their lives, if they were fully rational. The problem now becomes that of explaining what kind of life it is with which a fully rational person would be contented. And in so doing we will have abandoned contentment as the standard by which the satisfactoriness or unsatisfactoriness of a life is to be judged, substituting for it some conception of the kind of life with which someone *ought* to be contented. Here we begin to feel the full weight of Mill's preference for Socrates dissatisfied over a fool satisfied and the threat that it presents to utilitarianism. Consider the case of Wittgenstein.

When Wittgenstein was dying, he sent a message to his friends: "Tell them I've had a wonderful life." And indeed it had been a wonderful life. But it had been a life racked by much unhappiness and discontent and by much moral dissatisfaction with himself. Yet who would not count such a life immeasurably more worthwhile than a life of mindless good feelings? So there is a crucial difference, fully recognized by Mill, both in his theory and in his own life, between a worthwhile life and a subjectively happy life.

None of those difficulties seem to be removed by substituting for the notion of happiness the notion of preference satisfaction. For someone's preferences may well be the result of miseducation and social conditioning, with the result that their preferences are what others who have shaped them—for example, advertisers and other propagandists—want them to be. And their preferences may in consequence be satisfied by consumption rather than by achievement. Yet perhaps after all this is not a conclusive objection. For there are quite those who are unmoved by such criticism, insisting that all preferences are to be treated as given, as brute fact, and that nothing is to be treated as worthwhile except insofar as it satisfies preferences. Are they able to provide us with a notion of preference satisfaction and of the maximization of preference satisfaction that is by utilitarianism's own standards unproblematic?

A central problem arises immediately. If to be practically rational is to maximize the satisfaction of one's own preferences, under what circumstances will it be rational for me to maximize preference satisfaction in general? Any plausible version of utilitarianism in which Bentham's or Mill's notions of happiness have been replaced by that of preference satisfaction must be able to deliver an answer to this question, since otherwise we shall have no account of why we should maximize preference satisfaction in general and nothing will have taken the place that Bentham and Mill gave to "the greatest happiness of the greatest number." Yet the only credible answers to it seem to be incompatible with utilitarian claims. For it is evident that, if it is practically rational for me to maximize my own preferences, then, so long as I am rational, I can have an interest in maximizing the preference satisfaction of others only so long as that maximization conduces somehow or other to the satisfaction of my own preferences. But social life is often such that there will be relatively few others in whose preference satisfaction it is rational for me to take an interest. And social life is sometimes such that there are others whose preferences are such, that if their preference satisfaction is maximized, my own prefaces will remain unsatisfied. I conclude that I cannot both treat the maximization of my own preference satisfaction as my rational good and also treat the maximization of the preference satisfaction of the greatest possible number as such a good. The notion of preference satisfaction therefore cannot supply what utilitarians need, if they are to replace rather than to reformulate the notion of happiness.

The difficulties with which utilitarians are confronted in this area are of course familiar. There is a huge philosophical literature in which they have been and will be discussed. Yet perhaps the time has come when, instead of wrestling with them further, the question should be asked: What is it about utilitarianism that exposes it to such objections and how is its vulnerability to them to be explained? The thesis that I am going to advance is that it is only by the use of resources from within the Thomistic Aristotelian tradition and in the perspective afforded by that tradition that this predicament of utilitarianism can be adequately understood.

Utilitarians had understood from the outset that they needed a concept that would serve two related functions in their account of moral rules. It would enable them to say what the point and purpose of conformity to those rules was. And, by specifying their point and purpose, it would provide a standard by appeal to which one could determine both whether or not a particular rule is indeed a binding rule and what the scope of that rule is. It was those two functions that the concept of happiness or any concept that might replace it was to discharge, and it was essential to such a concept being able to fill the double role that utilitarians had assigned to it that we should be able to make sense both of the notion of happiness—or of whatever notion had taken its place—and of that of maximizing the general happiness—or of whatever else had taken its place. Abstract any such concept from utilitarianism, and it ceases to be utilitarianism. Yet the problem, as we have seen, is that utilitarians have been unable to give a defensible account of that central concept. Why *this* difficulty?

I want to suggest that utilitarians were and are in the right in claiming that any adequate account of—and defense of—moral rules requires just such a concept. But I also want to suggest that they looked for that concept—were in fact forced by their cultural circumstances to look for that concept—in the wrong place. As I noticed earlier, the moral rules that they inherited had, by the time that Bentham and others began their work of radical moral revision, been abstracted from the context in which in earlier predecessor cultures they had been at home. In those earlier cultures it had been recognized that moral rules were justifiable only insofar as they had point and purpose and the concept that had been used to elucidate that point and purpose was the concept of *eudaimonia* or *beatitudo* as an end *(telos, finis),* understood as Aristotle and Aquinas had understood it.

Whatever has an end has the end that it has by virtue of its specific nature, the kind of thing that it is. (Here I am following closely the account of ends given by Robert Sokolowski in "What Is Natural Law? Human Purposes and Natural Ends," *Thomist* 68, no. 4 [October 2004].) Something moves towards the achievement of its specific end when it develops as such a thing must, if it is to be perfected and completed. Plants and animals, human beings and a whole range of arts and institution, may be said to have ends. The end of a plant or an animal is the development and exercise of its powers, so that it becomes an example of its own specific type of flourishing by passing through the stages of its natural life cycle. Everyone who is able to distinguish a healthy and flourishing cabbage from a wilting or diseased cabbage or a healthy and flourishing wolf from an injured or undernourished wolf is relying in so doing on their implicit understanding of the specific ends of cabbages or wolves, even if they have never used the word *end* or any cognate expression.

Human beings are rational animals and the powers which they need to develop and exercise, if they are to flourish, are both animal and rational. So they have to find a place for a variety of goods in their life. What makes each such good a good is the fact that its achievement conduces to or partly constitutes their flourishing *qua* human being. What makes someone engaged in such achievement good is that she or he is directed towards their specific end. "Good," as Aquinas argues in the fifth question of the first part of the *Summa Theologiae,* is defined in terms of the concept of an end and the standards of goodness are in consequence what they are, independently of the desires, choices, and purposes of agents. The names that we give to the state of having achieved our end are, according to Aristotle and Aquinas, *eudaimonia* and *beatitudo,* words that have been translated in English by "happiness"—as it happens, unfortunately—and what is thus named is something at which all human beings aim. But, as I noted earlier in my discussion of Aquinas, they disagree about what it consists in and, when they are mistaken, it is characteristically because they suppose that it consists in the satisfaction of such desires as those for money, pleasure, honor, and power.

That this is a mistake and what kind of mistake it is are only to be understood by those already able in their practice to distinguish between directedness towards their end and directedness towards the satisfaction of their desires, and the making of this distinction at the level of practice is possible only for those who have already developed to some significant degree those qualities, those intellectual and moral excellences, by which we direct ourselves towards our end *qua* human being. It is a distinction embodied in a variety of institutionalized practices. I noted earlier that not only plants and animals, whether nonhuman or human, have ends, but also arts and institutions. So the end of the art of medicine is the health of the physician's patients and the end of a school is the education of its students. Particular physicians and teachers may be motivated by a wide range of desires: for money, for prestige, for power, but it is only insofar as they pursue the end of the medical art or the end of the school that they are good physicians or good teachers. Once again the relationship between the concept of good and that of an end is exemplified.

In cultures in which this distinction was widely and firmly grasped it became at the level of practice an essential part of a shared understanding of moral rules. Moral rules were understood as just and only those precepts conformity to which is either a constitutive part of or conducive to the achievement, first of those relationships and those common goods that are the relationships and goods of families and of political communities, and secondly of the final ends of individuals. They are therefore precepts without which human beings will be unable to achieve not only their final end and good, but a variety of the shared goods constitutive of the way of life through which in that particular culture the human end is to be achieved. And in such past cultures the theoretical articulation of the practical understanding of moral rules was often broadly Aristotelian in form.

Suppose however that within such a culture, one in which practice had presupposed a substantive conception of the human end and in which theoretical understanding had taken a broadly Aristotelian form, a series of radical transformations had occurred, religious, political, and economic, so that in each of those areas it had become difficult to continue to think of and to theorize about human beings in this particular way. Suppose that for theological reasons it came to be widely believed that the sinfulness of human nature was such that the *imago Dei* had been blotted out and that human beings could have no rational grasp of or derive guidance from knowledge of their natural end (Luther, Calvin, Jansen, Pascal). Suppose that politics became widely thought of as a sphere in which conflicting and competing wills, motivated by a desire for power or glory, aspire to defeat one another (Machiavelli). And suppose that economic life was increasingly understood as a competitive arena, in which acquisitiveness was the mark not of the vices of *pleonexia* and *avaritia,* as formerly, but of the character of the admirable entrepreneur.

In such a cultural climate it would appear at best eccentric to continue to think of human beings as having an end that was theirs by nature and it would be unsurprising if a perceptive observer of the social scene were to conclude that "I put for a general inclination of all mankind, a perpetuall and restlesse desire of Power after power, that ceaseth only in Death" and that "there is no such *Finis ultimus,* (utmost ayme,) nor *Summum Bonum,* (greatest Good,) as is spoken of in the books of the old Morall Philosophers" (Thomas Hobbes, *Leviathan* I, xi). What the new moral philosophers confronted was a new task, that of constructing an account of morality from nothing more than first a set of inherited moral rules—perhaps standing in need of revision, perhaps radical revision—and secondly a psychological account of human beings as motivated by their passions and inclinations. The problem was that there were two different and incompatible ways in which this task could be undertaken and both confronted large difficulties. *Either* the moral rules were taken to be binding independently of the passions and inclinations *or* they were taken to be binding in virtue of their relationship to the passions and inclinations. If the former alternative was chosen, it was difficult, and perhaps insuperably difficult, to explain how human beings could be motivated to conform to moral rules, and, if the latter type of account was defended, it was difficult, and perhaps insuperably difficult, to explain how the particular passions and inclinations of an individual could motivate her or him to have the kind of impersonal and universal regard for the persons, interests, and needs of others that moral rules enjoin. The first set of difficulties was addressed by the rationalists and by Kant, the second by Hume and by the utilitarians.

The peculiar difficulty that confronted the utilitarians was this. The concept that they needed to give point, purpose, justification, and motivating power to moral rules could now be spelled out only in psychological terms, in terms of the passions and the inclinations. And certainly happiness was easily the most promising candidate for that conceptual role, both because happiness was still often conceived as that at which everyone aims and because in English "happiness" is often used as the name of a psychological state, a state of feeling. Yet there is no such thing as happiness as such. To be happy—as contrasted with feeling happy—is always to be happy in virtue of something or other, something done or suffered, something acquired or achieved. When translators have supplied "happiness" as the English translation of *eudaimonia* or *beatitudo,* they have had in mind that type of happiness which supervenes upon and is made intelligible by the achievement of a completed and perfected life of worthwhile activity, the achievement of the human end.

Detach the notion of happiness from that of happiness-in-virtue-of-such-and-such, and you have a concept too indeterminate to function as utilitarians needed it to function, since what it had to replace was the highly determinate concept of the human end and of happiness as the state of having achieved that end. And this it could not do. From this arise not all, but some of the central and, I suggest, fatal difficulties for utilitarianism, whose character can only be understood when the historical relationship of the concept of an end to that of happiness has been understood.

How then should we formulate the Thomistic and Aristotelian claim that I am advancing? Thomistic Aristotalians agree with utilitarians that moral rules have to be understood teleologically. They agree with Mill—or rather Mill agreed with them—that there is no inconsistency in asserting of certain kinds of action both that they should be

done for their own sake and also for the sake of achieving some further end. (It is significant that Mill took Aristotle to be a "moderate
utilitarian" and that this was also how he would have described his
own position.) But the kind of finality that an *end* possesses, so that it
is not only that for the sake of which actions are performed, but also
that by appeal to which we can understand which types of actions
should be performed and why, cannot belong to any psychological
state. So the project of constructing a moral teleology that has been
evacuated of its metaphysical content by the erasure of the notion of
an end turns out to be an incoherent project.

That this is so can only be adequately grasped by those who have
understood and know how to find application for the concept of an
end. And to grasp this involves a commitment to a large set of interre-
lated concepts and judgments, both theoretical and practical, those
concepts and judgments through which, on a Thomistic Aristotelian view, human beings express their beliefs and guide their actions
when their lives are in good order. From that standpoint we have good
reason to understand ourselves and other living beings in terms of
the concept of a specific and natural end. But from the standpoint of
utilitarianism there are the best of reasons for rejecting that concept as
part of the discredited apparatus of an Aristotelian worldview, the
same worldview that was, so they take it, discredited by the defeat of
impetus theory. The claim that I am advancing is that the failure of
utilitarians to overcome the difficulties that arise from their use of the
concept of happiness, or of some substitute for it, provides Thomistic
Aristotelians with sufficient reason to judge that they are able to understand the truth about utilitarianism better than utilitarians can.

Yet utilitarians, as I have already suggested, have thereby been
given no reason at all for agreeing with this verdict. Given their
starting-point and the nature of the problems which they have been
and are addressing, given the constraints imposed by their commitment to a naturalistic understanding of human beings, there is no way
in which they could be open to arguments that would put in question

their whole project. And we should note that in the long-standing and ongoing debates between utilitarians, Kantians, and contractarians no arguments have emerged that have convinced the most open-minded adherents of any of those contending parties of the rational superiority of the views of their opponents. Since what utilitarians, Kantians, and contractarians share by way of assumptions and presuppositions is much greater than what any of them share with Thomistic Aristotelians, it would be surprising if they were open to admitting the force of Thomistic Aristotelian arguments.

XI

What I have left undone in this essay is quite as notable as anything that I have done. I have provided no more than sketches of some arguments, some of them arguments that have been developed at greater length by others elsewhere, but some of them arguments that still stand in need of a considerably fuller statement. And it is not only critics and opponents who will be disquieted by this. For the outcome of my arguments is notably at odds with what some Thomistic writers have claimed and many others have presupposed, namely that Thomists have resources that should enable them to refute their opponents in ways that are or should be compelling to *any* rational individual, whatever her or his standpoint. This I am committed to denying.

I do indeed believe that Thomistic Aristotelionism provides us all a well-founded and rationally justified moral philosophy, but I also believe that in the forums of rational public debate, by the best standards available for such debate, it will often be unable to defeat its critics and opponents. Note, however, that by allowing that this is so I am not committed to withdrawing and I do not withdraw the theses that I asserted in section VI of this essay about the motivated irrationality of denials of the authority of the precepts of the natural law.

What the defense of the precepts of the natural law therefore requires is not an attempt to demonstrate the falsity of the conclusions of the public defenders of those denials. For such an attempt is bound to fail. What is needed instead is attention to the premises from which they argue and an attempt to undermine belief in those premises by demonstrating the flaws and confusions that inform those premises, flaws and confusions exemplified, so I have suggested, by the utilitarian use of the concept of happiness and of cognate concepts. The best defence of natural law will consist in radical philosophical, moral, and cultural critiques of rival standpoints. Someone may at this point object: if this were to be a successful strategy, might not its effect be to promote moral skepticism, to undermine belief in *any* moral standpoint? To which the answer is that this might well be the unfortunate outcome, but only if moral skepticism was not itself subjected to radical critique, as it can and should be. But how to do this is another story.

Note

Sections I–VI of this essay are a slightly rewritten version of "Aquinas and the Extent of Moral Disagreement," published as chapter 4 of volume 2 of my *Selected Essays* (Cambridge: Cambridge University Press, 2006). It is reprinted here by the generous permission of the Cambridge University Press. The arguments about moral and philosophical traditions and the resolution of disagreements between rival traditions in sections VIII–X are versions of arguments that have been advanced in various places, including "Epistemological Crises, Dramatic Narrative, and the Philosophy of Science," first published in the *Monist* 60, no. 4 (1977), and reprinted in volume 1 of my *Selected Essays;* and "The Rationality of Traditions," chapter 18 of *Whose Justice? Which Rationality?* (London: Duckworth; Notre Dame: University of Notre Dame Press, 1988).

CHAPTER 2

Does the Natural Law Provide a Universally Valid Morality?

Jean Porter

For some time now, it has been apparent that Western societies are divided by deep, seemingly intractable disagreements over moral questions, especially but not only those pertaining to sexual expression, marriage, and family relations. More recently, we in the West have begun to see that we are divided from much of the rest of the world over still more fundamental questions having to do with some of our most cherished values, including human rights and the value of democracy. Of course, the reality and the extent of the relevant disagreements are themselves very much in dispute, and the universality of so-called Western values finds many defenders both in the West itself and elsewhere—all appearances to the contrary. But appearances certainly are contrary, at least sufficiently so to lead others to speak of the failure of the Enlightenment project to enact a universal morality through a kind of worldwide consensus of all rational persons.[1] At any rate, it is apparent that the existence of a universally valid moral system, compelling as such to any rational and well-disposed individual, can no longer be taken for granted. It must be defended, presumably through appeals to foundations for normative judgment that are themselves accessible to all men and women, regardless of their particular religious or cultural presuppositions.

The venerable tradition of reflection on a natural law would seem to offer one such basis for defending a universal morality. After all, the claims of a natural law morality, if successfully vindicated, would rest on human nature itself, and would be developed through the exercise of rational capacities that are themselves grounded in that nature. What could be more fundamental, or more likely to provide a touchstone for agreement, than our shared nature as human beings and our rational capacities to function as such? It is hardly surprising, therefore, that beginning in the last decades of the previous century, the natural law has enjoyed something of a renaissance, among philosophers and jurists as well as theologians. More recently still, Pope Benedict XVI has called for a return to the natural law as a basis for a universal morality that can bridge the dangerous divides in world society. Of course, in doing so he speaks as the representative of a religious tradition that has long based its moral claims on a natural law, but he insists that this natural law ethic is itself defensible in purely rational terms, without the need for supernatural grace or special revelation.

In his challenging essay, "Intractable Moral Disagreements," Alasdair MacIntyre argues that the natural law, as interpreted and defended by Thomas Aquinas, does indeed provide a universally valid set of moral norms which can be apprehended as such by all rational persons. Nonetheless, he goes on to say, the natural law presupposes a particular view of practical rationality which may or may not be shared by all, and for this reason its claims will not be compelling to those philosophers who begin with a significantly different view of rationality, especially (but not only) utilitarians and other sorts of consequentialists. This concession to the appearances of deep moral disagreement is perhaps not as far-reaching as it may initially seem. MacIntyre does think that the validity of the natural law can be vindicated through rational arguments, which might not be compelling to all rational persons (as a mathematical proof, for example, would arguably be), but which would be nonetheless rationally defensible, even to those who do not initially share the presuppositions informing these arguments. (Presumably such a defense, if successful, would lead one's interlocutors to revise their presuppositions, in accordance with processes of rational reflection across the boundaries of tradition set out by MacIntyre in his earlier works.)[2] What is more, he suggests that to some extent, at least, the account of practical rationality defended by utilitarians may stem in part from nonrational factors, including especially an unwillingness to abandon a view that is central to their continued allegiance to utilitarianism. Most important, MacIntyre focuses throughout on the possibilities and limitations of rational consensus among Western philosophers, who after all do share a broader context of philosophical and cultural assumptions. He barely acknowledges the possibilities of deep moral disagreements among different cultures and communities, and indeed seems to presuppose that most men and women, uncorrupted by the seductions of theory, will more or less agree on basic moral precepts such as those forbidding murder, adultery, lying, or theft.

At any rate, I do not intend to pursue MacIntyre's engagements with utilitarians and other contemporary philosophers in this paper. I disagree with him on a more fundamental point—that is to say, I am not persuaded that the natural law as Aquinas understands it is tantamount to, or can be made to yield, normative precepts that are both specific enough to be put into practice and valid and binding in all times and places. At the very least, the textual evidence on this point is inconclusive. Aquinas does not engage the questions that motivate contemporary debates over moral pluralism and the possibilities for a universal ethic, except obliquely in pursuit of a different agenda. But what he does say about the possibilities and limitations of certainty with respect to the precepts of the natural law does at least suggest a greater scope for a genuine and legitimate moral pluralism than many of his interpreters would allow, and at some points he himself seems explicitly to acknowledge as much.

This may seem to be a surprising claim. As MacIntyre rightly notes, Aquinas affirms the permanence and immutability of the natural law in no uncertain terms. The first principles of the natural law cannot be changed in the sense of being fundamentally altered, even though they can be supplemented by divine and positive law (*Summa Theologiae* I-II 94.5); by the same token, at the level of first principles, the natural law cannot be extirpated from the human heart; that is to say, it can in no way become so obscured as to be altogether lost to rational reflection (*ST* I-II 94.6; except where otherwise noted, all further references to Aquinas are taken from the *Summa Theologiae*). At the level of secondary precepts, the natural law can become inoperative in one way, through the agent's incapacity to function as a rational agent at all, and in another, more specific way, through sinfulness, personal weakness, or bad customs (*ST* I-II 94.6)—the implication being that so long as an agent is both rational and well disposed, even the secondary precepts of the natural law will be accessible to him.

Yet in the same question, Aquinas gives us reason to ask whether the natural law really provides a universally valid moral system. In a much-discussed article, he asks whether the natural law is the same for all, and he responds that it is neither the same for all, nor is it known equally to all. With respect to the knowledge of the natural law, he argues—as we might expect—that even with respect to those matters concerning which the natural law is the same for all, the knowledge of the natural law can be corrupted by personal sin or vice, or by depraved customs. However, he also says explicitly that at the level of concrete precepts, the natural law is not the same for all:

> [A]s was said above, those things pertain to the law of nature, to which the human person is naturally inclined; among which, it is

proper to the human person that he is inclined to act in accordance with reason. Now it pertains to reason to proceed from what is more general, to what is more specific. . . . Speculative reason is oriented towards this in one way, however, and practical reason in another. Since speculative reason deals chiefly with that which is necessary, which cannot be otherwise than it is, the truth is found without any defect in specific conclusions, as it is in general principles. But practical reason deals with contingent things, among which are human operations, and therefore, even if there is some necessity in its general starting points, the more one descends to specifics, the more defect is found. . . . [W]ith respect to things that are done, there is not the same truth or practical rectitude for all with respect to specifics, but only with respect to what is general; and with respect to those things about which there is the same rectitude in specifics, it is not equally known to all. (I-II 94.4)

Admittedly, what Aquinas chiefly has in mind here are clearly applications of natural law precepts to particular cases. Nonetheless, he at least leaves open the possibility that this diversity with respect to "rectitude"—that is to say, with the normative substance of the natural law—might be reflected at a communal level, and not just at the level of particular applications.

This may appear to be a relatively insignificant concession to the complexities of moral decision making in unusual or complicated cases—complexities that MacIntyre certainly recognizes. But the implications of Aquinas's remarks at this point go well beyond this point. In order to appreciate why this is so, it is important to note that for Aquinas, the first principles of the natural law are made up of formal principles without which reason could not operate in practical matters at all—including, but not limited to, "Good is to be sought and done, and evil avoided" (I-II 94.2). These he regards as comprising the natural law in the primary sense, and in this sense it is indeed true that the natural law is accessible to all human beings and can in no way be abolished from the human heart. Understood in this way, the first principles of practical reason, like the first principles of speculative reason, are constitutive elements of the human intellect: they cannot be eliminated so long as the human creature continues to exist.

Yet the precepts of the Decalogue are *not* included among the primary precepts of the natural law, nor much less are further specifications of these precepts such as, "The direct killing of an innocent person is always forbidden." Aquinas claims that the precepts of the Decalogue can be derived from the first principles of the natural law (most immediately, from the injunctions to do no wrong to anyone and to fulfill one's particular obligations), with only a minimum of reflection (I-II 100.3 ad 1; cf. I-II 95.1), but in contrast to his teacher Albert the Great, he explicitly denies that these are *per se nota* (Albert's position is set out in *De Bono* V 1.1). What is more, the precepts of the Decalogue are still not specific enough to guide action. They must be further specified through either divine (that is to say, revealed) or human law in order to be put into practice (*ST* I-II 91.3, 99.3 ad 2, 99.4). In this way, Aquinas flags what I believe to be the key issue in contemporary debates over moral universalism; that is to say, what is the relationship between normative principles formulated at a high level of abstraction and the concrete specifications that must be provided if these are to be put into practice?

It is easy to make a case for a universal morality if one is willing to pitch one's arguments at a sufficiently high level of generality. MacIntyre, in contrast, makes a more substantive and interesting case, defending the universality of the natural law understood at a fairly specific level. He does so in the first instance by arguing that the first principle of practical reason is specified through the immediate apprehension of those goods toward which the human person is naturally inclined—specified in such a way that the relevant precepts carry the same self-evident force as the first principle itself does. In this way, he joins forces with a widespread, although controversial, interpretation of what may well be the most well known passage in Aquinas's whole discussion of the natural law, namely, I-II 94.2.

I. The Origin and Unity of the Natural Law

The text which is most frequently cited in connection with Aquinas's discussion of the natural law is I-II 94.2. In this article, Aquinas addresses the question of whether or not the natural law is one unified law; after setting out a series of objections in support of the essential diversity of natural laws, he begins his analysis by observing that "just as was said above [I-II 91.3], the precepts of the law of nature stand in the same relation to practical reason, as the first principles of demonstrations stand to speculative reason, for in either case, they are particular self-evident principles. However, something is said to be self-evident in two senses; in one way, in itself, and in another way, with respect to us." A proposition is self-evident in itself, he explains, if its predicate is in some way implied by the *ratio* of the subject, but a proposition that is self-evident in this way will not necessarily be self-evident to all persons. In particular, it will not be self-evident to someone who does not know the correct definitions of its terms. Thus, while some propositions will indeed be self-evident to all persons (Aquinas gives the example, "Every whole is greater than its parts"), others will be self-evident only to "the wise" (for example, "An angel is not circumscribed in space").

Aquinas then goes on to apply his analysis of self-evident propositions to the first practical principles of the intellect. The text is worth quoting at some length.

> Now a certain order is found in those things which come under every apprehension. . . . [J]ust as being is that which first comes under apprehension simply speaking, so the good is that which first comes under the apprehension of practical reason, which is directed towards something that is done; for every agent acts on account of an end, which has the rational character of good. And therefore the first principle in the practical reason is that which is grounded in the rational character of good, that is,

"good is that which all desire." This is therefore the first precept of law, that the good is to be done and pursued and the bad is to be avoided. And on this are founded all the other precepts of the law of nature, inasmuch as all things to be done or avoided, which practical reason naturally apprehends to be human goods, belong to the precepts of the law of nature.

Because good has the rational character of an end, whereas bad has the rational character of the contrary, hence it is that all those things to which the human person has a natural inclination, reason naturally apprehends as good, and consequently to be pursued through action, and the contraries of these as bad and to be avoided. Therefore, the order of the precepts of the law of nature is in accordance with the order of natural inclinations. For there is first of all an inclination in the human person towards that good which is in accordance with the nature which he shares with all substances, insofar as every substance desires the preservation of its being in accordance with its own nature. And in accordance with this inclination, those things through which the life of the human person is preserved, and what is contrary to it is impeded, pertain to the natural law. Secondly, there is an inclination within the human person towards more specific things, in accordance with that nature which he shares with the other animals. And according to this, those things are said to belong to the natural law which nature teaches all animals, such as the union of male and female, and the education of offspring, and the like. In a third sense, there is an inclination in the human person towards the good in accordance with the nature of reason, which is proper to the human person alone; as for instance the human person has a natural inclination towards this, that he should know the truth about God, and this, that he should live in society. And according to this, those things regarding inclination of this kind pertain to the natural law, such as, that the human person should avoid ignorance, that he should not offend those with whom he must interact, and other things of this kind which regard this.

It is generally agreed that this passage represents, in Pamela Hall's words, Aquinas's "core treatment of the contents of the natural law."[3] There is, however, less consensus on exactly what Aquinas is saying here, and more particularly, what he says or implies about the precepts of the natural law. Most commentators assume—as MacIntyre does—that the inclinations set forth in I-II 94.2 are themselves normative specifications of the first principle of practical reason, or at least provide the immediate justifications for relevant norms. Given this line of interpretation, we might readily conclude that the norms stemming directly from the inclinations share in the rational transparency and cogency of the first principle itself—and this is just the line taken by one of the most influential contemporary theories of natural law, the "new natural law" theory developed by Germain Grisez, John Finnis, and their collaborators. On this view, concrete precepts of the natural law follow from the first principle of practical reason by way of specification, guided by our natural inclinations towards certain basic goods.[4] That is, in experiencing the basic good of life (for example), we rationally apprehend that life is worthy of pursuit and should never be destroyed or prevented from coming into existence. On this view, the specific precepts of the natural law are not conclusions deduced from the first principle of practical reason, but that does not mean that we do not know what they are; while they do not quite share in the degree of certainty proper to the first principles themselves, they are very nearly certain and can be formulated with a high degree of precision.[5] Hence, on this view the natural law is comprised of concrete moral norms which are not only knowable, but rationally compelling—offering, therefore, the strongest possible foundations for a universal ethic.

But in recent years, a number of commentators have defended a very different interpretation of I-II 94.2. According to Daniel Nelson,

Aquinas is here "merely restating in slightly more detail his claim that the law of our nature is always to act for the sake of an apprehended good. Although he identifies several broad categories of good, those categories have no direct implications for specific moral judgments."[6] Similarly, Hall remarks that in this article, "Aquinas does not so much as spell out some of the actual rules of the natural law. Instead, he is concerned with establishing a fundamental link between any precept of the natural law and the goods to which the precepts are ordered."[7] Hence, for both Nelson and Hall, I-II 94.2 is a general statement of the relationship between the natural law and human goods which tells us little or nothing about the actual content of the natural law. For both of them, therefore, I-II 94.2 provides strong evidence that the substantive content of the natural law can only be established through prudential judgments.[8]

When we take account of the range of interpretations of I-II 94.2, we find not only conflicting but also essentially contrary readings of the same text. When this happens, it is usually a sign that something has gone wrong at an early stage of interpretation. What has gone wrong in this case, I would suggest, is that these scholars, together with many other recent interpreters of Aquinas's moral theory, read I-II 94.2 as if it were intended as an account of the way in which the precepts of the natural law are grounded in or derived from a first principle.[9] But if we take seriously what Aquinas himself says in this article, it becomes apparent that this is not its point.

Consider the question with which Aquinas begins this article: "Whether the natural law contains many precepts, or one only?" As we have seen, he goes on to argue that the diverse precepts of the natural law can all be understood as expressions of one fundamental precept, "Good is to be done and pursued and evil is to be avoided." Hence, "All these precepts of the natural law, insofar as they are referred to one first precept, have the rational character of one natural law" (I-II 94.2 ad 1). Certainly, Aquinas presupposes a particular account of the normative content of the natural law, but he does not here give us that account, much less justify it, because he is attempting to make a different point. For this reason, any interpretation of Aquinas's account of the natural law which takes this article as a paradigmatic statement of the content of the natural law is likely to be distorted or incomplete.

Perhaps scholars have overlooked or downplayed the way in which Aquinas frames the issue to be addressed in I-II 94.2 because it is hard to get a sense of the context for Aquinas's discussion. Grisez points out that the question with which Aquinas begins this article was not a standard topic for discussion among the scholastics of his time.[10] While this is true, there was a similar question which was a standard topic, namely, the question whether there are many laws of nature, or only one. This discussion, I want to suggest, provides the immediate context for I-II 94.2, and we cannot understand the significance of the issue Aquinas raises here unless we take this context into account.

On its face, the question whether there are many laws of nature, or only one, seems even odder than the question whether the precepts of the natural law are one or many. Yet this question was a real problem for the scholastics in the twelfth and thirteenth centuries. In order to appreciate why, it is helpful to recall an obvious but important point, namely, that scholasticism is grounded in textually based procedures of inquiry, which aim to harmonize conflicting strands within sets of authoritative texts. In this case, the relevant textual tradition with which the scholastics were working was particularly difficult to harmonize, because it included a number of different and seemingly incompatible definitions of the natural law. For example, Cicero describes true law as right reason in accordance with nature (*De re publica* III 12.33), whereas the jurist Ulpian, quoted in Justinian's *Digest,* claims that the law of nature comprises whatever nature teaches to all animals (*Digest* I 1, 1.3), clearly implying that the natural law is *not* to be equated with right reason. Alongside these conflicting strains in the classical sources, from patristic times there was a distinctively Christian understanding of the natural law as somehow contained in Scripture. Writing in about 1140, Gratian began his analytic compilation of the canons of the church, the *Decretum*, with a definition drawn from this strand of the tradition: "The natural law is that which is contained in the law and the Gospel, by which each person is commanded to do to others what he would wish to be done to himself, and forbidden to render to others that which he would not have done to himself."[11]

Faced with this diversity of meanings, it is not surprising that the scholastics readily spoke in terms of multiple senses of the natural law. The canonist Stephen of Tournai, writing around 1160, is the first to offer a list of these multiple definitions, but he is scarcely the last.

> And it should be noted that the natural law is spoken of in four senses. For we speak of a natural law which is introduced by nature itself, and is not placed only in the human person, but also in other animals, from which derive the union of male and female and the procreation and education of children. The law of nations, which takes its origin from human nature alone, as it were beginning with it, is also said to be a natural law. The divine law, which our highest nature, that is, God, taught us, and placed before us through the law and the prophets and the gospel, is also said to be natural law. We also speak of a natural law which includes at once both human and divine law, and also that law which is placed in all animals by nature. And according to this last understanding, something is established "by natural law, that is, by divine, and that other primitive law." Or, if you can stand a fifth understanding of the natural law, understand, that is said to be the natural law which is placed by nature in human persons alone, and not the other animals, namely, a faculty directed towards doing good and avoiding evil. This is, as it were, a part of the divine law.[12]

Subsequently, the scholastics were not usually content simply to compile the traditional definitions; rather, they attempted to bring some coherence to the diversity of traditional accounts of the natural law. One approach was to identify one of the traditional definitions of the natural law as paradigmatic, and then to explain others in relation to it. Thus, the canonist Huguccio of Ferrara, writing about 1188, interprets the natural law as a power of rational judgment, arguing that the other traditional meanings of the natural law should be related to, or understood in terms of, this paradigmatic definition:

> And because different people have different views on the natural law, let us set forth its different meanings. Thus, the natural law is said to be reason, insofar as it is a natural power of the soul by which the human person distinguishes between good and evil, choosing good and rejecting evil. And reason is said to be a law *[jus]*, because it commands *[jubet]*; [also, it is said to be] law *[lex]* because it binds *[ligat]* or because it compels [one] to act rightly *[legitime]*; [it is said to be] natural, because reason is one of the natural goods, or because it agrees supremely with nature, and does not dissent from it. . . . Now in the second place, the natural law is said to be a judgment of reason, namely, a motion proceeding from reason, directly or indirectly; that is, any work or operation to which one is obliged by reason, as to discern, to choose, and to do good, to give alms, to love God, and those sorts of things. . . . But in this sense, "natural law" is improperly said, because anything which we have said to be contained in this sense is rather an effect of the natural law, or derives from it, or is something that one is bound to do by natural law, rather than being itself natural law. Likewise, in a third way the natural law is said to be an instinct and order of nature by which like things are propagated by their like . . . and do other things which they have to do in accordance with sensuality, that is, a natural appetite. Concerning this law, the jurist says, "the natural law is that which nature teaches all animals;" this law is common to all animals, while in the aforesaid two senses, it is only appropriate to rational beings. . . . Likewise, in a fourth sense, the natural law is said to be divine law, that is, what is contained in the law of Moses and the evangelical law; thus it is taken at the

beginning; and this is said to be natural law, because the highest nature, that is, God, transmitted it to us and taught it through the law and the prophets and the gospel, or because natural reason leads and impels us even through extrinsic learning to those things which are contained in the divine law. Hence, if I may speak boldly, I say quite certainly that this law is said improperly to be natural, because the natural law, that is, reason, compels one to do those things which are contained in it, and one is obliged to do those things by reason.[13]

Another approach organized the various definitions of the natural law in accordance with the different ways of understanding nature. We find an example of this approach in the writings of Aquinas's fellow Dominican Roland of Cremona, writing around 1230:

I say that, just as nature is analyzed by philosophers, just so, the manifold natural law ought to be analyzed. For there is a certain law or a certain universal nature, according to which it is said that all things naturally desire to be, or desire the good. Such a desire is universal nature, and the universal law of nature, and this is in all creatures, and perhaps this law or this nature proceeds from species, mode and order, of which enough has been said at the end of the second book. And there is a certain other nature, or particular law, which is in plants. . . . There is another more particular law in animals, by which each and every animal is united to one similar to itself, as Boethius says; and certain other laws are particular to certain kinds of animals, as for example, it is by nature that the spider weaves that she might catch the flies that she eats. And there is a more particular law, that is synderesis, in the human person.[14]

In fact, this last is Roland's preferred definition of the natural law, as we read further on:

Rather, we should say, just as we have said, that synderesis itself is indeed natural law in the particular way; and according to this, we grant that "one should be united to one alone" is of the natural law, that is, the natural law prescribes that so it should be done, on account of synderesis.[15]

When we turn back to the *Summa Theologiae* I-II 94.2, it is apparent that Aquinas combines these approaches in order to defend the rational coherence of the natural law. He begins his analysis of the natural law by identifying a first principle in terms of which other precepts of the natural law are to be related. This first principle is itself a variant on the definition of the natural law as a rational power of discriminating good and evil to which Huguccio gives pride of place, and which was subsequently widely adopted.[16] Within the framework of his taxonomy of human inclinations towards the good, Aquinas then finds a place for other traditional accounts of the natural law. The first inclination, which we share with all other creatures, is associated with the natural law understood as a universal tendency towards existence or goodness mentioned by Roland. The second inclination, which we share with other living creatures, is associated with Ulpian's natural law, to which pertain reproduction and the care of the young. Finally, the properly human natural law, including those precepts relating to life in society and worship of a divine being, are associated with distinctively human inclinations to live together and to engage in intellectual activity, which were central to Cicero's conception of the natural law and were subsequently incorporated into scholastic reflection by early canonical commentators on Gratian's *Decretum*.

At the same time, I-II 94.2 also represents an analysis of the different senses of the natural law in accordance with different understandings of nature, similar to that which we find in Roland. The first precept of practical reason is the distinctively human expression of the desire for the good to be found in all creatures, which is expressed in the first instance as a tendency towards the attainment of one's specific form of perfection, and then as a tendency to seek one's place in the universal order of things. Inanimate creatures express this general desire for goodness as a tendency to maintain themselves in existence, and animate creatures manifest it through their tendencies to stay alive and to reproduce their kind. The human creature, in turn, exhibits analogues of each of these tendencies, as well as displaying distinctively human tendencies which presuppose rationality. Seen in this light, I-II 94.2 is clearly an application of this general principle, developed in order to defend the rational cogency of the natural law.

To sum up the argument so far, there are very striking parallels in both approach and substance between I-II 94.2 and the discussions of the different laws of nature to be found in Huguccio, Roland, and many other scholastic canonists and theologians. These parallels strongly suggest that these discussions form the immediate context for Aquinas's argument in this passage. Furthermore, they indicate that his analysis is motivated by a similar concern to bring coherence to a variety of traditional understandings of the natural law. As such, it exemplifies what we might describe as the scholastic project, to bring the widest possible range of traditions and practical considerations into a "perfect system of knowledge" unified by reference to scripturally mediated revelation.[17] In this context, we can identify a second, more specific concern to safeguard a conception of nature as a coherent and intelligible system of causal principles—a concern that was again shared by the scholastics generally, but which is particularly important for the Aristotelian natural philosophy that undergirds Aquinas's account of the natural law. He thus argues for the unity of the natural law by analyzing it in terms of the complex yet rationally comprehensible causal tendencies exhibited by the human person as a creature and an animal of a distinctive kind.

In addition, Aquinas has a further, and from our standpoint a still more important, reason for defending the rational coherence and unity of the natural law. We see this most clearly when we turn from I-II 94.2 to a passage which occurs slightly later, that is, I-II 99.1. Here once again we find Aquinas asking whether a particular law, in this case the Old Law revealed to Moses, contains only one precept.

On the face of it, this question is even stranger than the near-parallel question which introduces I-II 94.2. Surely it is evident that the Old Law, that is to say, the Hebraic law as recorded in Scripture, contains multiple precepts? Yet as Aquinas observes in the first objection, a law is a precept, and since Scripture speaks of the Old Law in the singular, this would seem to imply that this law contains only one precept. This objection reflects Aquinas's general definition of a law, set forth at I-II 90.4: "Law is an ordinance of reason directed towards the common good, from one who has responsibility for the community, and promulgated." If the Old Law is to be a genuine law, that is to say, an ordinance of reason, then it must be susceptible of being analyzed as one unified precept, intelligible as such in terms of the purpose for which it is promulgated. Otherwise, we would not be able to grasp and act upon the precepts of the Old Law, at least not in accordance with our proper mode of functioning as rational agents (I-II 6.2). Aquinas thus argues that many things may be necessary to, or expedient for, the attainment of a given end, and in this sense, one unified law may contain many precepts, which are given rational coherence by the ultimate end towards which they are directed. Hence, in his reply to the first objection he says, "the Old Law is said to be one on account of its ordering to one end, and yet it contains diverse precepts, on account of the diversity of those things which it orders towards an end" (I-II 99.1 ad 1).

A similar concern to preserve the rational unity of the natural law lies behind I-II 94.2. The first objection under this article similarly points out that since "law" is contained in the genus "precept," then if there were many precepts of the law of nature, there would likewise be many laws of nature. As the text from Stephen of Tournai illustrates, many of Aquinas's immediate predecessors and contemporaries did indeed refer to multiple natural laws. For Aquinas, however, this line of analysis cannot account for the rational coherence of the natural law.

Accordingly, his aim in I-II 94.2 is to show the rational unity of the natural law through an analysis of the ways in which diverse precepts of the natural law may be said to be expressions of one fundamental precept, directed at the most general end of action, namely, the good itself. It is only from this perspective that men and women can understand and implement the natural law in a manner appropriate to their status as free individuals and participants in God's providential care for themselves and others.

What is more, the specification of the precepts of the natural law—whether the first principles or the precepts of the Decalogue following immediately from these—presupposes some grasp of the overarching purpose in terms of which they are unified into one law. As he says, "this pertains to right reason, that one should make use of those things which lead to an end in accordance with the measure which is appropriate to the end" (II-II 152.2), and we cannot determine the concrete applications of normative conflicts without taking account of the appropriate ordering of the diverse values that they incorporate (see, for example, II-II 101.4). More specifically, Aquinas appeals to the purposes of the precepts of the Decalogue in order to address the much-debated question of whether these admit of dispensation. Most of Aquinas's immediate predecessors and contemporaries held that these precepts do in fact admit of divine dispensation; Aquinas, in contrast, flatly denies this, on the grounds that these precepts express the intention of their legislator, who is of course God, in such a way that they can never be abrogated: "For the precepts of the first tablet, which order to God, contain the very order to a common and final good, which is God; and the precepts of the second tablet contain the very order of justice to be observed among human persons, that is, that nothing undue should be done to anyone, and that to each should be rendered what is due. For the precepts of the Decalogue are to be understood in accordance with this rationale. And therefore the precepts of the Decalogue do not in any way admit of dispensation" (I-II 100.8).

In the third objection, Aquinas offers what seems to be a decisive argument that not only God, but even human persons, can dispense from the precepts of the Decalogue: "the prohibition of homicide is contained among the precepts of the Decalogue. But it would seem that this precept receives dispensation from human persons, for example, when according to the precepts of human law, human persons are legitimately killed, for example, wrongdoers or enemies." He goes on to respond:

> [K]illing a person is prohibited in the Decalogue insofar as it has the character of something unjustified; for the precept contains the very rationale of justice. And human law cannot grant this, that a person might licitly be killed without justification. But the killing of malefactors or enemies of the republic is not unjustified. Hence, this is not contrary to a precept of the Decalogue, nor is such a killing a murder, which the Decalogue prohibits. . . . And similarly, if something is taken from another, which was his own, if he is obliged to lose it, this is not theft or robbery, which are prohibited by a precept of the Decalogue. . . .
>
> So therefore, these precepts of the Decalogue, with respect to the rational character of justice which they contain, are unchangeable. But with respect to some determination through application to individual acts, whether for example this or that is murder, theft or adultery, or not, this indeed is changeable; sometimes only by the divine authority, namely in those things which are instituted by God alone, as for example marriage and other things of this sort; and sometimes by human authority, with respect to those things which are committed to human jurisdiction. For with respect to those things, human persons act as the vicar of God, not however with respect to all things. (I-II 100.8 ad 3)

Thus, the precepts of the Decalogue are always binding, but that does not mean that we can proceed immediately from these to a correct judgment in every instance of moral choice. In many cases, we will be able to do so, but in other cases we will find it necessary to reflect carefully on the meaning of moral concepts such as murder, theft, or adultery, seen in the light of the overarching intention behind the promulgation of the corresponding precepts. In this way, moral reasoning proceeds through a process of specification, through which general moral concepts are given concrete meaning through prudential reflection aimed at practical application.[18]

The basic moral concepts sketched out in the Decalogue provide immediate starting points for much of this reflection, but as we have already noted, these concepts are themselves specifications of first principles which comprise the natural law in its primary sense. Because these are formulated in the context of the most fundamental claims and needs of human life, they are quite general and fall within reach of everyone's capacities, even though even these general precepts are too specific to be regarded as strictly speaking self-evident to all. Still more concrete moral norms are derived from these general norms through the same process of specification, seen in the context of a comprehensive assessment of the meaning of the human good as applied to particular cases. The further this process descends to details, the more it is subject both to contingency—because general moral concepts can be legitimately applied in more than one way—and to error— since in some cases even the most astute may find it difficult to discern an acceptable course of action. That is why the natural law at the level of concrete precepts admits of both legitimate variability and mistaken application, as Aquinas has already pointed out (I-II 94.4).

If my interpretation of I-II 94.2 is correct, we can more readily see why it has proven so difficult to derive an account of the specific normative content of the natural law from this article. Aquinas does not attempt here to develop such an account. Rather, he is defending the rational unity and coherence of the natural law, in the process also setting forth his interpretation of the various senses of the natural law which were current in the discussion at the time.[19] So far, it might seem that Aquinas is committed to what is essentially a modern conception of morality, understood as a systematic set of principles derived from, and unified by reference to, a fundamental principle. But this conclusion would be too quick. Aquinas does believe that the precepts of the natural law comprise a rational unity, but that does not imply that they are unified by being derived from some first principle in a systematic way, such that the logic of their derivation and their interconnections could be spelled out in advance. The concrete precepts of the natural law represent specifications of first principles, but their status as such, and their comprehensive unity seen from the standpoint of the purposes of those specifications, must be defended—and defended in terms of a contentious metaphysical theory, developed within an overarching theological context.

II. The Normative Significance of the Inclinations

We have just observed that for Aquinas, the natural law in its primary sense is equated with the first principles of practical reason, including, but not limited to, "Good is to be sought and done and evil is to be avoided." The inclinations enumerated in I-II 94.2 cannot plausibly be construed as natural law precepts, and yet they are clearly connected in some way with the first principle of practical reason. What then is their normative significance?

According to the interpretation developed by Grisez and Finnis, the inclinations to which Aquinas refers are significant because they provide the agent with knowledge of basic goods, including life, knowledge, and human interrelationships, which are self-evidently known to be good as soon as they are experienced. These basic goods, in turn, provide the basis for the derivation of moral norms, in accordance with the first principle of practical reason. At a minimum, once these goods have been apprehended, it is self-evident that their pursuit is desirable, and that it is wrong to act in such a way as to destroy or impede an instance of a basic good. It is important to underscore the point that for Grisez, and even more for Finnis, practical reason operating through the rational apprehension of basic goods generates moral norms through its own proper operations.[20] As Alan Donagan has observed, on this interpretation Aquinas's account of natural law is similar to Kant's account of practical reason, at least in its commitment to the autonomy of practical reason.[21] The resultant account deserves to be described as a version of natural law because reason is after all one component, indeed the definitive component, of human nature. But on their view it is a fundamental mistake to read Aquinas as if he regarded natural law precepts as grounded in human nature more comprehensively considered. As Finnis remarks, "Aquinas' moral arguments never run from 'natural' to 'therefore reasonable and right,' but always from 'reasonable and right' to 'therefore natural.'"[22]

MacIntyre appears at first to reject this line of interpretation, correctly noting that Aquinas's account of the natural law presupposes an account of what constitutes human happiness, understood as the distinctively human form of perfection. On closer examination, it is not so clear what role this account plays in shaping actual moral judgments, on MacIntyre's reading. If I have understood him correctly, MacIntyre holds that speculative accounts of the human good are normatively important for Aquinas because they provide starting points for shared deliberation—yet it is the deliberative processes themselves, rather than the perspectives and judgments they yield, which immediately yield the basic precepts of the natural law. (Or perhaps—since these precepts are self-evident, on MacIntyre's view—it would be more accurate to say that they manifest and display, and in that way clarify and confirm, these principles.) Mutual deliberation can only take place in a context of mutual equality and security, and this in turn presupposes the parameters set by the precepts of the Decalogue, which serve to guarantee my personal and social security, my freedom from inappropriate forms of influence, and the like.

Considered on its own merits, this argument is at best underdeveloped. It proves too little, or too much. If MacIntyre is simply claiming that deliberation presupposes some degree of security and pre-dictability, then it would seem that he has at most established the need for some framework of shared expectations and restraints—but not necessarily the framework set out by the specific natural law precepts that he cites. If he wants to claim that deliberation requires complete security and full mutual equality, he has set himself a very high bar-rier indeed—first, to show that these are indeed conditions for shared deliberation, and secondly, that these conditions can be secured, through these specific natural law precepts or any others. At any rate, I can find no textual evidence that this way of analyzing the precepts of the Decalogue represents Aquinas's own explicit or implicit views on the matter.

As noted above, the precepts of the Decalogue can be derived with minimal reflection from certain self-evident principles of prac-tical reason, namely, to wrong no one and to fulfill one's obligations. But as we have already seen, even the precepts of the Decalogue, which comprise the immediate concrete formulations of the natural law, are as they stand too general to be put into practice. They must be further specified by a lawgiver, whether human or divine, in the light of an overarching purpose which gives them both coherence and specificity (I-II 91.3, 99.3 ad 2, 99.4). The purposes of the lawgiver, in turn, pre-suppose some overall account of the meaning and point of human life and the ways in which a community can foster the attainment of that purpose. Once again, we are reminded that for Aquinas, normative judgments presuppose speculative knowledge—and correlatively, it is these judgments and the supporting framework of (hopefully true) beliefs themselves that generate moral precepts, rather than the pro-cesses through which these are derived.

This brings us back to the question of the normative significance of the inclinations. MacIntyre is right to underscore the centrality of the inclinations for our knowledge of the human good—a point that is also made, albeit in a very different way, by Grisez, Finnis, and others. At the same time, we can only appreciate the significance of the inclinations and draw out their normative implications by way of placing them in a wider philosophical and theological context. This does not imply that the inclinations can only be recognized as such, and given some normative significance, on the strength of an overarching speculative theory; on the contrary, the unreflective experiences and practices through which we individually and collectively apprehend and pursue these inclinations provide the immediate context for any kind of theoretical reflection on their significance and normative import. At the same time, however, the relevant theories cannot be elicited from these experiences themselves, or the processes through which we reflectively incorporate them into our lives.

This becomes apparent when we realize that Aquinas himself appeals to an overarching philosophical and theological framework in order to explain the significance of the inclinations. In I-II 91.2, "Whether there is in us a natural law?" he observes that all creatures are said to be "ruled and measured" by the eternal law, insofar as they are subject to divine providence:

> [I]t is manifest that all things participate in some way in the eternal law, insofar, that is, as they have inclinations to their proper acts and ends through its impression on them. Among the others, however, the rational creature is subject to divine providence in a certain more excellent way, insofar as it becomes in a sense a participant in providence, being provident for itself and for others. Hence in the rational creature also there is a participation in the eternal law, through which it has a natural inclination to its due act and end. And such participation in the eternal law on the part of the rational creature is called the natural law. (I-II 91.2)

We might say that the inclinations mediate the eternal law to creatures, insofar as they embody and express the ordered patterns of activity proper to the kind of creature in question—which, as Aquinas elsewhere observes, represents the creature's specific mode of participation in the divine goodness (I 6.1). In the rational creature, the inclinations can only be pursued through choices grounded in rational reflection, and for this reason, Aquinas identifies the natural law more specifically with "the light of natural reason," explaining that this light, "through which we discern what is good and evil, which pertains to the natural law, is nothing other than an impression of the divine light in us" (I-II 91.2). This point is surely not unconnected with the fact that only the rational creature can consistently, and as it were deliberately, pursue its inclinations in perverse and corrupted ways, which undermine its attainment of its true end. That is why each natural inclination corresponds to a particular virtue, disposing it to operate in an appropriate way (II-II 108.2). Nonetheless, as I-II 91.2 indicates, Aquinas interprets human inclinations in such a way as to underscore the parallels between human action and the patterns of ordered activity which stem from and express the proper forms of other kinds of creatures, through which they move towards their specific modes of perfection. This parallel is drawn even more clearly in an earlier text, his commentary on the *Divine Names* of pseudo-Dionysius:

> It may happen, however, that some prince, who may be desirable in his own person, will nonetheless give onerous laws to his subjects, which he himself does not keep, and therefore his subjects are not effectively subjected to him. But since this is excluded from God, [Dionysius] adds that he sets *voluntary laws* over *all;* for the law of God is the proper natural inclination placed in every creature to do that which is appropriate to it, in accordance with nature. And therefore, since all things are held by divine desire, so all are held by his law. (*De Divinis Nominibus* X, 1.1, 857)

By the same token, Aquinas explicitly draws a parallel between the inclinations of nonrational creatures and the inclinations of intellectual as well as rational creatures, observing that the latter can be understood by comparison with the former: "The natural inclinations in those things devoid of reason make manifest the natural inclination belonging to the will of an intellectual nature" (I 60.5). This remark clearly indicates that Aquinas sees the inclinations as reflecting, at least in part, aspects of our nature which we share with other kinds of creatures. Thus, characteristic patterns of human action can fruitfully be analyzed, up to a point at least, through comparison with analogous patterns of behavior and movement in other kinds of creatures. Indeed, this line of analysis can even shed light on the proper inclinations of incorporeal creatures, the angels, which comprise the subject of the article from which this remark is taken. And clearly, this line of analysis will presuppose some set of theoretical claims in terms of which the relevant analogies can be identified and their significance assessed—Aquinas's own Aristotelian philosophy of nature and metaphysics, or some other.

The difficulty lies in determining just how we are to fulfill our nature and achieve our specific form of perfection by acting on these inclinations. At this point, we need once again to remind ourselves that Aquinas does not attempt in I-II 94.2 to set forth concrete natural law precepts, or to explain how we arrive at such precepts on the basis of the first principle of practical reason. Rather, he is arguing here for the rational coherence of the natural law, which he spells out in terms of the relationship of specific precepts to the first principle of practical reason. To be sure, this line of analysis presupposes that the natural law has specific content, and that we know something about what that content is. Even so, Aquinas does not here refer to specific norms. The inclinations themselves are not moral norms, nor do they give rise to precepts apart from rational reflection on their place in human life taken as a whole. But Aquinas does say that we can correlate the inclinations with the precepts stemming from them, in such a way as to see the rational coherence of the latter. Hence, he says that precepts "pertain to" *(pertinere)* the natural law or they "regard" *(spectare)* the natural law—the assumption being that we already know what these precepts are, and now need to be shown how they stem from and express the first principles of the natural law.

When we look further at the scholastic writings which form Aquinas's context, we see that he is not the only one who speaks of the specific precepts of the natural law in this way. It is instructive to compare Albert with Aquinas at this point:

> The natural law is nothing other than the law of reason or obligation, insofar as nature is reason. When, however, I say that nature is reason, it is possible to understand it more as nature, or more as reason, or equally as nature and reason. If however it is taken as nature, then it would be the principle of actions pertaining to the continuance and well-being of the one in whom it is, and of the rational consideration of those things which pertain to the well-being of the individual, as for example, food, clothing, a house, a bed, the care of health and the procuring of medicine, and other things of this sort which we seek for ourselves through rational consideration. Similar to these are those things pertaining to the well-being of the species, such as a wife and children, and care and provision for each of them. For when reason is said to be nature, and more nature than reason, I do not exclude reason. And because the law does not establish injury, I always assume right reason with regard to these things. On this account, the desire of gluttony and adultery and stealing would not be in accordance with the natural law nor according to nature spoken of in this way, because right reason is that which is rationally discerned about natural things, that is to say, things pertaining to nature, through the natural law. (*De Bono* V 1.2)

Clearly, Albert's point is that human activities carried out in pursuit of the well-being of the individual and the species can be understood as expressions of the natural law, so long as this aim is pursued in a reasonable and appropriate manner. He is not deriving norms about self-preservation and procreation from the natural law but rather, interpreting these activities as manifestations of a natural law.

Similarly, in I-II 94.2, Aquinas's point is that the specific precepts of the natural law can be understood as expressions of a complex but ordered human inclination towards goodness. Given a correct theoretical understanding of human nature, it becomes apparent that the diverse precepts of the natural law are in fact expressions of the first principle of practical reason, but this does not mean that those precepts can be derived *ab initio* from the first principle, taken together with an intuitive knowledge of basic human goods. That is why he begins the main body of the article by distinguishing between those propositions which are self-evident to everyone and those which are self-evident to the wise; as he subsequently explains, there are indeed some moral precepts which are self-evident to all (that is, the Golden Rule), but others call for minimal reflection in order to be grasped (the precepts of the Decalogue), and still others can only be grasped by the wise (the specific applications of these precepts; see, respectively, I-II 100.3 ad 1 and 100.3 passim). Thus, Aquinas does identify specific moral precepts as precepts of the natural law, understood in a secondary but legitimate sense as expressions or specifications of the natural law properly so called, that is to say, the first principles of practical reason. The precepts of the Decalogue are analyzed in these terms, as are all acts of virtue, albeit with qualifications (I-II 94.3, 100.1). Indeed, any legitimate moral rule can be said to be a precept of the natural law, at least insofar as it reflects the exigencies of reason (I-II 94.3, 100.1)—although this does not imply that the natural law is grounded in anything like "pure practical reason" in a Kantian sense, as Grisez and Finnis (among others) suggest.[23]

More specifically, Aquinas makes it clear that reason in its practical operations always presupposes a rational desire for some perceived good, which in turn presupposes an intellectual grasp of the good in question as both attainable and in some way consistent with the agent's overall happiness.[24] Thus, reason in its practical operations presupposes a whole array of judgments, more or less well developed and articulated, about the final end of human life, the individual's own proper path to this end, and the way in which the desideratum at hand relates to the attainment of this end (I 1.1; II-II 4.7). These judgments, in turn, presuppose the operations of speculative reason, as informed both by natural processes of inquiry and by the virtue of faith—a virtue, we should note, of speculative reason (II-II 4.2 ad 3). Aquinas makes this point explicitly at the very beginning of the *Summa Theologiae,* in the context of a discussion of the necessity of theology for human life. Men and women cannot attain their last end, he notes, unless they have some idea of what it is that this last end involves (I 1.1). Since our last end is supernatural, he goes on to say, we cannot discover it for ourselves; God must reveal it to us, and Scripture is the medium for that revelation. At the same time, the exigencies of human reason are such that we need some orderly development of the data of revelation, if we are to act on these in an effective way (I 1.8 ad 2). That is one function of the science of theology, and that is why theology can legitimately be described, albeit in a secondary sense, as a practical science (I 1.4).

It might be said that while speculative knowledge of the relevant kind is necessary for salvation, it is not a necessity of human action as such. Considered in themselves, human desire, choice, and action can be analyzed in terms of inclinations towards basic goods, which can be grasped as such by reason, independently of any kind of speculative theoretical account of human nature. I have come to believe that there is a sense in which this claim is true, although it needs to be carefully qualified. Before pursuing this point, however, we should note that Aquinas says without qualification that human action properly so called—which is to say, fully rational action—presupposes some conception of a final end, towards which all one's specific choices are directed in some way or other (I-II 1.1, 1.6). This is so even when the concept of the final end in question is incomplete or mistaken; hence, the need for a concept of the final end is a constitutive element of rationality in action rather than a requirement that obtains only in the supernatural order of grace.

Let me turn now to the relation between the inclinations and practical reason. Aquinas certainly holds that the human person, like every other creature, is directed towards his or her final end through inclinations towards a species-specific form of goodness. The inclinations are thus dynamic expressions of the specific form of the creature, which as such display its intelligibility and goodness as a creature of a particular kind. As such, they reflect a natural ordering, through which the complex operations of the creature are sustained through time in a coherent and unified existence. The ordering of the inclinations is certainly accessible to reason, but that does not mean that it is established through reason. Rather, this ordering is discerned through the operations of (speculative) reason, in part through a comparison between the inclinations of intellectual or rational creatures and those manifested by nonrational and even nonliving creatures (*ST* I 60.5). In the human person, this natural ordering incorporates both more universal and foundational inclinations (towards existence, and for animals, towards nutrition and reproduction) and more particular and species-specific inclinations (including in our case all those presupposing rationality, most notably political life and worship of a divine being; see I-II 94.2). That is why the inclinations proper to a rational or intellectual creature (that is, an angel) can be analyzed, up to a point, by comparison to the inclinations manifested in nonrational and even nonliving creatures; to a considerable extent, rational and nonrational creatures share the same kinds of inclinations, even though presumably these are expressed in distinctive ways for each kind of creature.

But—it will be said—surely the ordinary man or woman neither knows nor cares anything about all this, and yet men and women seem to be perfectly capable of acting in pursuit of the proper objects of the inclinations. Quite right; the objects of the inclinations are natural objects of the will, and the human person spontaneously desires and pursues them, even before he or she is capable of rational reflection and action properly so called. This implies that with the advent of rational reflection, the human person will spontaneously affirm the desirability of these objects and will make room for their pursuit in the overall conception of human happiness which will govern his or her rational choices and acts. Thus, there is indeed a sense in which experiences of the inclinations, and the spontaneous rational apprehension that the objects of these inclinations are desirable, precede and inform speculative knowledge about human nature. Yet none of this implies that all our knowledge about human nature depends on these kinds of apprehensions, or that our empirical and philosophical knowledge about human nature has no relevance for the practical operations of reason. On the contrary, Aquinas indicates clearly that our speculative knowledge about ourselves can and should inform our practical judgments, above all by offering arguments of the relevant kind himself— to explain why rational creatures naturally love both the good of the universe and the divine goodness of God more than themselves as individuals (I 60.5); to justify giving preference to one's kin and close associates in acting out of charity, on the grounds that such preferences reflect inclinations that can be observed in all creatures (II-II 26.2); to condemn suicide and to defend killing in self-defense (II-II 64.5, 7); and, famously, to work out a sexual ethic on the basis of the order implicit in the inclination towards reproduction (II-II 154.11).

The desire for, and voluntary pursuit of, the objects of the inclinations does not presuppose a speculative theory, about the inclinations or anything else; to this extent, at least, those who would ground the precepts of the natural law in the spontaneous apprehension and pursuit of the natural aims of human life are right. Nonetheless, at this level, desire and voluntary activity have not yet risen to the level of fully rational human action: we are here in the realm of the higher animals, children, and (perhaps, and in a qualified way) immature and unreflective adults (I-II 6.2). In order to attain a capacity for fully rational action, an individual must arrive at some kind of speculative account concerning the proper end of human life, and of his or her life in particular. It is not necessary to have a sound empirical and philosophical theory of human nature in order to develop such an account, but all things being equal, one's account of the overall end of human life will be more adequate, the more securely it is grounded in such a theory. By the same token, our expanding speculative knowledge and understanding of human nature can and should inform and correct our concept of the final end of human life, in this way informing practical judgment. The relation between practical judgment and speculative knowledge is thus reciprocal and mutually correcting; we do come to understand what it means to be human through our experiences of practical judgment, choice, and action, but at the same time, our speculative knowledge of what it is to be human likewise guides and directs those practical judgments.

III. NATURAL LAW AND MORAL PLURALISM

We might well wish that Aquinas had addressed the question of the universality of the natural law, and the extent and limits of legitimate cross-cultural pluralism, more squarely and directly than he does. But given his own context and concerns, these were not key questions either for him or for his immediate forebears and interlocutors. Early scholastic reflection on the natural law emerged in a period of rapid and far-reaching social transformations and institutional reforms, all taking place within the broad framework of a shared normative and theological tradition. In this context, the scholastics were especially concerned to adjudicate among diverse and incompatible expressions and developments of a shared tradition—and they did so, at least to a considerable extent, by analyzing and adjudicating among these diverse practices as more or less acceptable conventional specifications of natural principles. They were thus particularly concerned to identify the diverse ways in which nature, comprehensively understood, finds expression in the conventions of a given society, and correlatively to develop normative criteria for evaluating and reforming those conventions. They had a great deal to say about the ways in which the natural law is expressed (or compromised) within a particular society, but—from our perspective—very little to say about the ways in which it might serve as a framework for normative judgments across the boundaries of diverse societies. The question of cultural pluralism only becomes a pressing theological question when Europeans are brought into contact with the very different ways of life exemplified by the peoples of newly discovered lands—and it is no coincidence that this is the point at which modern theories of the natural law, which are centrally focused on questions of universal ethics and international law, begin to emerge.

Nonetheless, the scholastics, including Aquinas, do address questions having to do with the universality of the natural law—if only because the natural law tradition as they receive it raises these questions. What is more, Aquinas himself offers a powerful and persuasive account of the ways in which human nature is both intelligible and normatively significant—in other words, a theory of the natural law— and to the extent that this account is persuasive, we might expect it to provide a starting point for understanding and coming to terms with cross-cultural moral pluralism. And so it does—not through providing a universally valid morality, but through suggesting fruitful ways in which the realities of moral pluralism can be understood and negotiated.

Let me begin by recalling an earlier point. Aquinas, together with the scholastics more generally, would give a qualified yes to the question whether the natural law comprises a universally valid and accessible law. The first principles of the natural law are accessible to all rational persons, because they are among the constitutive structures of the rational soul. But by the same token, they are too general to yield concrete norms for conduct, taken by themselves. The precepts of the Decalogue are not themselves self-evident, but they can be derived from first principles with only a minimum of reflection (I-II 100.3 ad 1; cf. I-II 95.1). Hence, they are readily knowable to all persons, and for this reason, Aquinas is prepared to say that they belong to the natural law without qualification (I-II 100.1).

Yet it does not follow that the natural law as Aquinas understands it can serve as the basis for a set of norms that are at one and the same time concrete enough to guide communal and individual action and universal in scope. Aquinas (together with almost all his scholastic forebears and contemporaries) is committed to holding that specific precepts of the natural law are rationally justifiable—that is to say, that they can be defended as legitimate expressions of the forms of life and purposes intrinsic to us as a natural kind of creature, *given* a more or less accurate grasp of the constitutive principles of human nature. It is less clear, however, that on his view the natural law yields concrete precepts that could be rationally defended apart from some such (necessarily contentious) theoretical framework, and what is more, defended as the only or the best possible specifications of the relevant natural inclinations. To put it another way, it is far from clear that Aquinas's theory of the natural law provides a basis for a compelling argument that an alternative cultural norm is simply wrong—for example, that we in the West are right and those in many Asian societies are wrong, to insist that the choice of one's marriage partner is an overriding individual right. It might be that contrary views on this question, taken together with the very different construals of marriage and family life that they reflect, represent two alternative ways of construing the human inclinations towards reproduction and kinship associations, each rationally defensible as a legitimate expression of human nature, but neither rationally compelling as the only, or even the clearly superior, alternative.

The precepts of the natural law fall along a spectrum of generality and rational certainty, from the first principle of practical reason, which is completely general and immediately self-evident to all, proceeding through direct and generally accessible applications of this principle comprising the precepts of the Decalogue, and then further to more specific applications, leading finally to determinations of correct action in particular instances of choice. At every level, this process will call for some determination of the concrete meaning of more general norms, and as such it will presuppose a more comprehensive principle as its starting point—thus even the most general moral precepts of the Decalogue cannot be regarded as strictly speaking foundational first principles. These precepts do reflect the immediate implications of first principles as these applied to the general needs and desires of human life, and as such everyone can readily grasp that they represent specifications of the foundational injunction to do good and to avoid evil. However, further levels of specification require greater understanding and prudence, which do not fall within the scope of everyone; that is why these processes require the judgment of "the wise." Correlatively, wise men and women will grasp that sound applications of basic moral concepts reflect specifications of the most general principle that good is to be done and the bad is to be avoided. In that way, these applications will be self-evident to them, since they correctly understand the terms in which they are framed, even though they will not be self-evident to the rest of us.

The question that arises at this point—for many of us, at any rate—is, just who are these "wise," and how do they go about the processes of applying and specifying the general precepts of the natural law? These are very much questions of our own time—yet Aquinas does suggest at least the beginnings of an answer in the text with which we began, I-II 94.4, in which he asks whether the natural law is the same for all. Consider his response to objection 2, which cites Aristotle's claim that what is just is not the same for all, in such a way as to rule out a legitimate diversity of laws—the laws of peoples, as the context makes clear. Aquinas responds that "the words of the philosopher are to be understood of those things which are naturally just not in accordance with common principles, but in accordance with certain conclusions derived from these, which maintain rectitude in most cases, and yet fall short in a few" (I-II 94.4 ad 2). This might appear from our perspective to be a fairly insignificant concession to diversity at the level of legal specification, which would of course be consistent with the claim that there is a universal morality. Yet on Aquinas's own terms, a legitimate diversity at the level of human laws is more significant than we might at first recognize. In his analytic taxonomy of kinds of law set out at I-II 90, he does not identify the moral law as a separate category, apart from natural law on the one hand and human and divine (that is to say, revealed) law on the other. We have already noted that the natural law, understood in its most proper sense, is comprised of foundational principles of practical reason, and therefore cannot be equated with a moral law in the modern sense. Aquinas does speak of moral precepts, but these are a subset of divine, that is to say, scripturally revealed law—even though they do reflect natural and reasonable exigencies of human existence. Moreover, the moral precepts, which he identifies at different points with both natural law and the proper acts of the virtues, are very general and must be specified through either human or divine law in order to be carried out (I-II 91.3, 99.3 ad 2, 99.4).

It would appear that the natural law is always specified by a lawgiver for Aquinas, whether human or divine. Narrowly understood, this is an implausible claim. However, if we take legislation broadly, to include communal processes of reflection, rational persuasion, and the formation of custom—and there is at least some reason to believe that Aquinas would accept such a move (see, most notably, I-II 97.3)—then we are left with a more persuasive account according to which normative precepts are always specified through communal processes, more or less explicit and authoritative, through which the general precepts of the natural law are given concrete meaning and force.[25] But at any rate, on this account concrete normative precepts are constructed, in and through communal processes of specification and determination. We cannot say that they are discovered, because prior to these processes, they do not even exist.

These considerations are reinforced by a second point. Recall that for Aquinas, reason in its practical operations necessarily involves judgments of priority and proper ordering among a range of diverse goods. In many cases, at least, it will be impossible to determine the concrete meaning of practical norms without making judgments of these kinds—determining when, for example, one's family obligations should override one's desire to pursue a life of perfection through religious vows, and when it does not. Again, when Aquinas considers these issues, he tends to do so in the context of individual deliberation and choice. Yet it would seem that exactly the same kinds of ordering and prioritizing operations would come into play at the level of legislation, and in the formation of social norms more generally. Here especially, it would seem, communally shared assumptions and judgments about the proper shape and form of human life, the desirable and worthwhile, and the like, would play an indispensable role in determining the concrete norms through which natural inclinations are channeled and expressed. As the philosopher John Gray observes, "Incommensurable values are by no means always constituted by social conventions. Some are anthropological universals. But universal human values are often rivals. When universal values collide there are no universal principles for settling their conflicts."[26]

The problem that we face, as men and women confronting one another in a context of deep moral disagreements, is not that of identifying a preexistent moral code that will settle these conflicts in some mutually acceptable way. Rather, we are challenged to construct a set of mutually acceptable norms through processes of shared reflection and negotiation—first of all, at the level of international law, but also within the increasingly permeable boundaries of our immediate political communities. This opens up the possibility that a universal ethic may still have validity—not as something we hope to discover, but something that we might jointly construct. To some extent, I would share this hope.

It might seem that this hope would be dashed by Aquinas's insistence that natural law reasoning presupposes a framework of speculative beliefs. Yet, paradoxically, this aspect of his thought suggests one way in which these processes of construction might proceed. In earlier writings, I have argued that any account of the natural law must draw on specifically theological elements in order to function prescriptively. My point was that we cannot understand the natural law, either theoretically or as a substantive, prescriptive account of practical norms, unless we take account of the ways in which the tradition of natural law reflection was decisively shaped by theological considerations at critical points. Correlatively, I argued that we cannot make theoretical sense, or practical use, of the natural law in purely rational or philosophical terms, without taking the contingencies introduced by theological considerations into account. I would still claim that the natural law cannot adequately be understood outside a theological context, but I now appreciate that the dichotomy between a theological and a philosophical account of natural law is too simplistic.

The more fundamental issue, it now seems to me, emerges between those who claim that practical norms can adequately (perhaps only) be analyzed in terms of an account of the autonomous functioning of practical reason and those who argue that any adequate account of such norms must rest on a more comprehensive philosophical, scientific, or theological account which locates them in a wider context of reflection and explanation. In my view, Aquinas's account of the natural law depends in part on philosophical claims, more specifically on a broadly Aristotelian philosophy of nature, which implies the actuality, the epistemic accessibility, and the normative significance of a shared human nature. As such, it does offer resources for defending and evaluating substantive moral claims on the basis of rational considerations that we might reasonably hope to be persuasive, even across the boundaries of distinct traditions of rational inquiry. Admittedly, these resources would not extend so far as to yield moral norms which are rationally *compelling* to all well-disposed persons. Yet if Aquinas's approach to the natural law is sound, that is just what we would expect. After all, he holds that practical norms are grounded in human nature, and our understanding and assessment of those norms will depend on the theory of human nature that we bring to bear on them. No such theory of human nature can expect to be so overwhelmingly well supported that it is rationally compelling to everyone who understands it. As MacIntyre rightly points out, no philosophical or broadly speculative theory, however good it is, can be so well developed as to dispel all doubts. Nonetheless, experience has shown that well-developed speculative accounts of the relevant kind can and do enjoy wide persuasive force, even across the boundaries of diverse intellectual traditions. So it may well prove to be in this case.

However, I remain convinced that even on the most optimistic showing, any attempt to specify the general precepts of the natural law will remain indeterminate and incomplete, apart from the traditions and practices of some specific community. In particular, the natural law as we Christians understand and formulate it will inevitably involve some degree of theological specification. What I have in mind, specifically, are claims about the centrality and value of certain aspects of human nature—namely, our capacities for self-direction grounded in rational judgment, identified by the scholastics as the very Image of God—and correlatively, strong commitments to the equal value of all persons (including those in whom the relevant capacities are damaged or undeveloped).[27] To the extent that this congeries of claims depends on specific theological commitments—as I believe they do— the norms stemming from them, including especially those connected to doctrines of natural or human rights, ultimately rest on specifically theological foundations. Yet it may well be the case that others who do not share these commitments may still find the relevant norms attractive and persuasive, and adapt them in such a way as to appropriate them into quite different traditions of thought and practice— just as we owe more than we can know to central practices of other traditions. There are many natural moralities, but all of them reflect something of the goodness and the attractive force of human nature itself, and as such they jointly constitute the patrimony of the human race.

Notes

Portions of this essay are taken from an earlier work, "A Response to Martin Rhonheimer," *Studies in Christian Ethics* 19, no. 3 (2006): 379–96, and are used by the permission of the editor of that journal. All translations are my own.

1. These include MacIntyre himself: for a recent discussion of the "Enlightenment project" and its failures, see *Three Rival Versions of Moral Enquiry: Encyclopedia, Genealogy, and Tradition* (Notre Dame: University of Notre Dame Press, 1990), 55–56. Similarly, the philosopher John Gray argues that the value pluralism he defends is simply incompatible with the universalist ideals of the Enlightenment; see *Two Faces of Liberalism* (New York: New Press, 2000), 1–33.

2. Most fully, in *Whose Justice? Which Rationality?* (Notre Dame: University of Notre Dame Press, 1988), 349–69.

3. Pamela Hall, *Narrative and the Natural Law: An Interpretation of Thomistic Ethics* (Notre Dame: University of Notre Dame Press, 1994), 33.

4. For Grisez's original account of the derivation of more specific precepts of the natural law, see Germain Grisez, "The First Principle of Practical Reason: A Commentary on the *Summa theologiae*, 1–2, Question 94, Article 2," *Natural Law Forum* 10 (1965): 178–201; Finnis provides a more detailed development of this line of interpretation in *Aquinas* (Oxford: Oxford University Press, 1998), 86–90, 103–31.

5. In "The First Principle of Practical Reason," 172, Grisez claims that many precepts of the natural law, and not just the first principle, are self-evident to all people. Subsequently, he and other proponents of this theory qualify this claim; as Robert George points out, *In Defense of Natural Law* (Oxford: Oxford University Press, 1999), 45, it is a mistake to assume that the specific conclusions of the natural law share in the same rational certainty as the first principle of practical reason and the norms through which it is specified. Nonetheless, it is clear that Grisez and Finnis would still claim that even the specific conclusions of practical reason have a very high degree of certainty, if not the absolute certainty of the first principles.

6. Daniel Mark Nelson, *The Priority of Prudence: Virtue and Natural Law in Aquinas and Its Implications for Modern Ethics* (University Park: Pennsylvania State University Press, 1992), 119. For a somewhat similar interpreta-

tion, developed however without specific reference to I-II 94.2, see John Bowlin, *Contingency and Fortune in Aquinas' Ethic* (Cambridge: Cambridge University Press, 1999), 130–36.

7. Hall, *Narrative and the Natural Law*, 33.

8. In saying this, I do not want to elide the differences between Nelson and Hall. According to Nelson, prudential judgment is an alternative to the application of moral rules, whereas Hall argues (more persuasively, in my view) that the moral rules of the natural law are discerned through the operations of prudence. Hence, Hall does believe that the natural law can be said to contain moral rules, insofar as its requirements are articulated through prudential judgment; see, in particular, *Narrative and the Natural Law*, 23–44.

9. Grisez does note that this article is set up to answer the question whether the natural law contains many precepts, or only one, but he then goes on to treat it as if it were meant as an explanation of how other precepts of the natural law are founded on the first principle of practical reason; see "The First Principle of Practical Reason," 169–70. On the other hand, Finnis rejects the "threefold order" of the inclinations as "an irrelevant schematization"; see *Natural Law and Natural Rights* (Oxford: Clarendon Press, 1980), 95. On the contrary, this "threefold order" is central to the point which Aquinas wants to make in this article.

10. Grisez, "The First Principle of Practical Reason," 169 fn. 3.

11. As Rudolf Weigand points out, the most immediate source for Gratian's definition is probably Hugh of St. Victor, *De Sacramentis* I 11.7; see *Die Naturrechtslehre der Legisten und Dekretisten von Irnerius bis Accursius und von Gratian bis Johannes Teutonicus* (Munich: Max Huber, 1967), 133; and cf. Hugh's text at 131.

12. Taken from Stephen's commentary on Gratian's *Decretum*, excerpted (in Latin) in *Die Naturrechtslehre der Legisten und Dekretisten*, 148. Weigand immediately adds that he is the first to offer such a list.

13. From Huguccio's commentary on Gratian's *Decretum*, excerpted (in Latin) in Odon Lottin, *Le droit naturel chez saint Thomas d'Aquin et ses prédécesseurs*, 2nd ed. (Bruges: Beyart, 1931), 109–10.

14. Taken from the text excerpted in Lottin, *Le droit naturel*, 115.

15. Ibid.

16. According to Brian Tierney, Huguccio was the first to equate natural law with reason, that is to say, with a rational power of moral discernment, but a consensus on this point quickly emerged among canon lawyers; see his *The Idea of Natural Rights: Studies on Natural Rights, Natural Law and Church*

Law, 1150–1625 (Atlanta: Scholars Press, 1997), 64–65; and, more generally, 43–77.

17. R. W. Southern, Scholastic Humanism and the Unification of Europe, vol. 1: Foundations (Oxford: Blackwell, 1995), 4; I rely largely on Southern for the characterization of European society during the early scholastic period.

18. As Hall persuasively argues; once again, see Narrative and Natural Law, 23–44.

19. In the first article of I-II 100, Aquinas seems to qualify his earlier claim that the natural law is grounded in the first principle that good is to be done and the bad is to be avoided. That is, in addition to this principle, he also identifies Jesus' commandments to love God and neighbor (Matt. 22:37–39), and correlatively the injunction to avoid wronging anyone, as self-evident principles of the natural law. It would appear that he holds that there are several first principles of the natural law, which would seem to undermine the defense of the rational unity of the natural law developed in I-II 94.2. However, the connection between these diverse principles is later clarified in the context of his analysis of the virtue of justice. There, we read that the injunctions to love and to forbear harming others are themselves specifications of the first principle of practical reason as applied to our dealings with other persons, while the first principle more generally construed is foundational for all the virtues, including those which refer only to oneself (II-II 79.1). This explains why these injunctions are associated specifically with the precepts of the Decalogue, since, as Aquinas goes on to say, these are the primary precepts of the virtue of justice (II-II 122.1). Thus, even the injunctions to love God and neighbor and to avoid harm, which are said without qualification to be self-evident to all, are specifications of the first principle to do good and avoid the bad; thus, they do not undermine the rational unity of the natural law.

20. Grisez develops this point in "The First Principle of Practical Reason," 190–96. Finnis likewise develops it both in Natural Law and Natural Rights, 33–34; and in Aquinas, 20–51.

21. Alan Donagan, The Theory of Morality (Chicago: University of Chicago Press, 1977), 60–66. But as will appear below, he was wrong to associate this view with Aquinas himself. Daniel Westberg likewise identifies the Kantian strain in the Grisez/Finnis theory but correctly disassociates this approach from Aquinas's conception of prudence; see Right Practical Reason: Aristotle, Action, and Prudence in Aquinas (Oxford: Clarendon Press, 1994), 10–11.

22. Finnis, Aquinas, 153 n. 91.

23. On the contrary, Aquinas analyzes many other moral norms in terms of their foundations in human nature more broadly construed, that is, in light of our proper inclinations considered as animals or even simply as creatures. For example, he condemns suicide because it violates the natural inclination of all living creatures to stay alive (II-II 64.5), and correlatively he defends killing in self-defense on the grounds that such an act is a legitimate expression of the inclination towards self-preservation common to all creatures (II-II 64.7). Similarly, he permits self-mutilation in order to preserve the health of the body, since the health of the organism is naturally preferable to its physical integrity (II-II 65.1). Vengeance, understood as the infliction of penal suffering for some good cause, is analyzed in terms of a general natural inclination to resist evil (II-II 108.1, 2). The obligations of obedience are limited by the natural inclinations and needs of the body, since with respect to such matters we are all equal (II-II 104.5). The virtue of temperance takes its norms from the natural necessities of human life (II-II 141.6); hence, fasting is an act of virtue when done for appropriate reasons, but it is vicious when taken to the extreme of actual harm (II-II 147.1 ad 2). And as is well known, Aquinas draws his norms for sexual behavior in part from a consideration of the natural purpose of human sexuality, as indicated by its expression in the life of other kinds of animals (II-II 154.11).

24. Of course, I do not mean to deny that reason in its practical operations takes its starting point from first principles, most important the principle that the good is to be pursued and what is bad is to be avoided (*ST* I 79.12; I-II 94.2; II-II 47.6). But these principles, taken by themselves, cannot lead to action apart from some desire for a particular good, which in turn depends on a judgment of the intellect that the desideratum in question is indeed good, and in some way consonant with the agent's overall happiness; see I-II 1.6, 8.1, 9.1, 10.1, 2; II-II 25.7.

25. Hall is one of the few recent commentators on Aquinas's ethic to develop this point in detail; again, see the illuminating discussion in *Narrative and Natural Law,* 23–44.

26. Gray, *Two Faces of Liberalism,* 45.

27. This point has frequently been made, by myself and others; I have been particularly influenced here by Brian Tierney, *The Idea of Natural Rights* (Atlanta: Scholars Press, 1997), 43–77; and by Basil Mitchell's unjustly neglected *Morality: Religious and Secular: The Dilemma of the Traditional Conscience* (Oxford: Clarendon Press, 1980); see, in particular, 107–37.

CHAPTER 3 | Moral Disagreement and
Interreligious Conversation

The Penitential Pace of Understanding

David A. Clairmont

A warning offered by Pope John Paul II about the
difficulties that inevitably accompany ecumenical dialogue provides
a helpful frame of reference for an examination of intractable moral
disagreements: "Christians cannot underestimate the burden of *long-
standing misgivings* inherited from the past, and of mutual *misunderstandings* and *prejudices. Complacency, indifference* and *insufficient
knowledge of one another* often make this situation worse. Consequently, the commitment to ecumenism must be based upon the conversion of hearts and upon prayer, which will also lead to the *necessary
purification of past memories.*"[1] While such purification by no means
denies or even relativizes the moral truths expressed in Christian faith
and signaled by Christian practice, attention to moral fragility and failure does afford us, for the short duration of our dialogues, an opportunity to examine our likeness to those with whom we disagree.

In this essay, I want to suggest that a Christian thinking about moral disagreement ought to take as her or his predominant influence and probable horizon the Christian practice of penance and reconciliation. I will also argue that it is precisely this kind of person-in-conversation—striving but exemplifying imperfectly the moral truths proclaimed—that those in the midst of moral disagreement long so desperately to hear. In perhaps one of the few ways that the sacramental life of the Church gestures to a dispositional parallel outside itself, in the kinds of persons it forms gradually and with a particular temporal sensitivity, the Christian practice of self-examination, confession, penance, and reconciliation offers a model for interreligious and religious-secular conversations about moral matters.

In order to develop this suggestion, I will offer two short comparisons with ideas developed by Alasdair MacIntyre, first on the notion of goods internal to practices and second on the place of moral enquiry in negotiating intractable moral disagreements. In response to the first, I will make two arguments: first, that we are able to think of interreligious conversation about moral matters roughly in line with how MacIntyre describes a practice with distinctive internal goods; and second, that the Christian practice that most resembles interreligious conversation about moral matters described in this way is that of penance and reconciliation. In response to the second, I will argue that MacIntyre's approach to moral disagreement offers a distinctive future-oriented focus for those engaged in moral enquiry, a focus that contrasts with the historically sensitive and past-oriented focus that he advocates for understanding rival traditions of moral enquiry. While this approach to moral disagreement rightfully argues that productive moral disagreement requires a necessary set of conditions that assures participants in the conversation that they will be free from coercion by their interlocutors or by the governing political powers, it does so at the expense of a proper sensitivity to the presuppositions that people often bring to such conversations—presuppositions about the unacknowledged failures by their partners in conversation to live up to the moral standards advanced. Here, the Christian practice of reconciliation (in distinction to the practices of Christian philosophical argumentation and apologetics) is again helpful in pointing out the depth of self-scrutiny and the pace of self-discovery that ought to govern the practice of moral enquiry.[2]

Instead of "intractable moral disagreements" (the title of MacIntyre's opening essay in this volume), I will use the phrase "interreligious conversation about moral matters," because it includes a wider account of the morally relevant subject matter for the parties in dialogue than the former term does. Because what I will be arguing is that part of the importance of the analogy to Christian penitential practice is its ability to include a wider scope of moral concerns and relevant actions within its moral scrutiny than an approach to moral enquiry that focuses primarily on actions and the precepts that govern them, I want to reflect in the language I use the breadth of these moral concerns. Indeed, as I suggest below, part of what is distinctive about interreligious dialogue as a practice is its ability to identify morally relevant issues that each tradition as party to that dialogue would not be able to account for exhaustively on its own. Therefore, I will employ the phrase throughout this essay, returning at the end to the notion of intractable moral disagreements to suggest what I judge to be the proper relationship between these two terms.

I. Goods Internal to the Practice of Interreligious Dialogue

MacIntyre's examination of intractable moral disagreements for this volume is, by his own characterization, intended to be no more than a systematic presentation of his thoughts on the topic scattered throughout his writings over the past thirty years.[3] Evaluations of this work by supporters, critics, and those who fall somewhere in between are well known, so I will not rehearse them here.[4] Instead, I want to suggest three points of departure from which we might initiate an examination of the practice of interreligious conversation about moral matters. The first focuses on MacIntyre's comments about why certain goods are called "internal" to practices, exploring what might constitute a preliminary list of such goods for interreligious conversation about moral matters understood as a coherent practice. The second briefly considers MacIntyre's challenge to those who presume to enter into a tradition of enquiry other than their own, expressing the difficulty involved even in approximating interreligious understanding. The third looks to MacIntyre's comments on the place of intractable disagreement in moral enquiry and highlights the conditions he thinks necessary for real moral enquiry to take place. I address the first two issues in this section and the third issue in the last section of this essay.

Toward the end of *After Virtue,* MacIntyre inquires into the meaningfulness of the concept of virtue in an age of radical moral disagreement and in a society structured to a significant degree by emotivist assumptions about moral discourse. "A virtue," he says, "is an acquired human quality the possession and exercise of which tends to enable us to achieve those goods which are internal to practices and the lack of which effectively prevents us from achieving any such goods."[5] For MacIntyre, a practice is "any coherent and complex form of socially established cooperative human activity through which goods internal to that form of activity are realized in the course of trying to achieve those standards of excellence which are appropriate to, and partially definitive of, that form of activity, with the result that human powers to achieve excellence, and human conceptions of the ends and goods involved, are systematically extended."[6]

Many theologians have examined the usefulness of this idea, especially for ethics, but relatively few have examined its importance for interreligious dialogue.[7] Perhaps most important, theologians tend to shy away from giving an account of why interreligious dialogue is worthwhile in the first place—especially what kind of human goods it advances and what the theological significance of these goods might be—beyond the frequently made and infrequently examined assumption that dialogue promotes peace and reduces overt religiously motivated violence. In other words, is interreligious dialogue a worthwhile practice for a Christian, and if so, what are the goods internal to it?[8]

What is distinctive about practices, MacIntyre says, is "in part the way in which the conceptions of the relevant goods and ends which the technical skills serve—and every practice does require the exercise of technical skills—are transformed and enriched by these extensions of human powers and by that regard for its own internal goods which are partially definitive of each particular practice or type of practice."[9] So practices extend human powers in ways characteristic of the practice, so that while such powers might have a relevant exercise outside the practice, the occasion for their development is linked most directly to the rules and events particular to the practice being considered.

In order to spell out more clearly what he means by goods *internal* to practices, MacIntyre offers the following important analogy to the game of chess:

> We call them internal for two reasons: first, as I have already suggested, because we can only specify them in terms of chess or some other game of that specific kind and by means of examples from such games (otherwise the meagerness of our vocabulary for speaking of such goods forces us into such devices as my own resort to writing of 'a certain highly particular kind of'); and secondly because they can only be identified and recognized by the experience of participating in the practice in question. Those who lack the relevant experience are incompetent thereby as judges of internal goods.[10]

Internal goods are, he says, "indeed the outcome of competition to excel, but it is characteristic of them that their achievement is a good for the whole community who participate in the practice."[11]

Now, I suggested above that we might consider interreligious conversation about moral matters a practice in MacIntyre's sense that it is a "coherent and complex form of socially established cooperative human activity through which goods internal to that form of activity are realized." It is easy enough to see that such conversations are activities (whether these conversations are spoken aloud or written, back and forth, in the form of letters or essays or commentaries). They are social to the extent that they often occur in groups, yet even when they occur between only two people the participants are drawing on narratives and cultural values that are socially mediated. But do such practices exhibit internal goods—that is, goods that can be identified and judged only by those who have participated in the practice, that are in some way analogous to rule-structured common activities like games, and that cultivate forms of human excellence that advance the whole community that participates in them in some way?

To summarize, then, extending MacIntyre's analogy of goods internal to practices, I propose formulating the three criteria for identifying goods internal to the practice of interreligious conversation about moral matters in the following way: (1) they will likely be identified or given a more refined description only by those experienced in the practice of interreligious conversations; (2) these internal goods are the result of some kind of skillful activity that occurs in interreligious conversation and is analogous to competition; and (3) achievement of these internal goods benefits the communities constituted by the practice (and also perhaps related communities). The first criterion we will leave aside for the time being because we need to establish a preliminary list of goods internal to the practice of interreligious conversation about moral matters before we refine it through experientially formulated correctives. What, then, are the internal goods that fit under the second and third criteria?

It is characteristic of such goods that they enable those involved in the practice to excel in ways analogous to a competitive environment, but in the case of interreligious conversation, this can mean one of two things or a combination of the two. Either those who engage in the practice become more excellent at the skills required to engage in the practice itself (for example, with respect to navigating the particular conversations), or they become more excellent with respect to that aspect of the practice which distinguishes it from other kinds of conversations—namely, the subject matter of morality, which would include possible religious grounding for moral behaviors. In the first case, we might imagine that intensive study of another tradition would be an important good: observing its practitioners' observances, scrutinizing their ways of living in the world, learning their languages, listening to their explanations about why they behave as they do, and listening to their descriptions of what they believe and why they believe as they do. We might also imagine that certain standards of respect for the dignity of the conversation would apply: listening quietly but attentively when the other person speaks, posing questions in a tone that indicates an attitude of search rather than destroy, posing thoughtful reformulations of what has been said to gain clarification, and accepting suggestions for correcting misinterpretations and opportunities for further study.[12]

In the second case of the conversation's subject matter (morality), a different kind of excellence pertains. Querying this excellence leads one to ask what is competitive about the moral life (as the second criterion indicated) and to ask how this competition benefits the community (the third criterion). Competition in the moral life urges one to struggle to live ever more closely to the standards of one's tradition, realizing that each person who struggles does so both to understand these standards more clearly (which may eventually result in a critical stance toward these standards) and to exemplify them more fully in their full range of actions. The community benefits from a more coherent witness, even as each of its members provides but one angle and a limited understanding of the shape and scope of the community's example.[13]

So, if the interreligious conversation is about "moral matters" broadly understood (realizing that for MacIntyre, the proper identification of a "moral matter" could likely only take place within a single tradition of rational enquiry), then it would seem that three kinds of goods might arise in the practice of this kind of conversation: the good of *moral understanding*,[14] the good of *moral consistency*, and the good of *moral scope*.[15] The good of moral understanding is closely related to the goods internal to conversation just mentioned. Excellence in interreligious moral understanding would include depth of knowledge about the meaning of moral terms in another tradition, about the motivations for certain moral statements and the religious beliefs that ground them, and at least some ability to predict how a tradition would respond to similar or as yet unforeseen moral challenges based on knowledge of how and why members of that tradition have responded in certain ways in the past. In other words, it would address the various ways in which religious traditions treat what MacIntyre emphasizes as a "naturalistic account of the good" and then examine how traditions describe and transform them.[16]

The goods of moral consistency and moral scope indicate slightly different concerns because they deal with how goods internal to the practice of interreligious conversation about moral matters relate to the personal histories and institutional affiliations of the conversation participants themselves. In this way, these goods relate to the first criterion for identifying internal goods mentioned above; that is, they can be identified and critiqued only by one experienced in the practice. If we step outside of the "ideal speech situations" one might be inclined to envision at this point, and look to the many instances of interreligious conversations across personal and political life, one feature of such conversations should be obvious: suspicion by one religious person of another because of his or her past moral failures and the moral failures of the religious groups of which he or she is a part. I am not suggesting that such failures are logically necessary, only that they are empirically common. Christians have deceived, manipulated, and killed people for personal and political reasons, with and without religious justifications, as have Muslims, Buddhists, and members of indigenous religions. This reason alone frequently has led secular or explicitly atheistic persons to discount the moral exemplarity of religious witness or even to point to religion as a source (some would say *the* source) of vicious behaviors in our time. Religious persons (universally, I would suggest) know that their traditions have had dark moments that offer, not logically but emotionally, a sort of counter-evidence to the moral truths they see in their own traditions. They know, when they speak about the moral ideals of their religious communities, that those from other communities or those who have no religious affiliation will scrutinize their past moral failures and those of their traditions more carefully and with greater detail than they will appreciate their triumphs. To think about moral consistency as a good internal to conversation practice is to recognize it as a prior condition for meaningful and constructive moral conversation but also as a good that is always partially unrealized in the midst of conversation, in other words, as a resulting ideal to be approximated more perfectly in future efforts precisely because of the effect it has in facilitating or interfering with the flow of conversation.

Moral scope, like moral consistency, has a personal as well as an institutional dimension as a good internal to the practice of interreligious conversation about moral matters. Individual persons, due in part to the complexity of the problems they confront and the effect of their own past experiences on their present thinking, have a tendency to establish certain moral priorities based on the set of concerns that they take to be morally relevant. Indeed, as MacIntyre suggests, one aspect of a tradition of enquiry is that it considers what, if any, final end exists for human beings and suggests how this final end reveals the way all proximate ends or goods a person pursues ought to be ordered to it. As he says, "[O]ur single final end is revealed in the way in which we organize those goods, in which good or goods it is to which we give the highest place, in what we are prepared to sacrifice for what, in our priorities."[17] Yet part of carrying on a tradition of enquiry is not only about the prioritization of goods already recognized; it is also about the recognition of morally relevant goods that might have escaped real deliberation by the tradition in the past.[18] In other words, the expansion of the scope of one's moral concern is a good internal to the practice of interreligious conversation about moral matters because it acknowledges that each tradition of enquiry cannot, because of the temporal and spatial limits of those who constitute it, foresee all the relevant moral problems and situations in which other real human goods are both affirmed and degraded. It requires the input of persons from other religious traditions if it is to keep the scope of its moral vision as wide as possible, and vigilant in searching out all the ways in which it has missed small but significant opportunities for exemplifying the tradition's basic values.

So there are at least three goods internal to the practice of interreligious conversation about moral matters: moral understanding, moral consistency, and moral scope. Yet it is important, at this point, to heed MacIntyre's warning about the difficulty of achieving any kind of understanding across religious or cultural traditions. Is not the sort of moral understanding just mentioned as a good internal to interreligious conversation about moral matters supremely difficult? And if it is so difficult, are we right to call it a good internal to the practice of interreligious conversation? As bookends to the long narrative of rival rationalities in Western philosophy, *Whose Justice? Which Rationality?* MacIntyre makes two telling comments on the function of comparative philosophy and of the possibility of interreligious understanding. At the beginning of the book he states that, in addition to the story he is telling in which the central protagonists are Thomism and the failed Enlightenment project, there are four other stories to be told: by members of the Jewish, Islamic, Indian, and Chinese traditions of enquiry.[19] "[T]o understand another tradition," he says, "is to attempt to supply, in the best terms imaginatively and conceptually available to one[,] . . . the kind of account which an adherent would give."[20] So the first difficulty in thinking through the possible goods internal to the practice of interreligious dialogue has to do with who tells the story of the history of a tradition's moral concepts and how it is told. MacIntyre seems to suggest here that one either needs to be a member of another tradition or needs to have cultivated certain habits of thinking so sensitive to another cultural context that one is able to narrate that tradition's history with minimal if any distortion. It remains an open question as to whether adherence to this tradition is necessary to give such an account. In other words, in order to be able to think within a tradition, as a native inhabitant would, is a history of religious practice in that tradition required, or must one be familiar only with its culturally specific form of philosophical reflection? Is some commitment to its long-term viability and the religious understanding of its people also required?

A second difficulty arises when we consider the specific training and skills needed to understand another religious tradition. Toward the end of the book, MacIntyre takes up the problem of understanding a tradition of enquiry that is not one's own: "[A]t the very least, understanding requires knowing the culture, so far as possible, as a native inhabitant knows it, and speaking, hearing, writing, and reading the language as a native inhabitant speaks, hears, writes, and reads it. . . . Gestures, modes of ritual behavior, choices, and silences may all on occasion express utterances, and utterances themselves will be one class of deeds, classified just as deeds are classified."[21] He seems to have in mind the sort of acquaintance that comes with years of living and working in a culture other than one's native community, or perhaps years spent in the rigors of academic anthropological investigations.

Yet it is worth asking at this point whether the spirit of enquiry is exhausted by the period of acquaintance. On the one hand, it would seem that what is required for one to understand the "traditions" of Western philosophy and their religious influences, on MacIntyre's account, is so daunting and complex for the ordinary religious person that relatively few could give an adequate account of their own tradition, much less an account of rival *religious* traditions. Yet MacIntyre's account also suggests that one need not spend all one's time in enquiry (indeed, few do, as most people do not pass the level of practical moral disagreements).[22] So are such people relegated to a religious insularity in communities of religious practice, assigning only the few qualified to undertake dialogue on their behalf? How are we to make sense of MacIntyre's warning at a time when interaction among religions is increasing rather than decreasing? It is here that the analogy to Christian practices of penance and reconciliation becomes helpful. For this is one area in the life of the practicing Christian where the benefit of engaging in the practice is not exhausted by what one is able to achieve, precisely because the kind of person formed by the practice, as much as the result of the activity itself, commends the practice to wider use and more careful consideration.

II. An Analogy between Interreligious Conversation and Penitential Practice

If, as I suggested above, it is proper to interpret interreligious conversation about moral matters as a practice with discernible internal goods, we must now ask what place such a practice ought to have in the life of the Christian. Here I think it is important to emphasize that why one enters into an interreligious conversation influences, to a significant degree, what might be gained through it. Let us suppose that there are, roughly speaking, three possible rationales for a Christian to enter into interreligious conversation about moral matters: moral enquiry aimed at the theoretical adjudication of claims arising from practical moral disagreements (the kind MacIntyre examines), the reduction of tension and the potential for violence among religious factions (the rationale frequently presupposed in many liberal proposals for such conversations), and the internal purification of a religious tradition and its members (the rationale most prominently stated, alongside evangelization through proclamation of the gospel, by recent documents of the Roman Catholic bishops).[23]

However, if one wants to position the activity of interreligious conversation about moral matters firmly in the context of the life of the Church, that is to say, in the midst of the practices that form Christian persons and cultivate in them certain distinctive habits, one must offer both a reason for the Christian to engage in dialogue and some assurance that preliminary limits in knowledge and understanding of one's own tradition and of the traditions of those with whom one will be in conversation will not ultimately interfere with productive discussion. While it is important to keep MacIntyre's warnings about such difficulties clearly in view, I suggest that what will ultimately draw a Christian into conversation is an awareness of shared goods and temporal similarities between sustained interreligious conversation about moral matters and the Christian practice of penance and reconciliation. It is here that one of the central sacramental activities of the Church has the capacity to prepare people for interreligious conversation, as well as to make important contributions to those conversations along the lines of the three goods internal to the practice just mentioned.

So let me return to the three goods internal to the practice of interreligious conversation outlined earlier—namely, moral understanding, moral consistency, and moral scope. Examining each of these goods in turn, I now want to suggest why the best analogy Christians have to both the process of interreligious conversation about moral matters and the goods internal to this practice is the sacrament of reconciliation.[24] This position is broadly compatible with the Thomist framework endorsed, in different ways, by Alasdair MacIntyre and the Roman Catholic bishops, but it requires a different set of theological emphases, ones closer both to the demands of contemporary life and to the practices of the Christian Church. Another way to put this problem is to say that whereas MacIntyre and others focus on the nature of the disagreements involved, I want to focus instead on what makes them intractable, beyond the fact of moral incongruities.

The practice of sacramental reconciliation and penance in the Church is too complex to summarize here, but I want to signal a few of its relevant analogical features. Yet before I do so, I want to caution that, with respect to the image involved, it is not the inside of the confessional so much as its doorway or threshold (in contrast to the pulpit or lecture hall or seminar room, for example) that signals the image's analogical importance in this discussion. I select this image purposefully because I want to emphasize that it is not what goes on in the confessional (here the process of interreligious conversation about moral matters has no direct correlate) but what goes on around it,[25] in the process of preparation and of execution of penance once one leaves, that is analogous to interreligious conversation.

In speaking of the sacrament of penance and reconciliation, the *Catechism of the Catholic Church* tells us that the pivotal event, the one that roots the practice of the sacrament in its scriptural meaning, is Jesus' call to conversion (par. 1427).

> Christ's call to conversion continues to resound in the lives of Christians . . . an uninterrupted task for the whole Church who, "clasping sinners to her bosom, [is] at once holy and always in need of purification, [and] follows constantly the path of penance and renewal." This endeavor of conversion is not just a human work. It is the movement of a "contrite heart," drawn and moved by grace to respond to the merciful love of God who loved us first. (Par. 1428)

The heart of this sacrament is the confession of sin and the interior penance that reconciles the sinner to God. But confession of sin requires a degree of self-knowledge about an evil done or a good avoided. It requires a period of preparation, an examination of conscience, and a fundamental modification of the pace at which self-reflection normally takes place. Reconciliation is not for the hurried or the easily inconvenienced. Indeed, it cultivates a habit of looking at oneself and the world in a measured, gradual, but nonetheless truthful way.

We can begin to imagine how moral understanding links the practice of interreligious conversation with the practice of penance and reconciliation. Moral understanding occurs when we gain clarity both through a comparison and contrast of moral ideas across traditions and through a comparison and contrast of what one believes and how one lives. Prayer forms the model of this penitential moral understanding. Just as by entering into conversation about our claims to moral truth, we invite those with whom we are in conversation to a kind of intellectual conversion, so too in the practice of penance we invite ourselves to listen to the call to ongoing conversion. Here, the teaching of the Roman Catholic bishops parallels closely MacIntyre's demands for an open, honest, noncoercive form of moral enquiry. The call to ongoing conversion does not coerce but invites truthful acknowledgment of the history of the person involved in the practice, something that is only possible with an appropriate level of suspicion about our past actions and an appropriate level of transparency about our merits and failings. Each penitential preparation, like each interreligious conversation, is a chance to ask again, "Do I really believe this, and do I live by what I claim to believe?"

Second, there is an analogy with respect to the internal good of moral consistency. When one approaches the sacrament of reconciliation, one does so with a sense of loss, of wanting to return with greater resolve to what one believes, and yet one is forced to ask, in the process of examining one's own past behaviors, whether in that moment of failure, of turning away from God, one really believed what one proclaims to others. This is akin to Luke Timothy Johnson's observation that in the moment of sin we are all practical atheists.[26] If interreligious conversation about moral matters is to continue and be rendered productive, it must relate to the hope on the part of each party that the persons with whom they speak either exemplify the moral truths they proclaim or that they might, as sincere participants in the conversation, come to exemplify it. The difference between a believer's moment of confrontation with her or his own sin and the confrontation of one person with another person who holds substantially different beliefs is, I think, a difference more in degree than in kind. Similarly, in the moment when one has resolved to sin no more, one is confronted with a degree of self-knowledge and renewed freedom that urges that person back into the world to restore the justice that was lost on the occasion of one's sin. Both the practices of reconciliation and of interreligious conversation aim at consistency, of making people better exemplifications of what they claim to be true.

The final internal good I mentioned was moral scope, and I argued that interreligious conversation has the capacity to widen the moral view of each participant in the conversation. The Christian practice of reconciliation intends a similar transformation. Indeed, the sacramental life of the Church is central to the cultivation of Christian virtue, and sacramental reconciliation is part of this work.[27] The one who develops the habit of examination of conscience and of imagining all the ways in which one's actions might violate the justice due to other people and the praise due to God becomes a person with a heightened capacity to see the world with moral sensitivity. I think this was the force of Thomas Aquinas's point that penance is the sacrament that is also a virtue and that it is a species of justice.[28] It widens the scope of our moral vision in a different way from interreligious conversation but to the same just end. For justice links the internal order of a person, as it is governed by the first principle of practical reason and the primary precepts of the natural law, to a just order outside oneself. As Christians move into increasingly complex situations in the modern world, ones filled with ever more ambiguous moral choices, they are faced with the possibility that the tradition's time-tested wisdom, although still relevant, must be constantly reexamined and assessed to ensure that the secondary precepts that govern our particular choices exhibit both sensitivity and broad scope.

III. MacIntyre's Thomist Standard for Future Moral Inquiry

In the first section of this essay, I discussed the important contribution that MacIntyre's explanation of goods internal to practices makes to our understanding of interreligious conversations about moral matters. I now want to suggest how MacIntyre's treatment of intractable moral disagreements, particularly his account of the conditions necessary for shared moral enquiry after one realizes that practical moral disagreements are not immediately resolvable, while helpful, also obscures a very important point about interreligious conversations— namely, how the participants past histories are revealed and challenged in the process. Moreover, this may actually point to a basic difference between rational enquiry as MacIntyre describes it and the kind of interreligious conversations I have been describing.

If we are to understand properly the dynamics of moral disagreement in the context of interreligious conversations, we must acknowledge two facets of such conversations. First, all participants are likely to be aware of their own past moral failures and the failures of those with whom they are in conversation. While these failures obviously do not count, in themselves, as arguments against the moral truths put forth by each party, they do cast a bidirectional shadow on the participants. In one direction, conversation participants are aware that each tradition contains a history both of vicious behaviors by its adherents and of instances in which, even despite great moral striving, those involved failed to live according to their tradition's highest moral ideals. In another direction, those involved in the conversation know that, whatever moral agreement might be reached, there is no guarantee (indeed, it is highly unlikely) that those parties to the agreement will live by the moral agreements that have been negotiated. In other words, in the dynamics of real interreligious conversations about moral matters, the personal histories of the participants and the institutional histories of the traditions from which those persons argue will inform the preconditions and the expectations about what the parties think about each other. What each party will reasonably expect in the future will be affected by each party's knowledge both of the other's past and of his or her own judgments about the likelihood of moral failure in the future. This bidirectional shadow can make it very difficult to know whether one has effectively moved from the realm of practical moral disagreements to the realm of moral enquiry.

It is interesting to ask, then, where is MacIntyre's focus—on the past or on the future, on the participants or on the rules governing their deliberation—when he lays out the conditions necessary for shared moral enquiry in the fact of disagreements arising from practical deliberations? To answer this question, we need to move on to a third set of comments by MacIntyre, those in his essay on intractable moral disagreements in this volume. MacIntyre argues that there are certain conditions under which people committed to rational enquiry operate that must be observed no matter what tradition they inhabit. While he specifically addresses hypothetical conversations with defenders of one strand of utilitarian philosophy, it is safe to assume that he would advocate these same conditions for similar conversations between religious traditions as well. "The good of truth," he says, must not be "overridden by other goods"; rational enquiry "has to find *some* continuing and significant place in our lives"; and neither of the prior two will be possible "unless we have been able to become disinterested, that is, to distance ourselves from those particular material and psychological interests that are always apt to find expression in those partialities and prejudices that are nourished by our desires for pleasure, money, and power. For those partialities and prejudices are apt to distort our thinking and always most effectively so when we ignore or are self-deceived by their influence" (pp. 21–22).

MacIntyre then proposes a form of life—we might call it a style and temporal orientation of life—characterized by what he calls "a form of intellectual and moral asceticism, both in our thinking and in the ways that we invite others to assent to our theses and arguments." He continues:

> We need to avoid allowing our own thinking to give expression to our prejudices and to abstain from a rhetoric that is designed to move others, not by the reasons adduced, but by the passions

to which the utterance of those reasons gives expression. . . . It is clear first of all that I will be unable to consider and to respond to your arguments impartially and impersonally, if I have good reason to fear present or future harm from you or from others, should I disagree with you. And for us to be able to engage in shared enquiry, so that my arguments and yours contribute to our common end, you too must have good reason to be assured that you are secure from harm or the threat of harm by me. It follows that a precondition of rationality in shared enquiry is mutual commitment to precepts that forbid us to endanger gratuitously each other's life, liberty, or property. And the scope of those precepts must extend to all those from whom we may at any time in our enquiry—and it is a lifelong enquiry—need to learn. (Pp. 22–23)

MacIntyre goes on to say that such precepts internal to the practice of honest moral enquiry also require commitment by each party to speak the truth as she or he understands it, to use plain rather than misleading speech, to honor our promises and make only those we intend to keep, and, if we continue in a community of enquiry for a long time, to make provisions for our common security.

This discussion of the conditions necessary for sustained moral enquiry falls in the middle of MacIntyre's essay, where he is arguing that Aquinas's account of the precepts of the natural law, "far from being inconsistent with the facts of moral disagreement, provides the best starting-point for the explanation of these facts" (p. 26), noting that for Aquinas sins are best understood as transgressions of reason. MacIntyre argues that succumbing to "the seductions and threats, the hopes and fears, that are generated by pleasure, money, and power will exhibit failures in practical rationality" (p. 26). In other words, moral enquiry may but should not be derailed by an excessive attachment to these worldly enticements. Such failures may infect moral enquiry, but they also might function to inhibit practical disagreements that precede theoretical enquiry. Yet MacIntyre does not acknowledge that, for the Christian, one of the central places where one becomes aware of these distractions in one's own life, as well as the history of how these have affected one's past dealings with other people in matters of moral concern, is in the sacramental practices of the Church. For the Christian who is attuned to her or his moral character and the landscape of past sins, it is difficult to separate one's thinking about moral truths from one's personal history of engagement with them and the examination of conscience that usually attends such thinking.

Even so, I think that MacIntyre's comments on the conditions necessary for moral enquiry have important points of contact with the goods internal to interreligious conversation and the penitential analogies to these goods outlined above. Let me suggest three such points. These three relations might be taken as specifications of what I mentioned earlier in terms of the third criterion for an internal good (that it benefits communities constituted by the practice) and that satisfaction of this criteria facilitates that excellence in the skills of conversation that are a good internal to its practice. Whereas the prior list of goods might be taken as goods of the practice itself, the following might be taken as a set of conditions that give the practice of interreligious conversation its proper temporal structure and its participants a proper personal and historical orientation. Yet each of these conditions necessary for the achievement of the goods internal to interreligious conversation is also, I submit, the same habit (or at least similar in important respects) that is formed through the Christian practice of penance and reconciliation.

First, there is the condition of an *appropriate pace* of conversation. This means that interreligious moral understanding is likely to happen only gradually, over the course of many years of effort and many failed attempts. Understanding requires that we not expect too much too soon, or that we refrain from moving on to new areas of conversation just because we have reached what we think are tentative agreements about this or that moral matter. In other words, we are always bound, if interreligious understanding is to be an aspect of seeking truth, to hold preliminary agreements as revisable and likely laced with elements of misunderstanding.

Moreover, the pace of conversation is a good internal to the practice of interreligious conversation about moral matters because it brings the one invested in it into a careful, gradual, constant reexamination of what one believes and the many ways in which the quest for material comfort in this world interfere with the search for truth. To a degree, this acknowledges MacIntyre's warning, but it also asks us what community, what form of life, is likely to cultivate this gradual cautious approach. For a Christian, the practice most immediately formative of one engaged in conversation is that which trains her or him in self-examination, in the gradual discernment of what lures one away from rationally chosen goods and toward forms of excessive or self-destructive desire. The practice of penance, I submit, orients oneself in new conversations in such a way that, whenever one holds out moral truths for consideration by others, one also calls to mind those times when one has failed to live according to those same truths. In other words, penance cultivates a kind of temporal realism about what one can expect from moral agreement and disagreement, from oneself and from those with whom one argues. Appropriate pace is the primary condition that penitential practice cultivates, but two other conditions flow from it.

The second is *appropriate transparency* in conversation, a measuredness and even-temperedness in the tone of our discussions and in the form of our rhetoric. MacIntyre is concerned, rightly I think, that what commonly sways people from one belief to another, especially in those instances when they have not taken the time to examine the reasons why they hold this or that position, is the persuasiveness of the rhetoric used to communicate the merits of a position and the drawbacks of its rivals. Yet there are those who will remain more convinced by the example of a moral life lived in an exemplary way without the explicit translation of this form of life into claims about its normative content and the place of such norms in the intellectual narrative of a tradition. Even so, the transparency and emotionally disinterested language for discourse that he advocates are goods internal to the practice of interreligious conversation because such norms for conversation counteract the performative and posturing aspects of much dialogue, that is, conversation severed from humility about the truths that one has learned.

Penitential practice forms a habit of transparency in similar ways as a kind of honest if painful self-knowledge. Repetition of the practice by Christians leads them to the development of a clearheaded (one might even say rational) view of themselves, one that indulges neither in excessive chastisement nor excessive self-consolation. Penance structures the Christian life in such a way that the moral exemplarity found in the Church is not a heroic type but rather a patient, struggling, occasionally inspiring type. While respecting the importance of MacIntyre's conditions for enquiry, I suggest that it is this kind of party to interreligious conversation and even disagreement, that is, one who admits frequent failure to abide by her or his community's moral norms, rather than the one who offers the better account of a rival intellectual tradition's difficulty in resolving its own internal conflicts better than the tradition itself, that has the best hope of convincing another to adhere to Christian truth claims. The penitent, in other words, offers the more compelling witness than the apologist, even if the Church must contain and support both.

Third, there is the condition of *appropriate suspicion* in conversation. MacIntyre's primary concern with respect to conditions for moral enquiry seems forward-looking; that is, one cannot converse well about moral matters if one is afraid for one's physical safety or if one feels that one is being manipulated or misled for reasons outside the goods internal to the conversation. In other words, MacIntyre's primary concern is future oriented, insofar as the recognition of truth might be obscured by what the partner in conversation might do or what the economic, military, and ideological powers in the surrounding society might do to interfere with the search for truth. We should also notice, however, that MacIntyre acknowledges a past-oriented or historical suspicion, both about one's partners in conversation and about oneself: "But we recognize easily enough in certain others, both in the present and the past, and sometimes in our own past selves, that what they now take or what we or they have in the past taken to be excellent reasons for judging such and such to be the good now to be pursued were held to be excellent reasons only because of the unacknowledged persuasions of pleasure, money, or power" (p. 26).

We might reframe this insight by saying that one good internal to the practice of interreligious conversation about moral matters is that such conversation forces each participant to review her or his own past moral failings and the moral failings of the religious tradition of which she or he is a part. Put differently, part of the temporal dimension of such conversations is the relationship of each conversation partner's place in the past of the other, which in turn affects her or his ability to hear what is being offered for consideration. I think we cannot overestimate how influential, in the dynamics of interreligious conversation about moral matters, this element of suspicion about the moral failings of the dialogue partner and her or his community has been. It is difficult work indeed to separate what has happened as a corruption of a tradition's own best moral insights from the limits of the insights themselves. This sort of problem, in a way, should be moderated by the previous warning about the transparency of conversation, but, again, it is perhaps the privilege of the academic life that its practitioners can hold such influences at bay for a time (although, occasionally, in classrooms and at conferences, we see them creep out).

If we return again to the analogy of penance, we can begin to see how to cultivate an appropriate suspicion for interreligious conversation. The examination of conscience that precedes confession and the resolve to avoid sin in the future cultivate a habit of seeing patiently and realistically, a habit that allows one to see that the tendency of all persons to fail to live by what they judge to be true is a serious obstacle to conversation and simultaneously a mark of solidarity, despite radical moral disagreement.[29] I label this "appropriate suspicion" because penance trains us to be wary of our patterns of past failure, and to evaluate carefully those who hold out moral truth as speaking beyond where they live. But we would be equally wise to avoid excessive suspicion in interreligious conversation about moral matters, lest we miss opportunities for real conversation about shared moral concerns because our pessimism overwhelms our hope.

I should note, in passing, that there are religious practices, analogous to my examination of penance, internal to other traditions (for example, the instruction for meditation in Theravada Buddhist manuals) that cultivate the same goods and highlight similar temporal conditions just mentioned, but I do not have room to comment on them here. I only mean to signal the importance of a central Christian practice that might strengthen Christian reasons and procedures for interreligious conversation about difficult moral questions, but I assume other insights will be found as other traditions think about their reasons and resources for conversation.

IV. CONCLUSION

There are two concluding notes I wish to make to clarify the usefulness of the analogy of the Christian practice of reconciliation and the practice of interreligious conversation about moral matters, one on the nature of truth and the other on the connection between penance and knowledge. First, I am *not* saying that one should not speak about what one judges to be true just because one has not successfully lived in accordance with the moral truths one holds. The existence of truth, as understood in Catholic Christianity, as well as in many other religious traditions, does not itself depend on our ability to apprehend it or live by it, either for the philosopher analyzing the content and meaning of truth claims or for the theologian analyzing the moral requirements of the gospel. In terms of the truth of the moral law, what might appear to be superhuman demands, or even strong human disciplines, do not mitigate our obedience to it. This is, again, why the logic of reconciliation (as confession, forgiveness, and penance) is so important to understanding moral disagreement. Both aim at and do not shy away from the difficulty of moral truth, yet both acknowledge that from a practical standpoint one does not hold truths easily. MacIntyre recognizes the many ways in which power, pleasure, and money (in any number of institutional settings) obscure the search for truth and our ability to maintain our close contact with it. The Catholic bishops, as noted earlier in this essay, assessed that interreligious conversation frequently is marred by the histories of personal and institutional sins that one brings to conversation. But this ought to intensify, rather than obscure, the search for moral agreement and ought to temper the despair that can arise in the face of intractable disagreement.

Second, I am *not* saying that one pursue interreligious knowledge, especially moral understanding, for the purpose of satisfying penitential requirements. This is only an analogy, which clearly breaks down when the structural requirement of the sacraments lose their footing in the theological discourse that gives them meaning. One makes restitution for the wrongs one has done, not so one has a clean slate and an easy conscience, but rather because the wrong done violates the just relations God intends for the human community. But if, as I suggested, moral understanding is one of several goods internal to the practice of interreligious conversations, then the practice demands satisfaction of the preconditions that make understanding possible. This means that Christians must find some basis on which to commit themselves to serious interreligious conversation at the pace and with the transparency that such conversations require. It is for this reason that I *do* think it appropriate for Christians to view interreligious knowledge and the intense study necessary to acquire it as an appropriate form of penance for the many individual and institutional sins for which they and their tradition must be held responsible. And those in conversation with them ought to acknowledge such an effort as work toward the restitution of the Christian's view of justice. If conversations about moral matters all aim, in the final analysis, at justice, then such a commitment does not instrumentalize religious others but provides evidence that Christians are indeed committed to the good of those persons in their integrity and are willing to bring those conversations analogously into their deepest internal confessions to their creator.

NOTES

1. John Paul II, *Ut Unum Sint,* promulgated May 25, 1995, par. 2.

2. I do not mean to say that apologetics has no place in the life of the Christian but merely to acknowledge that apologists frequently make two assumptions about the nature of argument: first, that the morally relevant issues for conversation can be easily and neatly identified prior to the actual interreligious discussion; and second, that the response to the truths pertaining to such issues has an either/or character both for the apologist and for the person with whom she or he is in conversation. Paul Griffiths reminds us of an important facet of ancient apologetics when he notes:

> When, for instance, the Buddhist doctrine *everything that exists is momentary* was challenged as being untrue because incoherent by Hindu philosophers in India, Buddhists did not respond as a Wittgensteinean believer would; they did not, that is, point to the profound difference in the forms of life inhabited by Buddhists and Hindus, and shake their heads regretfully at the impossibility of communicating or coming to understand in what the difference consists. No, they argued: they defended both the coherence and the truth of their doctrine, and did so with arguments that they apparently expected to be comprehensible (and perhaps even convincing) to their interlocutors. And this kind of response, which has traditionally gone under the name of apologetics in the Christian world, appears to be typical of religious communities.

See Paul J. Griffiths, *Problems of Religious Diversity* (Malden, MA: Blackwell, 2001), 48. While I agree that religions are truth-claiming vehicles of human life, I want to emphasize that the complexity of contemporary life requires that we not think of this activity as the exhaustive dialogical activity. It also fails to account for the various ways in which people become resistant to accepting as true, or living by what they judge to be true, in part because of their own moral failure and the history of moral failure in the apologists' communities. While behavioral inconsistency is nothing new to human life, I think that the context of contemporary interreligious dialogue renders it much more problematic and acute, for reasons of scope and scale, than it was in the times from which Griffiths draws his examples.

3. It is noteworthy that MacIntyre specifies "practical" disagreement, by which I take him to mean either disagreement about practical moral problems such as those he outlines at the beginning of his book, *After Virtue: A Study in Moral Theory*, 2nd ed. (Notre Dame: University of Notre Dame Press, 1984), 6–7, or disagreement that participants in dialogue identify only when they are actually participating in the practice of dialogue. Now, it is clear that he means the former kind of disagreement. However, the point of this essay is to examine what are the conditions that would be required to investigate practical moral disagreement that emphasize practices of dialogue rather than practical moral problems.

4. Among the articles that have been most helpful to me in appreciating the positive contributions as well as the limits of MacIntyre's diagnoses of contemporary moral discourse and his proposals for its future are Jeffrey Stout, "Virtue among the Ruins: An Essay on MacIntyre," *Neue Zeitschrift für systematische Theologie und Religionsphilosophie* 26 (1984): 256–73; Jeffrey Stout, "Homeward Bound: MacIntyre on Liberal Society and the History of Ethics," *Journal of Religion* 69, no. 2 (April 1989): 220–32; Jean Porter, "Openness and Constraint: Moral Reflection as Tradition-guided Inquiry in Alasdair MacIntyre's Recent Works," *Journal of Religion* 73, no. 4 (October 1993): 514–36; Jennifer A. Herdt, "Alasdair MacIntyre's 'Rationality of Traditions' and Tradition-Transcendental Standards of Justification," *Journal of Religion* 78, no. 4 (October 1998): 524–46. In addition, although not directly related to MacIntyre's writings, I have found it helpful to compare MacIntyre's thoughts on communities of virtue with Jonathan Z. Smith's comments on the place of comparison in the work of historians of religions (a tradition committed to a different set of practices): see Jonathan Z. Smith, "In Comparison a Magic Dwells," in *Imagining Religion: From Babylon to Jonestown* (Chicago: University of Chicago Press, 1982), 19–35; Jonathan Z. Smith, "Adde Parvum Parvo Magnus Acervus Erit," in *Map Is Not Territory: Studies in the History of Religions* (Chicago: University of Chicago Press, 1978), 240–64.

Both of these articles offer striking similarities in source materials to what MacIntyre considers in *Three Rival Versions of Moral Enquiry: Encyclopaedia, Genealogy, and Tradition* (Notre Dame: University of Notre Dame Press, 1990), setting up an alternative story, contrary but plausible.

5. MacIntyre, *After Virtue*, 191.

6. Ibid., 187.

7. Here I would identify especially the work of Bradford Hinze, *Practices of Dialogue in the Roman Catholic Church: Aims and Obstacles, Lessons and Laments* (New York: Continuum, 2006), 13–18. In his brief "word about method," Hinze suggests that what he means by practices will be determined inductively from the actual practices of dialogue about various subjects in the Roman Catholic Church (of which interreligious dialogue occupies a relatively small place). However, he does mention MacIntyre's definition, as well as Gustavo Gutiérrez's focus on historical praxis, supplemented by Pierre Bourdieu's explanation of the term *habitus*, to give fuller expression to his use of the term. However, the central problem of this essay—in what sense is the practice of interreligious dialogue a human good with theological significance?—goes unanswered as it is not the central focus of Hinze's study. The other significant work on this topic, more a piece of systematic theology than Hinze's intraecclesial ethnography, is Michael Barnes, S.J., *Theology and the Dialogue of Religions* (Cambridge: Cambridge University Press, 2002). Barnes also finds MacIntyre's notion of goods internal to practices helpful, extending them to the area of interreligious dialogue; see pp. 27–28.

8. MacIntyre differentiates goods internal to a practice from those external to a practice by analogy to certain games such as chess: "External goods are therefore characteristically objects of competition in which there must be losers as well as winners. Internal goods are indeed the outcome of competition to excel, but it is characteristic of them that their achievement is a good for the whole community who participate in the practice" (MacIntyre, *After Virtue*, 190–91).

9. MacIntyre, *After Virtue*, 193.

10. Ibid., 188–89.

11. Ibid., 190–91.

12. I take these aspects of the practice to specify what James Fredericks has described as the vices opposing the virtue of "interreligious friendship": namely "despising, ignoring, or caricaturing" those of other religious affiliation. See his "Interreligious Friendship: A New Theological Virtue," *Journal of Ecumenical Studies* 35.2 (Spring 1998). This is related to, but not the same as,

what Lee Yearley has described as the "virtue of spiritual regret." See his essay, "New Religious Virtues and the Study of Religion," Fifteenth Annual University Lecture in Religion, February 10, 1994 (Arizona State University, Department of Religious Studies), 12–16.

13. I take it that this is the significance of Paul addressing the Corinthian Christians (1 Cor. 9:24–27) on the subject of the likeness of the Christian life to the challenges of the imperial games. It is important that this passage follows Paul's discussion of the pedagogical effectiveness of acknowledging his own weakness and of the effect this has of binding the community in a unified moral witness, despite its stance that it has been freed from the law by faith in Jesus Christ.

14. It is admittedly odd to speak of moral understanding as a good, if one takes seriously writings in the tradition of theological hermeneutics (as in Gadamer, Ricoeur, and Schweiker) that understanding is not something that one achieves or attains but rather a process that is constantly in the state of revision and rearticulation. I express it here as a good internal to the practice of interreligious conversation to respond to MacIntyre's pattern of thinking about goods internal to practices. While I think this is helpful for the purpose of exploring the way moral disagreement is affected by past injustices by and to partners in conversation, I think that in the final analysis this will not prove a sufficiently complex way of interpreting the human activity of conversation.

15. Although this is not the proper place to explore related areas of study in detail, we must note that in the related field of comparative religious ethics, the central motivation for engaging in comparative scholarship at all seems primarily, if not exclusively, in the service of increasing moral understanding. I have previously identified various rationales or motivations for comparative thinking about moral matters: *facilitative motivation* (where comparison is pursued for the sake of personal and institutional efficiency in material transactions), *persuasive motivation* (where comparison is pursued for the sake of proselytization), *dialectical motivation* (where comparison is pursued for the sake of enlightened cultural sensitivity, perhaps most closely related to what I am here describing as the internal good moral understanding), *reconstructive motivation* (where comparison is used to reconstruct the resources of one's own tradition to address previously unforeseen moral problems), and *transformative motivation* (where comparison is used to bring one back to a closer witnessing to the greatest moral ideals in one's own tradition). See my initial mapping of this issue in "Comparative Religion, Ethics,

and American Family Life: Concluding Questions and Future Directions," in *American Religions and the Family: How Faith Traditions Cope with Modernization and Democracy*, ed. Don S. Browning and David A. Clairmont (New York: Columbia University Press, 2006).

16. Here it is worth quoting MacIntyre's summary statement of the meaning of "good": "Good is ascribed . . . both to what benefits human beings as such and to what benefits human beings in particular roles within particular contexts of practice." See Alasdair MacIntyre, *Dependent Rational Animals: Why Human Beings Need the Virtues* (Chicago: Open Court, 1999), 78, 65. What I am suggesting here about interreligious conversation can be reasonably understood as goods internal to one's pursuits when one inhabits interreligious conversation as a role. In this way, we can begin to think analogically about the roles that people play within religious traditions that speak on their behalf, and so the excellence accruing to the conversation participant can redound to the tradition.

17. Alasdair MacIntyre, "Intractable Moral Disagreements," 13.

18. In terms of MacIntyre's own tradition of Roman Catholic–inspired Thomism, I would press two areas of moral concern that, while there are resources in the tradition to identify them, the Thomist tradition (broadly understood) has not as yet addressed in anything like a comprehensive and systematic way: environmental degradation and racism. For an incisive critique of the teaching of the Roman Catholic bishops on racism, see Bryan N. Massingale, "James Cone and Recent Catholic Episcopal Teaching on Racism," *Theological Studies* 61 (2000): 700–730.

19. Alasdair MacIntyre, *Whose Justice? Which Rationality?* (Notre Dame: University of Notre Dame Press, 1988), 11.

20. Ibid., 11.

21. Ibid., 374.

22. MacIntyre, "Intractable Moral Disagreements," 21: "I do not of course mean by this that the pursuit of truth always takes precedence over all other types of activity. That would be absurd. There is a time to enquire and a time not to enquire, but instead to catch fish or to sing the blues or whatever." Although I take it that by this point MacIntyre just means there need to be times for recreation, this indicates to me an attitude of general dismissiveness toward "lower" activities, which are at best instrumental in clearing the mind and calming it for enquiry. Surely there are others for whom singing the blues is not a break from, but rather the substance of, moral enquiry. As James Cone explains about the centrality of blues music and African spirituals in

the struggle of black people to affirm their moral and religious agency under conditions of oppression, "What did it mean 'to steal away to Jesus' when one had been stolen from Africa and enslaved in white America? What did it mean to 'work on a building that is a true foundation' or to 'hold up the blood stained banner for the Lord' when one had no building to call his or her own, and one's blood was stained with slavery? What did it mean to be a 'child of God' and a black slave in a white society? All of these questions touch the very substance and 'gut' of black religion as reflected in the spirituals." See James H. Cone, *The Spirituals and the Blues: An Interpretation* (Maryknoll, NY: Orbis Books, 1992), 3. Certainly we must at least be open to the possibility that the blues, and other activities, more closely resemble "enquiry" than they do "whatever."

23. The statements of the Roman Catholic bishops are much more complicated than this typology suggests, but this rationale is clearly stated in the Pontifical Council for Interreligious Dialogue's 1991 statement, *Dialogue and Proclamation*. As it says, "While entering with an open mind into dialogue with the followers of other religious traditions, Christians may have also to challenge them in a peaceful spirit with regard to the content of their belief. But Christians too must allow themselves to be questioned. Notwithstanding the fullness of God's revelation in Jesus Christ, the way Christians sometimes understand their religion and practice it may be in need of purification" (par. 32). While the primary horizon for dialogue must always remain proclamation of the gospel, dialogue always requires that this proclamation be linked with an effort of inner purification by the Church: "It must be remembered that the Church's commitment to dialogue is not dependent on success in achieving mutual understanding and enrichment; rather it flows from God's initiative in entering into a dialogue with humankind and from the example of Jesus Christ whose life, death and resurrection gave to that dialogue its ultimate expression" (par. 53).

24. While I developed this analogy in an attempt to think through which Christian practices met both MacIntyre's concerns about the conditions for the search for moral truth and the bishops' warnings that this search is always bound to how the parties in conversation understand their own struggle to know and live the Christian faith more fully, my first hint that the practice of sacramental reconciliation might have a kind of temporal parallel to other moral practices started with a paper by Maria Morrow titled "Pornography and Penance" (unpublished) given at the sixth annual New Wine, New Wineskins Symposium, July 28, 2007. Morrow's argument, which I agree

with only in part, is that penance in the Catholic tradition has the formal quality of concretization, which tends to counteract the abstraction involved in producing and viewing pornography. My response to Morrow at the time was that the structural parallel is only one way to understand what "abstraction" means (namely, making a person into a body or then into an image of a body). But other forms of abstraction, namely, analogical thinking, are not the destructive abstractions of the kind she identifies. Moreover, any effort to find common elements or generalizations from particulars (i.e., efforts to find or to produce form) can often be in the service of enhancing rather than reducing the complexity of real persons, which was the real worry that Morrow identified in the paper (the reduction of personhood to abstract, manipulatable, instrumentalizable images). My view of the applicability of confession, reconciliation, and penance to interreligious conversations about moral matters draws its initial inspiration from my discussions with her.

25. I say there is no direct analogy, but there is one important parallel. In his book *The Creed: What Christians Believe and Why It Matters* (New York: Image/Doubleday, 2003), Luke Timothy Johnson offers a helpful typology of atheism. He distinguishes between two kinds of "humanistic atheism": one based on the judgment that "[b]elief in God is wish fulfillment that hides from people their real condition" and another that "rejects belief in God because of the pervasive presence of evil in the world" (p. 69). He contrasts these forms of atheism with "practical atheism," which "is based on a decision of the heart rather than a conclusion of the mind, and is expressed by serving oneself and oppressing others. Practical atheists have their 'gods'—all humans must center their lives somewhere—but they are gods that are crafted according to their own desires. Practical atheism finds its expression in idolatry" (p. 70). I think that if we think about the meaning of practical atheism in the context of confession, we find a parallel. What one brings to an examination of conscience is not unlike two selves that adhere to two different judgments about God in the moment of action, and to confess that one has given oneself to something that is not God. Call it momentary practical atheism. The point is that it is difficult, in the process of interreligious conversations about moral matters, not to think that similar conversations, with different "religions," go on within oneself, throughout life, and that the skills that one acquires in making sense of this phenomenon help to think oneself back into the interreligious conversation. At least this is the basic experiential claim on which this entire essay is based.

26. Johnson, *The Creed*, 69.

27. I should note that while I isolate the practice of penance as one of a number of sacramental practices that might inform the reasons for and ways of engaging in interreligious conversation, I do not mean it to be exclusive. I think the temporal habituation in liturgy serves a similar function, and there are certainly penitential moments in the Mass that focus the person in similar ways. My purpose in highlighting penance is that it is perhaps temporally distinct and distinctly Roman Catholic, even as I acknowledge that changing sacramental theologies suggest that how the faithful practiced penance in, say, Aquinas's time is not the same as how it is practiced today.

28. Thomas Aquinas, *Summa Theologica,* III, q. 85, a. 3:

[P]enance is a special virtue not merely because it sorrows for evil done (since charity would suffice for that), but also because the penitent grieves for the sin he has committed, inasmuch as it is an offense against God, and purposes to amend. Now amendment for an offense committed against anyone is not made by merely ceasing to offend, but it is necessary to make some kind of compensation, which obtains in offenses committed against another, just as retribution does, only that compensation is on the part of the offender, as when he makes satisfaction, whereas retribution is on the part of the person offended against. Each of these belongs to the matter of justice, because each is a kind of commutation. Wherefore it is evident that penance, as a virtue, is a part of justice.

29. 1996 C.E.

CHAPTER 4 | Prophetic Rhetoric

and Moral Disagreement

M. Cathleen Kaveny

In his groundbreaking book, After Virtue, *the* philosopher Alasdair MacIntyre argues that "the most striking feature of contemporary moral utterance is that so much of it is used to express disagreements; and the most striking feature of the debates in which these disagreements are expressed is their interminable character."[1] In support of his claim, he gives examples from three well-known and seemingly interminable debates of our time: the debate over whether it is ever just to wage war, the abortion debate, and the debate about the relative priority of social equality and individual liberty.[2]

What has caused such disagreement? According to MacIntyre, it is the loss of a coherent tradition of moral reasoning once provided by Western Christianity. In the wake of the religious wars of the early modern era, the Enlightenment project aimed to provide the West with a rational, secular foundation for moral norms that was both universally applicable and universally acceptable. With its failure, we are left with bits and pieces of incompatible moral traditions, the flotsam and jetsam from the shipwreck of innumerable attempts to formulate a coherent framework for moral reflection.

In my view, MacIntyre's diagnosis of the cause of moral disagreement is correct. It is, however, also incomplete. In the United States at the turn of the twenty-first century, our difficulties do not stem solely from the challenge of brokering the rival moral claims of Kantians and utilitarians, or negotiating the tension between hedonists and stoics. We also confront serious moral disputes among persons who see themselves as belonging to the same moral tradition, and as holding themselves accountable to the same values and the same account of the virtues. More specifically, we confront serious moral disputes among those who proclaim Jesus Christ their Lord and Savior and who allow their consciences to be shaped by both Scripture and the Christian tradition.

Needless to say, identifying the source, nature, and gravity of moral disagreement among Christians is a complicated task. Doubtless, some self-proclaimed Christians are shaped more by the secular culture than they are by the gospel. Furthermore, no Christian theologian can deny that human sinfulness, particularly a distorted form of self-interest, can contribute not only to an inability to act in accordance with our moral obligations but also to an incapacity to recognize and acknowledge those obligations. As St. Thomas Aquinas observed, moral blindness due to sin can afflict entire communities, as well as individuals.[3]

At the same time, however, Aquinas reminds us that not all moral disagreements about how to handle specific cases are rooted in the disordered self-interest of one or all parties to the disagreement. We ought to expect, he tells us, greater levels of disagreement about morality as we move from general principles to judgments about what to do in specific situations. Why is that the case? Following Aristotle, Aquinas notes that prudence, which is right reason about things to be done, does not operate with a complete set of general laws that cover all cases without exception. Prudence deals with specific actions, which are what Aristotle calls "contingent singulars."[4] What counts as the prudent course of action frequently depends on one's assessment of the background factual situation in cases of uncertainty. People of goodwill often differ in their assessment of the relevant facts, particularly in their predictions of the consequences of a certain course of action.

Nonetheless, setting the cases of good faith disagreement about the facts between and among committed Christians aside does not eliminate the problem. We continue to find ourselves faced with deep clashes of moral judgment among well-educated, committed adherents of the same religious tradition. Moreover, these clashes do not give rise to fruitful discussion about differences but instead signal the breakdown of conversation, and frequently even the breakdown of the bonds of community. The painfulness of these breaks in personal relationships frequently make it impossible for those involved to collaborate on behalf of the common good.

In my view, at least some of these clashes, and some of these ensuing breakdowns, are due at least as much to moral style as they are to disagreements about moral substance. More specifically, in making their case in the public square, many American Christians draw upon the passionate rhetoric exemplified in the prophetic books of the Hebrew Bible, the rhetoric that Matthew Arnold (1822–88) called the language of "fire and strength."[5] As Arnold himself acknowledged, prophetic rhetoric is an essential complement to the language of "sweetness and light"—the cooler, reasonable discourse we owe to Greek philosophers and Roman lawyers.[6] At the same time, however, prophetic rhetoric can be dangerous. The frequently ad hominem nature of prophetic indictments can set brothers and sisters in Christ against one another, while the harsh and uncompromising nature of their demands can exacerbate moral disagreements.

In sum, prophetic rhetoric is like moral chemotherapy. On the one hand, its use is necessary to combat certain grave moral cancers threatening a society's collective ability for sound moral deliberation.

On the other hand, it is dangerous medicine; if not applied judiciously, it can cause more harm than benefit to the moral health of the society in question.

In the first section of this essay, I will situate the place of prophetic rhetoric in American political discussion, noting the prominent but unexpected contribution that Roman Catholics have made to the renewed influence of this form of discourse since the year 2000. This contribution, in my view, is attributable to the broad resonance of Pope John Paul II's 1995 encyclical, *Evangelium Vitae*, among American Evangelical Protestants and other conservative Republicans, particularly the encyclical's opposition of the "culture of life" and the "culture of death."[7] In the second section, I will probe more deeply into the nature, function, and dangers of prophetic rhetoric for the moral discourse of our political community. In the third section, taking abortion as an example, I will argue that the "culture war" rhetoric in American political discourse has exacerbated moral disagreement among Christians. Consequently, it has made the full moral and political vision outlined in *Evangelium Vitae* less likely to be realized in American public life.

What, then, is the way forward? In the final section, I will suggest that *Evangelium Vitae* can provide necessary guidance—if we American Catholics look at it with fresh eyes. The first step is to recognize that the true home of *Evangelium Vitae* is *not*, in fact, the American tradition of prophetic rhetoric. Rather, its true home is the thoroughly Christocentric and sacramental vision of *Lumen Gentium*.[8] A Christocentric understanding of prophetic rhetoric opens new possibilities that can ameliorate the consequences of bitter moral disagreement.

I. Prophetic Rhetoric in the American Context

The American political experiment was begun by refugees from England seeking a pristine land where they would be free to organize a polity on the basis of their religious commitments. From the very beginning, their political speech was inherently religious, as scholars of American religious history such as Perry Miller,[9] Sidney Ahlstrom,[10] and Jon Butler[11] have recognized. Political sermons reflecting on the state of the covenant between God and the people were common in colonial New England, as settlers articulated their vision of themselves as a "new Israel," living out a new and eternal covenant with God. In *The American Jeremiad*,[12] the social historian Sacvan Bercovitch traces the uniquely American development of a form of prophetic speech regularly used by Puritan preachers in order to call their flock to live up to their obligations under the covenant. Named in honor of the prophet Jeremiah, whose passion it both imitates and channels, the jeremiad is defined by Bercovitch as a "lament over the ways of the world. It decried the sins of 'the people'—a community, a nation, a civilization, mankind in general—and warned of God's wrath to follow."[13] The American Puritans put their own stamp on this genre, mixing anxiety with an unwavering conviction of America's divinely given mission and a promise to propel their flock forward on their theological and political mission.

In *The Prophetic Tradition and Radical Rhetoric in America,* James Darsey traces the use of prophetic rhetoric in the American political context beyond its origins in Protestant sermonizing.[14] He demonstrates that it has been deployed by a wide range of American political activists, including pamphleteers for the American Revolution, the abolitionist Wendell Phillips, and the socialist Eugene Debs. Degraded forms of prophetic rhetoric also can be found in Joseph McCarthy's anti-Communist tirades, as well as the rhetoric of Robert Welch, the founder of the conservative, libertarian John Birch Society.

According to Darsey, the availability of prophetic rhetoric within a particular political community depends upon a bedrock sense of common values, upon which prophetic speakers can ground their cause in a common dedication to moral righteousness.[15] Writing in the early 1990s, Darsey argued that our society is increasingly pluralistic and materialistic; it is held together largely by self-interest rather than firm and unwavering moral commitment. In this context, he says, appeals to prophetic indictments make no sense, because there are no fundamental values to proclaim and uphold. "There is no communion," observes Darsey, "in money."[16]

In my judgment, Darsey is squarely on target in his claim that prophetic rhetoric in the United States is not the exclusive province of any one political party or social movement. He spoke too soon, however, about its demise as a form of political rhetoric. In the 1960s prophetic language was used by so-called religious progressives, the high-water mark of which was the Reverend Martin Luther King's "I Have a Dream" speech in support of civil rights given on the steps of the Lincoln Memorial in August 1963.[17] Forty years after that speech, prophetic rhetoric is used most prominently by religious conservatives. The resurgence of explicitly religious discourse, especially prophetic discourse, after the 2000 presidential election is too extensive to be ignored.

Much of that rhetoric has been shaped by the language of Pope John Paul II in *Evangelium Vitae,* in particular his vivid language of "the culture of life" and "the culture of death." The pope writes:

> [W]e are facing an enormous and dramatic clash between good and evil, death and life, the "culture of death" and the "culture of life." We find ourselves not only "faced with" but necessarily "in the midst of" this conflict: we are all involved and we all share in it, with the inescapable responsibility of *choosing to be unconditionally pro-life.*[18]

Repackaged as a battle cry in the "culture wars," that language has been adopted by a wide range of cultural conservatives of all denominations to encapsulate their moral and political demands. In the context of American political life, these demands have been pressed into service by the Republican Party in its political struggle against the Democrats.[19] At the advice of politically conservative Catholic advisors, such as Fr. Richard John Neuhaus of the monthly journal *First Things* and Deal Hudson of *Crisis* magazine, George W. Bush began inserting "culture of life" and "culture of death" language into his public speeches soon after he assumed the office of President of the United States in 2000. One of his goals was to appeal to Catholics, and thereby to solidify a political coalition between conservative Catholics and conservative Evangelical Protestants. The political use of the culture war language reached its height in the 2004 presidential election, when President Bush sought reelection against the Democratic presidential candidate, John Kerry. Drawing upon the language from *Evangelum Vitae,* many prominent conservative Catholics, including some members of the hierarchy,[20] contended that a good Catholic could not in good conscience vote for Kerry, because of his support for legalized abortion rights. They claimed that no other issues or set of issues, including the by-now-acute questions of the Iraq War, could trump the question of abortion.[21] There is no doubt that the efforts of the Republican Party to court conservative Catholics and evangelicals made a difference in the election, although careful and nuanced analysis is needed to specify this difference with any degree of certitude.[22]

In contrast, the dominant tone of the "culture of life" / "culture of death" language in the American political context owes more to this country's strong tradition of Protestant prophetic political rhetoric than it does to *Evangelium Vitae*. More specifically, the focus on a few sharply defined practices (abortion, euthanasia, stem cell research), the tendency to reduce the moral significance of these issues to securing legal prohibitions against the practices they define, and the tendency to divide the "righteous" and the "wicked" into clearly defined and opposing camps reflect the way in which prophetic indictments frequently operate in American political discourse. To understand why they operate in this way, it is necessary to consider in more detail the manner in which prophetic rhetoric functions.

II. The Language of "Fire and Strength": The Nature, Function, and Dangers of Prophetic Rhetoric in Political Discourse

To give a straightforward, albeit circular, definition of prophetic discourse is to say that it is the discourse characteristic of prophets. As I am using them here, the paradigmatic meaning of the terms *prophet* and *prophecy* centers on the prophetic writings in the Old Testament, or Hebrew Bible. The term *prophetic discourse* refers in the first instance to the rhetorical forms and substantive concerns that are characteristic of the biblical prophet.

What sort of discourse is characteristic of the biblical prophets? Here, it is helpful to note that four terms are commonly used to describe them in the Hebrew Bible: *hōzeh* (seer), *rō'eh* (diviner), *'îš hā' ĕlōhîm* (man of God), and *nābî'* (prophet).[23] In general, the first term refers to someone who receives divinely ordained visions; the second refers to someone who can discern helpful information from the divine world. Broadly speaking, these two terms account for the fact that we often use the term *prophet* to refer to someone with the power to predict future events. The third term, which is prominent in the stories of Elijah and Elisha, refers to men who "possess the power of the holy and hence are dangerous, powerful, and due appropriate respect."[24]

The fourth term, *nābî'*, is the most common term used in the Hebrew Scriptures for a prophet. What does it mean? Scholars note that it has a very broad range of meanings which over time came to overlap the three other terms. Nonetheless, the root meaning of this term, *nāb-*, which means "to call," appears to be significant.[25] A prophet is someone who is called and commissioned by God, usually to deliver a message to God's people. That message frequently pertained to God's perspective on the relationship between God and Israel, and more specifically, to the ways in which his chosen people were fulfilling—or failing to fulfill—the obligations of their covenant at a particular time and place in their history.

It is this aspect of prophetic discourse that is of particular interest to us here, for it is the aspect which strives to function as an impetus for social critique and reform. I shall refer to it as the language of prophetic indictment. As the great Jewish thinker Abraham Joshua Heschel stated, "The prophet was an individual who said No to his society, condemning its habits and assumptions, its complacency, waywardness, and syncretism. His fundamental objective was to reconcile man and God. Why do the two need reconciliation? Perhaps it is due to man's false sense of sovereignty, to his abuse of freedom, to his aggressive, sprawling pride, resenting God's involvement in history."[26]

One can speak "prophetically" in the sense described by Heschel without appropriating for oneself the mantle of a prophet. To put the point another way, persons who do not claim actually to be delivering particular messages from God can and do draw upon the forms and the themes of prophetic discourse preserved in the Old Testament. They do so in order to call attention to the moral and political challenges confronting their respective societies. Such persons do not believe God has directly conscripted them to communicate a new message to the community on his behalf. They do, however, tend to see themselves as following in the footsteps of the biblical prophets, as illuminating the moral dangers of the current situation by drawing upon the themes and style of discourse of the biblical prophets.

What are the characteristics of prophetic indictments as a rhetorical form? The Protestant ethicist James Gustafson noted three characteristics. First, "they usually, though not always, address what the prophet perceives to be the *root* of religious, moral, or social waywardness, not specific instances in which certain policies are judged to be inadequate or wrong."[27] Second, prophetic indictments employ "language, metaphors, and symbols that are directed to the 'heart' as well as to the 'head.' The prophet usually does not make an argument; rather he demonstrates, he shows, he tells."[28] Third, prophetic indictments are usually utopian in nature. Gustafson does not use this term technically, but merely to indicate that "prophets sometimes proclaim and depict an ideal state of affairs which is radically in contrast with the actual state of affairs in which we live together in society."[29] Prophetic indictments frequently decry a social evil without providing a clear plan for its amelioration. Following Darsey, I would add a fourth characteristic: those who use prophetic discourse tend to presuppose, tacitly or explicitly, that they are speaking into a moment of communal crisis—a moment of decision with enormous consequences for the community. Quite often, this moment of crisis is presented in the starkest possible terms: either turn from your wicked ways or be destroyed. There is no time to waste.

What is the relationship of prophetic indictments to ordinary moral discourse—what Arnold called the discourse of "sweetness and light"? The first point is that prophetic indictments are not ordinary moral discourse; instead, they are a form of radical discourse. Prophetic indictments are radical in the original sense of the term. The overarching goal of the prophet is to call the community back to its fundamental moral commitments, and to renew its dedication to the bedrock principles upon which the society is based. Prophetic discourse is, in an important sense, about the foundations of moral discourse, not about its upper floors. If the foundations are not steady and strong, any moral reasoning grounded upon them is likely to be unstable and dangerous.

The definitive example from the Old Testament is the sin of idolatry, excoriated again and again by the Hebrew prophets. Nowhere is the grievousness of the sin of idolatry more vividly portrayed than in the Book of Hosea. Instructed by God to take a temple prostitute for a wife, Hosea passionately conveyed God's sense of outrage and betrayal at Israel's dalliances.

> Protest against your mother, protest!
> for she is not my wife,
> and I am not her husband.
> Let her remove her harlotry from before her,
> her adultery from between her breasts,
> Or I will strip her naked,

leaving her as on the day of her birth;
I will make her like the desert,
reduce her to an arid land,
and slay her with thirst.[30]

The prohibition against idolatry stands at the foundation of the Israelite religion. Those who do not realize why idolatry is a grievous offense against Yahweh clearly do not perceive who Yahweh is—the one true God, who led the Israelites out of captivity and provided for them through their wanderings in the desert. They do not grasp the exclusive nature of the covenant Yahweh made with people on Mount Sinai. They do not understand either the folly or the betrayal involved in chasing after false gods. Consequently, they are unfit for more advanced forms of moral reasoning. Having shown themselves blind to the fundamental nature of that covenant, they are in no position to adjudicate more difficult questions of loyalty and obedience that are to be decided on the basis of that covenant.

In addition to calling people back to the fundamental commitments of their moral and political world, prophetic indictments serve a second fundamental purpose. They are frequently used as a form of moral shock treatment. In their very harshness, they force people to recognize the truth about thoroughly corrupt patterns or practices of behavior, a truth to which they have become blind or callous. This function of prophetic indictments is illustrated by the second overarching theme in the Hebrew prophets: the scandalous exploitation of the poor by the privileged upper class. In many cases, this exploitation was not due as much to maliciousness as to moral senselessness; consequently, the prophets assailed minds and hearts numb to the tribulations of other people. Nothing is more powerful than the words of the prophets themselves. Consider the words of the prophet Isaiah:

The Lord rises to accuse,
standing to try his people.
The Lord enters into judgment

with his people's elders and princes:
It is you who have devoured the vineyard;
the loot wrested from the poor is in your houses.
What do you mean by crushing my people,
and grinding down the poor when they look to you?
Says the Lord, the God of hosts.
The Lord said:
Because the daughters of Zion are haughty,
and walk with necks outstretched,
ogling and mincing as they go,
their anklets tinkling with every step,
The Lord shall cover the scalps of Zion's
daughters with scabs,
and the Lord shall bare their heads.[31]

If we examine the books named for the Hebrew prophets, it appears that the basic functions of prophetic indictments are two: (1) to demand that wayward citizens make a renewed commitment to the moral basis of that community—in the case of the Israelites, the covenant with the one true God; and (2) to shock wayward members of the community out of their indifference to their own flagrant pattern of sins, and to the harm those sins cause to other members of the community. As Matthew Arnold recognized, these functions are essential for the moral health of a community, not only in the times of Judah and Israel, but also in our own times. If a society is threatening to abandon key elements of its entire moral framework, or if its members manifest a pattern of sustained indifference to human injustice, prophetic indictments may be the only medicine strong enough to overcome the danger to its moral fabric.

Strong medicine, however, is also dangerous medicine. When a human body is ravaged by cancer, chemotherapy can be the only hope of restoring life and health. At the same time, chemotherapy can have destructive consequences. Unless the physician is extremely judicious in its use, it can do more harm than good; in some circumstances, it can even kill the patient. So too with prophetic indictments, which I believe function as a type of moral chemotherapy. They can be absolutely necessary to preserve the fundamental moral fabric of the community. At the same time, they can rip a community apart, setting mother against son, sister against brother. Any reflection on the function of prophetic indictments, therefore, must come to terms not only with their appropriate use but also with their great potential for abuse. This destructive potential is intimately connected with the inner logic of prophetic indictments; it arises from the way in which prophetic interventions affect the ongoing conversation. Let me sketch, therefore, four key characteristics of this inner logic.

First, by their very form and content, prophetic indictments radically constrain the possibilities for acceptable response on the part of the listeners. Remember that the true prophet is claiming to be a messenger of God; the prophet also claims that the message he or she is delivering is divinely mandated. From the prophet's perspective, therefore, the only acceptable response is obedience and repentance on the part of the audience. How else can one respond to an unequivocal message from the Supreme Being? Hearers who do not obey and repent are functionally in the position of making an ad hominem attack on the prophet. In effect, they are calling the prophet a liar, or at the very least, an unreliable messenger. Their very recalcitrance proclaims their belief that the prophet is not, indeed, a messenger from God, or that the prophet distorted or truncated the message in some significant way.

Second, and relatedly, it is important to note that prophetic indictments often forestall the possibility of dialogue or compromise. This is the case with respect to the substance of the message. The prophet believes that he or she is uttering God's own message; it cannot, therefore, be quibbled with or debated. Consider, for example, this passage from Jeremiah:

> For I will stretch forth my hand
> against those who dwell in this land, says the Lord.

Small and great alike, all are greedy for gain;
prophet and priest, all practice fraud.
They would repair, as though it were nought,
the injury to my people:
"Peace, peace!" they say,
  though there is no peace.
They are odious; they have done abominable things,
yet they are not at all ashamed,
they know not how to blush.
Hence they shall be among those who fall;
in their time of punishment they shall go down, says the Lord.[32]

There is no conversational space in this indictment for an interlocutor to ask, "Well, wait a minute, now. What exactly counts as 'greedy'?" Moreover, the questions "Do you have anything specifically in mind with the term *abominable things*?" and "Is their commission a specific-intent offense?" are not likely to be met with a measured and thoughtful response from the prophet. Those who ask such questions merely prove "they know not how to blush."

Third, and consequently, prophetic indictments leave scant room for careful, casuistic distinctions common in both law and ordinary analysis of moral problems. Consider, for example, the prohibition against idolatry, which I identified earlier as the fundamental moral prohibition of the ancient Israelites. Does it count as "idolatry" to eat meat sacrificed to idols if the eater doesn't actually believe in other gods? This is a casuistic question, probing the precise boundaries of the definition of *idolatry*. It was a live question for St. Paul.[33] It is not one, however, with which the writers of the Book of Isaiah or Jeremiah or Hosea would have had much patience. To ask the question would be to demonstrate that one had not fully grasped the full horror of the sin of idolatry; anyone who did recognize that horror would want to stay as far away from it as possible, not only in internal beliefs, but also in external acts.

Fourth, and most important, the use of prophetic indictment generally marks the end of civil discussion. Those who, for whatever reason, do not acknowledge the speaker's identity as a true prophet are likely to react with indignation to the prophet's stinging words. Consider the foregoing passage from Jeremiah as an example. The experience of being called "greedy" or "odious" by a person whom one does not consider a true prophet is likely to produce indignation and insults in return, at least from the vast majority of people not blessed with saintly patience. The prophet, filled with righteous anger, calls for obedience and repentance. One or two members of the audience might comply. But the rest are incredulous and skeptical; they believe themselves to have been calumniated and respond accordingly. The quality of the conversation disintegrates apace.

Consequently, those concerned about the common good need to think carefully before addressing their fellow citizens with sustained prophetic invective. Would-be prophets first need to consider whether their cause is not only just but also sufficiently grave. If their target is those who disagree with them about a moral precept, they need to ask themselves whether that precept stands at the center of the community's moral framework, or whether it is an ancillary issue about which people of goodwill could be expected to disagree. If their target is the callous behavior of other people, they need to consider whether there is another, more charitable explanation for that behavior. They also need to consider whether they are acting with right intention. It is all too easy to move from a give-and-take discussion to prophetic rhetoric because one's arguments are weak in their details. It is all too tempting to conceal one's own moral flaws by wrapping oneself in the righteous mantle of the Hebrew prophets. Finally, would-be prophets need to consider whether the deployment of prophetic indictments is likely to be successful. Given the particular people involved in the conversation, are the prophetic indictments likely to touch the minds and hearts of their opponents, or merely to harden their opposition? Is hardened opposition likely to preclude all possibility of gradual growth, and to darken a dawning recognition of moral truth?[34] In some cases, perhaps many cases, the fruits of reflection on these questions should cause would-be prophets to rethink their rhetoric.

III. Abortion, the United States, and the Culture Wars

In January 1973 the Supreme Court of the United States handed down its decision on *Roe v. Wade;*[35] it held that a woman possesses a constitutional right to privacy that encompasses a right to abortion in a broad range of circumstances. The decision invalidated restrictions on abortion in all fifty states, setting off a firestorm of controversy between "pro-life" and "pro-choice" activists that continues to this day. At the same time, examination of the polling data since that time suggests that these culture wars have had very little effect on the position on abortion held by the American population as a whole; in fact, that position has been remarkably stable over the past forty years. A recent report from the highly respected Pew Research Center for the People and the Press encapsulates the situation:

> Public opinion about the legality of abortion is largely unchanged from previous polling. While about one-in-three (31%) prefer for abortion to be generally available to those who want it and one-in-ten (11%) take the opposite position that abortion should not be permitted at all, most Americans fall in between, preferring what might be described as a "legal but rare" stance. One-in-five (20%) say that abortion should be available but under stricter limits than it is now, while about one-in-three (35%) say that abortion should be illegal except in cases of rape, incest or to save the woman's life.[36]

In short, a stable two-thirds of Americans appear to be open to a more restrictive regime with respect to abortion than we have today. Why, then, has there been so little progress on the part of the pro-life movement in the United States? The paramount reason stems from the fact that the legalization of abortion in this country was not achieved by legislation but rather by a judicial decision at the highest level of the federal court system. Given the political structure of the nation, undoing the effects of such a decision is an extremely complicated process. Short of banning abortion by an amendment to the American Constitution (an event highly unlikely to occur), what was done can only be undone by a decision of the Supreme Court reversing or greatly restricting its own decision in *Roe v. Wade*.

Such a significant judicial reversal is likely to come about only by a substantial change in the composition of the Supreme Court. But this sort of change is not easy to effect, for three reasons. First, Supreme Court justices are not elected by the American people; instead, they are appointed by the American president. Second, appointments to the Supreme Court are lifetime, not term, appointments. Consequently, there is no guarantee that any given president will have the opportunity to make an appointment during his or her term of office. Third, candidates for appointment to the Supreme Court routinely refuse to answer specific questions about what they would do in particular cases likely to come before them. Providing such answers is improper, because it seems to entail rendering judgment in a case before considering all the evidence and law relevant to the decision. Consequently, a president is liable to make a mistake about how an appointee to the Court will vote in any given case, particularly since an appointee's views may well evolve over time.

The analysis in section I of this essay helps us to understand the responses of some prophets for the pro-life position to this situation, as well as the tensions their responses generate in the broader political conversation. As Heschel reminds us, a prophet is someone who says "No" to the great evils of his time; to such a prophet, any response that hints of nuance or compromise merely reveals either the willful blindness or culpable ignorance of his or her interlocutor. In the context of the abortion debate, this "No" tends to take three forms. First, it takes the form of an absolute prioritization of the issue of abortion over all other issues. Many pro-life activists in the United States have long argued that the election of a president who will appoint Supreme Court justices willing to overrule *Roe* must be an absolute moral priority for the electorate. No other issue should be allowed to trump the moral demand to eradicate *Roe*.

Second, some of those who adopt a prophetic stance on abortion resist any attempt to draw casuistic distinctions regarding both the act of "abortion" and the circumstances surrounding the act. Just as St. Paul's attempts to probe the meaning and boundaries of the prohibited practice of "idolatry" would have met with hostility from the prophet Isaiah or Hosea, so too the arguments of serious Christians to probe the meaning and boundaries of the prohibited practice of "abortion" have met with hostility from many prophetic opponents of abortion. The influential American Life League, for example, opposes all abortion—without exception—in cases of rape, incest, and even if necessary to preserve the life or health of the mother.[37] I could find on their Web site no explicit acknowledgment that in some cases (e.g., removal of a fallopian tube in the case of an ectopic pregnancy) physicians might take action which they foresee but do not intend to result in the death of the unborn child. According to traditional Catholic moral theology, such a case would count as an "abortion" medically, but not morally.[38]

Third, some prophetic opponents to abortion judge that the only acceptable policy solution is a legal framework that precisely mirrors the absolute moral commitments of the prophetic stance. Some pro-life scholars have argued that one must vote against any law that appears by its wording, on its face, to permit a particular class of abortions, despite the fact that its concrete effect in a particular society will be to reduce the number or type of abortions that are legally available.[39]

A prophetic approach to the law is not confined to the realm of scholarly debate. In March 2006 the governor of the state of South

Dakota, for example, passed a law prohibiting all abortions except those necessary to save a woman's life—the strictest abortion law in the country.[40] The pro-lifers responsible for the law judged that it would not only express a salutary uncompromising attitude to abortion but also provide the Supreme Court with an opportunity to reconsider *Roe v. Wade* with the participation of two new members appointed by President George W. Bush, Chief Justice John Roberts and Associate Justice Samuel Alito.[41] As other pro-lifers predicted, the strategy backfired. In November 2006 the citizens of South Dakota rejected the law, which had been placed by its opponents on the South Dakota ballot, by a majority of 56 percent to 44 percent.[42]

Not surprisingly, the prophetic stance on abortion frustrates and alienates those who, while sympathetic to the moral problem of abortion, situate the effort to deal with it politically in the context of other social questions and responsibilities. For example, consider the first aspect of the prophetic stance described above, namely, the claim that overturning *Roe v. Wade* must trump all other considerations for a morally virtuous American citizen. Many persons sympathetic to the case against abortion see the political situation as demanding a more nuanced response. More specifically, many believe that in light of the dominant role of the United States on the global stage, prudent selection of the nation's president must necessarily take into account factors in addition to his or her stance on abortion rights. Furthermore, because Supreme Court justices are appointed for life, many Americans believe that assessment of a president's selection of Supreme Court justices must encompass far more than a candidate's likely response to *Roe*.[43]

Furthermore, the second aspect of the prophetic response to abortion, the refusal to engage in the practice of drawing careful distinctions in so-called hard cases, can alienate many Americans who are appalled by a widespread practice of abortion on demand. They are alienated not only by the negative judgment prophetic pro-lifers reach about abortion in these cases but also by their sense that pro-lifers cannot see any moral distinction in the gravity of evil between abortion after rape, on the one hand, and abortion after consensual sex in college, on the other.

Finally, the refusal on the part of many of the most vocal pro-life prophets to recognize that in many cases the legal framework around abortion cannot perfectly mirror prophetic moral standards frustrates potential allies. As Aquinas recognized in the *Summa Theologica,* sound positive law must not contradict the moral law, but it cannot expect to correspond with it in every respect. In particular, sound positive law must "be in accordance with the custom of the country"; otherwise, it will not be enforced, or it will be enforced only haphazardly, thereby undermining respect for law as a whole.[44] As Mary Ann Glendon has argued in *Abortion and Divorce in Western Law,* the most successful regime to protect unborn life includes a range of legal and social measures providing support for women who find themselves pregnant in difficult circumstances, not merely criminal prohibitions.[45]

In my judgment, then, there is significant tension between the few but vocal pro-life prophets, on the one hand, and the majority (two-thirds) of Americans who support significant but not absolute restrictions on abortion, on the other. Moreover, as the analysis of the effect of prophetic rhetoric upon interpersonal relations in section I suggests, the tension is not simply one between and among positions; there is also a tension between and among persons. The prophets believe the moral character and moral judgment of those who color their approach to abortion in shades of grey to be substantially flawed. Their motto is, "If you are not for us, you are against us." Needless to say, this motto does not sit well with those whom it judges. Moreover, those who are judged begin to make some judgments themselves.

The severest judgment, of course, would be to conclude that the pro-life prophets are false prophets; that their message contains nothing of value, only snares and delusions. This is the conclusion reached by activists on the other side of the debate—the mirror image of the pro-life prophets. They, however, are not our focus. We are concerned about the substantial majority of Americans who are uneasy with abortion on demand but who are not pro-life prophets—the group whose support is necessary in order to make any substantial changes in a representative democracy. In my judgment, they ultimately find the pro-life prophets admirable (for strongly advocating a worthwhile value) but politically unacceptable (for acknowledging only that value). During the periods in which the pro-life prophets have no political power, the majority are content to acknowledge that they make an important moral point. During the period in which it seems that the pro-life prophets are taking control, however, they balk; they worry about other values that are being sacrificed to achieve this goal. They begin to fear what life will be like in a political system dominated by prophetic concern with only one issue. So rather than collaborate with pro-life prophets in order to achieve some improvement, they move in an entirely different direction.[46]

IV. A Way Forward: Toward a Christocentric Understanding of Prophetic Rhetoric

Is there a way forward? Is there a possibility of forming a broader coalition of prophetic pro-life activists and ordinary pragmatic Americans who have significant reservations about abortion on demand? I have no solution, but I do have a suggestion. I think it will be very helpful for American Catholics to retrieve an understanding of prophetic discourse that is firmly rooted in the Catholic sacramental tradition rather than borrow uncritically from the American tradition of political rhetoric, influenced as it is by a less sacramentally focused Protestant tradition. It is obviously the Catholic tradition that best accounts for *Evangelium Vitae* itself, which includes not only a prophetic rejection of legal regimes which condone abortion and euthanasia but also a clear encouragement of incremental, practical steps to reduce both the desirability and the incidence of these practices. Consequently, the use of the prophetic contrast between the "culture of life" and "culture of death" in the encyclical is significantly different from its use by conservative partisans in the American political scene, particularly around the time of the 2004 presidential election.[47]

In my judgment, there are three basic differences between the pope's understanding of prophetic rhetoric and that of its use by American conservatives. First, Pope John Paul II's description of the "culture of life" and the "culture of death" takes seriously the nature of *culture* as an interpenetrating set of values, habits, practices, and institutions that shape the conditions under which persons make their own choices. A dominant culture affects everyone who lives within it; it is not something which particular individuals or families can easily step into and out of, although they can support or resist it. In contrast, the political use of "culture war" language tends to reduce cultures to opposing "teams" with distinct membership rosters, sometimes equated with the Democrats and the Republicans. Unfortunately, this tendency trivializes what is at stake in creating a life-affirming culture; it is not simply a matter of changing one's political affiliation. Moreover, it tends to exaggerate the moral gulf between oneself and one's political opponents, thereby diminishing opportunities for creative collaboration. After all, who could collaborate with a political operative whom one believes to be a minion of the culture of death?

Second, the conservative religious culture warriors vocal in American politics have a small and defined set of issues upon which they focus their consideration: abortion, stem cell research, euthanasia, and, increasingly, same-sex marriage. For them, a politician who opposes the legalization of these practices is in favor of a "culture of life"; their stand on other issues is secondary at best. Yet Pope John Paul II's vision is not so constricted. In addition to opposing these practices, he opposes the death penalty, at least in countries where it is otherwise possible to defend a society against the violence that its criminals would perpetrate.[48] Moreover, he explicitly ties the "culture of death" to widespread indifference to global suffering, such as the suffering of those beset by natural disasters. Quite strikingly, the pope describes as victims of "violence" those who are starving as a result of the unjust distribution of resources between the developing and the developed worlds. He notes the plight of those trapped by "violence, hatred and conflicting interests," such as in war and genocide. These too are victims of the "culture of death."[49]

What, then, accounts for the attention given to abortion and euthanasia? The pope states that he is focusing on these issues, not because their *victims* are somehow more worthy of attention, but because the *perpetrators* of those acts no longer believe that they are morally wrong.[50] It is the special moral blindness of the perpetrators to the plight of the vulnerable that is his overriding concern, not the special suffering of the victims.[51] Consequently, for religious conservatives to argue that a political figure can rightly ignore the plight of the other *victims* of injustice while focusing exclusively on abortion and euthanasia is to miss the larger point of the encyclical: the call for solidarity with *all* human beings, especially those who are vulnerable and suffering.

Third, for Pope John Paul II, the touchstone that distinguishes the "culture of life" from the "culture of death" is the fate of the vulnerable—those who by definition cannot take care of themselves. Consequently, he recognizes that the promotion of a culture of life must go beyond securing legal prohibitions against abortion and euthanasia; it must also assure that women facing difficult pregnancies and people facing suffering and death receive the assistance they need.[52] As has frequently been pointed out, however, the Republican culture war agenda in the United States is limited to enacting legal prohibitions of abortion, stem cell research, and euthanasia. There is little attention paid to providing women and families with the positive assistance they need to care for their more vulnerable members, or to care for those who have no one to look out for them. In fact, President Bush aimed to reduce essential social services for the poor and the elderly that directly affect "culture of life" issues—the Medicare and Medicaid programs that provide health care to elderly and impoverished Americans.[53]

These differences are crucial. While *Evangelium Vitae*'s use of the "culture of life" / "culture of death" language possesses undeniable prophetic elements, the very breadth of its vision opens up the possibility for collaboration with people of goodwill who may not share its vision on every point. This possibility is enhanced by the encyclical's recognition of the fact that a culture is not a team, which discourages a division of people into wheat and chaff, a division in which *we* are the "culture of life" and *they* are the "culture of death." Furthermore, the encyclical's emphasis upon the positive duty to assist the weak and the vulnerable encourages those committed to promoting a culture of life to contemplate areas in which they themselves are ripe for moral improvement.

What accounts for the clear differences between the use of the culture of life/culture of death rhetoric in *Evangelium Vitae*, on the one hand, and the contemporary American culture wars, on the other? In my judgment, the difference in rhetoric has its roots in a deeper difference in theological and sacramental perspective. John Paul II's use of prophetic rhetoric is deeply shaped by, and in fact transformed by, the Catholic theological and sacramental vision that is articulated in *Lumen Gentium*, Vatican II's Dogmatic Constitution of the Church. The meaning and use of prophetic rhetoric is ultimately governed by the reality of Jesus Christ's victory over sin and death. The same cannot be said, however, for the use of prophetic rhetoric in the American culture wars. In the following paragraph, I will elaborate upon this fundamental theological difference and its consequences, although I cannot do them full justice here and now.

First, as clearly expressed in *Lumen Gentium*, Jesus Christ is the fulfillment of the Old Testament prophetic books. He is the ultimate and decisive prophet, because he not only proclaimed the kingdom of God but also brought that kingdom into existence by his suffering, death, and resurrection.[54] Consequently, a Catholic use of prophetic rhetoric has to take into account the fact that the kingdom cannot be located entirely in the future, to rise from the ashes after a wrathful God inflicts certain destruction for our sins. The kingdom of God is already in our midst, and our connection with its inauguration is renewed each and every time we participate in the Mass.

In contrast, much of the prophetic rhetoric out of the American Protestant tradition tends functionally to absorb without much alteration the worldview of the Hebrew prophets—including their certain prediction of God's chastisement if immediate and radical changes are not made. That tradition of prophetic rhetoric tends to see American Christianity as the "New Israel," treating it as a more successful iteration of the original Israel, more capable of meeting the demands and predictions outlined by the Hebrew prophets. It fails, in my view, to take seriously the way in which the coming of Christ fundamentally altered the context in which human beings relate to God. From a Catholic perspective, the Church did not merely step into the shoes of the original Israel, carrying forward its relationship with God without any difference. Christ decisively transformed the relationship. In their oracles of woe to Israel and Judah, the Hebrew prophets vividly proclaim the ever-widening gulf between God and humanity caused by human sin. They frequently portray the cause of the Jewish people as hopeless, because they remained mired in their sinful ways. The birth of Christ, however, brought new hope, both for forgiveness and for new life.

By his redemptive death and resurrection, Christ ensured that human sinfulness would no longer be an insuperable stumbling block in the relationship between God and humanity. After Christ's resurrection, prophetic indictment of sin needs to proceed in a manner that acknowledges the decisive cosmic defeat of sin and death. In *Evangelium Vitae*, we see what this manner would look like most beautifully in Pope John Paul II's words to women who have had abortions: "If you have not already done so, give yourselves over with humility and trust to repentance. The Father of mercies is ready to give you his forgiveness and his peace in the Sacrament of Reconciliation. You will come to understand that *nothing is definitively lost* and you will also be able to ask forgiveness from your child, who is now living in the Lord."[55]

Undergirding this last sentence is the heart and soul of Catholic Christian faith, the Good News of the gospel. The mother-child relationship, which appeared decisively broken by the act of abortion, can be repaired and restored by the boundless and life-giving grace and mercy of Jesus Christ.

Second, and relatedly, a Christocentric prophetic rhetoric must be essentially positive, not negative, both with respect to its descriptions and with respect to its demands. While *Evangelium Vitae* is unhesitating in its condemnation of the "culture of death," it devotes far more attention to a thick description of the "culture of life." This concentration of attention is striking; as Gustafson noted, most indictments modeled on those found in the Hebrew prophets tend to convey a far clearer idea of the behavior which they condemn than the behavior which they would put in its place. A Christocentric prophetic rhetoric must not suffer the same fate. Pope John Paul II develops an account of the culture of life which is not limited to condemning practices such as abortion and euthanasia but recognizes that "[n]ot only must human life not be taken, but it must be protected with loving concern."[56] It is not enough to refrain from killing the most vulnerable members of the community. They need our attention, care, and love.

Third, that the kingdom of God is already in our midst gives us a way to put the imperfections and enduring moral evils of this society in perspective. They are serious, but not fatal, because God has already reestablished the relationship with humanity in the most secure way possible, which is through the body and blood of his own Son. At the same time, we know that we cannot expect to eradicate evil before the end of time,[57] although we are called to minimize its effects upon vulnerable persons by practicing the corporal and spiritual works of mercy.[58] Prophetic discourse ought not to be used in order to separate the wheat from the chaff, the good from the bad, or the saved from the damned. As St. Augustine tells us, that separation will be carried out at the end of time, in God's time, not in our own.[59]

We see tacit recognition of the "already but not yet" nature of the kingdom of God operating in *Evangelium Vitae*'s recognition of the need to invoke the principles governing cooperation with evil in assessing how to deal with imperfect legislation on life issues.[60] Whereas the prophetic indictments of the Old Testament characteristically reject all contact with moral evil as unacceptable, the Catholic casuistic tradition recognizes the possibility of drawing distinctions. The makers of that tradition, which was centrally designed to assist priests hearing confessions, formulated an analytic matrix designed to facilitate moral evaluation of cases in which one agent's action contributes to the wrongful act of another agent—a situation which they called "cooperation with evil."[61] Formal cooperation with evil—intentionally furthering another's wrongdoing—is never permitted. Material cooperation, which involves facilitating the wrongful act of another while foreseeing but not intending the commission of that act, is sometimes permissible, sometimes not, depending upon a number of factors. These factors include both the good to be achieved and the harm to be avoided by cooperation, evaluated in both a short-term and a long-term perspective. From the perspective of a prophetic rhetoric reshaped in a Christocentric manner, casuistic distinctions of the sort involved in the principle of cooperation are not snares but useful tools for responding to both the Kingdom's presence in our midst and the delay of its full manifestation.

Fourth, and finally, it seems to me that a prophetic rhetoric which takes seriously the decisive difference made by the life, death, and resurrection of Jesus Christ would adopt a different attitude toward those who are neither hostile nor totally sympathetic. The rhetoric of indictment in the Hebrew prophets tends to manifest the motto, "If you are not for us, you are against us."[62] While Jesus' own use of the motto demonstrates that there may from time to time be situations in which it is appropriate, it seems to me that a Christocentric prophetic rhetoric would adopt a strong presumption for the motto, "If you are not against us, you are for us."[63] If we know that the whole course of salvation history is destined toward the ultimate reconciliation of humanity to God, if we understand that human beings have been decisively redeemed from sin and death, we can afford to risk collaboration with those who see the truth only partially. For we too see through a glass darkly, but we know that one day we will see face-to-face.[64]

Moreover, precisely because we believe that the God who created us and the God who redeems us are one and the same, we can afford to interpret mistaken moral arguments charitably, if they are made in good faith. Prophetic pro-lifers may never agree with those who argue that abortion ought not to be legally prohibited in hard cases such as rape. At the same time, they ought to be able to acknowledge that such arguments do not necessarily depend upon either a denial of the humanity of unborn children or a cavalier insensitivity to their suffering on account of abortion. Along with Augustine, we can acknowledge that all human beings pursue their ends *sub specie boni,* even if they are mistaken about what constitutes the (higher) good in a particular instance. The very fact that they will the good provides us with a point of contact and common ground with them.

My suggestion, therefore, is to reclaim *Evangelium Vitae* from the American Protestant tradition of prophetic rhetoric. By explicitly situating the prophetic claims of the encyclical within the thoroughly Christocentric vision of *Lumen Gentium,* we may open avenues for cooperation with an entire segment of American society, which is morally uneasy about abortion, although not willing to impose a ban in the "hard cases." In so doing, we will do justice to the fundamental optimism of Pope John Paul II, an optimism which is rooted not in confidence in autonomous human progress but in deep faith in the boundless grace and mercy of God.

NOTES

1. Alasdair MacIntyre, *After Virtue: A Study in Moral Theory* (Notre Dame: University of Notre Dame Press, 1981), 6.

2. Ibid., 6–7.

3. St. Thomas Aquinas, *Summa Theologica*, II-II, q. 94, a. 4.

4. Ibid., II-II, q. 47, a. 3; q. 49, a. 2, rep.ob. 1.

5. Matthew Arnold, *Culture and Anarchy*, ed. Samuel Lipman (New Haven: Yale University Press, 1994).

6. I examine the conflict between the two forms of rhetoric in greater detail in M. Cathleen Kaveny, "Prophecy and Casuistry: Abortion, Torture, and Moral Discourse," *Villanova Law Review* 51, no. 3 (2006): 499–580.

7. Pope John Paul II, *The Gospel of Life (Evangelium Vitae)* (Boston: Pauline Books and Media, 1995).

8. Vatican II, *Dogmatic Constitution on the Church (Lumen Gentium)*, in *Vatican II*, 2nd ed., ed. Austin Flannery, O.P. (Dublin: Veritas, 1988), 350–440.

9. Perry Miller, *Errand into the Wilderness* (Cambridge, MA: Belknap Press, 1956).

10. Sydney E. Ahlstrom, *A Religious History of the American People*, 2nd ed. (New Haven, CT: Yale University Press, 2004).

11. Jon Butler, *Awash in a Sea of Faith: Christianizing the American People* (Cambridge, MA: Harvard University Press, 1990).

12. Sacvan Bercovitch, *The American Jeremiad* (Madison: University of Wisconsin Press, 1978).

13. Ibid., 7.

14. James Darsey, *The Prophetic Tradition and Radical Rhetoric in America* (New York: New York University Press, 1997).

15. Ibid.

16. Ibid., 9.

17. Martin Luther King, "I Have a Dream," August 28, 1963, available at www.youtube.com/watch?v=PbUtL_ovAJk. I have argued that King is in fact the gold standard of the American tradition of political rhetoric, precisely because he avoids some of the pitfalls described here. See M. Cathleen Kaveny, "Democracy and Prophecy: A Study in Politics, Rhetoric, and Religion," in *Law and Democracy in the Empire of Force*, ed. H. Jefferson Powell and James Boyd White (Ann Arbor: University of Michigan Press, forthcoming).

18. Pope John Paul II, *Evangelium Vitae,* par. 28.

19. For example, a Republican Catholic public intellectual, Ramesh Ponnuru, recently published a book titled *The Party of Death: The Democrats, the Media, the Courts, and the Disregard for Human Life* (Washington, DC: Regnery, 2006).

20. See, e.g., David D. Kirkpatrick and Laurie Goodstein, "Group of Bishops Using Influence to Oppose Kerry," *New York Times,* October 12, 2004, available at www.nytimes.com/2004/10/12/politics/campaign/12catholics .html. The article focuses on Archbishop Chaput of Denver and Archbishop Burke of St. Louis.

21. See, e.g., this comment by two prominent Catholic academics: "To vote for John Kerry in 2004 would be far worse, however, than to have voted against Lincoln and for his Democratic opponent in 1860. Stephen Douglas at least supported allowing states that opposed slavery to ban it. And he did not favor federal funding or subsidies for slavery. John Kerry takes the opposite view on both points when it comes to abortion. On the great evil of his own day, Senator Douglas was merely John Kerry-lite." Robert P. George and Gerard V. Bradley, "Not in Good Conscience," *NRO,* www.nationalreview.com/comment/george_bradley200410120849.asp,

22. See, e.g., David E. Campbell, ed., *A Matter of Faith* (Washington, DC: Brookings Institution Press, 2007). For a brief analysis, see Pew Research Center for the People and the Press, "Religion and the Presidential Vote: Bush's Gains Broad-Based," December 6, 2004, available at http://people-press.org/commentary/display.php3?AnalysisID=103.

23. My descriptions of these terms and the roles associated with them are taken from David L. Petersen, *The Prophetic Literature: An Introduction* (Louisville, KY: Westminster John Knox Press, 2002), 5–7.

24. Petersen, *The Prophetic Literature,* 6.

25. See, e.g., Petersen, *The Prophetic Literature,* 6; Joseph Blenkinsopp, *A History of Prophecy in Israel* (Louisville, KY: Westminster John Knox Press, 1996), 28–29; Bruce Vawter, C.M., "Introduction to Prophetic Literature," in *The New Jerome Biblical Commentary,* 188–89 (Raymond E. Brown, S.S., et al., eds., 1990).

26. Abraham Joshua Heschel, *The Prophets* (New York: HarperCollins Perennial Classics, 2001), xxix.

27. James M. Gustafson, *Varieties of Moral Discourse: Prophetic, Narrative, Ethical, and Policy* (The Stob Lectures) (Grand Rapids, MI: Calvin College, 1988), 8.

28. Ibid., 11.

29. Ibid., 13.

30. Hos.: 2:4–5. All scriptural passages quoted or cited in this essay are taken from *The Catholic Study Bible,* gen ed. Donald Senior (New York: Oxford University Press, 1990).

31. Isa. 3:13–17.

32. Jer. 6:12–15.

33. 1 Cor. 10:14–32.

34. It will no doubt be noted that these criteria parallel important criteria for the waging of a just war. This resemblance is not accidental. In many cases, the sustained use of prophetic rhetoric may well mark the beginning of a verbal war and the consequent breakdown of a community of conversation and deliberation.

35. Roe v. Wade, 410 U.S. 113 (1973).

36. Pew Forum on Religion and Public Life, "Pragmatic Americans Liberal and Conservative on Social Issues," August 3, 2006, available at http://perforum.org/docs/?DocID=150#2. The study observes, "Abortion continues to split the country nearly down the middle. But there is consensus in one key area: two out of three Americans (66%) support finding 'a middle ground' when it comes to abortion. Only three-in-ten (29%), by contrast, believe 'there's no room for compromise when it comes to abortion laws.' This desire to find common ground extends broadly across the political and ideological spectrum."

37. American Life League, www.all.org/.

38. Other hard cases can be dealt with casuistically as well. For example, it can be argued that a woman's decision to use RU486 after being raped is best understood, not as intentionally killing an unborn child, but instead as choosing not to subject her body to the additional trauma of a pregnancy after the trauma of a rape. Under some circumstances, particularly after rape during war or rape of very young girls, such a decision may be justified, with the death of the unborn baby being *praeter intentionem.* The Catholic casuistic tradition has not embraced this line of argument. It is important to note, however, that the argument neither denies the "personhood" of unborn life nor accepts the unjust claim that it is permissible *intentionally* to kill the innocent. Consequently, even those casuists who reject the soundness of the argument ought to recognize that it stands on very different footing from an argument that justifies abortion because it does not involve the taking of a human life.

39. The moralist Colin Harte, from the United Kingdom, takes this position. See his debate with John Finnis, in Helen Watt, ed., *Cooperation, Complicity and Conscience: Problems in Healthcare, Science, Law and Public Policy* (London: Linacre Centre, 2005).

40. South Dakota HB 1215, "Women's Health and Human Life Protection Act," available at http://news.findlaw.com/cnn/docs//abortion/sdabortionlaw06.html.

41. See Monica Davey, "South Dakota Bans Abortion, Setting up a Battle, *New York Times*, March 7, 2006, A1, available at www.nytimes.com/2006/03/07/national/07abortion.html.

42. Patricia Gray, "Controversial South Dakota Abortion Law Overturned by Voters," available at www.law.uh.edu/healthlaw/perspectives/2006/(PG)SDAbortionBill.pdf.

43. President George W. Bush's appointments to the Supreme Court, for example, have appeared to oppose constitutional protection for abortion rights. Yet they have also supported an expanded account of the power of the executive branch vis-à-vis the legislative and judicial branches that threatens to eviscerate the constitutional systems of checks and balances among the three branches of government. If left unchecked, the result of this approach to the separation of powers would be an imperial American presidency—a situation with long-standing and serious consequences not only for the nation but also for the world.

44. Aquinas, *Summa Theologica*, I-II, q. 95, a. 3. For more elaborate analysis, see my essay, "Toward a Thomistic Perspective on Abortion and the Law in Contemporary America," *Thomist* 55 (1991): 343–96.

45. Mary Ann Glendon, *Abortion and Divorce in Western Law* (Cambridge, MA: Harvard University Press, 1987.

46. In my view, the Terri Schiavo case, which came to a head in early 2005, increased Americans' alienation from prophetic pro-lifers. Many Americans disagreed with the parents' judgment that it was impermissible intentional killing to remove her feeding tube. Instead, they viewed it as the morally permissible withdrawal of medical treatment. The more serious problem, however, was the extent to which the pro-life movement was willing to go in order to vindicate their position. Although decisions regarding both guardianship and medical treatment are quintessentially matters for state government, not the federal government, they brought the matter to Congress. In turn, the Republican-dominated Congress passed a highly unusual law giving the federal courts jurisdiction over this one case—despite the fact that the case had been fully aired over many years in the Florida state court

system. This extreme disregard for the normal practices and procedures of our federalist system of government created great fear about the willingness of pro-life prophets to disregard the legal framework of American society in order to achieve their ends.

47. See, e.g., Paul Lauritzen, "Holy Alliance? The Danger of Mixing Politics and Religion," *Commonweal*, March 24, 2006, 14–17, available at www.commonwealmagazine.org/article.php3?id_article=1570; Amy Sullivan, "Compassionate Conservative," *Salon.com*, April 2, 2005, available at http://dir.salon.com/story/news/feature/2005/04/02/pope/.

48. Pope John Paul II, *Evangelium Vitae*, par. 56.

49. Ibid., par. 10.

50. Ibid., par. 11.

51. Ibid.: "Here though we shall concentrate particular attention on *another category of attacks*, affecting life in its earliest and in its final stages, attacks which present *new characteristics with respect to the past and which raise questions of extraordinary seriousness.* It is not only that in generalized opinion these attacks tend no longer to be considered as 'crimes'; paradoxically they assume the nature of 'rights,' to the point that the state is called upon to give them *legal recognition and to make them available through the free services of health-care personnel.* Such attacks strike human life at the time of its greatest frailty, when it lacks any means of self-defense. Even more serious is the fact that, most often, those attacks are carried out in the very heart of and with the complicity of the family—the family which by its nature is called to be the 'sanctuary of life.'"

52. Ibid., par. 90: "Here it must be noted that it is not enough to remove unjust laws. The underlying causes of attacks on life have to be eliminated, especially by ensuring proper support for families and motherhood. *A family policy must be the basis and driving force of all social policies.* For this reason there need to be set in place social and political initiatives capable of guaranteeing conditions of true freedom of choice in matters of parenthood. It is also necessary to rethink labor, urban, residential and social service policies so as to harmonize working schedules with time available for the family, so that it becomes effectively possible to take care of children and the elderly."

53. See, e.g., Robert Pear, "Bush Seeks Big Medicare, Medicaid Saving," *New York Times*, February 2, 2007, available at www.nytimes.com/2007/02/02/washington/02budget.html.

54. See, e.g., *Lumen Gentium*, par. 3 (citations omitted):

The Son, accordingly, came, sent by the Father who, before the foundation of the world, chose us and predestined us in him for adoptive sonship. For it is in him that it pleased the Father to restore all things. To carry out the will of the Father Christ inaugurated the kingdom of heaven on earth and revealed to us his mystery; by his obedience he brought about our redemption. The Church—that is, the kingdom of Christ already present in mystery—grows visibly through the power of God in the world. The origin and growth of the Church are symbolized by the blood and water which flowed from the open side of the crucified Jesus, and are foretold in the words of the Lord referring to his death on the cross: "And I, if I be lifted up from the earth, will draw all men to myself." As often as the sacrifice of the cross by which "Christ our Pasch is sacrificed" is celebrated on the altar, the work of our redemption is carried out. Likewise, in the sacrament of the eucharistic bread, the unity of believers, who from one body in Christ, is both expressed and brought about. All men are called to this union with Christ, who is the light of the world, from whom we go forth, through whom we live, and towards whom our whole life is directed.

55. *Evangelium Vitae*, par. 99; my emphasis. I am working with the first English translation of the text, based on the original Italian version. This translation continues to be available on the official Vatican Web site: www .vatican.va/edocs/ENG0141/_INDEX.HTM.

When the Latin text was published in the *Acta Apostolicae Sedis* 87 (1995), Pope John Paul II's imaginative and empathetic message of consolation to women who had obtained abortions was significantly tempered. More specifically, there is no Latin equivalent for the sentence, "You will come to understand that *nothing is definitively lost* and you will also be able to ask forgiveness from your child, who is now living in the Lord." In its stead appears this sentence: "Infantem autem vestrum potestis eidem Patri eiusque misericordiae cum spe committere," which I translate as "Moreover, you are able to entrust with hope your baby to the same Father and His mercy." The Latin text can be found on the Vatican Web site: www.vatican.va/holy_father/john_ paul_ii/encyclicals/documents/hf_jp-ii_enc_25031995_evangelium vitae_lt.html.

A second English translation was then issued, and is also available on the Vatican Web site: www.vatican.va/holy_father/john_paul_ii/encyclicals/ documents/hf_jp-ii_enc_25031995_evangelium-vitae_en.html. The key sentence here is, "To the same Father and his mercy you can with sure hope entrust your child." Obviously, it corresponds to the Latin version; nonetheless, by its translation of *spes* as "*sure* hope" (my emphasis), it gravitates toward the same generous compassion expressed in the pope's original message. Both English versions count as "official" versions, and both can be used in scholarly reflection. The second version is most relevant to ecclesiologists. Clearly, the purpose of the second version was not to blunt Pope John Paul II's pastoral empathy with women who have had abortions but rather to avoid announcing a new doctrinal stand on the eternal fate of unbaptized persons—a question on which the Church has not taken a definitive doctrinal stand.

56. Ibid., par. 81.

57. See *Lumen Gentium,* par. 48 (citations omitted): "The Church, to which we are all called in Christ Jesus, and in which by the grace of God we acquire holiness, will receive its perfection only in the glory of heaven, when will come the time of the renewal of all things. At that time, together with the human race, the universe itself, which is so closely related to man and which attains its destiny through him, will be perfectly reestablished in Christ."

58. See *Lumen Gentium,* par. 8 (citations omitted): "[T]he Church encompasses with her love all those who are afflicted by human misery and she recognizes in those who are poor and who suffer, the image of her poor and suffering founder. She does all in her power to relieve their need and in them she strives to serve Christ. Christ, 'holy, innocent and undefiled' knew nothing of sin, but came only to expiate the sins of the people. The Church, however, clasping sinners to her bosom, at once holy and always in need of purification, follows constantly the path of penance and renewal."

59. St. Augustine, *The City of God,* bk. XX.

60. *Evangelium Vitae,* par. 74: "[I]t can happen that carrying out certain actions, which are provided for by legislation that overall is unjust, but which in themselves are indifferent, or even positive, can serve to protect human lives under threat. There may be reason to fear, however, that willingness to carry out such actions will not only cause scandal and weaken the necessary opposition to attacks on life, but will gradually lead to further capitulation to a mentality of permissiveness. In order to shed light on this difficult question, it is necessary to recall the general principles concerning *cooperation in evil actions.*"

61. The matrix is abstruse and difficult. For a helpful introduction, see Anthony Fisher, O.P., "Co-Operation in Evil," *Catholic Medical Quarterly* 44, no. 3 (February 1994): 15–22.

62. See Matt. 12:30; Luke 11:23.

63. See Mark 9:40.

64. 1 Cor. 13:12.

CHAPTER 5

After Intractable Moral Disagreement

The Catholic Roots of an Ethic of Political Reconciliation

Daniel Philpott

Moral disagreement is at its most intractable when it descends into interstate war, genocide, civil war, dictatorship politics, massacres, bombings, torture, rape, unlawful detentions, and ethnic cleansing. Such descents abounded in the twentieth century and have not abated in the twenty-first. Their global profile has evolved gradually, from grand ideological struggles between liberal democracy and fascism and communism to wars fought between ethnic, national, and religious groups over territory, minority rights, and religion's role in politics.[1]

At the end of the past century and the beginning of this one, a wave of these episodes came to an end. A "third wave" of democratization terminated dictatorships—Communist, right-wing military, and apartheid—in more than forty countries in Eastern Europe, Latin America, Africa, and East Asia—and a wave of peace settlements has ended civil wars around the world.[2] After the violence associated with intractable moral disagreement comes to an end, a common task arises: to construct a stable and just peace in a landscape strewn with wounds, bodily, emotional, spiritual, psychological, political, economic, and cultural. Common dilemmas attend the task. Should elections and free markets be established immediately or only after stability and consensus has been achieved? Should war criminals receive amnesty in return for their assent to a peace agreement? What sort of punishment do human rights violators merit? May heads of state or political factions apologize on behalf of their people? Do living representatives of dead victims merit reparations? Can states practice forgiveness? Ought anyone to practice forgiveness? Common solutions have sprouted: international peacekeeping and reconstruction forces; monitored elections; schemes for demobilization, disarmament, and reintegration of armed troops; truth commissions; international tribunals; a permanent international criminal court; reparations schemes; official apologies; dramatic statements of forgiveness; museums; memorials; and sundry seminars, forums, and initiatives conducted by nongovernmental organizations (NGOs) and other civil society organizations. But common answers are still lacking. National politicians and international officials, citizens and activists, scholars and lawyers still disagree deeply over the ethics of peacebuilding. Much is at stake, for failed peacebuilding begets further intractable moral disagreement and perhaps further descents into violence. Where to turn?

Alasdair MacIntyre's lifetime of scholarship and his essay that opens this volume have taught me the importance of traditions for thinking about politics, ethics, and philosophy. Like MacIntyre, I am convinced that the Catholic tradition offers answers to contemporary problems that are both distinct from other traditions—Kantian, utilitarian, others—and intellectually and morally satisfying. In MacIntyre's present essay, what the Catholic tradition, particularly the Thomist natural law tradition, offers is a set of precepts that make possible shared rational enquiry into solutions to moral disagreements (p. 23). He is skeptical, though, that members of rival traditions will agree to these precepts, at least insofar as they continue to adhere to their tradition's own standards of practical rationality.

In just this spirit, I want to argue that the Catholic tradition offers the building materials for an ethic of peacebuilding in the aftermath of massive political violence—one that is distinct from and, I argue, improves upon the "liberal peace" paradigm that is grounded in the Enlightenment and that now dominates the thinking of the United Nations, Western governments, international organizations such as the World Bank, and many NGOs involved in peacebuilding.[3] Popes John Paul II and Benedict XVI, along with other Catholic as well as Protestant theologians, have laid the foundations for such an ethic in their teachings on the political significance of forgiveness and reconciliation. But more is needed: a development of the tradition. Catholic thought has offered little guidance through the difficult moral dilemmas that political reconciliation and forgiveness typically involve.[4] No pope has written an encyclical about peacebuilding in the wake of massive violence and injustice.

I devote most of this essay to an outline of an ethic for peacebuilding, at least its key ideas and its broad contours, and seek to show how it can be grounded in the Catholic tradition. Its unifying concept is reconciliation. Its foundations are the two main sources of Catholic social thought: natural law and the Bible, a source that has only robustly reentered Catholic social thought in recent decades but which is crucial for the concept of reconciliation.[5] To tap the Scriptures is to pursue just the sort of development that traditions make possible—retrieving from the cellar a once-popular wine that has been forgotten but is now apposite for just the current gathering. A model for success is the Catholic tradition's ethic for war, one that is grounded in philosophical and theological sources, that offers a robust set of practical guidelines for statecraft, and that has come to be accepted widely in international law, in political discourse, and in military establishments.

But is such widespread acceptance a likely prospect for a Catholic ethic of peacebuilding, especially one based significantly on biblical texts? Although Catholic populations participated disproportionately in the Third Wave of democratization and have played a part in many civil wars, in a great many transitions Catholics are uninvolved, inhabit religiously plural populations, or even form one side in a civil war. If a Catholic ethic of peacebuilding faces as much difficulty sharing its ideas across traditions as MacIntyre believes Thomistic natural law and utilitarianism have in pursuing enquiry together, the ethic will be limited in its reach. MacIntyre himself does not give up hope. But his own strategy for overcoming intractable moral disagreement— Thomists persistently exposing the conundrums of utilitarianism, showing that natural law reasoning is precisely the answer to these conundrums, insisting upon the fruitlessness of further theory-rescuing epicycles, hoping that accumulated anomalies will bring utilitarians to declare surrender and face up to a Kuhnian paradigm shift—may well take decades; Sudan, Iraq, and Afghanistan demand solutions today. But I am more optimistic than MacIntyre that ideas can find agreement across traditions, at least in political matters. In the final section of this essay I explain why.

A Catholic Ethic of Political Reconciliation

When UN troops seek to secure stability in Kosovo or monitor elections in Cambodia, when U.S. government officials strive for stability in Iraq, when the World Bank structures loans for postconflict reconstruction in places such as El Salvador and East Timor, when human rights activists and international lawyers demand the punishment of human rights violators in Argentina, Rwanda, Bosnia, or South Africa, they typically speak the language of the "liberal peace," the approach to peacebuilding that dominates the world's most powerful institutions. At least seven tenets, all reflecting its Enlightenment provenance, describe it.[6] The first is a Hobbesian one: A ceasefire or settlement of armed conflict is required. The second is more Lockean or Kantian: The rule of law, human rights, democracy, adherence to international law, and free market institutions are to be pursued. Elections are a key desideratum. Third, international organizations such as the United Nations and the World Bank, as well as powerful liberal democracies such as the United States, are key actors in constructing peace in societies that have suffered from massive violence. Though not all proponents or even describers of the liberal peace concern themselves with justice for past crimes, their underlying commitments make them close cousins of human rights activists and international lawyers whose approach to transitional justice yields the fourth and fifth tenets: punishment for human rights criminals, justified through a combination of Kantian retributivism and consequentialist arguments for the importance of accountability in establishing new regimes based on the rule of law; and reparations for victims. Sixth, liberals have argued that personal and spiritual healing, the transformation of emotions, and interpersonal reconciliation are fitting for the "private" realm but not for public, political efforts to build peace.[7] Seventh, and finally, rationales for the liberal peace are typically expressed in secular language, either because their proponents consider religious language inappropriate for the public realm or just because, in the logic that MacIntyre has articulated so consistently, religious language is simply not the language of their tradition.[8]

Different language and different arguments about peacebuilding have come from Archbishop Desmond Tutu, chair of South Africa's Truth and Reconciliation Commission (TRC); from Catholic Archbishop Juan Gerardi, who formed and conducted his own truth commission in Guatemala and was assassinated for it; from Popes John Paul II and Benedict XVI; from the Yale Protestant theologian Miroslav Volf, author of one of the pioneering contemporary theologies of reconciliation; from Jewish scholars such as Rabbi Marc Gopin; and from Muslim scholars such as Mohammed Abu-Nimer.[9] These voices inhabit religious traditions. In both their participation in and their analysis of peacebuilding efforts in the past generation, they have established a different paradigm, one whose focus is reconciliation. This paradigm resonates with the one that I propose here.

Liberal peace and reconciliation: It is not an absolute contrast. Religious voices often incorporate human rights and other liberal commitments into reconciliation, while some liberal human rights activists have come to favor reconciliation processes as a complement to punishment and reparations.[10] Secular voices can be found among both critics of the liberal peace and advocates for reconciliation.[11] But if they overlap, the two paradigms reason from different centers of gravity, from different core commitments, and from different sorts of traditions.

BIBLICAL AND THEOLOGICAL ROOTS

At the core of a Catholic ethic of peacebuilding is a concept of justice that is distinct from, though it includes elements of, what modern liberals mean by justice. It is found in the Bible. Crucial to its meaning is the linguistic fact that in both the Old Testament and New Testament, in both Hebrew and Greek, the words that translate into justice also frequently translate into righteousness (*sedeq* and *mishpat* in Hebrew, the family of words beginning with *dik-* in Greek)—a righteousness that includes all members of a community living in right relationship, in their political, social, economic, legal, familial, cultic, and professional affairs, as set forth by God's covenant.[12]

In turn, the biblical meaning of reconciliation, a term that appears fifteen times in the New Testament *(katallage* and *katallosso)* is either restoration of right relationship or the condition of right relationship that results from this restoration; importantly, reconciliation is both a process and a state.[13] If right relationship, or righteousness, is the biblical meaning of justice, then reconciliation can also mean the restoration of justice or a resulting state of justice. Reconciliation, then, is a concept of justice—the core claim of a Catholic ethic of peacebuilding.

In a biblical understanding, reconciliation is also a vision of peace. Both the Hebrew *shalom* and the Greek *eirene* connote comprehensive righteousness in a community.[14] Peace is the aspect of reconciliation that involves a state of right relationship. Reconciliation also corresponds to the biblical concept of mercy. In contrast to mercy in the Enlightenment tradition, where it is understood narrowly and conditionally as a discharge from deserved punishment, a departure from justice, biblical mercy is, as Pope John Paul II defined it in *Dives in Misericordia,* "manifested in its true and proper aspect when it restores to value, promotes and draws good from all the forms of evil existing in the world and in man." This is a far broader, transformational virtue that indeed looks like the justice of reconciliation. Mercy is the aspect of reconciliation that involves a process of restoration of right relationship.[15]

It is not only biblical language that manifests reconciliation as justice—and as peace, and as mercy—but also Scripture's description of God's response to evil. This response is not a logical "solution" to the problem of evil of the sort that philosophers since the Enlightenment have offered but a response of action, holistically restorative action, involving, variously, punishment, forgiveness, restoration of the rights of the poor, and the renewal of creation.[16] In the Old Testament, it is through all these modes that God renews his covenant, performing *tikkun olam,* or a repair of the universe. In the New Testament, Jesus identifies himself as the fulfillment of Isaiah's prophecy of a servant who brings justice to victory.[17] His victorious justice, involving forgiveness, a judgment upon evil, hope for the poor, and the renewal of creation, culminates in his death and resurrection. Theologians have sought to plumb the meaning of Christ's atonement in very different ways over the course of Church history. Early Church fathers such as St. Irenaeus and St. Athanasius understood it as a victory over sin, evil, and death, and indeed, as a restoration—or "recapitulation," as Irenaeus put it—of humanity and creation. Far less restorative was an interpretation that St. Anselm adumbrated but that the Calvinist reformation brought to a climax, one that held that in dying on the Cross, Christ pays that penalty that humanity deserves for its sin in order to appease the wrath of God the Father and secure a not-guilty verdict for humanity, but in doing so does not actually restore persons or relationships: sanctification is a separate, subsequent process. In the twentieth century, though, in the midst of and in reaction to episodes of gargantuan war and political injustice, there arose a revival of thinking much like the early Church's victory model but with an additional twist: a more explicit application of Christ's restorative triumph to the social and political realm. The renewal can be descried in the Protestant theologies of P. T. Forsythe, Karl Barth, Dietrich Bonhoeffer, Jan Milic Lochman, and Jürgen Moltmann.[18] It can be seen in the emergence of what is known as restorative justice, a concept that arose in Western juvenile criminal law, which has been articulated best by the Mennonite tradition but also endorsed by the U.S. Catholic bishops and was then famously applied to political orders by Archbishop Tutu in his leadership of South Africa's TRC. In the Catholic tradition, it surfaced in Pope Benedict XV's call for European states to practice reconciliation and forgiveness publicly after World War I, was revived in the writings of Pope John Paul II, who proposed reconciliation and forgiveness for politics in the final section of *Dives in Misericordia* and in subsequent addresses for the World Day of Peace, and has been continued through numerous statements by Pope Benedict XVI.[19]

How, though, is a biblical notion of justice as reconciliation—a holistic restoration of right relationship, animated by mercy, to a comprehensive state of peace—to be realized in modern politics? In Catholic social thought, political authority, situated today primarily in the state but also in international law, the United Nations, and the European Union, is essential for the common good. If reconciliation restores and promotes the common good, then political authority pursues reconciliation legitimately—but also with limits. Political authority properly promotes that portion of the common good that is furthered by law, which is only a subset of comprehensive, biblical righteousness. In the political order, right relationship is a condition in which human rights and the rule of law are recognized and respected between and among citizens and governments. Still, this reconciliation that political authority properly performs is more comprehensive than the mere creation of institutions and constitutions. It also involves redressing the wide range of wounds inflicted though the violation of victims' rights and performing a wide range of practices designed to restore these wounds and, through this very repair, restore citizens to their rightful status as subjects of the rule of law. Consistent with the teachings of the Second Vatican Council, the Church itself also has a rightful role in promoting political reconciliation, which it in fact has done in many places in the world through its direct work with citizens, its public pronouncements to states, and its leaders serving in official roles, such as that of truth commissioner.

Just what are the wounds of political injustice that reconciliation seeks to repair? Political injustices themselves may be understood much as they are in most contemporary political transitions: as violations of the human rights and laws of war that are embedded in numerous international conventions. Today, the magisterium of the Church not only endorses these standards but also places them on the uniquely strong foundations of human dignity rooted in the image of God, exceptionless moral norms, and natural law.[20] But if political injustices take their definition from these rights, laws, and norms, the respects in which they wound their victims are far more textured and multiform. There are at least six:

1. *Violation of the victim's basic human rights.* This first dimension echoes the very definition of a political injustice. Since the legal guarantee of a person's human rights is itself an aspect of his human flourishing, this violation constitutes a form of woundedness.

2. *Harm to the victim's person.* These include death; the death of loved ones; permanent bodily injury; grief; humiliation; trauma; loss of wealth and livelihood; the defilement of one's race, ethnicity, religion, nationality, or gender; sexual violation; and many other harms.

3. *Victims' ignorance of the source and circumstances of the political injustices that harmed them.*

4. *Failure of members of the community to acknowledge victims' suffering, either through ignorance or indifference.*

5. *The "standing victory" of the perpetrator's political injustice.* Political injustices leave behind not only harms to the victim's person but also a victorious, unchallenged message of disregard for the victim's dignity, a further harm to the victim and to the shared values of the community.

6. *The wounded soul of the perpetrator.* Deep in the Catholic tradition is the idea that evil injures the soul of the wrongdoer. Often, this injury will be manifested in severe psychological damage.

Reflecting harms that political injustices inflict directly, these six forms of diminishment may be called "primary wounds." But these wounds also stir emotions of fear, hatred, resentment, and revenge that lead citizens and their leaders to commit further political injustices or to withhold legitimacy from fledgling constitutions—"secondary wounds" that arise from memories of the original injustices themselves and that further stunt the project of building just and stable political orders.

In response, political reconciliation aims to heal and restore the range of wounds, primary and secondary, that political injustices inflict. It involves a matching multiplicity of restorative practices—six of them, as I shall describe—each of which aspires to restore one or more distinct dimensions of diminishment. Insofar as they heal wounds that political injustices inflict directly, these practices bring about what may be called "primary restorations." These very restorations, though, can then redound in strengthened assent to and trust in the political order and a greater willingness to participate in democracy and identify with the national community, forms of social capital that may be thought of as "secondary restorations." It is essential not to forget original sin: restorative political practices will always be partially achieved, compromised by power and irreducible differences over justice, and hampered by their sheer magnitude and complexity, as contemporary experience shows. But neither are the practices utopian. Each of the six that I describe has occurred in multiple settings over the past generation, however partially. It is indeed just this complex combination of actual practice and dirty politics, of breakdown and breakthrough, that calls for an ethic.

Six Practices of an Ethic of Political Reconciliation

Reflecting still another feature of MacIntyre's thought, the ethic is enacted through practices rather than pure principles.[21] Multiple, independent, and complementary, the practices model the holistic and active response to evil that characterizes God's justice. In their political realization, though—in Rwanda, Germany, East Timor, and Guatemala—the practices will always be partially achieved and adapted to circumstances, much in the manner of bricolage. Here, I can only describe the broad contours of each of the six practices, its moral logic and how it approaches some of its attendant ethical dilemmas.

Building Socially Just Institutions

After massive injustices, building and maintaining socially just institutions, based on human rights, constitutional democracy, international law, and a commitment to a just economic distribution, is indispensable to the restoration of right relationship in political orders. This practice restores the wound inflicted through the political order's failure to protect human rights and dignity, a primary restoration, and creates legitimacy for the political order, a secondary restoration. It is the values promoted by this practice—human rights, democracy, and the like—on which the Church's teaching, especially since the Second Vatican Council, converges most strongly with the Enlightenment, international law, and indeed the principles of the "liberal peace."[22]

The practice's most difficult dilemmas arise from the tension between the peace and stability that socially just institutions require and other practices that restore justice in other respects. "Cheap reconciliation," cry critics of politicians who promote the reconciliation of peace and stability without punishment for human rights violators, acknowledgment or reparations for victims, repentance, or even aspects of socially just institutions like democracy. "No peace without justice," the Church agrees, in the words of Pope Paul VI. The biblical, holistic peace and justice of reconciliation seeks to restore right relationship in all these respects through its several practices.

But what is to be done when it appears that a genocidal war or brutal dictatorship can be brought to a close by awarding amnesty to military commanders or dictators in return for their consent to a peace agreement or willingness to depart from power? The dilemma has arisen in locales as diverse as Argentina, South Africa, Bosnia, Kosovo, and Uganda. A holistic ethic of reconciliation must always begin with a presumption against forgoing punishment—one of the six practices, as we shall see. But if the choice between ending massive ongoing injustices and punishment is truly unavoidable, this presumption might be overcome and amnesty granted. But we must always ask if amnesty is truly required. Recent history offers examples of countries where prosecution was forgone to secure an agreement but later resumed through judicial processes, often international ones. To the extent possible, the possibility for each practice to be enacted ought to be preserved.

Acknowledgment

The wounds of political injustice are compounded when the community fails to acknowledge them or the victim himself remains ignorant of them. These deficiencies are themselves primary wounds but can also beget alienation from and revenge against political orders, secondary wounds. Through authoritative acknowledgment, communities publicly recognize victims' suffering, name the wound as an injustice, communicate empathy, confirm victims' restored citizenship, nullify the perpetrator's message of injustice, and seek to transform public memory of the injustice so that it becomes commonly recognized as just that—an injustice not to be repeated. Acknowledgment mimics the recognition of the poor, the victimized, and the forgotten that God manifests through Jesus Christ and puts into practice the virtue of solidarity taught by the Church.[23] Undertaking acknowledgment most thoroughly among public forums is the truth commission, a relatively new form of political institution that has arisen more than thirty times around the globe in the past generation. Taking the testimony of victims, sometimes holding public hearings, almost always publishing a report of its investigations, the truth commission establishes a public record of the injustices of a war or dictatorship. Monuments, museums, public burials, commemorations of various sorts, and sometimes public deliberation about past injustices through media and government forums are other forms of public acknowledgment.

The chief virtue of acknowledgment, reflecting the virtue of solidarity, is personalism. Public recognition is at its most powerful when it is thorough, direct, and personal. Personalism is at its weakest when a victim is accorded only a brief mention or statistic in a voluminous truth commission report. It is strong when victims are acknowledged directly by fellow citizens and even stronger when acknowledged by perpetrators. Guatemala's Recovery of Historical Memory Project

(REMHI), organized by that country's Catholic Church, was conducted by "agents of reconciliation" who traveled to villages to interview victims directly, but also to offer them emotional, spiritual, and psychological support.[24] Truth commissions that involve victims in public hearings also practice personalism, more strongly when these hearings are conducted in local communities, as they were in East Timor.

Reparations

Reparations involve a transfer of material goods—money, mental and physical health services, and the like—from perpetrators, the state, or both to victims. They have become increasingly common over the past generation.[25]

One argument for reparations is, quite simply, that they compensate victims for what they lost. They address the harm, economic, physical, and psychological, that the injustices caused to the person of the victim. The logic is much like that underlying the practice of penance that the Church prescribes as a form of repair to the harm from sin. Though the actual harm that terrible injustices inflict, especially when it involves death or permanent injury, can never be reversed, at least a partially restorative compensation can be conferred. So have thought successor regimes to dictatorships and civil war in post-Communist Europe, Rwanda, Latin America, and elsewhere. But as these cases have proved, determining amounts can be a difficult task, especially when the original victims are dead and property has changed hands many times.

A separate rationale for reparations views the practice as being much like acknowledgment, involving a community's recognition of victims' suffering and its will to restore them to full citizenship. On this argument, the amount of reparations is less important, though not irrelevant. The theological dimension of this rationale is much the same as the rationale for acknowledgment; it only adds God's will for material restoration. In the Old Testament jubilee tradition, for instance, slaves are set free, debts are forgiven, and the rights of the poor and the oppressed are vindicated.

Reparations are at their ethical best when they are accompanied by other practices of reconciliation such as acknowledgment and apology. If not, then they risk being labeled "blood money" by victims, for example, attempts by governments to purchase victims' silence about evils that money can never eradicate. In this way, the multiple practices are ethically interdependent.

Punishment

In recent debates about dealing with the past all over the world, punishment has been spoken of as inimical to, not a component of, reconciliation. Retribution versus reconciliation, justice versus mercy, justice versus forgiveness, accountability versus amnesty: Such a field of dichotomies characterizes the liberal peace paradigm, which itself takes the side of punishment. In their justifications, as mentioned above, the paradigm's proponents oscillate between the two chief modern arguments for punishment: retributivism, which demands punishment simply on grounds of desert, and consequentialism, which stresses the benefits of punishment for the criminal and for society— here, the establishment of the rule of law.

In the biblical texts, though, lies a "restorative" concept of punishment that, both in theory and in practice, comports with an ethic of reconciliation. Though it affirms with retributivism that criminals deserve proportionate punishment, it justifies the hard treatment of imprisonment and other deprivations as a communication of censure that defeats the standing message of the perpetrator's message of injustice and invites him to participate in the restoration of his own soul and of right relationship in the political community through recognizing his injustice, apologizing, and eventually becoming a full citizen again. But contrary to consequentialism, the validity of punishment does not ride on these results. Even if perpetrators remain unrepentant—in today's transitions, many do—punishment still serves as a community's penitential communication. Thus modeled is God's punishment, whose purpose is to constrain evil and restore relationships of *shalom* among the people of Israel, not to exact a measure-for-measure repayment of sin. Several passages in the Old Testament indicate God's willingness to forgive the repentant sinner without a prior payment of debt.[26] Reasoning similarly, the *Compendium of the Social Doctrine of the Church* avers that "there is a twofold purpose here. On the one hand *encouraging the reinsertion of the condemned person into society,* on the other, *fostering a justice that reconciles,* a justice capable of restoring harmony in social relationships disrupted by the criminal act committed."[27]

For political societies in transition from war and dictatorship, restorative punishment envisions forms of accountability that do not apply a balancing punishment to a perpetrator one-dimensionally but rather address an array of wounds experienced by an array of parties, including perpetrators, victims, citizens, and political orders at large. It allows for lengthy imprisonment for the masterminds of human rights violations, but for them, as well as perpetrators at all levels, it calls for complementary forums that expose perpetrators' deeds, shames them, acknowledges victims, and facilitates the reintegration of perpetrators, especially those guilty of less serious crimes, into communities. Practicing this possibility are Sierra Leone, East Timor, Germany, Rwanda, and, to some degree, South Africa; they have adopted a combination of imprisonment and public forums designed for reconciliation. In addition, Africa, North America, and Australia have used the reintegration rituals of certain native peoples in its restoration practices. What restorative punishment has little sympathy for is blanket amnesties, which forgo punishment, and hence its restorative potential, altogether. At most, when political circumstances require it, restorative punishment can allow a conditional amnesty, such as South Africa's, that partially compromises the practice of punishment in order to elicit other practices such as acknowledgment and apology.

Apology

Public apologies, like reparations, are becoming more common. Individual perpetrators, heads of state, and other leaders speaking in the name of corporate entities practice them. The political scientist Barry O'Neill amassed a database of 121 "apology incidents" in an interstate context from 1980 to 1995; numerous apologies have also occurred within domestic states in the past generation.[28]

Much like repentance in the Church's sacrament of reconciliation, an apology has a restorative thrust: The perpetrator nullifies his regnant commitment to his injustice and commits to the healing of his own soul and to repairing the wrong done to the victim insofar as he can. The public dimension of apology reinforces the community's acknowledgment of victims and helps to establish legitimacy for new institutions in place of the old. Perhaps the biggest ethical question regarding public apology is its corporate nature. What justifies a head of state apologizing for the deeds of its members or perhaps those of a previous head of state who is now dead? "Memory and Reconciliation," the paper that the International Theological Commission prepared for the Jubilee Year 2000 to clarify the Church's mea culpas for a variety of its historical sins, proposes a promising answer. The Church—and, I argue, other corporate entities—may apologize for the misdeeds that members have performed in its name, but it cannot apologize for the perpetrator's "subjective" decision to commit the misdeed. Individuals retain the prerogative to endorse, echo, or refuse the leader's apology.[29]

Forgiveness

Forgiveness is the rarest and most surprising and controversial of the six practices of political reconciliation. President Nelson Mandela of South Africa may be the only head of state to have practiced it. More commonly, political, religious, and civil society leaders have urged it and citizens have practiced it in South Africa, Chile, East Timor, El Salvador, Guatemala, Rwanda, Sierra Leone, Bosnia, Northern Ireland, Poland, Germany, and elsewhere. Of the six practices, forgiveness has the weakest pedigree in modern liberal thought and politics.

In a rich Christian understanding, forgiveness involves not merely a victim's renunciation of anger, resentment, and outstanding claims against a wrongdoer but also his or her will to look upon the wrongdoer as a person "in good standing" and to invite his apology, repentance, reparations, and restoration of soul. Forgiveness is not merely a cancellation of debt; it is also a construction of right relationship. It does not condone or forget evil or involve a return to a condition of vulnerability to violence or other mistreatment. As with all the practices, the reconciliation that forgiveness effects may well be partial. Theologically, forgiveness is not only a matter of obedience to Jesus' injunction to forgive but of participation in God's forgiveness in Jesus Christ, the action through which God restores right relationship and the peace of *shalom,* defeats evil and injustice, and exercises the mercy that wills the healing of all that is broken.[30] Forgiveness effects the justice that is reconciliation—a startling claim to modern ears.

More than anyone else in the contemporary Catholic Church, it was Pope John Paul II who advocated forgiveness as a political act. Forgiveness indeed promotes social reconciliation through restoring several of the wounds of political injustice. Because it names and condemns evil, it defeats the perpetrator's injustice. Through defining a new moral reality, victims become restored in their agency and are often freed from debilitating anger. Sometimes forgiveness can lead a perpetrator to repent and apologize, if he has not already done so. All this helps to restore a right relationship of respected citizenship between victim and perpetrator and may foster the secondary restoration of harmony in the political community.

Forgiveness and the other five practices complement one another in a holistic ethic of peacebuilding. Full reconciliation demands that forgiveness be combined with apology and reparations. Forgiveness never implies the relinquishment of a struggle for social justice where it is egregiously compromised. In an ethic of reconciliation, and again in contrast to the liberal paradigm, forgiveness is even compatible with punishment. Because each practice is justified restoratively, a victim could will both forgiveness and punishment consistently. She seeks punishment not out of a claim that the perpetrator owes her something but out of her desire to defeat the standing victory of the injustice. That the state, not the victim, carries out punishment on behalf of the community and its laws only deepens the compatibility of punishment and forgiveness. In a division of restorative labor, victim, perpetrator, and state each seek to defeat injustice and restore right relationships from a different direction and in a different way.

Forgiveness is the final practice in an ethic for healing the wounds of intractable moral disagreement in the political realm. It is an ethic that might be practiced within states, as most of the examples above envision, or between states, as it has been practiced between Germany and Poland and France and Israel, or through the efforts of international institutions, as the United Nations and European Union have done in places like El Salvador and Bosnia. Though the institutional context may vary, the principles are the same.

BUT CAN TRADITIONS THEMSELVES BE RECONCILED?

I have addressed the problem of intractable moral disagreement from a somewhat different angle than MacIntyre does in his essay in this volume. MacIntyre's dilemma is how members of competing traditions can arrive at philosophical agreement on moral issues. The dilemma of political reconciliation is how the wounds of massive, violent, intractable moral disagreement can be healed so as to establish just and stable political orders. But the problem of just restoration itself cannot avoid the problem of moral agreement. The ethic of peacebuilding outlined here is grounded in the Catholic tradition. But could it find application in populations that are not Catholic, within organizations that play important roles in promoting transitional justice but typically operate in secular language, or in settings such as Bosnia or Sudan, where Catholics constitute one disputant in a civil war? If it cannot find application here, then the ethic might frequently prove irrelevant or even divisive—the last thing to be desired from an ethic of reconciliation.

But I am more optimistic than MacIntyre that members of different traditions can forge agreement. There are at least two grounds for a reasonable hope that members of different traditions can agree upon something very much like the principles of reconciliation that I have derived from the Catholic tradition. First, the sort of agreement sought here is less demanding than the deep philosophical agreement that MacIntyre considers in his essay. In pluralistic societies recovering from war and dictatorship, members of one tradition need not enter another tradition and attempt the hard work of convincing its members of its conundrums. What is needed, rather, is legitimacy for practices—truth commissions, reparations regimes, and the like—that foster political restoration. Legitimacy, in turn, requires not agreement on the deep principles that ground these practices but rather an "overlapping consensus" in which members of diverse traditions offer their common assent to their functioning. Although I take this term, *overlapping consensus,* from the philosopher John Rawls, I do not agree with him that attaining this consensus requires that religious people translate their rationales into secular language or into "political" rather than "metaphysical" concepts. Rather, as the philosopher Charles Taylor argues, an overlapping consensus can and ought to arise from a convergence among interlocutors arguing from their tradition's deepest warrants.[31] In settings of political recovery, of course, these deep principles might also be mixed with pragmatic arguments. It is quite possible, too, that citizens will agree upon the same practices but for different reasons. Often compromises will result in practices that are more truncated than any one tradition's principles favor. Christians may have to concede to Muslim fellow citizens that political forgiveness will only occur after a perpetrator has apologized. Christians and Muslims may agree upon incorporating some human rights into their new constitution but not others. But the wider the consensus among the members of a population and the more deeply they hold it, the more legitimacy the practices will enjoy.

In 1948 just such a consensus emerged among the countries of diverse religious and philosophical traditions to sign the Universal Declaration of Human Rights. One participant in the politically and philosophically complex negotiations preceding the Declaration was the famous Catholic natural law philosopher Jacques Maritain. In his reflection on the proceedings, he described how the compromise occurred:

> How is an agreement conceivable among men assembled for the purpose of jointly accomplishing a task dealing with the future of the mind, who come from the four corners of the earth and who belong not only to different cultures and civilizations, but to different spiritual families and antagonistic schools of thought? Since the aim of UNESCO is a practical aim, agreement among its members can be spontaneously achieved, not on common speculative notions, but on common practical notions, not on the affirmation of the same concept of the world, man, and knowledge, but on the affirmation of the same set of convictions concerning action. This is doubtless very little, it is the last refuge of intellectual agreement among men. It is, however, enough to undertake a great work; and it would mean a great deal to become aware of this body of common practical convictions.[32]

"We agree about the rights, but on condition no one asks us why," Maritain also commented. Precisely. It is possible, too, that members of "different spiritual families and antagonistic schools of thought" might come to an agreement on how to deal with the past in a given setting.

The second reason for optimism lies in the fact that traditions other than Catholicism do in fact contain some of the same conceptual materials out of which I have constructed the ethic of peacebuilding here. Virtually all the arguments I have offered could in principle be endorsed—and, as my notes show, many of them have in fact been inspired—by Protestant Christians. Orthodox Christians could support most of them, too. Jews, whose Scriptures contain *sedeq, mishpat, shalom, hesed* (mercy), and *tikkun olam,* could easily join in an overlapping consensus on an ethic rooted in these concepts. Native peoples around the world—in Australia, New Zealand, North America, and Africa—practice rituals that reflect a concept of reconciliation similar to the one proposed here. I argue that the ethic can also be expounded in secular language; several philosophers have made compelling secular arguments for forgiveness, for instance.[33] The point is not that the arguments and warrants of different traditions are identical or even equivalent but rather that they are similar enough to forge consensus for practical politics. The Second Vatican Council's own landmark statement on dialogue, *Nostra Aetate,* encourages the hope that such overlaps exist. Even members of the Enlightenment tradition, the one that I have presented as being most at odds with Catholic reconciliation, might endorse several of the practices, if not the corresponding grounding principles, that I have proposed—human rights, reparations, punishment, and acknowledgment—and, in a given compromise, might allow, as long as they do not conflict with the other practices, apology and forgiveness. If consensus between members of different traditions is possible in principle, though, the extent of its actual occurrence always depends upon the particular circumstances, beliefs, and passions at play in any given setting of recovery.

MacIntyre would not necessarily reject the possibility of overlapping consensus on political practices. Again, it is a different, less demanding sort of agreement than the resolution of intractable moral disagreement between the natural law tradition, Kantianism, and utilitarianism. How confident he would be that any given two traditions can forge an agreement on political practices, though, I cannot say. More straightforwardly consistent with his thinking is my general project: to reason about an urgent contemporary political issue from within one tradition. I have done so in the hope that if the members of a tradition become convinced that certain political practices comport with their deepest commitments, they will then be prepared to share, and to enter into a consensus upon, these practices with members of other traditions. It is up to other traditions, of course, to develop their own thinking about restoring political orders, whose conclusions they may then offer up in reciprocal fashion. Here, I have sought to contribute in a small way to this grand conversation by seeking to develop the thinking of one tradition, the Catholic tradition.

Notes

1. After peaking at the end of the Cold War, though, the global number of communal conflicts has since declined. See *The Human Security Report: War and Peace in the 21st Century* (Oxford: Human Security Centre, 2005).

2. The exact number of countries that have become democracies since the Third Wave began in 1974 is not clear. In his *The Third Wave: Democratization in the Late Twentieth Century* (Norman: University of Oklahoma Press, 1991), Samuel P. Huntington documents 30 transitions between 1974 and 1989. Freedom House reports that the number of "free" countries increased by 13 from 1989 to 2004. See "Russia Downgraded to 'Not Free,'" press release, Freedom House, Washington, DC, 2004; Freedom House, *Freedom in the World 2005: The Annual Survey of Political Rights and Civil Liberties* (Washington, DC: Freedom House, 2005). The democracy theorist Larry Diamond estimates that in the period 1974–96, between 36 and 77 states became democracies, depending on how one counts democratization exactly. See his "Is the Third Wave of Democratization Over? An Empirical Assessment," Working Paper #236, Kellogg Institute, University of Notre Dame, March 1997.

3. See Roland Paris, "Bringing the Leviathan Back In: Classical Versus Contemporary Studies of the Liberal Peace," *International Studies Review* 8 (2006): 425–40; Daniel Philpott, "Religion, Reconciliation, and Transitional Justice: The State of the Field," in *SSRC Working Papers* (2007); Oliver P. Richmond, "The Problem of Peace: Understanding the 'Liberal Peace,'" *Conflict, Security, & Development* 6, no. 3 (2006): 291–314.

4. Exceptions are William Bole, Drew Christiansen, and Robert T. Hennemeyer, *Forgiveness in International Politics: An Alternative Road to Peace* (Washington, DC: United States Conference of Catholic Bishops, 2004); Stephen J. Pope, "The Convergence of Forgiveness and Justice: Lessons from El Salvador," *Theological Studies* 64 (2003): 812–35.

5. On the sources of Catholic social thought, see Pontifical Council for Justice and Peace, *Compendium of the Social Doctrine of the Church* (Washington, DC: United States Conference of Catholic Bishops, 2004), par. X. On the increasing importance of the Bible for Catholic social thought, see John R. Donahue, S.J., "The Bible and Catholic Social Teaching: Will This Engagement Lead to Marriage?" in *Modern Catholic Social Teaching: Commentaries and Interpretations,* ed. Kenneth R. Himes (Washington, DC: Georgetown University Press, 2005), 9–40.

6. Here again, I draw from Paris, "Bringing the Leviathan Back In"; Philpott, "Religion, Reconciliation, and Transitional Justice"; Richmond, "The Problem of Peace."

7. Timothy Garton Ash, "True Confessions," *New York Review of Books* 44 (1997): 37–38; Rajeev Bhargava, "Restoring Decency to Barbaric Societies," in *Truth v. Justice,* ed. Robert Rotberg and Dennis Thompson (Princeton, NJ: Princeton University Press, 2000), 60–63; David A. Crocker, "Retribution and Reconciliation," *Philosophy and Public Policy* 20, no. 1 (2000): 6, David A. Crocker, "Truth Commissions, Transitional Justice, and Civil Society," in Rotberg and Thompson, eds., *Truth v. Justice,* 108; Amy Gutmann and Dennis Thompson, "The Moral Foundations of Truth Commissions," in Rotberg and Thompson, eds., *Truth v. Justice,* 32–33; Michael Ignatieff, "Articles of Faith," *Index on Censorship* 25, no. 5 (1996): 111–13, 21–22.

8. Kent Greenawalt, "Amnesty's Justice," in Rotberg and Thompson, eds., *Truth v. Justice,* 199; Gutmann and Thompson, "The Moral Foundations of Truth Commissions."

9. Mohammed Abu-Nimer, *Nonviolence and Peace Building in Islam* (Gainesville: University Press of Florida, 2003); Marc Gopin, *Between Eden and Armageddon: The Future of World Religions, Violence, and Peacemaking*

(Oxford: Oxford University Press, 2000); Desmond Tutu, *No Future without Forgiveness* (New York: Doubleday, 1999); Miroslav Volf, *Exclusion and Embrace: A Theological Exploration of Identity, Otherness, and Reconciliation* (Nashville, TN: Abingdon Press, 1996); Miroslav Volf, "The Social Meaning of Reconciliation," *Interpretation* 54 (2000): 158–68.

10. See Juan E. Méndez, "National Reconciliation, Transnational Justice, and the International Criminal Court," *Ethics and International Affairs* 15, no. 1 (2001): 25–44.

11. See Paris, "Bringing the Leviathan Back In"; Elizabeth Kiss, "Moral Ambition within and beyond Political Constraints: Reflections on Restorative Justice," in Rotberg and Thompson, eds., *Truth v. Justice*, 68–98.

12. See Elizabeth Achtemeier, "Righteousness in the OT," in *The Interpreter's Dictionary of the Bible*, ed. G. A. Buttrick (Nashville, TN: Abingdon Press, 1962), 80–85; Christopher D. Marshall, *Beyond Retribution: A New Testament Vision for Justice, Crime and Punishment* (Grand Rapids, MI: Eerdmans, 2001).

13. John W. De Gruchy, *Reconciliation: Restoring Justice* (Minneapolis: Fortress Press, 2003), 46, 51.

14. Ulrich Mauser, *The Gospel of Peace: A Scriptural Message for Today's World* (Louisville, KY: Westminster/John Knox, 1992); Perry Yoder, *Shalom: The Bible's Word for Salvation, Justice, and Peace* (Newton, KS: Faith and Life Press, 1987), 10–23.

15. Pope John Paul II, *Dives in Misericordia*, Encyclical Letter (1984), par. 6. MacIntyre finds a similar concept of mercy in the thought of Thomas Aquinas. See Alasdair C. MacIntyre, *Dependent Rational Animals: Why Human Beings Need the Virtues* (Chicago: Open Court, 1999), 124–25.

16. See Susan Neiman, *Evil in Modern Thought: An Alternative History of Philosophy* (Princeton, NJ: Princeton University Press, 2002); Jon D. Levenson, *Creation and the Persistence of Evil* (Princeton, NJ: Princeton University Press, 1988).

17. Matt. 12:20.

18. On the history of theories of the atonement, see De Gruchy, *Reconciliation*, 67–76; Colin Gunton, *The Actuality of Atonement* (Grand Rapids, MI: Eerdmans, 1989); MacIntyre, *Dependent Rational Animals*.

19. Joseph Ratzinger, *Values in a Time of Upheaval* (New York: Crossroad and Ignatius Press, 2006), 104–6, 7, 19, 24, 25. As pope, Benedict XVI has spoken of reconciliation in his statements on the war in Lebanon in summer 2006, in his letter to the Catholic Church in China in 2007, and in his

explanation for his choice of his name in his address shortly after he became pope, "To Reflect on the Name I Have Chosen," on April 27, 2005.

20. See Pope John XXIII, *Pacem in Terris,* Encyclical Letter, par. 259; Second Vatican Ecumenical Council, *Gaudium et Spes,* Pastoral Constitution, par. 27.

21. Alasdair MacIntyre, *After Virtue: A Study in Moral Theory,* 2nd ed. (Notre Dame: University of Notre Dame Press, 1984).

22. Pope Benedict XVI's own ambivalence toward the Enlightenment includes the acknowledgment, "One must welcome the true conquests of the Enlightenment, human rights and especially the freedom of faith and its practice, and recognize these also as being essential elements for the authenticity of religion." This quote is taken from his address to the Roman Curia, much of it dealing with Islam, on December 22, 2006.

23. Pope John Paul II, *Solicitudo Rei Socialis,* Encyclical Letter (1988), par. 565–66.

24. Michael Hayes and David Tombs, eds., *Truth and Memory: The Church and Human Rights in El Salvador and Guatemala* (Leominster: Gracewing, 2001), 34, 107, 25; Paul Jeffrey, *Recovering Memory: Guatemalan Churches and the Challenge of Peacemaking* (Uppsala, Sweden: Life & Peace Institute, 1998), 51; Recovery of Historical Memory Project, *Guatemala: Never Again!* (Maryknoll, NY: Orbis Books, 1999), xxiii–xxix.

25. Elazar Barkan, *The Guilt of Nations: Restitution and Negotiating Historical Injustices* (New York: Norton, 2000), xx.

26. Generally, I follow here the arguments of Marshall, *Beyond Retribution.*

27. Pontifical Council for Justice and Peace, *Compendium,* par. 403.

28. Barry O'Neill, *Honor, Symbols, and War* (Ann Arbor: University of Michigan Press, 1999), 178–82.

29. International Theological Commission, "Memory and Reconciliation: The Church and the Faults of the Past" (December 1999), par. 5.1.

30. See Alan Torrance, "The Theological Grounds for Advocating Forgiveness and Reconciliation in the Sociopolitical Realm," in *The Politics of Past Evil* (Notre Dame: University of Notre Dame Press, 2006), 45–86.

31. See John Rawls, *Political Liberalism* (New York: Columbia University Press, 1993); Charles Taylor, "Modes of Secularism," in *Secularism and Its Critics,* ed. Rajeev Bhargava (Oxford: Oxford University Press, 1998).

32. Michael Novak, "Human Dignity, Human Rights," *First Things: A Monthly Journal of Religion & Public Life,* no. 97 (1999): 40.

33. See, e.g., Robert D. Enright and Joanna North, eds., *Exploring Forgiveness* (Madison: University of Wisconsin Press, 1998); Trudy Govier, *Forgiveness and Revenge* (London: Routledge, 2002); Margaret R. Holmgren, "Forgiveness and the Intrinsic Value of Persons," *American Philosophical Quarterly* 30 (1993): 341–53.

CHAPTER 6 | Moral Disagreement

and the Limits of Reason

Reflections on MacIntyre and Ratzinger

Gerald McKenny

Persistent moral disagreement seems to be a
characteristic feature of modern liberal democratic societies. In the
United States the polarization between people with diverse moral
views on issues such as abortion, research using embryos, homosexuality, and the structure of the family and its role in society may finally
be subsiding after more than two decades of rancorous debates, but
the disagreement itself shows no sign of abating. In Europe similar
disagreements regarding abortion, genetic testing, embryo research,
reproductive technology, the implications of justice and equality for
family relationships, and public religious expression appear to be the
latest episodes in a long struggle between Europe's Christian and Enlightenment legacies that is still not put to rest.

Disagreements such as these are extraordinarily complex. Sometimes they turn on factual or conceptual issues. Are the unborn and

the severely impaired human beings in the full moral sense or not? Does withholding or withdrawing a feeding tube from someone in a persistent vegetative state count as killing or not? At other times there is disagreement over whether a moral obligation binds absolutely, that is, in all conceivable circumstances, or whether there are circumstances in which it might be overruled or outweighed by other factors. Is the intentional killing of an innocent human being morally wrong in all conceivable cases, or can it be justified when the rights or well-being of others is at stake, or when someone who is suffering greatly from a terminal illness gives consent for lethal intervention? In still other cases what is at stake is the meaning or application of a moral principle. Nearly everyone agrees that economic activity is subject to principles of justice, but what do these principles require? Are they limited to respect for individual liberty and enforcement of contracts, or do they require substantive standards of fairness or equality? Finally, there is disagreement over which principles are relevant to the moral evaluation of a kind of activity or relationship. Are relationships involving sexual intimacy subject only to principles of just treatment, the consent of each party, and mutual affection, or are they also subject to norms of lifelong fidelity, the complementarity of man and woman, and openness to procreation?

For citizens of liberal democracies moral disagreement of these kinds poses a serious question: How can people who disagree so deeply on so many moral issues form a political society on grounds other than coercion? It is difficult to imagine how a stable and just social order is possible without some agreement on matters as fundamental as the dignity of human life, the ordering of marital and family relationships, and the basic rules of economic activity. In the absence of moral agreement these matters seem destined to be decided on purely political grounds: either by the decree of the state or by the power of majorities or the influence of interest groups. The first option is antithetical to the very idea of liberal democracy, which excludes any such role for the state. As for the second option, when this kind of power or influence is exercised by majorities or interest groups apart from a social consensus, it usually indicates a corruption of liberal democracy. For these reasons liberal thinkers from John Locke to John Rawls have held that a liberal political order depends on a broad consensus supporting the moral principles underlying basic social and political institutions.

Disagreement on these fundamental moral matters poses a special problem for many Christians. Both the Catholic Church and the major Protestant traditions rooted in the Reformation era have historically held a high view of the capacity of human reason to know the basic requirements of a just social and political order. Catholics and Protestants of this variety have agreed on this point in spite of their profound disagreements over whether this capacity and this knowledge can achieve anything that is of ultimate worth in the eyes of God. This high view of moral reason has seemed to these Christians to follow quite clearly from Romans 2:14–15, where the apostle Paul attributes moral knowledge to Gentiles who have not received the revealed law of Scripture: "When Gentiles, who do not possess the law, do by nature what the law requires, they, despite not having the law, are a law to themselves. They show that what the law requires is written on their hearts, to which their own conscience bears witness." Based in part on this passage, the Roman Catholic tradition has elaborated a well-known doctrine of natural law, which is "present in the heart of each man and established by reason," to repeat the phrase from the Church's catechism quoted by Alasdair MacIntyre at the beginning of his essay in this volume. While the principles of this law may be rejected, "it cannot be destroyed or removed from the heart of man. It always rises again in the life of individuals and societies."[1] What is less widely known is that the Protestant reformers Martin Luther and John Calvin taught something roughly the same as this doctrine.[2] But as MacIntyre points out, if these claims regarding natural law are true, we should expect to find widespread agreement among human beings, at least over time, on basic moral values or principles. This would

especially be the case, we might suppose, in societies in which the revealed law of Scripture, which enables reason to grasp the moral law
more clearly, has become widely known due to the influence of Christian faith.

This essay examines two attempts to resolve this question of
whether and how the claims these Christians have made about moral
reason can be consistently maintained in the face of moral disagreement. One attempt is by Alasdair MacIntyre, the other by Joseph Ratzinger. Because the writings of Ratzinger that I consider in this essay
were all written prior to his elevation to the papacy in April 2005, I
refer to him by the name in which they were written and not as Pope
Benedict XVI. Before examining the positions of these two thinkers in
detail, I want to place their solutions to the problem in a broader range
of possible solutions.

I. Moral Disagreement and the Claims of Reason:
Three Solutions to the Problem

Confronted with the apparent contradiction between the claims made
on behalf of reason and the facts of moral disagreement, there are two
obvious solutions. The first solution is to deny that moral disagreement is either as deep or as persistent as many people assume. Consider that for well over a century the United States was sharply divided
first over slavery, then over the right of women to vote, and finally over
the civil rights of its citizens of African descent. While moral disagreements continue to surround race and gender, these particular disagreements, all of which must have seemed at the time as intractable
as our current ones seem to be, no longer polarize Americans. There is
no reason, therefore, to assume that our current disagreements over issues such as abortion and homosexuality will not also be resolved. If
moral disagreements do seem to arise more frequently in modern societies, this is because rapid social change and constant technological

innovation keep posing new challenges to settled convictions while the lack of any official moral authority means that agreement will have to be reached through common deliberation over time. This is roughly the view held by Jeffrey Stout.[3]

The second obvious solution is to deny that reason gives us the kind or degree of knowledge of what is morally good which the Catholic tradition and its Protestant counterparts have claimed that it gives us. This solution comes in two versions. One version holds that it was a mistake all along to think that reason is capable of telling us what we need to know to live morally worthy lives. In its simplest form this position holds that reason was so badly damaged by the Fall that it is no longer a reliable source of moral insight, which must be sought instead from Scripture. This is the position taken by many American Protestants today. It faces the daunting challenge of establishing the Bible as authoritative in the political order. In a more complex form this version of the second solution holds that reason was meant, in God's plan for humanity, to operate in dependence upon God's self-revelation, so that strong claims about the capacity of reason to know the good are theologically mistaken. By God's providence, reason acting independently of revelation may be sufficient to hold society together after the Fall, but it can know what is morally good only in a minimal sense or in approximation to the truth of the good. It is finally only in Jesus Christ that the good of human life is revealed and known. At the same time, and also by God's providence, there has been and continues to be a historical influence of Christian witness to Christ on political and social arrangements, especially but not only in Western societies, and the results of this historical influence are easily mistaken for products of reason independent of revelation. Various aspects of this version are held by Karl Barth, Oliver O'Donovan, and John Howard Yoder. The other version of this second solution does not attempt to limit the claims made on behalf of reason by placing reason in the context of revelation but rather holds that the good as reason knows it is a very general or indeterminate notion, offering broad outlines or directions, so that if we want specific answers to questions about how we should live, we will need to look to particular ways of life in which the good attains specificity, one of which is the Christian tradition of thought and practice. We can, by the exercise of reason, gain reliable knowledge of the conditions for human flourishing, but these conditions will often allow for an indefinite number of ways of life and social and political arrangements as compatible with human flourishing. This does not mean that there is no truth of the good or that reason is incapable of grasping it, but it does mean that this truth, or at least our grasp of it, is general. This position has been articulated by Jean Porter.[4]

A third solution to the apparent contradiction is also possible. One can accept both the facts of moral disagreement and the claim that reason is capable of knowing what is morally good to the extent that the Catholic Church and other Christian traditions have claimed, if one can also offer an explanation, in the form of an error theory, of why many people at least appear not to be in a position to see clearly what reason in principle tells us about the good. Once again there are two versions of this solution. One version points to the inability of reason since the early modern period to secure agreement on a single conception of the good human life. In the aftermath of Enlightenment attempts to ground morality in reason alone, it is now clear that reason is inseparable from the particularity of history and tradition. In this situation multiple historical traditions of moral thought and practice claim the support of reason, yet none of them are able to appeal to a universal standard of reason that transcends history and tradition. However, this need not preclude the possibility that a tradition of moral thought and practice, such as the Thomistic tradition of natural law, may have grounds for claiming rational superiority over other traditions, even though adherents of these other traditions may have no reason to accept this claim, and thus may not be in a position to see what reason, according to the Thomistic tradition, tells us about the good. This, roughly, is the view of Alasdair MacIntyre. The second version of this third alternative also identifies the Enlightenment effort to ground morality in reason alone as a critical point in its explanation of moral disagreement and rejects the assumption that reason is utterly independent of historical traditions. It argues that while moral truth is in principle accessible to reason, in practice it can be concretely recognized as truth only as it is embodied in a historical tradition. If appeals to reason fail to arrive at moral truth, this is due at least in part to the modern separation of reason from the historical traditions in which alone moral truth is effectively recognizable as such. This is the view of Joseph Ratzinger.

For both MacIntyre and Ratzinger, then, moral reason has a close relationship to history, and this historical factor is central to the explanation of why moral disagreement occurs despite the capacity of reason in principle to know the good. In what follows I examine their respective versions of this third solution to the problem of reason and moral disagreement.

II. Reason, Tradition, and Moral Disagreement: Alasdair MacIntyre

To understand MacIntyre's position, it will help to point out the extent to which he shares with much of modern liberal thought the view that any reflective account of morality today must come to terms with moral disagreement as an ineradicable feature of modern life. Moreover, MacIntyre and his modern liberal opponents share key strands of a common narrative about the origins of this disagreement and its implications. Prior to the modern era, this story goes, there was wide agreement that the kind of being we as humans are determines the ends we should pursue if we are to live praiseworthy and fulfilling lives. Knowing these ends makes it possible for us to distinguish between what we in fact simply happen to desire and what we would desire if we were adequately informed about the kind of being we are and properly trained, and thus to have a conception of *the* good of human life. Knowledge of the ends that are in accordance with our nature is in principle available to us by reason, though for Christian thinkers, of course, this knowledge must be supplemented by the revealed law of Scripture, just as the orientation of our desires to their proper ends requires the assistance of divine grace. Despite this qualification, it was reasonable for people holding these beliefs about the good to expect that rational persons would be able to agree on what kind of human life is worth living.

For modern people, the story continues, it is no longer reasonable to expect such agreement. The belief that the moral life consists in the pursuit of certain ends set by human nature was discredited by numerous factors in the early modern era, including the decline of Aristotelian science, which had provided the metaphysical scheme of nature, end, and desire on which this moral vision rested; the growing influence of theological schools at odds with Aristotelianism; and the effects of the great social and political upheavals of the age. On a theoretical level, human nature came to be regarded as too indeterminate and contingent to serve as a basis for morality, and without any ground in human nature it appears futile to look for a common morality in the seemingly endless variety of human desires. In the absence of a conception of human nature to order these desires, a diversity of conceptions of human fulfillment is unavoidable, and moral disagreements over the good will therefore be incapable of rational resolution. Meanwhile, on a practical level, the bloody conflicts that accompanied efforts to impose conceptions of the good by force left thoughtful people searching for a moral basis for society that did not rest on any such conception. The result of all these developments was that the basic moral principles that ensure the unity of a society and supply the foundations of the political order would now have to be formulated independently of conceptions of the good. In the words of John Rawls, the task now was "to answer the question: how is social unity to be understood, given that there can be no public agreement on the one rational good, and a plurality of opposing and incommensurable conceptions must be taken as a given?"[5]

It is here that MacIntyre and modern liberalism diverge. The answer given by Rawls, along with many other modern liberal thinkers, involved establishing for the basic political, social, and economic institutions of society principles of justice that are independent of comprehensive conceptions of the good.[6] For Rawls and other liberal thinkers, political liberalism thus supplies for people who strongly disagree over what a good life is grounds for cooperating with each other without either giving up their particular views of the good or forcing others to live according to them. For their critics, of course, political liberalism simply expresses one such view of the good and leaves us with the kind of society many people today find profoundly dissatisfying, one that is constantly preoccupied with questions of who owes what to whom and who is entitled to what, and relegates questions of what is and is not worth having or what ways of life are and are not worthy of living to the domains of individual taste or private conviction. What is sometimes forgotten in these debates over liberalism is that a liberal theory that sets out to establish principles of justice in independence of comprehensive conceptions of the good may proceed either by deriving those principles from reason in abstraction from any historical tradition or community or by arriving at them through rational reflection starting from intuitive convictions about justice in a historical community. In his later work Rawls explicitly identified his theory with the second alternative, but MacIntyre consistently identifies liberalism with the first alternative. For him what is most distinctive about this moral and political vision is its confidence that the problem posed by moral disagreement can be overcome by looking to reason alone, abstracted from conceptions of the good, as well as from the historical traditions and relations of authority to which moral conceptions were heretofore bound, to establish basic principles of justice. This kind of theory holds that unlike conceptions of the good, on which rational persons may disagree, the basic principles of justice, insofar as they are established by reason alone, command the agreement of all rational persons as such. Yet it is an obvious fact that the theories which purport to establish these principles of justice on the basis of abstract reason have proposed rival and incompatible principles of justice. It is at this point, where Enlightenment reason is confronted with its failure, that MacIntyre finds occasion to reopen the question of moral rationality.

MacIntyre begins by impressing his readers with the incoherence of the moral discourse of everyday life in modern societies. In a typical debate about justice, for example, appeals may be made to notions of merit or desert, to inalienable rights or entitlements, and to the concept of utility. Our moral debates are interminable, he argues, because their premises derive from conceptions of justice that are in conflict with each other. When we turn to moral reflection to resolve these conflicts we are left to choose between, on the one hand, the Enlightenment view that moral claims can be justified only to the extent that they can in principle secure the assent of all rational persons and, on the other hand, the anti-Enlightenment view that moral convictions are rooted in the ways of life of historical communities and are not capable of rational justification at all. The basic outline of MacIntyre's diagnosis of this situation is well known: Our ordinary moral discourse is incoherent because it consists of fragments of once-coherent moral visions which were shattered by the project undertaken by Enlightenment thinkers, who in the face of the moral disagreement bequeathed by the early modern era sought to justify moral claims in abstraction from the traditions in which our moral concepts were once at home. The failure of this project has left us with the scattered remnants of those moral visions. Meanwhile, the other alternative—to deny that moral claims are susceptible of any rational justification—ultimately makes morality a purely arbitrary affair.[7]

MacIntyre's effort to rehabilitate tradition is sometimes portrayed by critics as an antimodern and even an antirationalistic endeavor, but his rejection of the second alternative shows how far off the mark this interpretation is. Far from being antirationalistic, MacIntyre's project is committed to understanding moral discourse as rational inquiry. For him the collapse of the Enlightenment project opens the possibility of considering a conception of moral rationality excluded by the Enlightenment conception. In MacIntyre's words, this is "a conception of rational enquiry as embodied in a tradition, a conception according to which the standards of rational justification themselves emerge from and are part of a history in which they are vindicated by the way in which they transcend the limitations of and provide remedies for the defects of their predecessors within the history of that same tradition."[8] Moral inquiry is discursive argumentation carried out not from an allegedly neutral stance but within particular historical traditions of inquiry each possessing its own standards of argument and justification, and also, at critical junctures, within encounters of these traditions with other traditions which have their own standards of argument and justification. With this conception, MacIntyre denies that there are rational standards independent of traditions of inquiry by which the claims of one tradition may be found true and those of another false and rejects the view that rational moral inquiry gives timeless answers to timeless questions. As for his alleged antimodern stance, what these denials and rejections make clear is that while MacIntyre's own allegiance to a tradition with premodern roots (specifically, to what he now refers to as the Thomist-Aristotelian tradition) becomes increasingly explicit in his work, he also recognizes that it is a certain kind of modern awareness, one not available to Aristotle or Aquinas, that enables him to understand this moral position as a tradition, and more generally to speak of moral rationality as constituted by traditions.[9] Whatever his intention may be, in all these respects this position is well designed to resolve certain modern tensions between reason and history, albeit from the standpoint of a particular tradition rather than from that of a Hegelian metanarrative.

However, if in MacIntyre's view moral rationality is dispersed into rival traditions each with its own standards, how can he overcome the fragmentation he himself has diagnosed or avoid suspicion that in his conception of moral inquiry reason is merely an honorific title conferred on nonrational moral conviction? Here, I believe, is where the attractiveness of MacIntyre's conception of moral inquiry is most evident. This conception promises to give us moral particularity without forcing us to give up moral truth, and it allows us to come to terms with moral pluralism without paying the price of moral relativism. I can retain my adherence to a particular tradition, refusing to make my commitment to it conditional upon its agreement with an allegedly universal standpoint, without thereby becoming a nihilist, and I can concede that adherents of other traditions may be rational without thereby becoming a relativist. With regard to nihilism, MacIntyre argues that the particularity of a tradition does not entail that its claims cannot be true or false; traditions can and do make claims, in terms particular to themselves, which entail the rejection of any incompatible claim made by any rival tradition. The status of these truth claims is clarified by MacIntyre's theory of truth, which echoes arguments of Charles Peirce. Truth for MacIntyre (as for Peirce) is a relation between mind and reality, expressed in judgments. By subjecting its judgments to dialectical testing, a tradition may be able to claim rational progress when comparing its present judgments to its previous ones; if so, it can understand this progress as an approximation of a final truth in which the mind is fully adequate to its object, though the inability to know that one has reached this state requires a continual openness to further dialectical testing of judgments.[10]

With regard to relativism, while MacIntyre does claim that each tradition possesses its own standards of rational justification, he rejects the relativist thesis that such a claim precludes the possibility of rational debate between traditions and leaves us with no rational grounds for adhering to one tradition rather than another. MacIntyre's reply relies on a complex account of how rational inquiry within a tradition entails commitments that under certain circumstances may lead it to an encounter with another tradition, an encounter in which one tradition may establish its rational superiority over the other tradition on the other's own terms. Insofar as a tradition takes the form of a rational inquiry committed to truth, it is bound to raise questions about the success of its own standards in resolving the problems it faces from within its own history of inquiry. If, as may and sometimes does happen, such a tradition finds itself at some point in its history without adequate resources of its own to resolve certain problems it now faces, it is reasonable for it to look to the resources of other traditions, both for a resolution of these problems and for an explanation of why it has found these problems incapable of resolution in its own terms. Given MacIntyre's strong claims about the incommensurability of standards of rational justification among diverse traditions, such a process requires a Herculean labor of understanding which requires adherents of one tradition to adopt the standpoint of the other tradition so far as this is possible. Yet what may emerge on the other end of this process is a situation in which adherents of the first tradition ultimately recognize that the second tradition is able both to resolve (or avoid) the problems faced by the first tradition and to explain how these problems are exactly those which would be expected to arise if the claims of the second tradition were true. In such a case the second tradition would be rationally vindicated over against the first in its claims to truth. Thus it is the case for any tradition that its commitment to truth entails the possibility of defeat at the hands of a rival tradition, and this possibility is sufficient to refute the relativist claim that the relativity of standards of rational justification to traditions renders rational debate between traditions impossible and leaves us with no grounds for choosing one tradition over another. Only the spectator who stands outside all traditions (who, for MacIntyre, is a figure of modernity), surveying them from above, as it were, is tempted by relativism.

However, once one has conceded, as MacIntyre has, that traditions of inquiry possess distinct standards of rational justification which may be incommensurable, it is difficult to keep relativism at bay. There are at least three considerations that seem to keep the question of relativism alive in relation to MacIntyre's position. First, in a successful encounter between two such traditions it may be unclear whether the adherents of one tradition have come to accept the rational superiority of the other from the perspective of their own standards or have rather simply decided to adopt the standards of the other tradition in place of their own. Has the former tradition been defeated or simply abandoned? Unless we can establish grounds for asserting the first alternative over against the second, the relativist can always claim that no genuine rational debate between traditions has occurred but that, instead, the adherents of the first tradition, facing a crisis, have simply jumped ship. Second, as MacIntyre acknowledges, centuries may pass without traditions meeting the kind of crisis that necessitates an encounter with another tradition, and even when such a crisis occurs the strenuous efforts required to overcome the incommensurability between the two traditions may fall short. It is de facto conditions such as these, as MacIntyre acknowledges, that will always tempt the spectator to credit the relativist stance.[11] A third consideration brings us to the major point of the essay that opens this volume. Here, MacIntyre argues that even when a tradition has been defeated its adherents may have no compelling reason to admit their defeat, and he thinks that such is the case in the encounter between the Thomistic Aristotelian tradition and utilitarianism. MacIntyre argues that the problems utilitarianism faces in its conception of happiness can be grasped and overcome only by those who understand and know how to apply the concept of a natural end. Yet he also recognizes that utilitarians have good reasons for rejecting any such concept; and so, while Thomistic Aristotelians can legitimately assert their rational superiority over utilitarians, the latter have not been given any reason for accepting this assertion. And, ironically, in cases like this one the spectator may be in a better position than an adherent of the defeated tradition to see what has happened.

In what follows I want to focus on the second and third of these considerations. Neither overturns MacIntyre's argument against relativism. Nevertheless, each has important implications that seem to entail a certain kind of relativism in practice, though not in principle. The second consideration implies that unless or until a tradition is rationally defeated by a rival tradition its adherents are, to borrow a term from Jeffrey Stout, rationally entitled to their beliefs, assuming that these beliefs are justified according to the rational standards recognized by the tradition. Stout argues that being justified in believing something differs from context to context, and on this basis he distinguishes being justified in holding a set of moral beliefs from holding a set of moral beliefs "that any human being or moral agent, regardless of context, would be justified in accepting."[12] If we substitute MacIntyre's "tradition" for Stout's "context" we have the same idea. Now, the third consideration implies that this rational entitlement may hold even when one tradition is defeated by another. In sum, as long as adherents of different traditions have good reasons, justifiable in accordance with their own standards, for retaining their moral beliefs, they are rationally entitled to those beliefs, even if those beliefs are false. It follows from this that while the Church, on MacIntyre's account, can rightly claim that its natural law doctrine is rationally superior to other forms of moral rationality if and insofar as the Thomistic Aristotelian tradition, or another natural law tradition like it, can rationally vindicate itself against its rivals, as MacIntyre thinks it can, there is nevertheless, on his account, no reason to hold that those who reject this doctrine, and the traditions in which it is embedded, are rationally compelled to accept it, so long as they have reasons, well founded in their own traditions of inquiry, for not accepting the premises on which its claim to rational superiority rests. In such cases they are rationally entitled to their rejection of this doctrine and these traditions. If so, then they are rationally entitled to reject at least some of the moral principles which the Church holds all persons must accept. And if that is the case, then it seems to follow that a state may be rationally justified in failing or refusing to acknowledge those principles as the moral foundation of political order or to incorporate them into its basic law. Thus, while MacIntyre shows how a natural law tradition can concede the ineradicable pluralism of moral reason in the modern world while nevertheless being able to claim rational superiority for itself, this concession, which amounts to a kind of relativism in practice, jettisons some of the most important implications that the Church claims follow from its doctrine of natural law.

We now turn to the third consideration. MacIntyre's argument that a tradition may be rationally vindicated without rationally compelling adherents of the defeated tradition to acknowledge their defeat raises another question: What if the defeated tradition not only refuses to accept the verdict pronounced by the victorious tradition but also puts forth its own claim to rational vindication against that tradition? When MacIntyre begins his essay it is not utilitarianism but the Thomistic Aristotelian tradition that faces an apparent crisis insofar as the facts of moral disagreement seem to conflict with claims Aquinas makes about the primary precepts of the natural law. Aquinas, as MacIntyre understands him, holds and is committed to holding that agreement on the moral content and normative authority of these precepts is virtually universal and dissent a rare and temporary occurrence, while in fact disagreement over these precepts is widespread and persistent. MacIntyre's solution to this crisis is to argue that while rational moral argument cannot directly resolve disagreements of this kind, which are deeply rooted in different conceptions of the ultimate ends of human life, it can show how practical reason in the face of such disagreement presupposes what Aquinas identified as the primary precepts of the natural law. Thus MacIntyre argues that inquiry into the truth of matters on which we disagree presupposes a disinterested stance which itself entails norms that secure the conditions under which participants in the inquiry can consider rival claims impartially. These norms include the protection of life, liberty, and property; truthfulness and promise keeping, and provision for common security. Moreover, these norms have certain formal characteristics. They are universal, exceptionless, identical for everyone, and necessarily presupposed. In other words, they are first principles of practical reason. In both form and content, then, these norms of inquiry are, according to MacIntyre, identical to Aquinas's primary precepts of the natural law.

And so, the Thomistic Aristotelian can face radical moral disagreement with the confidence that his tradition can be rationally vindicated, if not directly, then at least indirectly, and perhaps somewhat unexpectedly, via a quasi-transcendental argument that establishes the primary precepts of the natural law as conditions for rational inquiry in the face of radical moral disagreement. Yet MacIntyre recognizes that the utilitarian will at some point conclude, based on the standards of her own tradition, that she has no reason for continued participation in the inquiry. Nothing good, she will at that point conclude, can come of an inquiry conducted on these terms. On MacIntyre's account, his argument has not provided her with a reason, given her own standards, for continuing, but he nevertheless insists on the "motivated irrationality" of her denial of the primary precepts of the natural law.

Imagine, however, that it is not a utilitarian but a believer in the basic moral underpinnings of liberal democracy who joins MacIntyre's inquiry. This liberal will first argue that even on his own account MacIntyre's conditions of rational discourse do not correlate exactly with his list of the primary precepts of the natural law. In particular, there is no obvious match between these conditions and the precepts having to do with sexuality and the rearing of children. She will then go on to argue that MacIntyre has not fully accounted for the requirements of disinterested inquiry. If, as MacIntyre suggests, disinterested inquiry occurs when each participant responds to the arguments of other participants "impartially and impersonally," then certain other norms are also implied. These norms include (at least) the prohibition of all forms of discrimination, the guarantee of toleration for minority and dissenting views, and the rejection of appeals to constituted authorities (whether persons or texts). In short, inquiry in the face of radical moral disagreement presupposes the very conditions of liberal discourse which MacIntyre has elsewhere criticized, and the liberal will point out that this is no accident—that it is precisely modern conditions of radical moral disagreement which must be resolved by rational inquiry alone, without appeal to metaphysical and theological conceptions or traditional authorities that justify liberal moral and political theories. She may argue, finally, that if the claims of her tradition are true, then one would expect the Thomistic Aristotelian to encounter exactly the problem with moral disagreement which he in fact does encounter and to be unable to resolve this problem in his own terms, that is, by appeal to the primary precepts of the natural law. MacIntyre might respond by arguing that the Thomistic Aristotelian has been given no reason for agreeing to these liberal conditions and at some point would conclude that there is no point in continuing in an inquiry under such conditions. The liberal would have to accept this, but she might continue to insist on the motivated irrationality of the Thomistic Aristotelian's refusal.

My point in this extended exercise is not to take the side of the liberal or to conclude with her that she has rationally defeated the Thomistic Aristotelian. It is only to point out that MacIntyre's position seems unable to avoid the kinds of disagreements that lead us to throw up our hands and call for the verdict of the spectator who stands outside the rival traditions and who, by MacIntyre's own account, may be in a better position to see what is the case than are the adherents themselves. Yet one of the advantages of MacIntyre's account of rationality is that it enabled us to avoid such appeals to the spectator. It is important to keep in mind here that it is the very nature of rationality as MacIntyre understands it, along with the commitment to truth his conception of rationality involves, which leads to these impasses. An adherent of a tradition which claims to have rationally defeated another tradition cannot help but ask, if he is rational on MacIntyre's terms, about the claim of the other tradition to have rationally defeated his own. If in such a case each tradition has reasons for not accepting the claim of the other, then once again it is difficult to see how relativism has been avoided in practice, even if it has been successfully avoided in principle.

III. Reason, History, and the Future of the Christian Moral Legacy: Joseph Ratzinger

We may, following MacIntyre, understand persistent moral disagreement by focusing on the synchronic diversity of rival moral traditions each claiming the sanction of reason. Such a condition confronts us with the de facto pluralism of moral reason, a pluralism that seems to be the historical fate of those who live after the loss of consensus on the metaphysical and theological convictions that once made it possible to secure widespread agreement on a conception of the good and the failure of the Enlightenment to restore rational moral unity on the basis of reason in abstraction from such convictions. MacIntyre, as we have seen, shows us how we can acknowledge the de facto pluralism of reason without succumbing to nihilism or relativism. However, we may also understand persistent moral disagreement diachronically, locating it at a particular point in time when an older, once-dominant moral vision shares historical space with a newer one which has not yet become dominant. From this viewpoint deep moral disagreement is a transitional phenomenon. Two moral visions clash, yet only for the duration of time it takes for one era of stable agreement to be replaced by another. A rather triumphalist version of this view is propounded by Peter Singer, who opens a popular book on the taking of human life by brashly declaring that "the traditional western ethic has collapsed" and attributing ongoing disagreement over issues such as abortion and euthanasia to the confusion caused by the temporary overlap of two moralities, one waxing and one waning.[13] At issue here is not the pluralism of moral reason but its secularization, the replacement of a Judeo-Christian ethic of the sanctity of life with a utilitarian ethic. Pluralism and the moral disagreement it involves will, on this view, presumably disappear once the new secular ethic has completed its overthrow of the "traditional western ethic."

Joseph Ratzinger is far from conceding either Singer's bifurcation between a traditional and a modern ethos or the inevitable triumph of the latter over the former. Nevertheless, he views the most important moral disagreements in contemporary Europe (and to some extent in North America) in light of the growing historical influence of one moral vision over another. He traces moral disagreement to a fraternal conflict between moral convictions historically embodied in Europe's Christian heritage and what he describes as a "new canon" of values rooted in an Enlightenment culture which increasingly asserts itself in Europe's moral identity and its legal institutions. The conflict is not, in Ratzinger's view, a conflict between Christianity and the Enlightenment as such. He repeatedly underscores the fundamental compatibility of much of the Enlightenment's moral and political vision, including its commitments to democracy, freedom of thought and belief, and the fundamental equality of human beings, with the Christian vision, and he credits the Enlightenment with restoring principles of religious liberty and the dignity of reason where they had been obscured by a form of Christianity which, "contrary to its own nature," failed to adhere to these principles.[14] This shared confidence in reason is what most fundamentally links Ratzinger, and indeed the Catholic tradition generally, to the Enlightenment, ironically uniting these old foes in a partnership against the widespread suspicion of reason among many post-Enlightenment secular thinkers and their Christian counterparts.

Yet if reason is what unites Christianity and the Enlightenment in Ratzinger's scheme, it is also what divides them. In Ratzinger's Augustinian-Platonist vision there is a rational order to the universe which human reason is capable in principle of perceiving. In this capacity of reason human beings resemble the divine Logos who created the universe and is reflected in its rational order and who is most fully manifested in Christ, the Logos made flesh, in whom rational order is ultimately revealed as love. Ratzinger identifies this human resemblance by reason to the divine Logos as the ultimate ground of human dignity and therefore of human rights. As for the Enlightenment, while it must be credited with "giv[ing] reason back its own voice" where this voice had been muffled, it did not uphold this Augustinian-Platonist vision.[15] In place of the perception of rational order, the Enlightenment reduced the role of reason to its empirical and technical employment in a fundamentally irrational universe, where reason is itself merely a by-product of irrational processes. As empirical and especially as technical, this form of rationality is the expression of human capability, so that a perverse resemblance to God in the form of power over external reality stands in place of the proper resemblance to God in the ability of reason to perceive truth. There is nothing wrong with empirical and technical rationality as such; Ratzinger acknowledges their great value. It is the reduction of reason to these empirical and technical uses that he rejects. The implications of this reduction for morality are especially troubling. With the reduction of reason to empirical and technical rationality, moral values are relegated to the subjective realm, leaving the calculation of the consequences of acts as the sole task of reason in the moral realm, while the possibilities of rational control of external reality underwrite an ideology of progress. And so, as Ratzinger sees it, Enlightenment reason authorizes and promotes a "new canon" of values, based on individual liberty, consequentialist moral reasoning, and the idea of progress, which together constitute a secularist-Enlightenment moral vision that increasingly asserts itself in Europe today against the Christian-Enlightenment moral vision and leaves Europe's commitment to human rights vulnerable and unstable.

Ratzinger's depiction of the crisis of moral reason in a society characterized by a technical-calculative reduction of rationality complemented by the subjectivity of values is a familiar one, reflecting the Weberian diagnosis of modernity as it was taken up by the Frankfurt philosophers Karl-Otto Apel and Jürgen Habermas during the 1970s and 1980s.[16] Apel and Habermas were Kantians who thought that only a postmetaphysical, purely procedural, yet noninstrumental form of rationality could restore a rational morality in the face of the subjectivity of value. For Ratzinger, by contrast, the only alternative to the subjectivity of moral values is an objective, rational moral order. Here he echoes the discussion of freedom and truth in the papal encyclical *Veritatis Splendor,* where John Paul II contrasts a genuine freedom grounded in objective moral truth with a spurious individual liberty grounded in the subject as the source of moral value.[17] Yet, while Ratzinger believes that reason is in principle capable of grasping the rational order of the universe, he acknowledges that it is incapable of making the moral truth grounded in this order fully credible or effectively persuasive. In practice, this "evidential" character of moral truth is not purely rational but requires embodiment in a historical tradition or community. Here Ratzinger makes a Kantian move of his own, acknowledging the practical necessity of a historical faith as the vehicle of moral reason. Moral reason is inextricable from the historical tradition or community that is the bearer of moral truth, and to uproot reason from this context is to claim for it a self-sufficiency that it does not possess. One of the most salient features of the kind of Enlightenment reason Ratzinger criticizes is precisely its claim to self-sufficiency, its assertion of independence from its historical roots. To the extent that it claims such independence, Enlightenment reason is in an unnatural, diseased state which we may refer to as a "pathology of reason."

This problem of the evidential quality of moral truth is central to Ratzinger's moral and political thought, and it is in his solution to this problem that he exemplifies the third approach to moral disagreement. In contrast to MacIntyre, Ratzinger is not principally occupied with the question of how moral claims can be rationally justified and vindicated in the face of rival claims but rather with how the truth of moral claims can become effectively persuasive. The importance Ratzinger assigns to this issue, I believe, indicates the central importance of a certain set of questions to which his moral and political thought is an answer. If the Church's claims about natural law are true, why has it proved so difficult in contemporary Western societies to secure rational agreement on what the Church teaches are the moral foundations of a just social and political order? Why is it so often the case that outside the Catholic Church and its magisterial authority the exercise of reason leads to judgments about moral issues that are inconsistent with those the Church attributes to reason? Why does it seem to people outside the Church (and to many people within) that the Church's moral teachings and even its doctrine of natural law itself reflect a merely parochial form of reason? These questions seem to lie just below the surface in Ratzinger's essays and lectures on morality and politics, and his answer, which as we have seen points to the inability of reason to supply this evidential quality of moral truth alone, apart from its historical vehicle, is a key to several of his major preoccupations, including the relationship of faith and reason, the role of Europe's Christian legacy in its moral and political identity, and the vocation of the Church in contemporary society.

Ratzinger's proposed solution to this problem of the evidential quality of moral truth is inseparable from his broader understanding of the relationship between moral reason and its historical vehicle in the modern era. His story begins in early modern Europe. Despite no longer sharing a common faith, Europe in this period did share a common morality; in this situation, in which reflective people disagreed over faith but agreed on morality, it was plausible to attribute the evidential quality of shared moral convictions to reason unaided by faith, and thus to suppose that reason is capable of grasping moral truth apart from Christian faith, which in any case was a matter of controversy and therefore unable to supply the needed ground for morality. It is in this light that Ratzinger views Hugo Grotius's much-discussed call for a morality whose validity would hold *etsi Deus non daretur* (even if God did not exist). The persistence of moral unity despite the radical disruption of religious unity in the early modern period lent credence to claims that a moral order could be established by reason alone, and yet, Ratzinger maintains, these claims were illusory; all along it was in fact the influence of Christian faith as the historical bearer of moral truth, and not independent reason, that constituted the evidential force of the moral convictions shared by nearly everyone. When we look back on this period from our own vantage point, two factors become clear. On the one hand, we can now see that with the early modern effort to articulate moral convictions in terms of reason alone the Enlightenment severance of reason from its roots was already under way. On the other hand, the early modern societal consensus on the truth of Christian moral convictions seems to have steadily eroded during the intervening centuries. In the light of these two factors it is now clear to us in a way that it was not clear to Grotius and his contemporaries that reason alone is unable to provide the evidential quality of the moral convictions Christians claim are derived from reason.[18]

Ratzinger proposes a twofold solution to this problem, one solution aimed at nonbelievers, the other at believers. First, he seeks to convince nonbelievers of the evidential character of the Christian moral tradition. To a society whose moral and political culture increasingly reflects what he sees as a one-sided Enlightenment legacy, he issues a call to acknowledge the roots of modern reason in Europe's Christian legacy, commending the Christian moral tradition as a historical embodiment of moral reason that still deserves recognition as such. The Christian moral tradition, he argues, has proved itself in history as a concrete form of moral rationality, and as such it merits a place in the articulation of Europe's moral and political identity. If the need to supply a ground for morality in the confessional turmoil of early modern Europe led Grotius to his axiom, the threat to humanity posed by the new canon of values derived from Enlightenment reason calls for a reversal of this axiom: those who no longer accept the claims of the Christian tradition "ought nevertheless to try to live and to direct [their lives] *veluti si Deus daretur,* as if God did indeed exist."[19]

Second, Ratzinger urges believers to conduct themselves in society in such a way that the evidential quality of moral truth is not altogether lacking. It is the political and cultural task of the Church in the present to supply this evidential quality of moral truth, giving it visibility and effective persuasive power by its comportment in the world. Let us consider these two parts of the solution in order.

Ratzinger asks those without Christian faith to acknowledge that we effectively perceive moral truth only by recognizing its manifestation in a historical tradition. But in what sense or on what grounds can these nonbelievers acknowledge this point if, as nonbelievers, they reject the fundamental claims of this tradition, including Ratzinger's Augustinian-Platonist belief in a rational moral order that reflects a divine creative Logos? Ratzinger is careful to distinguish the recognition of moral truth in a historical tradition, which is an activity of reason, from belief in the truth of Christian revelation, which requires faith.[20] However, his proposal to the nonbeliever presupposes both that Christianity *as a historical tradition* has embodied moral truth in such a way as to supply its evidential character and that this evidential character remains even where the fundamental theological and metaphysical claims of this tradition have been rejected. Both of these presuppositions are subject to objections, but it is the second that presents the most interesting difficulty. For Ratzinger the actual capacity of reason to grasp moral truth is inextricable from Christianity as a historical and cultural force, though he readily acknowledges that in different cultural contexts other religious traditions may also function as historical bearers of moral truth and argues that in a globally connected world dialogue among historical faith traditions is necessary for the reestablishment of an adequate conception of moral reason. Yet the more Ratzinger emphasizes the de facto dependence of moral truth on its historical vehicle, the more plausibility he lends to the suspicion that the moral values to which he is committed are derived from a historical tradition rather than from a created moral order that is in principle accessible to reason. A comparison with Ratzinger's own interpretation of the early modern era is appropriate here. When the historical and cultural influence of the Christian moral vision was pervasive, it seemed plausible, even if it was in fact false, to ignore the role of historical tradition altogether and to hold that the truth of Christian moral convictions could be grasped by reason alone. But when the moral vision Ratzinger claims is in principle accessible to reason is in reality affirmed only where its embodiment in Christian faith and practice has visible influence, it will seem plausible to many, even if it is false, to suppose that this moral vision is the product of a particular historical tradition. Like Kant, Ratzinger is clear about the distinction between the moral law itself and its historical vehicle, yet, again like Kant, where the metaphysical (and in Ratzinger's case, the theological) underpinnings of this distinction are rejected, it collapses, and the Christian moral vision will appear as a mere product of history. This is how it must appear to the nonbelievers to whom Ratzinger addresses his appeal. But if these addressees already see themselves as having progressed beyond this Christian history, then it is difficult to know what motivation they have to respond to this appeal. The evidential force of the Christian tradition seems, after all, to depend on the fundamental theological and metaphysical claims Ratzinger has so eloquently articulated.

Ratzinger's very pleas for contemporary Europeans to acknowledge the continuing significance of the Christian moral tradition imply that the evidential character of this tradition is currently lacking, as he is well aware. This awareness no doubt explains his repeated emphasis on the role of the Church in supplying this evidential quality. This brings us to the second part of Ratzinger's solution, the part that is addressed to believers. It is significant that whereas Ratzinger's appeal to nonbelievers rests on the hope that the Christian moral legacy can still be recognized as a rational principle by society at large, it is now as a "creative minority" in society that the Church plays its role.[21] This point brings us to a more general observation. I believe that we should think of Ratzinger's solution as the latest in a long line of attempts to preserve the moral order of Christendom in the absence of the ecclesial-political order that once upheld it. His is a nuanced solution, advanced in full awareness of the difficulties it faces, yet not succumbing to despair or resentment. It is attuned to some of the complexity of the reasons for the Church's loss of moral authority, and it attempts to regain that authority through rational persuasion rather than through simply asserting it. Wherever it can do so it credits Enlightenment culture and even adopts the latter's terminology. Yet, at the same time, the very tone of Ratzinger's plea to contemporary Europe to acknowledge its Christian legacy and the nature of his appeal to the Church to uphold the evidential quality of moral truth betray an awareness that the era of Christendom as a moral order has already passed, at least in any form Ratzinger would consider adequate. He seems torn over whether to cling to whatever remains of a rapidly diminishing Christendom or to accept the Church's marginal status and draw on it as a creative force. In practice, of course, he does both, hoping that the Church will play the role of a creative minority that ignites a moral transformation in the society at large, but his double gesture also seems to be an interim solution, reflecting the uncertainty that characterizes a time of transition between two eras. In the past half century the case for retaining Christendom as a moral order in the absence of Christendom as an ecclesial-political order has shifted from Maritain's confidence in the pervasive influence of the Christian moral vision on the social and cultural life of Europe to Ratzinger's hope that Christians will influence culture by exhibiting a moral vision that is now in conflict with the one that is increasingly dominant.

Ratzinger shows how it is possible consistently to hold to the Catholic Church's claims about natural law while recognizing the reality of persistent moral disagreement. He does so by distancing the Catholic natural law tradition from notions of reason as autonomous and self-sufficient—notions which the Christian natural law tradition generally has not always been willing or able to reject. In this respect Ratzinger contributes to a trend in recent magisterial teaching on natural law.[22] The limits of moral reason are clear: "It is perfectly possible for reason to lose sight of essential values."[23] Left to itself, reason may well move in different directions from those indicated by the Christian moral vision, leading to judgments that disagree with the judgments which follow from that vision. And if this is so, it is because reason was never meant to be left to itself. But what, then, accounts for the self-assertion of reason in the first place? How is it that reason comes to embody a claim to autonomy, namely, the rejection of a transcendent moral order in which reason participates, as well as a claim to self-sufficiency, namely, the rejection of the need for a historical vehicle to make moral truth credible and effectively persuasive? Is Enlightenment reason an aberration? Or was the disciplining of Stoic moral reason by scriptural revelation and Christian tradition an aberration, historically speaking, after which Stoic reason once again shows its true color? Can the Christian natural law tradition secure its conception of reason as participating in an order that both transcends human reason and, as itself rational, is accessible to human reason? Or are autonomy and self-sufficiency inherent in the Western Logos, at least in the Stoic form which exercised such a great influence on the Christian natural law tradition, as Ernst Troeltsch famously argued?[24]

There are at least two ways to answer these questions which deserve more attention than Ratzinger has given them. One way is to understand Enlightenment reason not in the essentialist terms implied in these questions but as a historical interlude which began, as in Ratzinger's narrative, with the early modern attempt to maintain the moral order of Christendom by appeal to pure reason and which has ended with the collapse of the Enlightenment project announced by MacIntyre, among others. From this perspective, we may question whether moral reason in Western liberal democracies is polarized between the Christian-Enlightenment and secularist-Enlightenment alternatives Ratzinger describes, and whether our options are limited to a renewed commitment to the former and a kind of totalitarian tyranny under the latter. Like MacIntyre, Ratzinger never seriously entertains the possibility that modern democratic arrangements have themselves come to constitute a historical tradition, sustaining forms of moral commitment, cultivation of virtue, and deliberation which, to be sure, will sometimes be at odds with the Church's moral vision, yet which do not conform to Ratzinger's description of Enlightenment reason and do not portend totalitarian tyranny.[25] In many respects, this is a more serious challenge to Ratzinger's position than is abstract Enlightenment reason, precisely because it has already made the turn to history for which Ratzinger calls and because it embodies a much more robust moral vision than the combination of individual liberty, consequentialism, and commitment to progress Ratzinger finds in the abstract Enlightenment moral vision. There is an argument to be made that this moral vision presents a more formidable challenge to Ratzinger's moral vision than does the abstract Enlightenment morality whose final banality he perceives so acutely.

A second answer to our questions goes to the heart of some of Ratzinger's concerns. If Ratzinger is correct that autonomy and self-sufficiency remain dominant characteristics of modern moral reason, then we may ask whether he contributes to the problem with his understanding of the relationship between eschatology and political reason. At this point we can only gesture toward a rich and complex theme in Ratzinger's political theology. For Ratzinger, eschatology marks out the space of politics, both giving the state its rights and limiting its scope and placing political ends in a broader context of human flourishing which cannot be realized through politics. At the same time, Ratzinger wants to affirm a kind of autonomy of reason in its own sphere, and this is especially the case in politics, where reason must be allowed its exercise without disturbance from the eschatological reality beyond its boundary.[26] But from a Christian perspective should not political reason be not only expected to acknowledge eschatology as its boundary and condition but also summoned to pay heed to its content? Does not the very moral legacy of Christianity which Ratzinger seeks to preserve bear positive traces of the impact of

Christian eschatology on political reason? Surely Christian eschatology has had a pervasive and often salutary effect on Western social and political institutions and practices, not least in its mitigation of criminal penalties and of paternal domination in the sphere of the household.[27] At times Ratzinger seems to allow for a narrowly circumscribed role of eschatology in the political realm.[28] It must also be said that his concerns for the autonomy of reason in the political sphere and the concern to avoid utopian historical projects rooted in misunderstandings of Christian eschatology are appropriate and even necessary. Yet his political theology is based on the twofold scheme in which eschatology plays complementary roles by delimiting politics while also safeguarding its autonomy in its delimited sphere, and it is precisely on these grounds that reason can assert itself in its own immanent content and capability, reduce its historical bearer to a merely contingent vehicle, and keep Enlightenment reason alive in spite of Ratzinger's efforts to restore the role of historical tradition.

IV. Conclusion

If any one thing has become clear from these considerations of MacIntyre and Ratzinger, it is that it will be futile for Christians simply to appeal to reason in the face of moral disagreement today. In this respect, the Christian natural law tradition appears to share the fate of the Enlightenment project itself, which proved unable to ground moral and political values in reason alone. MacIntyre and Ratzinger both show how certain claims traditionally made by the Christian natural law tradition may continue to be affirmed, yet we have also seen that both are unable to show in a convincing way how this tradition can effectively overcome moral disagreement today. And in this respect one of the most important advantages often claimed for the natural law tradition is questionable. This does not, of course, amount to an argument that this tradition itself is questionable. But it does raise in a new way the question of the extent to which the moral content of the Christian natural law tradition is attributable to revelation or to history—or, more precisely, to reason guided by revelation and embedded in history—rather than to what every rational person or moral agent can know in principle. However this question is finally answered, its centrality to the thinking of MacIntyre and Ratzinger implies that they are closer to the two versions of the second alternative described in section I of this essay than they are to most of the versions of natural law thinking that have prevailed since the early modern period.

NOTES

1. *Catechism of the Catholic Church,* 2nd ed. (Vatican City: Libreria Editrice Vaticana, 1994), par. 1956, 1958.

2. John Calvin, *Institutes of the Christian Religion* II.8.1; Calvin, *Commentary on Romans 2:14.*

3. Jeffrey Stout, *Democracy and Tradition* (Princeton, NJ: Princeton University Press, 2004).

4. Jean Porter, *Natural and Divine Law: Reclaiming the Tradition for Christian Ethics* (Grand Rapids, MI: Eerdmans, 1999); Jean Porter, *Nature as Reason: A Thomistic Theory of the Natural Law* (Grand Rapids, MI: Eerdmans, 2005).

5. John Rawls, "Justice as Fairness: Political, not Metaphysical," in *Collected Papers* (Cambridge, MA: Harvard University Press), 388–414.

6. See John Rawls, *Political Liberalism* (New York: Columbia University Press, 1993).

7. See Alasdair MacIntyre, *Whose Justice? Which Rationality?* (Notre Dame: University of Notre Dame Press, 1988), 1–12. A similar argument with different emphases is found in Alasdair MacIntyre, *After Virtue: A Study in Moral Theory,* 3rd ed. (Notre Dame: University of Notre Dame Press, 2007), 1–22.

8. MacIntyre, *Whose Justice? Which Rationality?* 7.

9. Ibid., 8.

10. See MacIntyre, *Whose Justice? Which Rationality?* 356–61, 367–68; Alasdair MacIntyre, *First Principles, Final Ends, and Contemporary Philosophical Issues* (Milwaukee, WI: Marquette University Press, 1990); Alasdair

MacIntyre, "A Partial Response to My Critics," in *After MacIntyre: Critical Perspectives on the Work of Alasdair MacIntyre*, ed. John Horton and Susan Mendus (Notre Dame: University of Notre Dame Press, 1994), 295.

11. MacIntyre, "A Partial Response to My Critics," 297.

12. Stout, *Democracy and Tradition*, 231.

13. Peter Singer, *Rethinking Life and Death: The Collapse of Our Traditional Ethics* (New York: St. Martin's Griffin, 1996), 1–2.

14. Joseph Ratzinger, *Christianity and the Crisis of Cultures* (San Francisco: Ignatius Press, 2005), 47 f.

15. Ibid., 48.

16. See Karl-Otto Apel, "Types of Rationality Today," in *Rationality Today*, ed. T. Garaets (Ottawa: University of Ottawa Press, 1979), 307–40; Karl-Otto Apel, *Towards a Transformation of Philosophy* (London: Routledge, 1980), 225–300; Jürgen Habermas, *Toward a Rational Society* (Boston: Beacon Press, 1970), 81–122; Jürgen Habermas, *Reason and the Rationalization of Society*, trans. Thomas McCarthy (Boston: Beacon Press, 1984), vol. 1 of *The Theory of Communicative Action*.

17. Pope John Paul II, *Veritatis Splendor*, par. 31–34.

18. Joseph Ratzinger, *Values in a Time of Upheaval* (New York: Crossroad and Ignatius Press, 2006), 49–50, 62–67; Ratzinger, *Christianity and the Crisis of Cultures*, 51–52.

19. Ratzinger, *Christianity and the Crisis of Cultures*, 51.

20. Ratzinger, *Values in a Time of Upheaval*, 64.

21. Ibid., 150; Ratzinger, *Christianity and the Crisis of Cultures*, 52–53.

22. See esp. *Veritatis Splendor*, par. 35–45.

23. Ratzinger, *Values in a Time of Upheaval*, 50.

24. Ernst Troeltsch, *The Social Teaching of the Christian Churches* (Chicago: University of Chicago Press, 1931), 1:161.

25. See Richard Rorty, *Achieving Our Country* (Cambridge, MA: Harvard University Press, 1998); Stout, *Democracy and Tradition*; Ratzinger, *Values in a Time of Upheaval*, 47–48, 60–62.

26. Ratzinger, *Values in a Time of Upheaval*, 22–23, 70–72, 120.

27. See Oliver O'Donovan, *Desire of the Nations* (Cambridge: Cambridge University Press, 1996); John Milbank, *Theology and Social Theory* (London: Blackwell, 1993).

28. See Joseph Ratzinger, *Eschatology: Death and Eternal Life*, 2nd ed. (Washington, DC: Catholic University of America Press, 1988), 100–101. I am indebted to Geoffrey Keating for alerting me to this passage.

CHAPTER 7 | # Ultimate Ends and Incommensurable Lives in Aristotle

Kevin L. Flannery, S.J.

I. Kenny and Defeasibility

In Will, Freedom and Power, *Anthony Kenny* sets out a very convincing understanding of the practical syllogism, according to which it functions quite differently from the standard syllogism. If a standard syllogism is of valid form, its premises give rise necessarily to the appropriate conclusion; if, on the other hand, a practical syllogism is set out as such a syllogism ought to be set out, its conclusion is defeasible ("defeatable"). As Aristotle understands the practical syllogism, the end sought appears as the major term, the means as the middle term (or middle terms), the action to be performed as the conclusion.[1] In considering the various means that might take one, by way of a concrete action, to the end sought, all sorts of obstacles and alternatives might present themselves. To use Kenny's own example, I may need to get to London from Oxford by 4:15 P.M., and decide quite reasonably to take the 2:30 train, but then recall that the 2:30 train is always crowded and not conducive to working during the journey; so I take instead the 1:30 train. Had I taken the 2:30, my practical syllogism would have been valid *as* a practical syllogism, but it was reasonable too to change my mind. So there was nothing *necessitating* that conclusion; my original plan was defeated by further considerations.[2]

But, although Kenny puts this forward as an analysis of the Aristotelian practical syllogism, he maintains that it is incompatible with the understanding of happiness (that is to say, of εὐδαιμονία) put forward not only by Aristotle but also by Thomas Aquinas: "Both Aristotle and St. Thomas sometimes write as if they thought that the first premise of a piece of practical reasoning must be a universal plan of life of this kind, specifying an all-embracing good. Indeed, the type of premise they had in mind was something not only universal, but also objective."[3] The problem, according to Kenny, lies not in the practical syllogism but in this objective, universal "all-embracing good": "But whether or not the objectivity of the designated value refutes the Aristotelian theory of practical reasoning, the universality of the postulated major premises seems to me to establish the theory's inadequacy."[4]

Earlier in the same book, Kenny has said that "satisfactoriness," which he regards as the key relation in the analysis of the practical syllogism, "unlike truth, is a relative notion."[5] Here he is more expansive regarding this same notion:

> The defeasibility of practical reasoning comes about because of satisfactoriness being—like explanation—a relative notion: something is not satisfactory *simpliciter,* but satisfactory relative to a given set of wants; just as something is not an explanation *simpliciter,* but an explanation of a given set of data. The only way to avoid defeasibility in practical reasoning would be to insist that the premise setting out the goal should be not only cor-

rect but also complete; that all the wants to be satisfied by one's action should be fully specified. If we could do this, then there would be no danger of some further premise being added— some further want turning up—which would negate the satisfactoriness of the action described in the solution.[6]

According to Kenny, then, Aristotle and Thomas lighted upon the one way of invalidating their own theory.

But Kenny is confused about where in the practical syllogism defeasibility has its bearing. Defeasibility cannot pertain to the end sought in a particular piece of practical reasoning, since an end is always fixed in the context of a particular piece of practical reasoning.[7] It pertains rather to the means. Consider the very example that Kenny employs, that of taking the train to London. Let us say that I want to go to London in order to attend a lecture at 4:15. Given that that is my end, many issues and alternatives might occur to me, but they all presuppose my desire to attend the seminar. Having reasoned perfectly validly that the 2:30 train is for me, that plan might be defeated by the thought that the 2:30 is always crowded, but what is defeated is that way of getting to London, not my desire to go to London. It is true that if all feasible means of getting to London by 4:15 appear defeated, my desire to go to London may subside or be suppressed; but, even in this case, what has been defeated is not the end but the means. The desire will in all likelihood be rekindled if feasible means present themselves. It makes no difference whether getting to London would satisfy just some of my desires or all of them: also in the latter case, a means settled upon, or even all such means, might be defeated.

If the end of going to London is defeated, it is defeated not *qua* end of a piece of practical reasoning but *qua* means to some other end.[8] Let us say that I want to attend the lecture in order to stay current with what they are saying at King's College about ancient logic but am told that I can see the lecture—and save time—by watching it on closed circuit television. In this case, while the valid reasoning regarding London and the trains is defeated, the desire to stay current with the state of ancient logic remains. Indeed, some such end will always remain if there is to be anything to be defeated, since any piece of practical reasoning involves a certain tension between a (for that context) fixed point of arrival and the prospect of performing an action. If the desire for the point of arrival vanishes, the whole piece of reasoning disintegrates as irrelevant. This is not defeat (or defeasibility), which is always among alternatives, but annihilation or vanishing.

As to the ultimate end (happiness, however conceived), its stability as end (assured since it comes at the end of a string of reasons and can never be a means) is a necessary presupposition of any piece of practical reasoning. But this is only to say that someone who has no desire whatsoever for happiness however conceived cannot act. Such a person would have to be asleep or drugged—and, indeed, in a way sufficient to blot out all desire to go forward toward anything, if such a state is even possible. An ultimate end of some sort is a precondition for the presence of any defeasibility at all, since defeasibility is a characteristic of practical reasoning and practical reasoning presupposes a fixed point of arrival. And, in fact, that point of arrival can never stop short—in principle—of a state of full satisfaction. How else can we explain the fact that no one, when faced with two descriptions of their final end, one of which is less satisfactory than the other, would choose the less satisfactory state? If, for instance, one description includes satisfactions A, B, and C, but a second lacks satisfaction B, no one prefers the second. One chooses the first state of things not because one just happens to have an innate or acquired desire for a final state that includes A, B, and C but because the desire for happiness is a desire for the most satisfaction possible: that is, for perfect satisfaction, if possible.

II. NONTHEMATIC FIXING UPON THE SUMMUM BONUM

Kenny's remarks, quoted above, contain another questionable presupposition, namely, that Aristotle (with Thomas) conceives of the major term representing the *summum bonum* as "complete," that is, "that all the wants to be satisfied" are "fully specified." But is it really necessary that one's understanding of happiness come into one's reasoning in this—what we might call—"thematic" way?[9] If in some sense we have to say that the *summum bonum* is the major term of any piece of practical reasoning, must the inadequacy of bad acts be immediately apparent to those who perform or contemplate them?

There are some passages that suggest an affirmative answer to this question. In *Nichomachean Ethics* i,12, for instance, Aristotle says of happiness that "it is a first principle; for it is for the sake of this that we all do everything else, and the first principle and cause of goods is, we claim, something prized and divine."[10] But here, when he refers to happiness as a first principle, Aristotle might certainly be talking about happiness in the sense intended by anyone—whether philosophically inclined or not—who is pressed in a progressive way to specify why he does or wants to do something (whatever it might be). Why are you going to the gym? In order to take a run. But why take a run? In order to stay fit and healthy. But why stay fit and healthy? I want to be happy. Before this series of questions, the person on his way to the gym may not even have thought about his health, much less about happiness; but his replies can nonetheless all be true ones. Identifying the first principle of all action *as* "prized and divine" is the product of philosophical reflection, as the immediately preceding discussion in *EN* i,12 reveals. It requires noticing that one praises noble actions but not that at which they aim: "no one praises happiness as he does justice, but rather calls it blessed, as being something more divine and better" (1101b25–26).

There is another reason to believe that Aristotle does not think that the *summum bonum* (however conceived) has to be thematically in the mind of the person who acts—and this time the point applies not just to individuals who may lack the philosophical acumen to attend to what they are doing but to others as well. In a couple of places in *EN,* Aristotle insists on the close relationship between a pleasure and the human activity to which it properly belongs. His approach to this issue is closely related to his refutation of the Platonic notion of a universal good in *EN* i,6. In that refutation, he argues that the analogical (or quasi-analogical) relationship that exists among types of being—among the categories—can be applied to talk about the good (or goods), since it is things in the categories that are good (or bad).[11] Thus, if we want to understand goodness, we must look not to the good per se but to the various things that are good (i.e., good as that which they are), for good is always embedded in natures. A similar thing can be said about pleasure, since, just as good attaches to beings, pleasure attaches to activities (which are engaged in for the sake of their proper goods). The activity of thought, for instance, differs from the pleasure of eating, and the pleasure of eating from the pleasure of sexual intercourse (see *EN* x,5,1175a21–26). Bearing in mind this close relationship between activity and pleasure gives one reason to monitor and moderate one's pursuit of pleasure because it gives one reason not to pursue pleasure for its own sake rather than for the sake of the intelligible activity to which the pleasure properly belongs.[12]

Aristotle uses a couple of analogies in order to depict this close relationship in ordered lives between pleasure and activity. In *EN* i,8, he says the life of the virtuous "has no further need of pleasure as a sort of adventitious charm, but has its pleasure in itself."[13] And in *EN* x,4, perhaps correcting himself a bit, Aristotle says that "pleasure completes the activity not as the inherent state [ἡ ἕξις ἐνυπάρχουσα] does, but as a sort of end [τι τέλος] which supervenes as the bloom of youth does on those in the flower of their age."[14] Whether or not the latter is a correction of the former (or vice versa), it is clear that for Aristotle such pleasures are very close to their activities (even if not inherent states) and that one legitimately pursues *them,* for they are ends (of a sort). Toward the conclusion of this chapter, he remarks, "But whether we choose life for the sake of pleasure or pleasure for the sake of life is a question we may dismiss for the present. For they seem to be bound up together and not to admit of separation, since without activity pleasure does not arise, and every activity is completed by pleasure."[15]

All this says a good deal about whether happiness need enter into anyone's practical reasoning in a "fully specified" way. When a philosopher sits down to pursue his favorite activity—reading or writing about philosophy—he need not think of this as "activity of the soul in accordance with virtue" (*EN* i,7,1098a16–17) or as anything else so thematically formulated. That which is found at the end of his practical syllogism as he sits down might be simply the pleasure he expects from his customary activity at that time of day. Of course, he may also *know* that that pleasure is attached to activity specified in a certain way, but that need not go through his mind.

There is a pertinent passage also at the very end of book nine of the *Nicomachean Ethics* in which Aristotle in effect draws a connection between the extended treatment of friendship in books eight and nine and the two major themes of book ten: pleasure and happiness. He is speaking about groups of friends:

> And whatever existence means for each class of men, whatever it is for whose sake they value life, in that they wish to occupy themselves with their friends; and so some drink together, others dice together, others join in athletic exercises and hunting, or in the study of philosophy, each class spending their days together in whatever they love most in life; for since they wish to live with their friends, they do and share in those things that they deem living well.[16]

It is obvious here that Aristotle is talking about these men's conception of the ultimate good, for he goes out of his way to say that they regard the good that gathers them together as existence itself (τὸ εἶναι—1172a1–2): that for which they value life. But it is unlikely that a major term *drinking* or *dicing* plays much of a part in the practical reasoning of these two groups, assuming that there's much of that being done there at all. And it is unlikely that, if asked, they would describe their *summum bonum* in quite those terms. So the *summum bonum* is not only removed from the thoughts of men in the sense that it often comes out only after progressive interrogation regarding reasons for action ("Why are you going to the gym?" etc.) but also in the sense that it may take another person, standing outside of a "way of life," to clarify to someone dwelling habitually within it what his reason for living is.

This sense of happiness (i.e., the final answer in a series of answers) is the sense that Aristotle, in his quest in *EN* i for an account of the happiness that men seek, dismisses:

> Verbally there is very general agreement; for both the general run of men and people of superior refinement say that it is happiness, and identify living well and faring well with being happy; but with regard to what happiness is they differ, and the many do not give the same account as the wise. (*EN* i,4,1095a17–22)

This sense—also referred to above when we spoke about desiring perfect happiness, as far as possible—does not serve Aristotle's immediate purposes in *EN* i, but he does not regard it as completely empty or meaningless. It is what allows a person to be questioned and led to acknowledge that what he *really* wants in life—that is, the happiness that at present he actually seeks—is more than just health or wealth, neither of which is demonstrably not ultimately satisfying.

It is true that such a truly *summum bonum* appears not a little Platonic and that Aristotle criticizes Plato's conception of the ultimate good in the very book of the *Ethics* we are considering. But it is important to be clear about what in Plato Aristotle rejects. He rejects the notion that the *summum bonum* is "something universally present in all cases and single" (1096a27–28; also 1096b25–26), but he does not reject the idea that there *is* a *summum bonum* or even that it is separate. We have already heard him saying that happiness is "a first principle" and that it is that divine thing for the sake of which "we all do everything else" (1102a2–4). He says similar things in book one of the *Eudemian Ethics:* "But the object aimed at as end is best, and the cause of all that comes under it, and first of all goods. This then would be the good *per se,* the end of all human action" (1218b10–12). And in *Metaph.* xii, 10, Aristotle asks how the universe contains "the good or the highest good" (1075a10–11) which all things love (xii,7,1072b3–4): whether it is "as something separate and by itself, or as the order of the parts." He answers: "Probably in both ways, as an army does. For the good is found both in the order and in the leader, and more in the latter; for he does not depend on the order but it depends on him" (1075a13–15). It is clear from these passages that Aristotle does not exclude the existence of a specific and separate *summum bonum.*

III. Good Lives, Bad Lives

Even when a person has an erroneous notion of happiness, and that notion is thematic, it is not necessarily *obvious* that his practical reasoning—or the way he conducts his life—is flawed, that is, that he is pursuing an erroneous path to the truly *summum bonum.* There is a very curious remark that Aristotle makes in the second chapter of the *Eudemian Ethics:*

> First then about these things we must enjoin every one that has the power to live according to his own choice [προαίρεσιν] to set up for himself some object for the good life to aim at (whether honor or reputation or wealth or culture), with reference to which he will then do all his acts, since not to have one's life organized in view of some end is a mark of much folly. (*EE* i,2,1214b6–11)

Aristotle is employing here his own technical (and nonstandard) sense of προαίρεσις (unavoidably translated "choice"), according to which one only makes a προαίρεσις if there is agreement between one's voluntary action and one's overall conception of living well. Any actions performed that do not correspond in this way (as when a man wants to be faithful to his wife but commits adultery out of weakness) are not really choices (or, rather, προαιρέσεις).[17] So Aristotle would be recommending that certain individuals make such a προαίρεσις, whatever their overall conception of the good might be, whether the pursuit of "honor or reputation or wealth or culture."

But could Aristotle really be counseling the positing of less than noble objects for the conduct of lives? Is he really recommending, for example, that someone resolve to do all for the sake of wealth? It is difficult to believe that: it would be incompatible with his belief that happiness is activity of the soul in accordance with virtue. It seems rather that he is making (maladroitly) a methodological point about how the argument of an ethical treatise ought to progress.[18] It is not impossible that he is imagining himself to be—or actually is—in a dialectical or teaching situation in which, in effect, he is saying to his interlocutors: To begin with, fix for yourselves an ultimate end: we will begin from there. That the remark is a methodological one is suggested by the passage's position in the *Eudemian Ethics* as a whole: it comes in the second chapter of the first book, where one expects methodological material. And, indeed, what in this chapter follows the remark about setting up an object for oneself has to do with how one should conduct an investigation ("we must first define to ourselves without hurry or carelessness in which of our belongings the happy life is lodged" [1214b11–13]) in order to get at the "causes of the disputes about happy living" (1214b24–25).

These latter remarks are closely related to remarks in *EE* i,8, where Aristotle criticizes the Platonists, not for positing a *per se* good independent of the other goods sought by things of various natures, but rather for the way that they make their argument:

> But we should show the nature of the good *per se* in the opposite way to that now used. For now from what is not agreed to pos-

sess the good they demonstrate the things admitted to be good, i.e., from numbers they demonstrate that justice and health are goods, for they are arrangements and numbers, and it is assumed that goodness is a property of numbers and units because unity is the good itself. But they ought, from what are admitted to be goods, e.g., health, strength, and temperance, to demonstrate that beauty is present even more in changeless things; for all these are order and rest; but if so, then changeless things are still more beautiful, for they have these attributes still more. (*EE* i,8, 1218a15–24)[19]

His own method, at least in the *Eudemian Ethics,* will be to start with plausible accounts of the *summum bonum* and work from there—that is, work *toward* the top, from which the Platonists begin. Aristotle is not denying the relevance of immaterial and changeless things to the analysis of good and of happiness. Indeed, he is suggesting that there is a way to get them into the discourse—or, perhaps better, for the discourse to get to them—although it is not an easy way.

Aristotle clearly does not think—and is right not to think—that less than perfect ways of organizing one's life are immediately apparent *as* less than perfect. It is true that he probably regards as obvious the inadequacy of (for instance) the life of the bibulous. The latter's thematic or nonthematic conception of the good life would be classed, when beginning the investigation of ethics, among the approaches not worth even considering (*EE* i,3,1214b28–1215a7). Aristotle would probably exclude such lives from consideration on the grounds that they involve incompatibilities among the various parts of the soul, "parts" being conceived in a very loose sense and including patterns of behavior and their attendant desires, the satisfaction of which interferes with the satisfaction of other, more natural desires.[20] But there are more reasonable approaches to life that Aristotle thinks must be included among the phenomena that go into the mix from which is extracted the correct understanding of the moral life (*EE* i,4,1215a25–b5). The man, for instance, whose life is ordered toward the acquisition of honors is not to be dismissed so out of hand. Nor the young man who regards nothing more valuable in life than love (i.e., erotic love). Much less an Eudoxus who, while leading an upright and disciplined life, maintains (quite thematically) that happiness *is* pleasure (*EN* x,2, 1172b9–11). As Aristotle begins his investigation into ethics in the *Eudemian Ethics*—and, in particular, into the nature of the good life—he accepts such approaches as coherent and, therefore, worth examining for their relative merits. Such ways of life are not immediately refutable, even when set beside the best way of life. It is not mere happenstance that human beings with radically different lifestyles live next to each other without one of the lifestyles crumbling because of (obvious) contradiction.

In *EN* x,5, Aristotle mentions that the lives of mere animals are much simpler than those of men: animals always pursue and enjoy the same things. We can hardly imagine a disagreement among dogs, for example, about what to devote themselves primarily to: eating or rolling in the grass, for instance. And even the lives of the most "intelligent" animals, such as dolphins and chimpanzees, are not plagued by disparity between the apparent good and the true good (for dolphins or chimpanzees) (*EN* iii,4,1113a15–b2). But with human beings, things are different: human beings might acquire a variety of "second natures."[21] Like any natures, these secondary ones need to be investigated as phenomena of nature (in the wider sense), each with its own inherent intelligibility.

In a sense, then, Kenny is right: just as one must consider on their own terms individual pieces of practical reasoning, such as do not admit of immediate assessment with respect to the *summum bonum*, so also the investigator of ethics must put on a sort of qualified—or, perhaps better, qualifiable—relativism as he begins his inquiry. Although (as I have argued) Kenny is wrong to suggest that the very positing of an objective universal *summum bonum* is incompatible with the defeasibility of the practical syllogism, he is right to suggest not only that we grasp the logic of the practical syllogism by attending to how it works in its localized context but also that larger units of practical reasoning such as lives—although not all of them—possess a certain sense in their own right. Candace Vogler, in arguing for the notion of the "rationally vicious," points out that even Thomas Aquinas acknowledges that a person might organize his life around a capital sin, such as avarice, which might provide a motive for falsifying accounts and neglecting one's family, or also keeping good accounts and being attentive to one's family, if doing so promises to be profitable.[22] The orderly investigator of ethics knows, as he begins his work, that he is in no position to condemn a life organized around honor, love, or even pleasure (provided the life so chosen is not obviously unsustainable as a good life); his attitude must be rather that of a person who says to himself, "Let us gather all the facts and see how they stack up against each another."[23]

IV. Aristotelian Methodologies

This way of taking into consideration the thought of others—or, at least, of all those who might make a genuine contribution to the resolution of a philosophical issue—although particularly evident in the *Eudemian Ethics,* is very much of a piece with the methodology Aristotle employs elsewhere, in particular, in the *Metaphysics.* That work begins, of course, with a consideration of Aristotle's predecessors' understandings of principles and causes, from which conglomeration of theories he sifts out his own theory of the four causes; and this study of his predecessors is followed (in *Metaph.* iii) by a list of puzzles, most of them involving positions that Aristotle does not hold and which are solved over the course of the larger work.[24] But the place where the logical character of Aristotle's methodology is most apparent is in the crucial shift from the treatise on material substances in books vii–ix to the discussion of immaterial substance in book xii.

It appears now fairly certain that book xii was written with a different context in mind from its present one and possibly as a single freestanding work;[25] indeed, book xii gives the impression of having been "parachuted in" by someone in order to fill a beckoning gap in the argument. But even independently of such accidents of history, Aristotle's immaterial substances come into his larger argument in a way that he believes is compelling—but *not* with the compulsion proper to demonstrations. Immaterial and immobile substances are put forward as explaining the ultimate order of the universe, but not in such a way that someone could not refuse to acknowledge them without forfeiting logical consistency. That sort of refutation is only available when someone has already accepted certain principles and refuses to accept their consequences; but here Aristotle is reaching *toward* the principles (or a principle) that he believes are (is) the best explanation of everything that is. Not accepting such a highest principle cannot draw down upon an interlocutor the opprobrium appropriate to one who refuses to draw or somehow avoids drawing the correct conclusion from scientifically established premises, since such a principle cannot *be* a conclusion of any but a nondemonstrative syllogism.[26]

Aristotle in effect acknowledges this as he sets up the arguments in *Metaph.* vii–ix that will lead (after one apparently out of place book and another containing summaries of arguments found elsewhere) to the gap filled by *Metaph.* xii. He says, that is, in *Metaph.* vi, that "if there is no substance other than those which are formed by nature, natural science will be the first science; but if there is an immovable substance, the science of this must be prior and must be first philosophy, and universal in this way, because it is first" (*Metaph.* vi,1,1026a27–31). But what follows is not, strictly speaking, a demonstration of the existence of immaterial and immovable first principles but rather a complicated exposition of the metaphysics of substance, then potency and actuality, that he believes provides strong reason to believe that immaterial and immovable first principles offer better ultimate explanations of why things are as they are than the first principles of natural science.[27] Near the end of this exposition, that is, in *Metaph.* ix,8, having laid before the reader his basic position—that is to say, having identified the core meaning of substance as form and actuality (1050b1–2) and having claimed that "it is obvious that actuality is prior in substance to potentiality, and as we have said, one actuality always precedes another in time right back to the actuality of the eternal prime mover"—even in that very chapter and with the former words still ringing in the reader's ears, he remarks, "Nor does eternal movement, *if there be such,* exist potentially; and, *if there is an eternal mover,* it is not potentially in motion" (*Metaph.* ix,8,1050b20–21; emphasis added). This is not to say that Aristotle does not believe that he has good arguments for his position, just that he is aware, for instance, that even the meanings of the words *potentiality* and *actuality* used in these arguments do not link up with scientific definitions but depend rather, as he says in *Metaph.* ix,6, upon "seeing the analogy" among types of potency and actuality.[28]

That Aristotle employs this methodology in his ethical writings, and specifically when considering the nature of genuine happiness, is apparent from passages we have already considered. His argument against the Platonists in *EE* i,8 is that they start at the wrong end of the stick, with their supposed numerical first principles;[29] they ought rather to start "from what are admitted to be goods, e.g., health, strength, and temperance, to demonstrate that beauty is present even more in changeless things" (1218a21–22). (The proper direction of the argumentation, one notices, is that of a practical syllogism: not from but toward the major term.) The word behind the translation "demonstrate" in this general passage (1218a15–24, quoted in full above) is δεικνύουσιν (1218a18), which is not the technical term used by Aristotle for a demonstration, which would be ἀπόδειξις (or some form of ἀποδείκνυσθαι). A few lines later, however, Aristotle does use the word ἀπόδειξις but only to say that these Platonists employ a "reckless" or even "deceitful" (παράβολος: 1218a24) demonstration. Such a "demonstration" is faulty since they have no right to talk about such abstract numerical entities—presuming that they exist—as good. They simply assume without argument that they are good and work down from there, applying the goodness of these first principles to the terms below and dependent upon them.

That Aristotle believes that even with arguments the nature of the highest good is not established with *unquestionable* certainty becomes apparent in a remark that comes a couple of lines later: "One should investigate this matter systematically and not assume anything without argument—things that are not easy to be convinced of even *with* argument."[30] The word behind the expression "investigate . . . systematically" is πραγματεύεσθαι. It connotes an organized procedure, certainly, but its meaning is more generic than "to demonstrate" (ἀποδείκνυσθαι). Aristotle has in mind the mounting of a many-faceted argument, with the aim of convincing someone to come over to a different position.

He discusses such matters also a couple of chapters earlier, in *EE* i,6:

> We must try in such matters to get conviction [πίστιν] by means of arguments, employing the phenomena as evidence and examples. It would be best if all men could clearly concur with what we are going to say; but, if that does not happen, then they should all at least concur in *some* way, which they will do if redirected [μεταβιβαζόμενοι—1216b30], for everyone has something of his own to contribute to the truth and, beginning from this, we must offer some sort of proof about these matters. (1216b26–32)

One notices here the word *conviction* (πίστιν), which also (in effect) appears in the remark about its not being easy "to be convinced of [πιστεῦσαι—1218a30]" some things even *with* arguments. The process of "redirecting" referred to here in *EE* i,6 is discussed a couple of times in the *Topics*, where Aristotle insists that it be done not in a contentious manner but in a way that involves argumentation and respectful consideration for the opinions originally brought to an argument.[31]

How then does Aristotle bring a reluctant interlocutor (or reader), whose sights are still fixed on lesser goods, to the understanding that true happiness is found in a life centrally featuring philosophical contemplation, as he concludes in *EN* x,7 (1177a12–18), or that that life is best which "will most produce the contemplation of god," as he concludes in *EE* viii,3 (1249b16–19)? How, that is, does he bring such a person to the realization that the *summum bonum* that the latter actually does desire is quite different from what he thinks it is? His key move in either case is not unlike the move we have just seen him making in the *Metaphysics*. There, having shown that the core of our understanding of even a material substance is form and actuality, he invites his interlocutor simply to kick away (like Wittgenstein's ladder) the incidental conditions of materiality and potentiality and to accept the idea of immaterial substances that are pure act.

In the ethical realm, he invites his interlocutor to acknowledge the fact that he has been pursuing the typically human *conditions* of happiness rather than happiness itself: its core intelligibility or essence. The as yet non-Aristotelian interlocutor has seen that no one who lives in penury and pain is happy—or, in any case, in his pursuit of happiness he would not seek out a similar state *as such*—but he has confused such conditions with what it *means* to be happy. Even if he does not characteristically pursue conditions that are obviously not happiness itself—drinking and dicing and going to shows—but cultivates rather the virtues, he does so because they lead to goods such as honor or reputation or wealth or culture. Aristotle's methodology is not simply to argue that these are means to an end and that as means they cannot constitute happiness itself; his methodology is rather to analyze these means, and the whole realm of human ethics, in a leisurely but systematic way, and to point out at the end that the whole complex makes sense if conceived of as heading toward something that is not a means and, indeed, that cannot be *part* of human life at all, since it necessarily stands at the end point of any piece of practical reasoning and any human pursuit.

He makes remarks to this latter effect in the concluding pages of both the *Eudemian* and the *Nicomachean Ethics*. In the former, he notes that human virtues such as justice and temperance and also their corresponding actions are praised, but the goods at which they ultimately aim are not praised (*EE* viii,3,1248b20–25).[32] In the *Nicomachean Ethics*, he says similarly that it would be strange and tasteless to praise (φορτικὸς ὁ ἔπαινος—1178b16) the gods since their activity, or that type of activity, is what we *aim* at; we praise men in so far as they perform actions that would bring them *to* that state.[33] His point is not that the calm and serene lives of the gods is irrelevant to the life of human beings but rather that they provide its defining focal point. Because man is a composite being (σύνθετον), a state of pure and constant contemplation is impossible for him (*EN* x,7,1177b28–29; also *EE* viii,3,1249b10); but what capacity he does have for that divine life is what distinguishes him from other animals and determines, therefore, his definition and essence. Anyone who locates his "existence" (to recall *EN* ix,12,1172a1–2) in drinking or dicing or going to shows is not doing what he was made to do.

That this is the general structure of (at least) the *Eudemian Ethics* is indicated in its final chapter, in which Aristotle claims in effect to have completed the task he set for himself long before, in *EE* i,2 (the chapter in which he speaks rather strangely about each man's positing "some object for the good life to aim at" [1214b7–8], whether it be honor or wealth or whatever). That introductory and methodology-laden chapter contains a prediction about where this itinerary will lead: "some regard as parts of happiness what are merely its indispensable conditions" (1214b26–27). In the final chapter of the work, Aristotle says that the man who "thinks he ought to have the excellences [ἀρετὰς] for the sake of external goods does deeds that are noble only *per accidens*" (*EE* viii,3,1249a14–16). His deeds are only noble *per accidens* because he does not see that the terms of his practical syllogism are out of order: virtue is regarded as a means to the major term (honor or wealth or whatever), whereas it ought to be the major term or end sought.

V. Conclusion

To sum up, then, although Aristotle (followed by Thomas Aquinas) has very specific ideas about the *summum bonum* (i.e., the end that ultimately makes sense of all practical reasoning), this specificity has no negative effect upon the defeasibility of the practical syllogism, since defeasibility pertains not to ends but to alternative ways of getting to ends (such as the *summum bonum*). And, in any case, the notion that a fully satisfying *summum bonum* would negatively affect defeasibility presupposes that the ultimate major term in a piece of practical reasoning is thematic, that is, fully specified in the mind of the person acting or considering action. In fact, the major term is rarely thematic, although this does not entail that the person is not seeking the *summum bonum*.

But even when a person has a thematic and erroneous notion of happiness, it is not necessarily *obvious*—either to himself or to an objective observer—that his way of life is flawed and that he is pursuing an erroneous path to the truly *summum bonum*. Acknowledgment of this fact is an essential presupposition of Aristotle's ethical methodology, which is not unlike the methodology he employs in the *Metaphysics*. It is true that in both of his major ethical works, the *Eudemian* and the *Nicomachean Ethics*, he presents strong arguments for understanding the *summum bonum* (sought also by those who are thematically in error about its nature) as he understands it. But he does not claim to be putting forward a demonstration (or demonstrations) in the strict sense.

This, I might add, makes a good deal of sense in discourse of this sort—discourse, that is, about what the *summum bonum* is and how we should lead our lives. Although the occasional self-intoxicated

philosopher will claim that it has been demonstrated that there is
no God or that the human soul in its entirety dies with the body or
that there is no single *summum bonum*, such vital issues are decided
in most people's minds—whether philosophers or not—by social factors: winks and nudges and nods suggesting that it is acceptable or not
to espouse a particular thesis. Even good methodology at this level
proceeds in a way not unrelated to this, although it does involve effective argumentation. It puts forward arguments not as *unquestionable*
but as sound reasonings suggesting that an interlocutor ought to
change his mind. Such suggestions might also imply criticism of the
interlocutor, should he fail to come over to the position held before
him—although the methodology itself presupposes that the position
he is coming from, and being urged to abandon, enjoys a certain re-
spectability in its own right.

Notes

My thanks to Fr. Stephen Brock for his helpful comments on an earlier version of this essay and to Alasdair MacIntyre for conversations on related
themes.

1. See *EN* iii,3,1112b15–20; also *MA* vii,701a17–20: "I need a covering, a
coat is a covering: I need a coat. What I need I ought to make, I need a coat: I
make a coat. And the conclusion 'I must make a coat' is an action." In this
essay, for translations of Aristotle I make use of the Revised Oxford Translation (Jonathan Barnes, ed., *The Complete Works of Aristotle: The Revised Oxford Translation* [Princeton, NJ: Princeton University Press,1984]), occasionally making adjustments. Abbreviations for works by Plato and Aristotle are
taken from the list of abbreviations found at the beginning of any edition of
H. G. Liddell and R. Scott, *A Greek-English Lexicon*.

2. Anthony Kenny, *Will, Freedom and Power* (Oxford: Blackwell,
1975), 91–92. See also Kevin L. Flannery, *Acts Amid Precepts: The Aristotelian Logical Structure of Thomas Aquinas's Moral Theory* (Washington,
DC: Catholic University of America Press; Edinburgh: T & T Clark, 2001),
8–12.

3. Kenny, *Will, Freedom and Power*, 93. Although the translation of εὐδαιμονία as "happiness" (or εὐδαίμων as "happy") is notoriously inadequate, I stick with it for (an equally notorious) want of a satisfactory alternative.

4. Ibid., 94.

5. Ibid., 82.

6. Ibid., 93.

7. *EN* iii,3,1112b11–20.

8. See Thomas Aquinas, *Summa Theologiae* (*ST*)1-2.14.2c. See also *ST* 1-2.14.6c, where Thomas notes that deliberation *(consilium)* cannot be infinite but is bounded at one end by "the end, about which there is no deliberation, but which is presupposed in deliberation as a principle" and at the other by "that which is immediately in our power to do." It is apparent in the same article that Thomas is aware of the defeasibility of practical reasoning. An objector argues, "Under the enquiry of deliberation falls not only what is to be done but also how to remove impediments. But any human action can be impeded, and the impediment can be removed by some human reasoning. Therefore, the search for impediments to remove will remain into infinity." In his response, Thomas does deny that deliberation is infinite (i.e., potentially infinite), but he insists that, practically speaking, it must come to an end: "Although a human action can be impeded, there is not always an impediment present *(non tamen semper habet impedimentum paratum)*. And, therefore, it is not always necessary to deliberate regarding an impediment to be removed" (*ST* 1-2.14.6 ad 2). I am grateful to Stephen Brock for pointing me to these texts.

9. I mean this in the sense—derived from the Greek words θέμα (proposition) and/or τιθέναι (to place)—of an idea that is explicitly formulated at least in the mind: posited or put into a proposition. At *ST* 1.1.6 ad 3, Thomas Aquinas appears to have in mind the distinction between thematic and nonthematic knowledge of the good; there he says that the wise man might make wise judgments in two ways: either *per modum inclinationis* (and he cites Aristotle's *EN* x,5,1176a17–19) or *per modum cognitionis*.

10. *EN* i,12,1102a2–4. See also *EE* ii,1,1219b11–16. This and other passages related to the means/end relationship are discussed in René-Antoine Gauthier and Jean Yves Jolif, *L'Éthique a Nicomaque: Introduction, traduction et commentaire* (Louvain-la-neuve: Éditions Peeters, 2002), II,2 863.

11. See *EN* i,6,1096a17–29 and 1096b26–29. In the first of these passages, Aristotle is speaking primarily of the way that the categories are ordered, and that is according to a πρὸς ἕν (toward one) relationship (see

Metaph. iv,2,1003b5–7). In the second passage, where he has in mind the relationship among types of goods, which in turn correspond to the various categories, Aristotle prefers to speak of analogy (ἢ μᾶλλον κατ᾽ ἀναλογίαν). It is apparent in this second passage that he regards πρὸς ἕν relationships as belonging to the same general class of relationships as analogical ones. See also *EE* i,8,1217b16–35, 1218a1–15. Michael Woods says of 1218a1–15, "This passage stresses that there is no common Form which is, in addition, *separate* from things that are serially ordered [his emphasis]. There is no suggestion that all things serially ordered lack a common character" (Michael Woods, *Aristotle: 'Eudemian Ethics,' Books I, II and VIII*, 2nd ed. [Oxford: Clarendon Press, 1992], 71). In lines 1218a1–2, it is clear that the problem is a common element that is *also* separate: οὐκ ἔστι κοινόν τι παρὰ ταῦτα, καὶ τοῦτο χωριστόν. Since the two passages (*EN* i,6 and *EE* i,8) are clearly parallel, the point can be applied to the argument in *EN* i,6 (but cp. Woods, *Aristotle*, 71).

12. Aristotle holds too that one should prefer the calmer pleasures corresponding to the higher activities (*EN* x,5,1175b24–1176a3), activities being ranked, like the categories, hierarchically (*EN* i,6,1096a19–22).

13. The phrase translated here as "like an adventitious charm" is ὥσπερ περιάπτου τινός (1099a16). A περίαπτος is anything, such as a necklace, which is "hung around" a person; it lies *on top* of the person.

14. *EN* x,4,1174b31–33; enlightening on this is Thomas Aquinas, *In decem ethicorum Aristotelis ad Nicomachum expositio*, ed. A. M. Pirotta (Turin: Marietti, 1934), par. 2030–31.

15. *EN* x,4,1175a18–21. One notices that Aristotle has in this passage with little ado slipped from talk of individual pleasures to talk of the pleasure of "life."

16. *EN* ix,12,1172a1–8. The Revised Oxford Translation reads ὡς οἷόν τε for οἷς οἴονται συζῆν in line 1172a8. But, although there is MS support for ὡς οἷόν τε, there is none for cutting out συζῆν. So I have kept οἷς οἴονται and adopted Bekker's suggestion of εὖ ζῆν for συζῆν.

17. See G. E. M. Anscombe, "Thought and Action in Aristotle: What Is Practical Truth?" in *From Parmenides to Wittgenstein* (Minneapolis: University of Minnesota Press; Oxford: Basil Blackwell, 1981), vol. 1 of *Collected Philosophical Papers*, 66–77; see also Kevin L. Flannery, "Anscombe and Aristotle on Corrupt Minds," *Christian Bioethics* 14 (2008): 151–64.

18. Regarding method in ethics, I have learned most from the following: Jonathan Barnes, "Aristotle and the Method of Ethics," *Revue internationale de philosophie* 34 (1980): 490–511; Terence Irwin, "Aristotle's Method

of Ethics," in *Studies in Aristotle*, ed. Dominic J. O'Meara (Washington, DC: Catholic University of America Press, 1981), 193–223; Enrico Berti, *Le Ragioni di Aristotele* (Roma-Bari: Laterza, 1989); Marco Zingano, "Aristotle and the Problems of Method in Ethics," *Oxford Studies in Ancient Philosophy* 32 (2007): 297–330.

19. On the object of Aristotle's criticism in this passage—Plato's "unwritten doctrines"? Xenocrates?—see especially Jacques Brunschwig, "EE I 8, 1218a15–32 et le περὶ Τἀγαθοῦ," *Untersuchungen zur* Eudemischen Ethik: *Akten des 5. Symposiums Aristotelicum (Oosterbeek, Niederlande, 21–29. August 1969)*, ed. Paul Moraux and Dieter Harlfinger (Berlin: De Gruyter, 1971), passim; also Woods, *Aristotle,* 74–77.

20. Showing that these would be Aristotle's grounds for excluding such conceptions of the good life would involve a lengthy argument, for which there is not space here. I intend to set out the argument elsewhere; it concerns *EE* vii,6 and *EN* ix,4.

21. One does not actually find in Aristotle's writings the expression "second nature." The *idea,* however, is found in a number of places, such as *EN* i,10,1100b11–17; ii,6,1106b14–16 (ὥσπερ καὶ ἡ φύσις). These remarks are made with reference to virtuous activity, but they might apply just as easily to nonvirtuous (or "less than perfectly virtuous") activity.

22. Candace Vogler, *Reasonably Vicious* (Cambridge, MA: Harvard University Press, 2002), 68–69. Vogler quotes *De malo,* q. 13, a. 3. (See Thomas Aquinas, *Quaestiones disputatae de malo* [Rome/Paris: Commissio Leonina/Librairie Philosophique J. Vrin, 1982], vol. 23 of *Opera Omnia* 252, lines 24–51.)

23. "What is needed is an argument that both gives us in the end the most likely views regarding these matters and also resolves the difficulties and contradictions. And this will come about if the contrary views are disclosed as reasonable. Such an argument will be most in accord with the phenomena. The contradictions will be left standing, if what is said is true in one sense, not true in another" (*EE* vii,2,1235b13–18).

24. For a list of the the puzzles and where they are solved, see Wilfred D. Ross, *Aristotle's* Metaphysics: *A Revised Text with Introduction and Commentary,* 2nd ed. (Oxford: Clarendon Press, 1953), I, 222–23.

25. See Michael Frede and David Charles, eds., *Aristotle's* Metaphysics Lambda: *Symposium aristotelicum* (Oxford: Clarendon Press, 2000), 1–5; also Enrico Berti, "Il libro *lambda* della *Metafisica* di Aristotele tra fisica e metafisica," in *Nuovi studi aristotelici: II - Fisica, antropologia, metafisica,* ed. Enrico Berti (Brescia: Morcelliana, 2005), 471–87.

26. See *APo.* i,13,78a22–b4.

27. At *Metaph.* xii,6,1071b12–22, however, there does appear to be a proof of the existence of an eternal mover whose substance is actuality.

28. οὐ δεῖ παντὸς ὅρον ζητεῖν ἀλλὰ καὶ τὸ ἀνάλογον συνορᾶν, ὅτι ὡς τὸ οἰκοδομοῦν πρὸς τὸ οἰκοδομικόν, καὶ τὸ ἐγρηγορὸς πρὸς τὸ καθεῦδον, κτλ (*Metaph.* ix,6,1048a36–b4).

29. On the identification of these Platonists, see above, note 19.

30. δεῖ δὲ περὶ τούτου πραγματευθῆναι, καὶ μὴ ἀξιοῦν μηθὲν ἀλόγως, ἃ καὶ μετὰ λόγου πιστεῦσαι οὐ ῥᾴδιον (*EE* i,8,1218a28–30). (This is my own translation, not what appears in the Revised Oxford Translation.)

31. See *Top.* i,2,101a32–34 (ἐκ τῶν οἰκείων δογμάτων ὁμιλήσομεν πρὸς αὐτούς, μεταβιβάζοντες ὅ τι ἂν μὴ καλῶς φαίνωνται λέγειν ἡμῖν); also viii,11,161a33–37. The former passage has linguistic similarities to *EE* i,6,1216b30–32. See also Plato's *Lg.* v,736D3–4, where the emphasis is on how slow the process is and how short the individual steps along the way.

32. *EE* viii,3,1248b16–26 is a complicated and obscure passage (see Donald J. Allan, "The Fine and the Good in the *Eudemian Ethics*," in *Untersuchungen zur* Eudemischen Ethik: *Akten des 5. Symposiums Aristotelicum [Oosterbeek, Niederlande, 21–29. August 1969]*, ed. Paul Moraux and Dieter Harlfinger [Berlin: De Gruyter, 1971], 63–72), but a few things are apparent: Aristotle is saying that some things are praised (ἐπαινετά), some things not, and that noble actions are among the former, *health* among the latter (1248b23). Why in this context should Aristotle be concerned with health rather than a nobler end such as ultimate happiness? (In fact, he goes on in the same chapter to speak of the contemplation of God as the best pursuit.) I believe it is simply because health is his standard example of an end and he knew that his audience would have understood what he was driving at. At *EE* i,7,1217a35–40, he draws an explicit connection between health (as an end) and happiness (εὐδαιμονία).

33. *EN* x,8,1178b7–23. We have already seen Aristotle making such remarks in *EN* i,12 and *EE* ii,1; see above, note 10.

CHAPTER 8 | # The Foundation of Human
Rights and Canon Law

John J. Coughlin, O.F.M.

The increasing recognition of human rights in
state and international systems of law constituted one of the most significant legal developments of the twentieth century. However, even as
this development continues to mature in the legal theory and practice
of the twenty-first century, disagreement persists about the moral
foundation of human rights. Alasdair MacIntyre writes about some
of the intractable moral disagreements which have characterized
philosophical discourse since the Enlightenment, especially among
Thomists, Kantians, and utilitarians. What MacIntyre describes from
a more general perspective is consistent with the lack of agreement
about the foundation of human rights. Indeed, this lack of agreement
seems to be a subset of the fifth major type of disagreement identified
by MacIntyre, which concerns rival conceptions of justice. During the
twentieth century, the Catholic Church assumed a voice in the discussion about the foundation of human rights. The Church has suggested

that both natural law and Christian theology serve as complementary grounds on which to secure human rights language.

Despite the growing influence of positivistic approaches to law which attempt to separate law from moral value, the Catholic Church has observed that the only stable foundation for the normativity of human rights law remains the dignity of the human person. In Pope Benedict XVI's words:

> [I]nternational discussions often seem marked by a relative logic which would consider as the sole guarantee of peaceful coexistence between peoples a refusal to admit *the truth about man and his dignity*, to say nothing of the possibility of an ethics based on the recognition of the natural moral law. This has led in effect to the imposition of a notion of law and politics which ultimately makes consensus between states—a consensus conditioned at times by short-term interests or manipulated by ideological pressure—the only real basis of international norms. The bitter fruits of this relativistic logic are sadly evident: we think, for example, of the attempt to consider as human rights the consequences of certain self-centered lifestyles; a lack of concern for the economic and social needs of the poorer nations; contempt for humanitarian law; and a selective defense of human rights.[1]

In drawing attention to the human person as the foundation of human rights, Pope Benedict's words are an affirmation of what Pope John Paul II referred to as the anthropological basis of law.[2]

Absent the anthropological basis, I believe that human rights are endangered in several ways. First, human rights that are dependent on a positivistic approach to law may be subordinated to the interests of state or party. In this regard, it should not be forgotten that human rights language originated in the context of modern Western legal systems. While the historical origins of human rights language remains complex, a watershed in its development may be traced to the 1776

Virginia Bill of Rights, which served as a prototype for the adoption of the Bill of Rights or the first ten amendments to the United States Constitution. Almost simultaneously, the language of human rights surfaced as an aspect of the legal theory of the French Revolution. Several centuries later, in 1948, this development culminated in the adoption of the Universal Declaration of Human Rights by the United Nations.[3] The language of human rights also served as a catalyst for the events of 1989 in Eastern Europe during which a peaceful revolution toppled an oppressive totalitarian system of government. As contemporary issues such as war, poverty, abortion, capital punishment, euthanasia, and torture—to name a few—demonstrate, mere positive law itself fails to guarantee that the nation-states of the Western world always act in accord with human rights.

Second, non-Western nations sometimes repudiate human rights precisely because their historical origin is particular to the West. In a *New York Times* op-ed, John L. Allen Jr., comments, "From China to Iran to Zimbabwe, it's common for authoritarian regimes to argue that rights like freedom of the press, religion and dissent represent Western—or even Anglo-American—traditions. If human rights are to be protected in a 21st century increasingly shaped by non-Western actors like China and the so-called Shiite axis from Lebanon to central Asia, then a belief in objective truth grounded in a universal human nature is critical."[4] The Church suggests that the normativity of human rights depends not on the particularity of their historical origin in Western modernity but on one universal human nature.

Third, without an objective moral foundation, human rights law could fall into disrepute. When human rights are subordinated to ideological interests based on reasons of state or party, employed to safeguard particular interests and privileges, manipulated as a publicity weapon without regard to individual dignity and the common good, skepticism about human rights language can only increase. Skepticism about natural law and religious belief is a hallmark of modernity. One of the consequences of modern skepticism renders it difficult, if not impossible, to establish an objective foundation for law in general and human rights law specifically. Again, in the Church's view, the antidote to this poisoning of the atmosphere which can sustain human rights is an appeal to a correct understanding of human nature and the human situation.

In this brief essay, I shall discuss the foundation of human rights from the perspectives of natural law, theology, and historical consciousness which are aspects of the methodology of canon law. First, in reference to MacIntyre's essay, I shall depict the objective foundation of human rights with regard to practical reason and free will, which are understood in the tradition of canon law as characteristics of human nature. At the outset, I want to point out that I am simply trying to sketch in broad strokes the anthropology of canon law. This is obviously intended neither as an exhaustive discussion of the traditional understanding of the human person which is drawn from Thomistic thought nor as an account of the many subsequent objections to the traditional understanding. Second, I shall describe the complementary foundation of human rights which may be derived from theology. In this section of this essay, I shall draw principally on the thought of Walter Cardinal Kasper, and I shall comment on the relationship between natural law and theology in terms of the foundation for human rights. Third, I shall attempt to portray the inner dialectic in canonical methodology between the transcendent and historical. The development of canonical equity illustrates the unity of natural law and theology through the proper function of historical consciousness. I shall suggest that canon law's receptivity to human rights also reflects this integration of the transcendent and historical.

Although now enjoying a record of pronouncements in defense of human rights, the Church initially expressed reticence about human rights language as it emerged from Enlightenment thought. While the seeds of human rights law may arguably be detected in the dignity of the human person recognized by the medieval canonists, it was not until the promulgation of the 1983 Code of Canon Law by

Pope John Paul II that canon law adopted an expressed list of human rights such as those embraced at earlier times by many nation-states and the United Nations. The foundation of human rights in canon law depends on a methodology that draws on natural law, theology, and historical consciousness. Given the limits of this essay, my focus is on the theory and methodology of canon law rather than specific canons and their practical application to concrete issues. This focus is also a result of my view that theory and method have the most to contribute to the discussion about the foundation of human rights. It is not intended to detract from the fact that the Church's credibility in the discussion depends at least in part on the extent to which human rights are safeguarded within the ecclesiastical community by the application of canon law. In the words of John Paul II, "[T]he task of the Church and her historic merit, which is to proclaim and defend in every place and in every age the fundamental human rights, does not exempt her but, on the contrary, obliges her to be herself a *mirror of justice (speculum iustitiae)* for the world."[5]

I. Natural Law and Human Rights

Canon law governs the Catholic Church, which from her origins remains a community based upon faith. Consequently, one might be tempted to conclude that canon law's contribution to the discussion about the foundation of human rights would be exclusively theological. This temptation might be bolstered by a strong argument that has been advanced in favor of religious values and language as the ground of human rights.[6] To yield to such a temptation, however, would be to underestimate that role which natural law plays as an element in the methodology of canon law. Perhaps the primary contribution of canon law to the discussion about human rights derives from the methodological principle that calls for reflection on human nature. During the course of its long historical development, canon law has adhered to the principle that human nature itself contains the foundation of law. Canon law assumes certain characteristics as essential to what it means to be a human person. In the classical anthropology systematically expressed in the work of St. Thomas Aquinas, the human person is understood as a dynamic unity of body and soul. The soul of the human person is endowed with reason in the intellect and freedom in the will. In accord with the classical anthropology, permit me to list several characteristics of the human soul which form the foundation of law.

First, a characteristic of the intellect is the human person's love for truth.[7] Ultimately, only truth can satisfy the intellect. In MacIntyre's words, "a more adequate understanding in respect of truth is always to be preferred to a less adequate, no matter how profitable it may be to remain with the less adequate or how painful it may be to exchange it for the more adequate."[8] This commitment to truth through the use of reason is precisely what forms the basis of scientific method. Even scientific method, however, must itself be open to inquiry about truth which sets limits on what science and technology can achieve, and how they offer at best significant but only partial accounts of the truth about the human good in particular circumstances or considered from the perspective of the ultimate end of the human person. The skepticism of scientific method ought not to be so absolute and pervasive as to result in an epistemological pessimism that eviscerates the law of the possibility for a deep moral foundation.

Second, reflection upon, evaluation of, and judgment about a specific course of action in light of the end of the human person exemplify practical reason.[9] Practical reason is reason for choice and action. It presumes an epistemological optimism through which the human agent is able to know the good upon which a particular choice is based. According to MacIntyre, practical reason, as with scientific method, depends on a certain disinterest which permits us "to distance ourselves from those particular material and psychological interests that are always apt to find expression in those partialities and prejudices that are nourished by our desires for pleasure, money, and power."[10] MacIntyre thus attributes to practical reason "a form of intellectual and moral asceticism."[11]

Third, such asceticism involves the work of the human will. It means putting aside self-interest to the extent that self-interest threatens to harm the fundamental well-being of the other. The practical reason of natural law recognizes "precepts that forbid us to endanger gratuitously each other's life, liberty, or property."[12] In accord with the classical Thomistic anthropological perspective, the will possesses the capacity to enter a lifelong commitment to certain negative laws that "forbid us ever to take innocent human lives, to inflict other kinds of bodily harm on the innocent, and to respect the legitimate property of others."[13] Intellectual and moral asceticism opens the way for the recognition of the principle that all human rights ultimately depend on the most basic natural right, the right to life. Moreover, the human will is able to act in accord with a commitment "to no deceptive or intentionally misleading speech."[14] Such a commitment on the part of the will is not only a necessary precondition for the orderly progression of rational inquiry; it is also essential to the trust between persons interested in enquiry that leads to the truth about the human good. As the human intellect is satisfied only by truth, the human will flourishes to the extent that it acts freely to trust others.[15] The asceticism embraced by the will is also not a solitary endeavor. Rather, it recognizes the inherently social nature of the human person whose *eudaimonia* or *beatitudo* depends upon relationships of trust with other individuals and the exercise of freedom as a participating member of communities and society.[16]

MacIntyre recognizes that the above described anthropological characteristics are "universal in their scope," "exceptionless," and "the same for everyone."[17] In other words, the anthropological characteristics claim objectivity. They presume one universal human nature shared by all human beings without regard to time, place, or subjective experience. Although the anthropological objectivity does not of itself require the recognition of specific legal norms, it offers the moral foundation upon which specific legal norms respecting human rights may be built. The anthropological characteristics are consistent with the following elements of natural law: (1) a universal human nature shared by each human being regardless of time, place, or circumstance; (2) the intellect's capacity for practical reason committed to the disinterested search for the truth; (3) the will's freedom to act for the good and the potential to trust; (4) the social nature of human persons for whom participation and solidarity in communities are necessary to flourishing; and (5) respect for the life, liberty, and property of others.

Faithful to its natural law underpinning, canonical methodology aims to ensure that practical reason rather than power forms the moral basis of the law. In the words of Aquinas, law is first and foremost "an ordinance of reason."[18] As MacIntyre indicates, the commitment to practical reason contrasts with systems of law that rely upon "inherited patterns of authority endowed with nonrational legitimacy or on some implicit or explicit social contract whereby individuals and groups, each trying to maximize their own advantage, arrive at some arrangement about allocations of costs and benefits."[19] The problem with all such alternative justifications for law is that "inequalities of power determine" what the law ordains for individuals, communities, and the larger society that the law is designed to regulate.[20] On account of its commitment to practical reason, canon law thus exemplifies a system of law underpinned by a reliable, nontheological, objective foundation. For the reasons that I described above, human rights law would be well served by this anthropological foundation.

II. The Theological Foundation of Human Rights

In the ongoing dialogue about the foundation for human rights, natural law offers the advantage that does it does not depend upon divine revelation for its authority. With broad strokes, I have just attempted to suggest that the authority of natural law derives from an account of the human person whose soul enjoys both the capacity for reason in the intellect and the capacity for freedom in the will. At the same time, canon law remains a system of religious law, and as such, it also draws on theological fonts. In this regard, the methodology of canon law embraces a unity of law and theology. As Eugenio Corecco has observed, the ultimate end of canonical methodology is not simply that of guaranteeing the common good based on practical reason, but of realizing *communio*. This *nova lex evangelii* aims to set the conditions in which the members of the ecclesiastical community are enabled to live a life based on the salvific message of gospel love.[21] Consistent with the unity of law and theology, canon law exemplifies a legal system in which reason and faith serve as complementary, and not exclusive, fonts of law.

Just as natural law corresponds to a certain anthropological perspective, canon law's unity of law and theology reflects a theological anthropology. Cardinal Kasper insightfully posits that theological anthropology affords a foundation for human rights.[22] The theological anthropology follows a biblical narrative starting with the creation of the human person in the *imago Dei*. The fundamental dignity of the human person was damaged but not completely destroyed by original sin. As Kasper puts it, "For even sinners, even the worst criminals, still have a claim to the respect of their fundamental rights as human persons. For example, they have the right not to be subject to degrading punishment, such as torture."[23] The biblical narrative proceeds to "the person of Jesus Christ, in whom God once and for all took on everything human and so bestowed a unique dignity on human beings."[24] To complement the Christological dignity bestowed on human nature through the Incarnation, Kasper highlights the personalist perspective expressed at Vatican II that Christ "has united himself with each man."[25] The dignity of the human person is further enhanced by a pneumatological one. The Holy Spirit gives dignity to the new person as one who enjoys the freedom of the children of God. To cite Kasper:

"For in Jesus Christ, all the natural differences that exist within humankind disappear, their self-alienating and discriminating character
is eliminated. There is neither Jew nor Greek, there is neither slave nor
free, there is neither male nor female (Gal. 3:28; 1 Cor. 12:13; Col. 3:11).
To this universal dignity of the children of God all women and men
are called."[26] Finally, the biblical narrative anticipates the consumma-
tion of time in which the vision of God's ultimate justice yet to come
serves as the incentive to work for justice in the here and now. Theological anthropology, with its commitment to individual human dignity, thus offers a firm foundation for human rights.

The anthropological perspectives of natural law and biblical
theology are intended as complementary and reinforcing. However,
Kasper believes that theological anthropology offers a better foundation for human rights than does that offered by natural law, for two
reasons. First, Kasper states that the theological foundation is advanta-
geous from an ecumenical point of view. It permits a common stance
not limited to Catholic natural law theory but open to all Christians.
Second, Kasper states, "[W]e Christians cannot counter the threat to
humanity merely by an appeal to a minimal consensus founded in
natural law. We must respond with all the concrete fullness and the
concentrated strength of our Christian faith, and mobilize all its forces
against the powers of injustice, violence, and death."[27] In canon law,
the theological and natural law foundations are part of a methodology
in which they admit no inherent opposition to one another. The scholastic maxim holds that grace builds on nature in order to perfect,
not to destroy, it. According to Kasper, since Vatican II the theological
foundation has increasingly taken precedence over the natural law argument in the Church.

Without in any way detracting from Kasper's important contribution to the discussion about human rights, one might question the
precedence of the theological over the natural law approach. Given the
broader global context in which the search for an objective and universally acceptable foundation for human rights now occurs, does the

natural law foundation enjoy a more comprehensive intellectual appeal than one based on Christian theology? The natural law foundation, with its appeal to an anthropological perspective not dependent on Christian revelation, has the potential to transcend religious differences in the pluralistic context of the present discussion about the foundation for human rights. Certainly, Christians remain free to bolster their efforts on behalf of human rights with the fullness of conviction that derives from faith. The Catholic tradition has developed in such a way that faith and reason are considered not to be in opposition but rather to reinforce each other.[28] The Catholic integration might certainly serve as an example for people of other faiths who seek to bring deeply held religious beliefs to bear on the discussion of human rights. However, commitment to human rights does not depend on faith, and for this reason, the natural law argument made on the basis of practical reason has the potential for universal appeal. In the global and pluralistic context of the contemporary discussion, this seems to me an indispensable characteristic of an objective moral foundation for human rights. This is clear when canon law is considered from the perspective of comparative legal study. In contrast to secular systems of law that have increasingly tended to adopt a positivistic approach which purports to separate law from morality, canon law serves as a counterexample of a system of law developed upon practical reason as an objective moral foundation. This in no way diminishes the significance of the complementary and powerful foundation of human rights offered by Christian theology.

III. Canonical Method, Historical Consciousness, and Human Rights

The anthropology of canon law drawn from natural law and theology facilitates the incorporation of transcendent truths about the human person into the law. This classical approach to law contrasts with the modern view that few if any immutable truths about the human person continue through history. The modern doctrine of historicity led to the conclusion that law does not rest on timeless truths but rather reflects cultural, economic, and temporal circumstances. In the words of Hegel, the modern doctrine rejects the classical approach as based upon "a heavenly truth alone, a Beyond."[29] However, the methodology of canon law may be described as consisting of a dialectic between the transcendent and historical.

In this final section of the essay, I shall discuss the methodology developed by the medieval canonists, illustrate it with the notion of canonical equity, and then suggest that the incorporation of an expressed list of fundamental rights into canon law is a more recent illustration of the enduring heritage of canonical methodology. Finally, I shall discuss the relation between the historicity and the objectivity of canon law.

The Methodology of the Medieval Canonists

Although canon law did not develop into a system of law until the eleventh century, the Church from its very origins has experienced the need for an order based upon the good of individuals and the community. The Christian Scriptures themselves, as well as the canons promulgated by several early Church councils, contain ample evidence of this necessity. In the third quarter of the eleventh century, the rediscovery of legal documents compiled under Emperor Justinian during the sixth century afforded the medieval canonist with a wealth of substantive and procedural provisions that led to a renaissance in the study of law. The rebirth of the law was evident at the emerging medieval universities in places such as Paris, Bologna, and Oxford. Harold Berman described the renaissance in law as a "papal revolution" which would lay the foundation for Western legal concepts up until the present day.[30] Whether or not papal revolution is the proper terminology, there can be no question that something new and dynamic emerged in the canonical methodology. The methodology continues to have enduring effects for the Church both *ad intra,* as it relates to canon law, and *ad extra,* in what canon law might contribute to the ongoing contemporary dialogue about human rights and their deeper philosophical foundation.

Gratian's *Decretum* exemplified the methodology of the medieval canonists. Consisting of more than 3,800 legal texts, the *Decretum* contained religious and secular legal provisions drawn from early Church sources and from those of the secular jurists of classical antiquity. Not merely a vast collection, the *Decretum* represents a methodology that attempted reconciliation among contradictory provisions, offered generalization while admitting exceptions, and recognized distinct disciplines within the field of law. The methodology also distinguished between divine, natural, and positive law. In this regard, it recognized the *ius gentium* as a law distinct from the positive law but in accord with the precepts of natural law as applicable to all persons and nations. The *Decretum*'s methodology discerned law that reflected immutable principles, as well as law shaped in response to particular historical circumstances of time, place, persons, and communities. Commenting on the methodology of the medieval canonists, Richard Helmholz has observed, "Whether one looks at their ability in mastering the relevant authorities, their proficiency in reasoning by analogy, their skill in analyzing precedents, their talent in drawing legal distinctions, or their energy in working through a large body of law, the canonists seem scarcely inferior to modern lawyers."[31]

Canonical Equity

The notion of equity was of particular importance to the medieval canonists. In the *Decretum* equity is linked with the practical reasonableness of natural law:

> Natural law is that which all nations share in common, by the very fact that it derives from the universal instinct of the human person, and not from any constitution; such is the union of man

and woman; the rights of succession and the education of children; . . . the freedom of one to possess and acquire those things which are taken from the sky, land, and sea; the disposing or returning of money which has been entrusted to someone; and the forceful repelling of violence. . . . [F]or all these things are never unjust, nor is anything similar to them unjust. Such are considered natural and equitable.[32]

The *Decretum* also recognized that rigor of the law could be tempered by evangelical mercy:

Love of one's enemies and mercy towards one's neighbors is an evangelical precept. . . . We command that love for one's enemies and having mercy on them is necessary; . . . that each one bear the burdens of others so that we do not become pertinacious and not persist in evil with impunity. We are not to be severe towards penitents, but we have been advised to be merciful. . . . Judge him without mercy who does not show mercy. . . . We have been ordered to be merciful. In the Church, when anyone is to be shown great mercy, he should also show a strong form of justice. . . . Man as man is to be shown mercy. . . . [T]he Bishop ruling his flock[,] . . . . the judge ruling his province, the king ruling his people . . . are not to help sinners because they are sinners, but . . . are to show human consideration to them because they are human.[33]

The methodology flowered in the thought of John of Ostia, who described equity as "justice tempered by sweet mercy."[34] For the medieval canonists, equity reflected a methodology that attempted to assimilate immutable principles of divine and natural law with historical circumstances. The canonical methodology underpinned the law with a moral objectivity while permitting it to develop in accord with historical circumstances. Both the objectivity and the historicity may be described as rooted in an anthropological perspective that posited a universal human nature even as it recognized specific circumstances of persons and communities.

Fundamental Rights in Canon Law

The historical consciousness of canonical methodology plays an important part in the recognition of the legitimacy of human rights. Although natural law and theology are now understood by the Church to offer an objective moral foundation for human rights, it must be acknowledged that the Church itself initially expressed reticence about the recognition of human rights. As I mentioned, human rights language in its modern manifestation first appeared in the secular context of Enlightenment thought. As the Pontifical Commission for Justice and Peace has recognized, several popes, including Pius VI, Gregory XVI, and Pius IX, were critical, and even hostile, to the modern development of human rights language.[35] The Church's initial hostility must be understood in the context of the anticlerical and secular character that often marked the emergence of modernity. As Kasper observes, it "led the Church to adopt a dubious defensive stance and pushed it into a dangerous isolation."[36] Despite the historical circumstances which occasioned the Church's initial reticence, the fundamental goals of human rights language and their objective foundation in the dignity of the human person were far from inconsistent with the Catholic anthropological tradition. In this regard, one might recall, for example, the link that St. Thomas Aquinas posited between human dignity and the person's capacity for truth and freedom.[37]

Starting with Leo XIII's *Rerum Novarum* in 1891, the Church became more receptive to the modern human rights movement. This receptivity is evident in a series of papal encyclicals that set forth the Church's social teaching. Pius XI's *Quadragesimo Anno* in 1931 is but one prominent instance of the transition in the Church's support for human rights language. John XXIII's *Pacem in Terris* of 1963 represents yet another milestone in the Church's journey to become an active participant in the discussion about the foundation for human rights. The transition may be said to have culminated at Vatican II with the Church's embrace of religious liberty for all persons in *Dignitatis Humanae* and the Pastoral Constitution on the Church in the Modern World, *Gaudium et Spes.* Since Vatican II, there can be no question that the Church considers the recognition of human rights to be normative and has been an active participant in the defense of such rights in particular circumstances, as well as in the theoretical discussion about the foundation of human rights. During his twenty-six-year pontificate, John Paul II served as a principal protagonist on the global stage for the defense of human rights based on the dignity of each human being.[38] Pope Benedict XVI has been equally courageous in this endeavor on behalf of humankind.

The promulgation of the 1983 Code of Canon Law, with the inclusion of the *lex ecclesiae fundamentalis,* represented the Church's official acceptance of human rights into canon law. This "fundamental law of the Church" appears in Canons 212 through 221 acknowledging the rights of the Christian faithful to freedom in speech, association, and assembly; education of children; expression of research; and basic due process. These rights are never absolute but are qualified, to be exercised always with due respect for the common good, faith and morals, and the proper reverence due to pastors.[39] They may be justified on the theological basis of baptism or as aspects of the natural moral order, and in either case, the rights in canon law trace their origin to the dignity of the human person. The 1917 Code of Canon Law did not include such a formal list of human rights. The inclusion of the present list of rights in the universal law of the Church represents a historical consciousness of the influence of secular documents such as the U.S. Bill of Rights and the UN Universal Declaration of Human Rights. On a deeper level, it may be said to reflect the integration of practical reasonableness, theological fonts, and historical consciousness in accord with canonical methodology. On account of its anthropological foundation in the practical reason of natural law, the canonical methodology already contained within itself openness to the historical development of human rights language.[40] Theological anthropology served to reinforce the methodology's openness to the recognition of human rights on the basis of individual human dignity.

The Objectivity of Law and the End of the Human Person

The function of historical consciousness in framing specific statutory provisions of law enables the law's adaptation to the circumstances of individuals and communities at given times and places. It means that specific formulations of the protection of human rights will not be identical in every system of law. The free speech right, for example, may be framed differently in the constitutional documents of different legal systems—just as it may be interpreted in different ways by these systems' judiciaries. In this regard, it seems helpful to recall that Thomas Aquinas thought that the precepts of natural law were translated into specific legal norms either directly or through *determinationes*. For example, the direct translation occurs when the proper legislative authority enacts a rule such as one that prohibits the taking of innocent human life in all circumstances. On the other hand, *determinationes* involve a process through which the legislative authority engages practical reason in a prudential process of decision making, which Thomas Aquinas compared to a craftsman who builds an edifice.[41] The particularities of the edifice of the law may vary in accord with historical circumstances.

However, historical consciousness as a feature of canonical methodology is not intended to diminish the objective moral basis of law. The fundamental precepts of the natural law remain unalterable even as they may point the way for development in the law. The same claim can be made of theological anthropology. In the canonical methodology, the normativity of law derives from the human person. This does not imply a subjective arbitrariness whereby human beings simply do as they please. Nor does the anthropological basis of canon law mean emancipation from the ethical order. Rather, it is a question of the emancipation of the ethical order from some merely positivistic purpose. Canonical methodology rests the foundation of the law on the end contained within human nature itself.

The end of the human person is expressed by Aristotle with the Greek word *eudaimonia* and by Thomas Aquinas with the Latin *beatitudo*. In English, these words are often translated as "happiness." Neither Aristotle nor Aquinas intended these terms to denote merely a psychological state based upon an individual's subjective preferences. Aristotle thought that the end of the human person was achieved through exercising reason in accord with virtue. He held that the more one acts in accord with virtue, the more one becomes virtuous.[42] Aquinas wrote that "[h]appiness itself, since it is a perfection of the soul is an inherent good of the soul; but that . . . which makes man happy, is something outside the soul."[43] MacIntyre faults various utilitarian approaches to moral value on the ground of the subjective conceptions of happiness that all versions of utilitarian theory must eventually embrace. In his words: "Detach the notion of happiness from that of happiness-in-virtue-of-such-and-such, and you have a concept too indeterminate to function as utilitarians needed it to function, since what it had to replace was the highly determinate concept of the human end and of happiness as the state of having achieved that end."[44] In adapting the law to historical circumstances, canonical method remains faithful to the Aristotelian-Thomistic understanding of a kind of objective happiness as the end of the human person. Correctly understood, the end of the human person constitutes the objective foundation of human rights.

Conclusion

What I have been describing as the anthropology of canon law might also be referred to as the *intellectus* or deeper meaning that anchors the outward form of the law. Absent this inner meaning, the law would reflect the rigid lifelessness of dry bones. When it is faithful to its animating *intellectus,* canon law serves a sacramental function in the ecclesiastical community. Canon law recognizes the *salus animarum* (salvation of souls) as the supreme law of the Church, and canon law promotes the salvation or objective happiness of individuals and communities to the extent that it honors the natural, theological, and historic elements of canonical methodology. With regard to human rights, canon law suggests that the anthropological *intellectus* would serve as an objective foundation on which the assertion of such rights might rest.

In light of the Catholic Church's initial reticence about human rights and the issue of the ongoing development of such rights in its internal life, the Church has reason for humility. The humility of the Church, however, does not mean that the Church has nothing of value to contribute to the broader discussion about the normativity of human rights. To the contrary, the anthropology of the Church's law, with its elements drawn from natural law and theology interpreted with due respect for historical circumstances, affords an objective moral foundation for law in general and for human rights law specifically. Given the radical moral and political disagreement about the foundation of human rights, the Church's contribution to the discussion reflects a concern that this disagreement "can easily lead to a decline or erosion of their value."[45] As MacIntyre indicates, the problem for the Catholic Church is not simply theoretical: "It is a problem of everyday practice, one arising in all those situations—debates about poverty, about social justice, about war and peace, about abortion and contraception, about capital punishment, and more generally about the common good—in which Catholics appeal to precepts of the natural law in arguing against positions incompatible with the Catholic understanding of human nature and the human condition."[46] The more the Church actively participates in the discussion *ad extra,* and at the same time facilitates the development of human rights in accord with the best tradition of canon law *ad intra,* the more she will be a *mirror of justice* that illuminates the truth about the end of the human person.

Notes

1. Pope Benedict XVI, "To the Representatives of the Holy See to International Organizations and to Participants in the Forum of Catholic-Inspired Non-Governmental Organizations," December 1, 2007; emphasis added. Available at www.vatican.va/holy_father/benedict_xvi/speeches/2007/.december/hf_benedict.

2. See, e.g., Ioannes Paulus Pp. II, "Allocutiones: Ad Rotae Romane Auditores coram admissos (Die 5 m. februarii a. 1987)," *Acta Apostolicae Sedis* 19 (1987): 1453, 1454–58. See also John J. Coughlin, O.F.M., "Canon Law and the Human Person," *Journal of Law and Religion* 19 (2003–4): 1, 3.

3. See Mary Ann Glendon, *A World Made New: Eleanor Roosevelt and the Universal Declaration of Human Rights* (New York: Random House, 2001), 136.

4. John L. Allen Jr., "What Pope Benedict Is Likely to Tell the United Nations," *New York Times,* December 23, 2007, A23.

5. Ioannes Paulus Pp. II, "Allocutiones: Ad Rotae Romane Auditores coram admissos (Die 17 m. februarii a. 1979)," *Acta Apostolicae Sedis* 71 (1979): 422–27. English translation in *L'Osservatore Romano, English Language Edition,* February 26, 1979, 6–7.

6. See Michael J. Perry, *The Idea of Human Rights* (Oxford: Oxford University Press, 1998), 11–41.

7. See John Paul II, *Fides et Ratio,* Encyclical Letter, September 14, 1998, 25–30, in *The Encyclicals of John Paul II,* ed. J. Michael Miller, C.S.B. (Huntington, IN: Our Sunday Visitor Press, 2001), 850, 865–67.

8. Alasdair MacIntyre, "Intractable Moral Disagreements," 21.

9. See John Finnis, *Aquinas* (Oxford: Oxford University Press, 1998), 65.

10. MacIntyre, "Intractable Moral Disagreements," 22.

11. Ibid.

12. Ibid., 23.

13. Ibid.

14. Ibid.

15. See John Paul II, *Fides et Ratio,* 31–32.

16. See Karol Wojtyla, *The Acting Person*, trans. Anna-Teresa Potocki (Dordrect: D. Reidel, 1979), 276–88.

17. MacIntyre, "Intractable Moral Disagreements," 24.

18. Thomas Aquinas, *Summa Theologica*, I-II, q. 90, a. 4, trans. Fathers of the English Dominican Province (Westminster, MD: Christian Classics, 1981).

19. MacIntyre, "Intractable Moral Disagreements," 20.

20. Ibid.

21. See Eugenio Corecco, *The Theology of Canon Law, a Methodological Question* (Pittsburgh, PA: Duquesne University Press, 1992), 137.

22. See Walter Kasper, "The Theological Foundation of Human Rights," *Jurist* 50 (1990): 148, 148–66. This biblical anthropology was articulated at Vatican II in *Gaudium et Spes*, 14.

23. Kasper, "The Theological Foundation of Human Rights," 158.

24. Ibid.

25. Ibid., 159, quoting *Gaudium et Spes*, 22.

26. Ibid., 159.

27. Ibid., 160.

28. See, e.g., John Paul II, *Fides et Ratio*, 104.

29. Armand Mauer, *St. Thomas and Historicity* (Milwaukee, WI: Marquette University Press, 1979), 32, citing *Hegel's Lectures on the History of Philosophy*, vol. 3, trans. E. S. Haldane and Frances H. Simson (London: Routledge and Paul, 1898), 52.

30. See Harold J. Berman, *Law and Revolution: The Formation of the Western Legal Tradition* (Cambridge, MA: Harvard University Press, 1983), 520.

31. R. H. Helmholz, *The Spirit of the Classical Canon Law* (Macon: University of Georgia Press, 1996), 397.

32. D. 1, c. 7 (from the Etymologies of St. Isidore), quoted in John J. Coughlin, O.F.M., "Canonical Equity," *Studia Canonica* 30 (1996): 403, 410.

33. C. 23, q. 4, c. 35 (from a homily of the Venerable Bede), quoted in Coughlin, "Canonical Equity," 410–11.

34. Hostiensis, *Commentaria in V Decretalium Libros*, I, c. 11, X, *De transactionibus*, I, 36 (Venetiis: Apud Iuntas, 1581).

35. See Kasper, "The Theological Foundation of Human Rights," 152, citing Pontificia Commissio, "Iustitia et Pax," *The Church and Human Rights*, Working Paper 1 (Vatican City: The Commission, 1975), 8.

36. Kasper, "The Theological Foundation of Human Rights," 153.

37. See, e.g., *Summa Theologica*, II-II, q. 64, a. 2 ad 3.

38. See George Weigel, *Witness to Hope: The Biography of John Paul II* (New York: HarperCollins, 1999), 289, 348; John J. Coughlin, O.F.M., "Pope John Paul II and the Dignity of the Human Being," *Harvard Journal of Law & Public Policy* 27 (2003): 65, 66–71.

39. See Canon 212 § 3, CIC-1983.

40. See Brian Tierney, *The Idea of Natural Rights: Studies on Natural Rights, Natural Law and Church Law, 1150–1625* (Atlanta, GA: Emory University Scholars Press, 1997), 343.

41. See *Summa Theologica*, I-II, q. 95, a. 2, corpus.

42. Aristotle, *Nicomachean Ethics* I, 7, in *The Complete Works of Aristotle*, vol. 2, ed. Jonathan Barnes (Princeton, NJ: Princeton University Press, 1984), 1734.

43. *Summa Theologica*, I-II, q. 2, a. 7 ad 3.

44. MacIntyre, "Intractable Moral Disagreements," 49.

45. Kasper, "The Theological Foundation of Human Rights," 149.

46. MacIntyre, "Intractable Moral Disagreements," 2.

CHAPTER 9

The Fearful Thoughts

of Mortals

Aquinas on Conflict, Self-Knowledge,
and the Virtues of Practical Reasoning

Thomas Hibbs

Some years ago now, Leonard Boyle proposed that
Aquinas devised the *Summa Theologiae* as a corrective to the genre
of confessors' manuals prominent in the early period of the Dominican order.[1] What worried Aquinas was a penchant for narrow casuistry
and a tendency to isolate moral matters from the rest of Christian theology. Boyle's accent on Thomas's relocation of practical, concrete
ethical questions within the full scope of speculative Christian theology might, on a superficial level, seem to confirm the basic thesis of
Marie-Dominique Chenu's famous interpretation of the structure
of the *Summa*.[2] Couched in terms of a sharp division between the necessary and the contingent, the speculative and the historical, Chenu's
reading proposes that the structure of the work mirrors the neo-
Platonic emanationist scheme of *exitus-reditus*, a going forth from,

followed by a returning to, God. The *exitus-reditus* structure relegates the Incarnation to a mere, and merely contingent, means in a return *(reditus)* to God seemingly anticipated within the coming forth *(exitus)* of nature. Similarly, ethics would express an abstract and universal unfolding of what is already inscribed within the order of nature.

But this is not a fair reading of Boyle's thesis, which is not that Aquinas's inscribing of ethics within an overarching theological account is meant to replace the examination of moral matters in concrete detail. Instead, Aquinas intends with the *Summa Theologiae* to make a distinct contribution to the very genre of the care of souls *(cura animarum)*. As is now generally acknowledged, Chenu's reading works only at the most general level of interaction with the text. Even within the *prima secundae,* there is the historical dialectic sin-law-grace that mirrors salvation history. The structure of the voluminous *secunda secundae* is not the abstract categories of the virtues and vices but intricately detailed accounts of the way in which the natural virtues are taken up and transformed by their relationship to the theological virtues and the gifts: "After the common investigation of the virtues and the vices . . . , it is necessary to consider singular matters in detail, since universal considerations of moral matters are less useful, than are those which examine actions in their particulars."[3] Aquinas's *Summa* is thus characterized not only by its ambitious scope, which includes the full spectrum of theology and locates ethical topics within a comprehensive theological vision of human life, but also by its range, from universal to singular. Of course, any theoretical account remains to some extent removed from the specific conditions of human action.

However attuned to particulars, no account of human nature or ethics, whether in the form of rules or virtues, can substitute for the non-rule-governed activity of prudence, whose chief task, Aquinas insists, is to bring about right action. Prudence, the capacity to appraise, judge, and command what ought to be done in concrete circumstances, is at the very heart of Aquinas's ethics. In this, Aquinas certainly follows Aristotle, for whom the wise individual is the measure of human acts. What a theoretical account of ethics can do is sketch broadly the moral precepts, the virtues, and the vices; it can of course also underscore the limits to its own inquiry. It does this in part by gesturing repeatedly in the direction of what exceeds its grasp: the proper order of human action. But it can do a bit more than this. It can give the careful reader a sense of the shape of practical reasoning, of the chief threats to its operation, and a description of the virtues whose cultivation tempers the dangers.

In the last matter, Aquinas goes much further than Aristotle in highlighting the limits to practical reason and the perils for human agency in the course of ordinary human life; indeed, Aquinas to some extent puts into question Aristotle's assumptions about the ease and delight of the activity of practical wisdom.[4] Following Augustine, Aquinas highlights the vulnerability of practical reason, its susceptibility to conflict, to the deceptions of evil, and, even, to tragedy. The dangers here are in part traceable to universal features of the human condition, but some are internal to the operation of human reason and will. Aquinas's ethical pedagogy thus imposes on the careful reader the task of self-appropriation by means of a more refined and more vigilant form of self-knowledge. What emerges is a decidedly Augustinian account of the manifold ways in which we resist self-knowledge; internal impulses, not just unruly passions but powerful vices, incline us, as Pascal would later put it, to "disguise ourselves from ourselves."[5] In his discussion of prudence, for example, Aquinas stresses the continuing need for counsel; in explicitly theological contexts, he subordinates the seemingly self-sufficient judgment of prudence to the gift of counsel. The theological re-formation of the cardinal virtues is further evident in the novel set of emerging alignments between the various virtues. In light of a specific set of threats to practical reasoning, Aquinas draws out the crucial role of courage as a virtue that plays a role in succoring practical reason, enabling reason to cling patiently to the good in the face of seemingly overwhelming evil.[6]

In what follows, I will begin with a sketch of the virtues in Aristotle; then I will turn to Aquinas's reworking of prudence; that reworking in turn will be shown to follow from Aquinas's embrace of Augustine's critique of the pagan philosophical project of eliminating or at least marginalizing the possibility of conflict and tragedy in the good life; and finally I will examine Aquinas's surprising reappraisal of the role of courage in the very activity of practical reason. Throughout I will attend to the way in which Aquinas implicitly conceives practical wisdom as a matter of self-knowledge, to which evils of various sorts block access. At least in this life, conflict is ineliminable and can even be seen to play a positive role in our progress toward self-knowledge.

I. Fearful Thoughts of Mortals: Prudence, Command, and Counsel

The cardinal virtues are temperance, courage, justice, and prudence.[7] These show up, usually alongside a host of other virtues, in pagan accounts of ethics. Aquinas states that the "whole structure of good works originates from the cardinal virtues."[8] Put with introductory brevity, we can say that temperance and fortitude rightly order the passions, especially regarding pleasure and fear, while justice rightly orders the will in relation to others and prudence perfects the activity of practical reason itself. Construed thus, temperance and fortitude can be seen as instrumental virtues, as means to the possession of other virtues. The very pursuit of virtue is not possible unless we can curb our inordinate desire for pleasure and overcome our fear of activities we find painful and difficult. Another way to see the secondary or propaedeutic character of these virtues is to focus on the powers that they perfect, the subrational parts of the human soul. But we must be careful here. As Aristotle puts it, the subrational part of the soul is subdivided into that part which is not susceptible to reason and another part that can partake of reason, be persuaded by it, and act in accord with it.⁹ The passions, perfected through the moral virtues of temperance and fortitude, reside here. Hence there is no necessary gulf between reason and passion; indeed, the presence of such a gulf is a sign that virtue has yet to be achieved. Yet the perfection of reason is more to be desired for its own sake than is the perfection of passion.

To divide passion and reason is for Aristotle to risk misunderstanding the very nature of practical reasoning, which he describes at the end of the *De Anima* as "desiring reason" or "reasoning desire."¹⁰ Prudence itself presupposes rightly ordered passion. In Aristotle's examination of the virtues, justice comes after temperance and fortitude but prior to prudence and the intellectual virtues. Whereas Aristotle is silent about the part of the soul that justice perfects, Aquinas locates justice in the will as a perpetual willingness to give others what is due them. Because justice regards others and ensures the proper social and political comportment of individuals in relation to one another, Aquinas goes so far as to call justice complete virtue (*ST*, II-II, 53, 3). In that respect, justice can be considered the highest of the virtues. In another respect, prudence, which resides in reason and orders the entire range of practical activities, is supreme.

Perhaps more than any other virtue, prudence has been badly distorted in modernity both by the dominant schools of ethics (Kantian or utilitarian) that reduce prudence to a calculative skill and by popular conceptions that see the prudent person as one who is particularly masterful at maximizing self-interest and keeping aloof from all unnecessary entanglements. So central is prudence to the entire scheme of the virtues that it surfaces implicitly in Aristotle's description of each of the virtues. The acts of temperance or courage must be performed in the right way, at the right time, and with respect to the right person. To act virtuously requires an attunement to, and discrimination of, the concrete circumstances of action. Prudence supplies precisely these capacities. Aquinas demarcates prudence from the moral virtues, because it resides in the intellect rather than the passions, and from the other intellectual virtues, because it is concerned with singular acts. Still, he writes, "prudence assists all the virtues and works in all; but this does not suffice to indicate that it is not a special virtue; for nothing prohibits the existence in a genus of a species that works equally in every other species of that same genus, as the sun exerts an influence on all bodies" (ST, II-II, 47, 5 ad 2).[11]

The authority of prudence with respect to the entire order of acts is clear from Aquinas's assertion that "command is the chief act of prudence" (ST, II-II, 47, 8).[12] Prudence encompasses three acts. Counsel, which involves inquiry ordered to discovery, is followed by judgment of what has been discovered. In light of counsel and judgment, practical reason commands what ought to be done in concrete circumstances. Only in this third act does the agent move from the speculative to the practical order properly speaking. The scope of the knowledge needed for wise action ranges from the universal or common principles of action, otherwise called the precepts of the natural law, to the concrete, contingent conditions of human acts. The negotiation of universal and singular, or rather the perception of the universal in the singular, is not peculiar to prudence; it is the very source of all human knowledge.[13] Aquinas includes *intellectus* as a part of prudence that involves a "right estimate of some particular end" (ST, II-II, 49, 2 ad 1).[14] Negotiation of singulars involves both understanding and sense. Aquinas states that the interior sense, which judges of singulars, performs a crucial mediating role in the exercise of prudence.[15]

Aquinas fleshes out the account of prudence in the question concerning the parts of prudence, the first of which is memory. Judging of the present and future in light of the past, memory is necessary that we might "take good counsel of the future" (ST, II-II, 49, 1 ad 3).[16] Prudence must reason not just from universal principles but from what is true in the majority of cases, evident to us only through experience and time. Moreover, Aquinas makes clear that memory involves more than passive receptivity. He takes up an important objection, namely, that whereas prudence can be perfected, memory is natural and thus should not be construed as a capacity to be developed in the way virtues are. Aquinas offers a lengthy response derived from Cicero's treatment of the arts of memory (*ST,* II-II, 49, 1 ad 2). Memory involves the active cultivation of certain arts: a knack for picking a suitable example; an arranging of memories so that we "might pass with facility from one memory to another"; a certain earnestness and active application of the mind to the things to be remembered so that we can impress them on the mind; and finally, an ongoing activity of reflection on the images stored in the memory so that we might "rapidly call them to mind, proceeding by a natural order from one to another."[17]

Memory plays a dual mediating role, between past and present and between singular and universal; its latter function indicates that it resides at the level of the singular reason, which is directly informed by sensible particulars. The singular reason, from which memories arise, is, of all the capacities involved in human knowing, most directly in contact with, and most influenced by, the passions: "memory is in the sensitive part of the soul" (*ST,* II-II, 49, 1 ad 2). Hence, the soul's dispositions with respect to virtue and vice determine to a great degree how an individual makes use of images. One of the reasons that Aristotle is skeptical about moral change for adults is that by the time we come to reflect seriously about our ends and our character, our habits are already deeply ingrained. These settled ways of interacting with the world influence not just our acts, but our knowledge of our very selves. One of the painful consequences of settled vice is that it blinds us to our own limitations and deformations, even to the way we actively, if rarely consciously, resist greater self-knowledge. For this reason, Josef Pieper speaks of "true-to-being memory," an attunement to the real that requires a "rectitude of the whole human being."[18]

The significance of habit for practical knowledge underscores the social role of moral formation in Aquinas. The mores of our regime, culture, religion, and family influence us before we can consciously assent or resist, or at least before we have a reliable conception of the good. To focus on the practical reason of the isolated individual is to court serious misunderstanding of the actual conditions of human development and action. From another vantage point, we can see that the natural understanding and memory of the individual do not suffice for prudence, which needs counsel precisely because of the sheer diversity of experience, what Aquinas calls the "infinite variety" of "particular matters of action." There is a dramatic tension here between, on the one hand, the complexity of experience, which requires lengthy time to be absorbed, and, on the other hand, the demand that we act here and now. Aquinas concludes that every individual "stands in very great need of being taught by others," particularly by older members of the community and by the sayings of the learned, to whose instructions we ought to apply ourselves "carefully, frequently, and reverently . . . neither neglecting them because of sloth, nor despising them because of pride" (*ST,* II-II, 49, 3 ad 2).[19] Another part of prudence is docility; its inclusion sparks the objection that docility is proper to disciples or beginners, not to teachers or those already capable of virtue. Aquinas responds that "even the learned need to be docile in some respects, since in matters of prudence no one is wholly sufficient" (*ST,* II-II, 49, 3 ad 3).[20] Aquinas here quietly undercuts any implication that the prudent person could be completely autonomous in practical matters.

The defense of counsel as an ineliminable part of prudence has important ramifications for Aquinas's understanding of the intellectual life, in both its practical and its theoretical dimension. Now, it might seem that counsel as allied to prudence would be irrelevant to the theoretical activity of the intellect since the latter is not directly concerned with action but only with the determination of truth, which does not depend on rectified appetite. But this is to conflate the order of demonstration with the order of discovery and to assume that all knowledge is universal and necessary rather than at times merely probable and contingent. In fact, in the order of discovery, the moral virtues can indeed play an important role in aiding us in the discovery of truth.[21]

Without courage or temperance, we are likely to be distracted by pleasures or stymied by fear of failure; without justice, we are likely not to take seriously the objections or rival positions or even simply the friendly advice of interlocutors. Moreover, Aquinas insists that in the realm of opinion or probable knowledge, that is, where knowledge falls short of demonstrative norms articulated in the *Posterior Analytics,* passion or will can play a crucial role in assisting or blocking our perception of truth. Indeed, in the discovery of knowledge, the path to the principles, and in the entire order of probable knowledge, there is need for the apt discrimination of singulars and hence for something akin to prudence. Thus, the account of counsel as intrinsic to prudence has implications for the entirety of the intellectual life. Perhaps the most interesting consequence has to do with the inherently social dimension of intellectual inquiry.

A certain inclination to inordinate, and potentially destructive, self-sufficiency would seem to be natural to those who are wiser than others. Highlighting a temptation never mentioned by Aristotle, Aquinas ends his treatment of the parts of prudence with a discussion of "caution," the authoritative source for which is Ephesians 5:15: "See how you walk cautiously" (*ST,* II-II, 49, 8). In contingent matters of action, "true is mixed with false and good is commingled with evil." In the practical order, "goods are often hindered by evil and evils have the look of good *(mala habent speciem boni).*"[22] The scriptural counsel concerning the uncertainty of human judgment comes to the fore in Aquinas's examination of the gift of counsel, the specific gift of the Holy Spirit associated with the cardinal virtue of prudence. The first objection in the first article concerning counsel urges that no divine assistance is needed in this case because the activity of taking counsel is "sufficiently perfected by the virtue of prudence" (*ST,* II-II, 52, 1, obj. 1).[23] Aquinas returns to a theme from the questions on prudence, namely, the limitations to human reason's apprehension of the singular and contingent conditions of human acts. The result is that, as the Book of Wisdom (9:14) puts it, "mortals' thoughts are fearful, and our counsels uncertain." If we were surprised at the prominence accorded to counsel as a part of prudence, we might be apt to find even more remarkable Aquinas's subordination of prudence to counsel in the theological order. No longer a subordinate part of prudence, counsel now reigns over prudence. We always have need, Aquinas insists, of taking counsel from those who are wiser than we are, particularly from God, "who comprehends all things."[24]

By the gift of counsel, the human soul is rendered docile to the promptings of the Holy Spirit. But this prompting does not replace or enslave the human intellect and will: "Their free choice being preserved, the children of God are moved by the Holy Ghost according to their mode. . . . Since the Holy Spirit instructs reason about what is to be done, the gift befits the children of God" (*ST,* II-II, 52, 1 ad 3).[25] Another objection takes aim at the association of prudence with counsel, which is the first and merely instrumental act of prudence, rather than with a gift of judgment or especially command, the latter of which is the proper act of prudence (*ST,* II-II, 52, 2, obj. 1).[26]

Counsel, rather than judgment, signifies that "the counselled mind is moved by another counselling it" (*ST,* II–II, 52, 2 ad 1).[27] Counsel befits the temporal condition of human action; it is proper to wayfarers who have neither sufficient knowledge nor experience to anticipate and respond appropriately to the infinite variety of concrete conditions they face in the order of action. Aquinas's response stresses the dependent and partial status of the human intellect in the order of things. The proximate rule or measure of human acts is human reason, but reason itself is a reflection of, and a participation in, the supreme rule, the eternal reason which is the divine essence.[28] Yet the inscribing of human reason within a more encompassing metaphysical order is not an obstacle to its proper operation but a condition of it. The gift of counsel provides knowledge and a greater capacity for discrimination of circumstances and discernment of fitting paths of action (*ST,* II-II, 52, 2 ad 3).[29] It also eases anxiety.

II. Augustine contra Gentiles: Virtue, Conflict, and the Vulnerability of the Human Good

Eases, but never quite eliminates. Even the possession of the virtues does not exclude the presence of some degree of uncertainty, deception, and conflict. Without adverting to the historical debate, Aquinas here addresses the topic of the role of conflict and tragedy in relation to the good life, the life of the practice of virtue. In order to see more clearly the distinctive features of Aquinas's account, it will help to have before us the inherited assumptions and opposing traditions about tragedy, virtue, and the good life. In a masterful way, unnoticed by most commentators, Aquinas reconstructs a novel account out of the opposed positions of Aristotle and Augustine, the latter of whom offers a devastating critique of Socratic rationalistic optimism, a critique that in certain respects anticipates Nietzsche's critique of Socrates in the *Birth of Tragedy*.[30]

When Socrates claims that nothing can harm him except his own commission of acts of vice, he equates virtue and self-sufficiency. Of course, such assertions need to be tempered by what he has to say about his own ignorance and his expression of a kind of indemonstrable faith in the ultimate justice of life after death, or at least a confidence that if there is a life after this one, the virtuous will not be harmed. As he proclaims at the end of the *Apology*, "nothing can harm a good man, either in life or after death."[31] Still, his assertions of invulnerability render him in this sense at least a worthy predecessor of the Stoics. In many of the dialogues, Plato juxtaposes Socrates to the Homeric hero. On one level, the effect of such comparisons, given Socrates' physical appearance and his lack of public office, render him a laughable competitor for heroic status; but, on another level, the comparison vindicates the superiority of Socrates' philosophical life, the life of one who pursues and practices the virtues and who thus is fearless in the face of death. Socrates' evident absence of fear, indeed his cheerful equanimity, raises the question whether the virtue of courage has not been rendered superfluous. If virtue were knowledge simply, then certain kinds of virtues, namely, the moral virtues that have to do with the ongoing education and formation of the passions, would be rendered otiose.

Aristotle, by contrast, insists on the necessity of the moral virtues and argues that part of the irrational soul, namely, the passions, can participate in reason. In contrast to Plato's Socrates, Aristotle admits the possiblity of tragedy even for the virtuous. There is, in his account, a hierarchy of goods, external, bodily, and psychic. Although the goods of the soul are superior to the goods of the body and external goods, the latter are genuine goods, whose loss constitutes a misfortune even for the virtuous. Tragic loss of nation, friends, or family or even severe physical deprivation can mar the happiness of the virtuous: "If the virtuous suffers many major misfortunes, they oppress and spoil his blessedness, since they involve pain and impede many activities. And yet, even here what is fine shines through, whenever someone bears many severe misfortunes with good temper, not because he feels no distress, but because he is noble and magnanimous."[32] So the good life cannot be achieved solely by the possession of virtue. A virtuous man will endure such tragedy nobly, but, after "many serious misfortunes," the "return to happiness . . . will take a long and complete length of time that includes great and fine successes."[33]

Aquinas inherits not just this pagan conception of the good life, self-sufficiency, and the role of tragedy but also a Christian conception of the good life as realizable only through the possession of the *summum bonum*, the highest good, God himself, to whom we can be united only in the next life and only by means of an unmerited gift. That is one of the lessons of Augustine's famous treatment of happiness in book XIX of the *City of God*. Just as is the case in the famous section of the *Confessions*, where Augustine summarizes what he did and did not find in the books of the Platonists, so too here Augustine's critique of the pagan account of the good reposes upon an affirmation and embrace of part of what the pagans assert. Some of them at least have accurately depicted the criteria for the ultimate end of human life: "[the] end of our good is desired for its own sake and other things for the sake of it" (*City of God,* bk. XIX, 1).[34] But Augustine's critique is devastating to the claim of the philosophers to teach authoritatively about the way of life constitutive of the human good. They have made promises that they cannot keep.[35]

Instead of simply repudiating (Plato's Socrates) or maginalizing (Aristotle) the vulnerability of human life to tragedy, Augustine underscores the persistent fragility of happiness and even virtue itself in the fallen, temporal world of human affairs.[36] As Augustine develops the description of happiness, he opts for Aristotelian inclusivity rather than Socratic exclusivity: "That human life, which enjoys virtue and other goods, both of soul and body, is blessed" (*City of God,* bk. XIX, 3).[37] Of course, that more complex, Aristotelian conception of happiness is precisely what exposes the individual to tragedy. Augustine goes much further than Aristotle; indeed, Augustine's depiction of the tragic vulnerability of the virtuous exhibits a greater affinity to Greek tragedy than to Greek philosophy. Augustine's correction of Aristotle is twofold. The first is a matter of degree. Augustine sees the possibility of tragedy nearly everywhere in human life, whereas Aristotle tends to depict it as marginal. The social condition of happiness—the way in which bonds of friendship, family, and politics contribute directly to our flourishing—involves the constant threat of tragedy. We cannot know with certainty "the interior dispositions of our friends." Even more unsettling is that no one "can rely utterly even on family affection." "Domestic disloyalty" is a nearly universal phenomenon, as is, in the wider community, the tragic failure in the execution of justice, whether through vice or ignorance (*City of God,* bk. XIX, 5–6).

The second difference involves the introduction of a different type of vulnerability, one intrinsic to the soul itself. While Aristotle admits that the happiness of the virtuous can be harmed by events outside his control, he does not conceive of the life of virtue itself as subject to internal conflict. Yet Augustine writes that the "life of virtue" is "a perpetual war with vice, not only exterior but also interior, not foreign but clearly within us arising from what is our very own" (*City of God*, bk. XIX, 4).[38] Such conflict, for Aristotle, is possible only for those who do not possess virtue. And it is precisely the possibility of any confident possession of virtue that Augustine wants to put into question. One way to state the contrast is to say that whereas Aristotle sees only external threats to the life of happiness for the virtuous, Augustine envisions a host of internal threats. He thus puts into question the adequacy of Aristotle's revised version of the Socratic thesis that virtue is knowledge. In his development of the teaching on incontinence, Aristotle distinguishes between the general awareness that a certain type of action is to be avoided or to be performed and an awareness in the concrete singular that this is an action of that sort.[39] The latter apprehension sustained through to performance or avoidance is what moves the agent to act. But that is precisely the sort of apprehension that is most derailed by pleasure or pain; thus, the incontinent, in one sense, possess knowledge but, in another sense, not. This is often presented as a conflict between general knowledge and specific passion, in which the latter clouds our awareness of the former or at least renders it impotent. But Augustine's account of the way evil inclinations arise within us and are "our very own" is much more complex than anything available in Aristotle's texts.

The final stages of Augustine's conversion, as detailed in the *Confessions*, are far too complex for simple summary. To see the point germane to our inquiry, we need only attend to a single scene that stands between Augustine's failed attempt at Platonic contemplation, in which he moves from the exterior to the interior and then ascends to the divine but is unable to sustain the ascent (VII, 10–17), and his experience of healing grace in the garden, in which the reading of St. Paul initiates the divine overcoming of his divided will (VIII, 11–12). As is true at every stage in Augustine's development, progress coincides with the reading of texts, the participation in a certain community, and the practice of a certain way of life. In a pivotal scene, Augustine describes a visit he made with his friend Alypius to the home of Ponticianus, who tells of reading by chance the life of Antony, the Eyptian monk. As he read, he "was changed inwardly." Augustine inscribes that story of the transformative reading of a story within his own story of his conversion. He writes:

> Ponticianus narrated these things. But You, Lord, between his words, were twisting me back upon myself, drawing me out from behind my back, where I had placed myself, for I wished not to see myself. You set me before my own face, that I might see how vile I was, how deformed and sordid, how stained and ulcerous. I saw and was horrified; but there was no way for me to flee from my very self. If I tried to avert my gaze, Ponticianus kept telling his story and you kept turning me back upon myself, thrusting me before my own eyes, that I might discover my iniquity and hate it. I already knew it, but I dissimulated, held it back, and thrust it into oblivion. (*Confessions,* VIII, 7)[40]

The remarkable passage reveals how radically Augustine transforms two fundamental features of the neo-Platonic path to the Good: the role of introspection and the analysis of the obstacles to self-knowledge. On the neo-Platonic model, the ascent is a matter of turning the intellect from the mutable realm of sensation to the interior realm of the immaterial intellect and moving on from there to the divine source of the intellect. Books and stories may prompt the turn, but they are thereafter discarded. Christian conversion by contrast involves a dialogue between external and internal, between the hearing of a story and the internal motions of the soul. The neo-Platonic manner of reorienting the soul involves a transition from the temporal to the eternal, the external to the internal, and on to the superior; this philosophical pedagogy glosses over self-knowledge of sin, understood not just as inordinate attention to the temporal, but rather as a willful refusal to acknowledge rebellion against the good. Augustine describes his coming to this knowledge as painful and horrifying, as something he desperately wants to avoid. This is much more than mere weakness, an acknowledgment of the gap between knowledge and action. Instead, this involves knowledge at war with knowledge: "I already knew it, but I dissimulated, held it back, and thrust it into oblivion" (*Confessions*, VIII, 7).

Alasdair MacIntyre describes the problem with resorting to simple introspection "in search of self-knowledge." What we encounter through introspection is "the self's self-serving presentation of itself to itself, a presentation designed to sustain an image of the self as well-ordered, free from fundamental conflict, troubled perhaps by occasional akratic difficulties, but for the most part entitled to approval both by itself and by others." Because self-presentation is typically selective, we find ourselves trapped. "To break out of this circle," we need "some standard that initially appears to be external to the self, even alien to it, in such a way as to occasion a particular kind of pain, . . . the pain felt by a self when treated by the prospect of having to acknowledge a truth about itself that it has not yet been able to bear." Here it is not so much knowledge in conflict with passion, as two sorts of knowledge at odds, the knowledge of memory that would confess one's evil deeds and the knowledge of pride that denies or revises what has been done.[41] Augustine makes this point in a subtle way when he describes the individual who brought to him the "books of the Platonists," books that proved instrumental, if finally inadequate, in his conversion from the sensible to the intelligible, as someone "swollen with monstrous pride" (*Confessions*, VII, 9).[42]

Augustine does not think natural virtue itself is consistently possible for fallen man. To hold that it is forces philosophers into the comic absurdities of the Stoics, who in their advocacy of suicide in the face of great evils assert simultaneously that life is "happy and unlivable" (*City of God*, bk. XIX, 4). The very function of certain virtues, fortitude, for example, is evidence that this life can never be freed from misery; the necessity of fortitude, which "compels us to bear misfor-tune with patience," provides ample "testimony" to the pervasiveness of human evil (*City of God*, bk. XIX, 4).[43]

In more restrained language, Aquinas countenances Augustine's central theses about moral progress, practical reason, vice, and self-knowledge. Aquinas's account of the wounds of nature resulting from sin, both original and actual, qualifies his embrace of Aristotle's claim that we are by nature suited to become virtuous: on account of origi-nal sin, "all the powers of the soul remain destitute of a proper order, by which naturally they are ordained to virtue, and this deprivation it-self is called a wound of nature" (*ST*, I-II, 85, 3).[44] The four wounds of ignorance, malice, infirmity, and concupiscence infect the powers of the soul, respectively, intellect and will, and the irascible and concu-piscible appetites. These are precisely the powers to be perfected by the cardinal virtues, but their disordered state presents greater obstacles to the inculcation of virtue than those provided by lack of practice.

As we shall see later, Aquinas will certainly take Augustine's point about the nature and necessity of fortitude as an indication that human life is best with unhappiness and misery. In contrast to the general principle that the possession and practice of virtue is pleasant, the activity of courage is inherently painful. What is also significant and too often overlooked in Augustine's account of the potential sources of tragedy is the way he construes the good life as intrinsically social. That communal dimension introduces types and degrees of de-pendency that render any boast of self-sufficiency comical. Augustine here anticipates Aquinas's critique of the self-sufficiency of practical wisdom. The social aspect of the good life is not just applicable to our earthly life; salvation itself is corporate. That is why Augustine opts for the Pauline languages of cities and speaks on behalf of the city of God.

Augustine does not eliminate the language of virtue, as excel-lence of soul, or happiness, as the enjoyment of the highest good; we shall have to wait for modernity for that. He thinks that we can retain the notion of happiness if we are honest about the sole place where it can ultimately reside, namely, in union with God. And he thinks that we can retain the language of virtue if we admit a different set of virtues from those celebrated by the pagan philosophers. Virtue consists "rather in the pardoning of sins than in the perfection of virtue" (*City of God*, bk. XIX, 27).[45]

III. Aquinas on the Pedagogy of Law: Aid and Accusation

The role of conflict and tragedy surfaces in Aquinas's ethical discourse, not only in his discussion of the virtues and the vices, but also in his treatment of law. Of course, the teaching on the natural law has seemed to undergird an overly confident conception of natural reason and its ability to arrive at moral truths unaided by grace or even training in the natural virtues. Aquinas does indeed insist that some portion of the natural law is universally available and that its fundamental precepts are self-evident or known in themselves, and not as inferences from more fundamental knowledge. He has in mind the fundamental precept—"do good and avoid evil"—and others that follow from this, such as the prohibitions against murder, theft, and adultery. But Aquinas notes a number of limitations to the universal availability of the natural law. Agreement, he observes, extends only to the intermediate precepts; the more we descend to particulars, the more disagreement there is likely to be. Moreover, apprehension of even intermediate precepts, such as the prohibition of theft, can be obscured by "passion and bad education" (*ST*, I-II, 94, 6).

There is an instructive overlap between the natural law and the revealed, divine law of the Decalogue. Applying the general principle that grace presupposes nature, Aquinas writes that the divine law presupposes the natural law (*ST*, I-II, 99, 2 ad 1). Indeed, the precepts of the natural law function as *praeambula fidei* parallel to the the speculative truths about God's existence, truths knowable by reason but nonetheless revealed.[46] Similarly, in the practical order, the prohibitions against murder, theft, and adultery are both knowable by reason and revealed: "The Old Law manifested the precepts of the natural law, and added certain precepts of its own" (*ST,* I-II, 98, 5).[47] Yet there is a striking disparity between the practical and the theoretical orders. Truths concerning the existence and nature of God are not self-evident but rather are the result of complicated chains of argument. As Aquinas notes, without revelation of God's existence, that truth would be known only by the few, after a long time, and even then with an admixture of error (*SCG,* I, 4).[48] Without revelation, the "human race would be left in the darkest shadows of ignorance."[49] So the fittingness of revelation duplicating what could be known by nature is, in this case, evident. But the precepts of the natural law are immediately given to human reason. Why, then, the need for revelation in this case?

God sent the law as a help *(auxilium)* when the "natural law began to be obscured by an exuberance of sin" (*ST,* I-II, 98, 6).[50] Aquinas sees the revealed law of the Decalogue as one moment, a transitional moment, in divine pedagogy. The pedagogical character of the law is clear from Aquinas's use of the term *praeceptum,* which means both rule and instruction or teaching. The Old Law was "given between the natural law and the law of grace" so that we might be led "from the imperfect to the perfect."[51] The precise timing of the revelation has to do with sin as a cause of forgetfulness: "the written law was necessary as a remedy for human ignorance" (*ST,* I-II, 98, 6).[52] Our ignorance is twofold: ignorance of the law and ignorance of our own ignorance.[53] The law aids or instructs by accusing (*ST,* I-II, 98, 6).[54]

One might describe divine pedagogy as ironic, in the Socratic sense that it involves a stepping back from progress in the discussion of the good, a retreat from an objective, detached inquiry. The first movement is not forward but backward to self-appropriation; the Socratic proposal is that we must first acknowledge our own ignorance and the multiple ways in which we are currently ill-disposed to make progress in the pursuit of the good. The wounds of nature—

ignorance, malice, infirmity, and concupiscence—characterize the condition of our souls from the moment of birth, a condition exacerbated by actual sin and habitual viciousness. The recognition of moral failure and of the way in which we ignore what we at some level already know is the first teaching of the law. While the recognition may arise from the reflection of natural reason, the cure for such internal division wholly exceeds the power of nature and reason. Aquinas is blunt: God gave "such a law that by our own powers we could not fulfill, so that, while presuming to rely on ourselves, we might discover ourselves to be sinners and, being humbled, might have recourse to the aid of grace" (*ST,* I-II, 98, 2 ad 3).[55] These passages support Augustine's conclusion: virtue consists "in the pardoning of sins rather than in the perfection of virtue" (*City of God,* bk. XIX, p. 480).

Augustine is the authority for the final article associating counsel with the beatitude commending mercy. He writes: "Counsel befits the merciful, because the sole remedy is to be uprooted from such great evils, to pardon others, and to give" (*ST,* II-II, 52, 4).[56] Aquinas stresses here that counsel directs mercy, which itself conduces to the end of human life. Indeed, the sense of uncertainty, the fearful thoughts of mortal men, in the face of the admixture of good and evil and the deceptive presentation of evil under appearance of good, render infallibility of judgment in matters of action impossible. Failure, both culpable and inculpable, gives rise to regret and remorse. For this universal human experience what is needed is not so much further prudence or greater counsel but rather mercy, the beatitude Aquinas associates with the gift of counsel.

The prospect of mercy is precisely what makes the tragic element in Christian theology but one moment in a more comprehensive narrative. Aquinas's account of the overlap between the natural law and the Decalogue testifies to the tragic gap, introduced by sin, between (a) what human beings long for in the way of happiness and what they are capable of achieving and (b) our sense of what we ought to do and what we can do in the way of fulfilling the law. The divine intervenes to make us acutely aware of that gap, but this does not leave us in a state of paralyzed awe in the face of inexorable fate. Instead, the accusation includes both an explanation of how the very frame of things became askew and an offer of forgiveness. Put slightly differently, the moment of recognition, which in classical tragedy leads to the downfall of the protagonist, here is an opportunity for the graced rehabilitation of our capacities to know and love.[57]

One might wonder what happens, in the theological order, to the final two acts associated with prudence, namely, judgment and command? Do these simply disappear as the human agent becomes docile to the promptings of the Spirit? Such an understanding of grace, as introducing heteronomy into the moral life, runs counter to Aquinas's metaphysics of creation, according to which divine generosity operates in a manner congenial to the natural mode of activity of the creature. Correlatively, Aquinas claims that the human creature achieves a greater degree of liberty under the influence of grace. In fact, the capacity of judgment and command surface at the very heart of the theology of the virtues, in the activity of charity, which is defined as the form of the virtues. Charity is the "mother of the virtues"; by commanding the other virtues, it brings forth the "acts of the other virtues, by the desire of the last end" (*ST*, II-II, 23, 8 ad 3).[58] Indeed, the gifts of the Holy Spirit originate and terminate in charity (*ST*, I-II, 68, 5).

While the commanding act of prudence presupposes rectified desire through the moral virtues, charity is *essentially* a matter of rightly ordered desire. Aquinas follows Augustine in defining charity as the "movement of the soul to the enjoyment of God for his own sake" (*ST*, II-II, 23, 2).[59] Charity involves temporality and community; it is, as Aquinas famously describes it, a type of friendship, based on the communication of mutual love: "there is communication between us and God, insofar as he communicates his happiness to us" (*ST*, II-II, 23, 1).[60] Charity is not just love, but the ordering principle of all other types and acts of love. It "commands the acts of every type of friendship, as the art about the end commands the arts concerning the means" (*ST,* II-II, 26, 7).[61] That charity itself is defined as a movement, not a resting, underscores the temporality, contingency, and fragility of the central virtue in human life. That is yet another way to get at a point stressed above in the treatment of the dangers afflicting practical reasoning, namely, the difficulty of clinging to the good in a world where every agent is to varying degrees beset by evils.

IV. COURAGE RE-FORMED: PATIENT ENDURANCE AND THE PERILS OF PRACTICAL REASON

Clinging to the good in the face of seemingly overwhelming evil is precisely the task Aquinas assigns to courage, which thereby becomes a crucial virtue, helping to preserve practical reason, within the life of the faithful Christian. That marks something of a transformation of the understanding and practice of the virtue from its pagan roots, where it is an instrumental and decidedly problematic virtue. The instrumental status of fortitude is clear from Aquinas's discussion of its status as a virtue, the fundamental purpose of which is to make human "works accord with reason" (*ST,* II-II, 123, 1).[62] While prudence helps to rectify reason itself and justice establishes rectitude in human affairs, courage and temperance "remove obstacles" to establishing the rule of reason. Courage enables us to overcome fear in the face of difficult matters. An abiding assumption of Aquinas's account, in contrast to the sort of account I suggested might be latent in Plato's Socrates, is that fear of bodily harm, especially loss of life, is natural and appropriate; indeed, Aquinas goes so far as to say that the exercise of courage is unpleasant even for the virtuous—a rather striking exception to the general doctrine that virtue, once possessed, enables its possessor to perform acts of virtue with ease and delight. Of course, the reading of Aquinas on prudence just given already involves an instructive qualification of the identification of virtue with ease and delight. The lingering presence of fear and moderate anxiety and the need for virtues such as repentance and mercy entail a critique of certain classical accounts of the self-sufficiency of the good life.

Complete insensivity to pain is not necessary for virtue, but the virtuous individual would not focus on the pain endured but rather on the good to be achieved; even in the midst of great sacrifice, perhaps especially in such a circumstance, the virtuous individual takes delight in doing what is right and noble. As I have noted, Aquinas's Augustinian account of the good life admits a greater possibility for tragedy than do the most influential pagan accounts; yet Aquinas stands with the ancients in exalting noble action and in seeing the greatest evil, not in physical pain, but in the performance of vice: "the courageous person experiences both delight and grief: delight from the act of virtue and from its end, grief from the loss of his own life" (*ST*, II-II, 123, 8).[63] To adapt a line from Aristotle about the desirability of partial knowledge of the highest and most noble things, we might say for Aquinas that the pursuit and possession of a noble end, with suffering, is to be preferred to a secure and comfortable possession of a lesser good.[64]

Aquinas holds that courage is one of the four cardinal virtues, a virtue without which human beings cannot even begin to flourish. In his consideration of whether courage is a special virtue, there is a hint of a more encompassing role for courage. Ambrose, Aquinas notes, construes courage "broadly, as denoting firmness of soul in the face of assaults of whatever sort" (*ST*, II-II, 123, 2 ad 2).[65] In this sense, fortitude is not so much virtue itself as it is "a condition of every virtue, since as Aristotle indicates, every virtue acts firmly and immovably" (*ST*, II-II, 123, 2).[66] But what distinguishes fortitude as a special virtue is firmness in bearing "grave dangers." Courage "holds the will to the good of reason against the threat of the greatest evils," particularly the fear of death, "the most terrifying of all bodily evils" (*ST*, II-II, 123, 4).[67]

But what do or ought we to fear, and how should we rank the many dangers we encounter throughout our lives? Virtue "ever tends to the good" (*ST*, II-II, 123, 5), so fears and dangers have to be understood in relation to an order of threats to the good. Fortitude is principally about the dangers of death in battle; in that case, it is most evident that the dangers come directly from the pursuit of a good, namely, that of "defending the common good in a just war" (*ST,* II-II, 123, 5).[68] Aquinas does not intend to diminish other situations of threat to life, but he notes that those who are able to withstand fear of death in battle also will "behave well in the face of danger of other kinds of death."[69]

What Aquinas's rather tidy binding of fears and dangers to the good and his quick reduction of the exercise of courage to the defense of the common good may obscure from view is the particularly problematic status of courage as a virtue in the ancient world. Courage is troublesome not just because it is a merely instrumental virtue but also because it has so little direct connection with reason. Of course, its exercise can help reason not to be overcome by fear, but the link between the virtue and reason is not nearly as close as it is in the case of another instrumental virtue, temperance, whose very name philosophers associate with the preservation of reason. Moreover, the spirit that is especially drawn to the exercise of courage, the warlike spirit, is one that is likely to be attracted to danger and battle for its own sake and not merely as a means of preserving the common good. So, for example, in Plato's *Republic* the danger of cultivating the thumotic part of the soul is that, in the absence of enemies external to the state, bellicose individuals may turn inward and do battle against the community. But there is an even greater danger, a peculiarly modern risk, that of a nihilistic embrace of the pursuit of danger, excess, and the overcoming of fear as an end in itself. Reckless abandon in defiance of petty convention turns courage into a kind of antiprudence—a willingness to risk safety and health as a mark of nobility.

Closely aligned with the spirit of battle is a sensitivity to questions of honor, which are most often self-regarding rather than other-regarding. Precisely that which is necessary to preserve the common good against deadly threats can turn against the common good in an affirmation of the good of one or of a certain class.[70] Another way to put the problem concerning courage is in terms of Aristotle's claim that virtue stands midway between two vices, one excessive and the other deficient. Despite the assertion of virtue's median status between two vices, it is typically the case that one of the two vices has a greater resemblance to the virtue and thus is more likely to be confused with it. With temperance, for example, the vice that most simulates the virtue is the deficiency rather than the excess. Drunkenness, lechery, and gluttony are unlikely to be confused with temperance, whereas abstemiousness may be. By contrast, not the deficient but the excessive vice is most likely to be erroneously taken as a virtue in the case of courage. Boldness or audacity rather than cowering passivity is most apt to be admired. Indeed, even as a vice it can inspire a kind of awe in witnesses of its exercise. Thus, the vice most associated with courage is closer to the noble than the vices associated with temperance, which always smack of the base.

Aquinas's corrective consists in identifying endurance rather than attack as the chief act of fortitude (*ST,* II-II, 123, 6). Aquinas explains:

To endure is more difficult than to attack, for three reasons. First, he who endures fends off invasion by a stronger opponent, while he who attacks invades from a position of greater strength. It is harder to contend with a stronger than a weaker opponent. Second, he who endures experiences an imminent threat, while he who attacks regards danger as at some distance in the future. It is more difficult not to be affected by the present than by the future. Third, to endure entails a long duration of time, while attack can arise from sudden movements. It is more arduous to remain immobile for a length of time, than to be moved suddenly to something strenuous. (*ST,* II-II, 123, 6 ad 1)[71]

We have already noted that the most deceptive simulacrum of the virtue of courage is not timidity but rashness or boldness. Shifting the emphasis in courage from attack to endurance serves to unmask the pretender to virtue, since boldness is incompatible with endurance. It is also clear from Aquinas's discussion that we should not consider endurance passive; instead, it is an active clinging to the good in the face of seemingly insurmountable evil. The connection between courage and activity is what makes it broader than, and superior to, patience. Fortitude, Aquinas writes, "not only endures vexation without disturbance, as is true of patience, but also fights against it if necessary. Hence he who is brave is patient, but not necessarily the converse; for patience is a part of fortitude" (*ST*, I-II, 66, 4 ad 2).[72]

In his discussion of the passion of fear, Aquinas highlights themes that we have already noted: the necessity of courage for the very operation of practical reason and the connection between courage, prudence, and counsel. The passions themselves can easily derail practical reason by leading us to imagine things falsely; under the influence of passion, Aquinas observes, something can "seem greater or less than it actually is according to the truth of the thing" (*ST*, I-II, 44, 2). Thus does the presence of fearful things afflict perception, judgment, and action—the entire order of practical reasoning. Given the pervasive threats to human agency in its pursuit of the good, courage would seem especially needed: "those things that incite fear are not simply evil but things that possess a certain magnitude, . . . things that are difficult to repel" (*ST*, I-II, 44, 2).[73] Although fear normally disposes us to be solicitous of counsel, in the case of great fear, we are likely to become so distraught that we fail to seek counsel (*ST*, I-II, 44, 2 ad 2).[74]

Among the cardinal virtues, courage is the one that most directly enables us to overcome difficulties in our progress in virtue. Regarding the quest for truth, whether speculative or practical, courage is necessary for progress in inquiry. Its ameliorating role is particularly pronounced in the human pursuit of the highest truths, those concerning God, which, we should recall, can be attained only by the few, only after a long period of investigation, and even then with an admixture of error. The temptation to despair is real. In the overcoming of despair at the outcome of the quest, courage is once again revealed to reach its pinnacle not in attack but in endurance. Indeed, courage understood as attack may be relevant where the refutation of fundamental error is necessary, but as part of the ethics of inquiry, truth as endurance is more significant. The most fundamental way in which all human beings can be said to possess a knowledge of God, if only in a general and confused manner, is through our natural desire for happiness. But this untutored desire can mistakenly take anything whatsoever as fulfilling that longing (*ST*, I, 2, 1 ad 1).[75] In this context, revelation itself might be seen as merciful counsel, enabling human beings to come to a knowledge, otherwise nearly inscrutable, of their end and the means to its attainment. Such counsel fosters courage even as it emboldens hope, which is a mean between "presumption and despair" (*ST*, I-II, 64, 4 ad 3).

For the Christian, the exemplar of courage is not the warrior defending the common good of the political order but the martyr testifying to the ultimate truths of human redemption.[76] It is not surprising that the distinction between endurance and attack figures in Aquinas's defense of martyrdom as an act of fortitude.[77] But the distinction is evident even on the natural level, in the case of warfare. If the courageous warrior is typically one who fights valiantly in battle by attacking the enemy, a superior degree of courage is manifest in the warrior who, taken captive and deprived of the opportunity to attack the enemy, refuses to provide information to the enemy, even under torture. Such a warrior endures rather than attacks. Given my earlier discussion of the ways in which the prospects of conflict and tragedy are ineliminable elements of the human condition, courage construed as clinging to the good in the face of seemingly insurmountable evil is a virtue crucial to the very activity of practical reason. In contingent matters of action, we recall with Aquinas, "false is found with true and evil mingled with good." Moreover, "good is often hindered by evil and evil itself has the look of good." As noted above, Aquinas infers from these facts the necessity of "caution" as a part of prudence. What we are now in a position to see is that caution is not to be construed as mere hesitation, much less as timidity. Instead, such caution is to be understood as patient endurance, itself a form of valiant vigilance. It is also to be understood, in the case of the patience of the martyr, as an exemplary act of friendship. Even in cases where martyrdom is not necessary for salvation, many holy martyrs, from the zeal of faith and from fraternal charity, offer themselves to God on behalf of others.[78]

It might seem as if the elevation of courage in Aquinas's theological re-formation of the cardinal virtues involves a regression to a pre-Socratic resignation of the tragic hero in the face of inscrutable fate. The case of the martyr belies such an interpretation. Aquinas argues that, while martyrdom is not itself one of the greatest acts, it is "among all virtuous acts . . . supreme evidence of the perfection of charity: since one's love for a thing is proved to be so much the greater, according as that which one despises for its sake is more dear, or that which one chooses to suffer for its sake is more odious" (*ST*, II-II, 124, 3).[79] But this is not blind submission. The martyr, for Aquinas, is analogous both to the warrior, who defends the common good of the *polis* in battle even to the point of death, and to the philosopher, whose desire to know the final cause of all things points beyond the *polis* to a transcendent truth. In a way that could never be true for the natural virtue of courage, the sacrificial fortitude and the loving patience of the martyr give witness to the highest truth about God and human life, the truth of faith (*ST*, II-II, 124, 5). To the philosopher, then, the martyr is or ought to be much more than a novel example of courage.[80] The martyrs' "heavenly battle," in which they conduct themselves, forgetful of bodily life, with "speech free from fear and mind unbowed," is a source of wonder. A puzzling paradox, the martyr sets before the philosopher disquieting theses concerning the perils of practical reason and the way in which purportedly rational self-knowledge can mask layers of internal conflict and self-deception.

NOTES

An earlier version of this essay was delivered at Boston College in April 2008, in a lecture sponsored by the Lonergan Center. I am grateful to the students and faculty, particularly Fred Lawrence and Arthur Madigan, S.J., for the stimulating discussion of the essay. I am also grateful to my graduate assistant at Baylor, Julianne Romanello, for her editorial work on the manuscript. Finally, I wish to express my gratitude to Alasdair MacIntyre whose superb essay provides the occasion for this volume. My own essay is not a direct response to his essay; it was well under way when I received the invitation from Larry Cunningham to contribute to this volume. Yet the topic of my essay and the issues with which it is preoccupied clearly bear the marks of the influence of Alasdair's writings. For me at least, it is inconceivable to work at the intersection of contemporary ethics and Aquinas's ethics without acknowledging an enormous debt to Alasdair's work.

1. Leonard Boyle, O.P., *The Setting of the Summa Theologiae of St. Thomas* (Toronto: PIMS, 1982). See also the much more detailed and comprehensive study by Boyle's student, Michele Mulchahey, *First the Bow Is Bent in Study: Dominican Education before 1350* (Toronto: PIMS, 1999); and Jean-Pierre Torrell, *Aquinas's Summa: Background, Structure and Reception* (Washington, DC: Catholic University of America Press, 2005).

2. Marie-Dominique Chenu, *The Scope of the Summa* (Washington, DC: The Thomist, 1958).

3. Post communem considerationem de virtutibus et vitiis et aliis ad materiam moralem pertinentibus, necesse est considerare singula in speciali, sermones enim morales universales sunt minus utiles, eo quod actiones in particularibus sunt (II-II, proemium). All quotations from the *Summa Theologiae* are from the Leonine edition of Robert Busa (Rome, 1888). All English translations from Latin are my own.

4. Pascal, *Pensees*, #655, trans. A. J. Krailsheimer (New York: Penguin, 1966). See John Bowlin, *Contingency and Fortune in Aquinas's Ethics* (Cambridge: Cambridge University Press, 1999). Bowlin's focus is on difficulty and contingency in practical reasoning and not so much on conflict, evil, and self-knowledge. He also has a different reading of natural law from the one I would advocate. But he is right to focus on Aquinas's supple treatment of courage. See especially his first chapter, "Virtue and Difficulty," 20–54. Also see Rebecca Konyndyk De Young, "Power Made Perfect in Weakness: Aquinas's Transformation of the Virtue of Courage," *Medieval Philosophy and Theology* 11 (2003): 147–80.

5. For an intriguing critique of much of contemporary ethics, especially virtue ethics, as bankrupt in the absence of the sort of theological

teleology found in Aquinas's ethics, see Candace Vogler, *Reasonably Vicious* (Cambridge, MA: Harvard University Press, 2002). Vogler focuses on Aquinas's treatment of the capital vices as taking genuine goods as their objects, as cultivated in such a way as to exhibit strength rather than weakness of will, and as organizing whole regions of human life in a rational way (pp. 38, 58). The implication is that contemporary attempts to demonstrate that the vicious or immoral must somehow be operating in ways incongruous with practical reason are bound to fail. Vogler may go further than Aquinas in insisting on the need for a theological basis for virtue, since he traces the basis of virtue not just to its ultimate ground in God but also to its proximate foundation in human nature; but of course even that account of nature points us not just ultimately but also inevitably in the direction of theology. She is also perhaps too taken with McDowell's account of "conversion" as a sort of inexplicable transition from one conceptual framework to another, in this case immoral to moral, as the only viable explanation of moral transformation (see Vogler, p. 186). The problem is not with the appeal to "conversion" but rather with McDowell's peculiar conception of it. For a corrective, see Alasdair MacIntyre's seminal essay, "Epistemological Crises, Dramatic Narrative, and the Philosophy of Science," published most recently in *The Tasks of Philosophy: Selected Essays, Volume 1* (Cambridge: Cambridge University Press, 2006), 3–23.

6. In his initial discussion of the cardinal virtues in the *Summa Theologiae*, Aquinas ranks courage above temperance because of the former's wider scope; it orders the passions to reason in matters of life and death (*ST*, I-II, 66, 4). Courage here is associated with, and praised on account of its subordination to, justice. Temperance, which is associated with the beautiful and the pleasant, is more closely associated with prudence itself.

7. The name "cardinal virtue" is of Roman rather than Greek origin. Aquinas finds both the term and the schema fruitful. In *ST*, II-II, proemium, he writes, "Aliae vero virtutes morales omnes aliqualiter reducuntur ad virtutes cardinales, ut ex supradictis patet, unde in consideratione alicuius virtutis cardinalis considerabuntur etiam omnes virtutes ad eam qualitercumque pertinentes et vitia opposita."

8. *ST*, I-II, 61, 2. Gregorius dicit, in II Moral., *in quatuor virtutibus tota boni operis structura consurgit.*

9. *Nicomachean Ethics*, I, 13 (1102b13–1103a10). All quotations of Aristotle's texts are from *The Complete Works of Aristotle: The Revised Oxford Translation*, vols. 1 and 2, ed. Jonathan Barnes (Princeton, NJ: Princeton University Press, 1984).

10. On the mutual interaction of reason and will throughout the stages of practical reasoning, according to Aquinas, see Daniel Westberg, *Right Practical Reason: Aristotle, Action and Prudence in Aquinas* (Oxford: Oxford University Press, 1994).

11. prudentia adiuvet omnes virtutes, et in omnibus operetur. Sed hoc non sufficit ad ostendendum quod non sit virtus specialis, quia nihil prohibet in aliquo genere esse aliquam speciem quae aliqualiter operetur in omnibus speciebus eiusdem generis; sicut sol aliqualiter influit in omnia corpora.

12. prudentia est recta ratio agibilium, ut supra dictum est. Unde oportet quod ille sit praecipuus actus prudentiae qui est praecipuus actus rationis agibilium. Cuius quidem sunt tres actus. Quorum primus est consiliari, quod pertinet ad inventionem, nam consiliari est quaerere, ut supra habitum est. Secundus actus est iudicare de inventis, et hic sistit speculativa ratio. Sed practica ratio, quae ordinatur ad opus, procedit ulterius et est tertius actus eius praecipere, qui quidem actus consistit in applicatione consiliatorum et iudicatorum ad operandum. Et quia iste actus est propinquior fini rationis practicae, inde est quod iste est principalis actus rationis practicae, et per consequens prudentiae.

13. For an interesting argument on behalf of the universal role of phronetic reasoning, even in the most speculative inquiries, see David Lachtermann, *The Ethics of Geometry: A Genealogy of Modernity* (New York: Routledge, 1989).

14. intellectus qui ponitur pars prudentiae est quaedam recta aestimatio de aliquo particulari fine.

15. Aquinas does not entertain a dichotomy between universals and singulars or between precepts and prudence. His account of prudence presupposes a metaphysical account of primary substance as a "this-such," a singular that is perceived and identified under some more general formality. In the works of Aristotle and Aquinas, it is common to find *nous* or *intellectus* associated exclusively with an apprehenson of universals. But even in the speculative order, Aquinas speaks of *intellectus* as reaching by a kind of reflection to the singular which instantiates the universal. Thus, the account of prudence in Aquinas entails both metaphysical claims and assertions about the nature of human knowledge and the human soul.

16. ex praeteritis oportet nos quasi argumentum sumere de futuris. Et ideo memoria praeteritorum necessaria est ad bene consiliandum de futuris.

17. ut Tullius dicit, in sua rhetorica, memoria non solum a natura proficiscitur, sed etiam habet plurimum artis et industriae. Et sunt quatuor

per quae homo proficit in bene memorando. Quorum primum est ut eorum quae vult memorari quasdam similitudines assumat convenientes, nec tamen omnino consuetas, quia ea quae sunt inconsueta magis miramur, et sic in eis animus magis et vehementius detinetur; ex quo fit quod eorum quae in pueritia vidimus magis memoremur. Ideo autem necessaria est huiusmodi similitudinum vel imaginum adinventio, quia intentiones simplices et spirituales facilius ex anima elabuntur nisi quibusdam similitudinibus corporalibus quasi alligentur, quia humana cognitio potentior est circa sensibilia. Unde et memorativa ponitur in parte sensitiva. Secundo, oportet ut homo ea quae memoriter vult tenere sua consideratione ordinate disponat, ut ex uno memorato facile ad aliud procedatur. Unde philosophus dicit, in libro de Mem., *a locis videntur reminisci aliquando, causa autem est quia velociter ab alio in aliud veniunt.* Tertio, oportet ut homo sollicitudinem apponat et affectum adhibeat ad ea quae vult memorari, quia quo aliquid magis fuerit impressum animo, eo minus elabitur. Unde et Tullius dicit, in sua rhetorica, quod *sollicitudo conservat integras simulacrorum figuras.* Quarto, oportet quod ea frequenter meditemur quae volumus memorari. Unde philosophus dicit, in libro de Mem., quod *meditationes memoriam salvant,* quia, ut in eodem libro dicitur, consuetudo est quasi natura; unde quae multoties intelligimus cito reminiscimur, quasi naturali quodam ordine ab uno ad aliud procedentes.

18. Josef Pieper, *Prudence,* trans. Richard Winston and Clara Winston (London: Faber and Faber, 1959), 27.

19. docilitas, sicut et alia quae ad prudentiam pertinent, secundum aptitudinem quidem est a natura, sed ad eius consummationem plurimum valet humanum studium, dum scilicet homo sollicite, frequenter et reverenter applicat animum suum documentis maiorum, non negligens ea propter ignaviam, nec contemnens propter superbiam.

20. etiam ipsos maiores oporteat dociles quantum ad aliqua esse, quia nullus in his quae subsunt prudentiae sibi quantum ad omnia sufficit.

21. See, e.g., Linda Zagzebski, *Virtues of the Mind: An Inquiry into the Nature of Virtue and the Ethical Foundations of Knowledge* (Cambridge: Cambridge University Press, 1996). I have tried to say something about the ethical implications of knowledge in Aquinas and how this view stands in relation to contemporary virtue epistemology, in "Aquinas, Virtue and Recent Epistemology," *Review of Metaphysics* 52 (1999): 579–94.

22. Sed contra est quod apostolus dicit, ad *Ephes.* V, *videte quomodo caute ambuletis.* . . . ea circa quae est prudentia sunt contingentia operabilia, in quibus, sicut verum potest admisceri falso, ita et malum bono, propter multiformitatem huiusmodi operabilium, in quibus bona plerumque im-

pediuntur a malis, et mala habent speciem boni. Et ideo necessaria est cautio ad prudentiam, ut sic accipiantur bona quod vitentur mala.

23. Dona enim spiritus sancti in adiutorium virtutum dantur; ut patet per Gregorium, in II Moral. Sed ad consiliandum homo sufficienter perficitur per virtutem prudentiae.

24. *ST,* II-II, 52, 2 ad 1. quia humana ratio non potest comprehendere singularia et contingentia quae occurrere possunt, fit quod *cogitationes mortalium sunt timidae, et incertae providentiae nostrae,* ut dicitur Sap. IX. Et ideo indiget homo in inquisitione consilii dirigi a Deo, qui omnia comprehendit. Quod fit per donum consilii, per quod homo dirigitur quasi consilio a Deo accepto. Sicut etiam in rebus humanis qui sibi ipsis non sufficiunt in inquisitione consilii a sapientioribus consilium requirunt.

25. filii Dei aguntur a spiritu sancto secundum modum eorum, salvato scilicet libero arbitrio, quae est facultas voluntatis et rationis. Et sic inquantum ratio a spiritu sancto instruitur de agendis, competit filiis Dei donum consilii.

26. Cum ergo consilium sit primus et infimus actus prudentiae, supremus autem actus eius est praecipere, medius autem iudicare; videtur quod donum respondens prudentiae non sit consilium, sed magis iudicium vel praeceptum.

27. Et quia in donis spiritus sancti mens humana non se habet ut movens, sed magis ut mota, ut supra dictum est; inde est quod non fuit conveniens quod donum correspondens prudentiae praeceptum diceretur vel iudicium, sed consilium, per quod potest significari motio mentis consiliatae ab alio consiliante.

28. The claim can be seen in the definition of the natural law as the participation of the rational creature in the eternal law (*ST,* I-II, 91, 2): Inter cetera autem rationalis creatura excellentiori quodam modo divinae providentiae subiacet, inquantum et ipsa fit providentiae particeps, sibi ipsi et aliis providens. Unde et in ipsa participatur ratio aeterna, per quam habet naturalem inclinationem ad debitum actum et finem. Et talis participatio legis aeternae in rationali creatura lex naturalis dicitur.

29. Unde mens humana ex hoc ipso quod dirigitur a spiritu sancto, fit potens dirigere se et alios.

30. See Friedrich Nietzsche, *The Birth of Tragedy,* trans. Walter Kaufmann (New York: Random House, 1967), esp. sections 12–16.

31. Plato, *Apology* (41d), trans. Hugh Tredennick, *The Collected Dialogues of Plato,* ed. Edith Hamilton and Huntington Cairns (Princeton, NJ: Princeton University Press, 1987).

32. *Nicomachean Ethics*, bk. I, chap. 10, 1100b1526–33.

33. *Nicomachean Ethics*, bk. I, chap. 10, 1101a11–14.

34. Illud enim est finis boni nostri, propter quod appetenda sunt cetera, ipsum autem propter se ipsum. All Latin texts of Augustine are from the Loeb Classical Library: *The City of God* (Cambridge, MA: Harvard University Press, 1960); *Confessions* (Cambridge, MA: Harvard University Press, 1912). Translations are my own.

35. See Augustine, *City of God*, bk. XIX, 4: ubi uirtutes ipsae, quibus hic certe nihil melius atque utilius in homine reperitur, quanto maiora sunt adiutoria contra uim periculorum laborum dolorum, tanto fideliora testimonia miseriarum. Si enim uerae uirtutes sunt, quae nisi in eis, quibus uera inest pietas, esse non possunt: non se profitentur hoc posse, ut nullas miserias patiantur homines, in quibus sunt (neque enim mendaces sunt uerae uirtutes, ut hoc profiteantur), sed ut uita humana, quae tot et tantis huius saeculi malis esse cogitur misera, spe futuri saeculi sit beata, sicut et salua. Quo modo enim beata est, quae nondum salua est? Vnde et apostolus Paulus non de hominibus inprudentibus inpatientibus, intemperantibus et iniquis, sed de his, qui secundum ueram pietatem uiuerent et ideo uirtutes, quas haberent, ueras haberent, ait: Spe enim salui facti sumus. Spes autem quae uidetur, non est spes. Quod enim uidet quis, quid et sperat? Si autem quod non uidemus speramus, per patientiam expectamus. Sicut ergo spe salui, ita spe beati facti sumus, et sicut salutem, ita beatitudinem non iam tenemus praesentem, sed expectamus futuram, et hoc per patientiam; quia in malis sumus, quae patienter tolerare debemus, donec ad illa ueniamus bona, ubi omnia iterunt quibus ineffabiliter delectemur, nihil erit autem, quod iam tolerare debeamus.

36. Aristotle's positive appraisal in the *Poetics* of the ethical impact of tragedy is often seen as a departure from Plato's ostracizing of the tragic poets from the ideal regime. But this overlooks the way Aristotle admits poetry only on Plato's terms; the description of tragedy in the *Poetics* has already purged it of elements Plato found problematic, namely, the role of fate, the gods, and necessity in the denouement of the action. See Stephen White, "Aristotle's Favorite Tragedies," in *Essays on Aristotle's Poetics*, ed. Amelie Rorty (Princeton, NJ: Princeton University Press, 1992), 221–40; and Amelie Rorty, "The Psychology of Aristotelian Tragedy," in *Essays on Aristotle's Poetics*, 1–22.

37. Haec ergo uita hominis, quae uirtute et aliis animi et corporis bonis, sine quibus uirtus esse non.potest, fruitur, beata esse dicitur; si uero et aliis, sine quibus esse uirtus potest, uel ullis uel pluribus, beatior; si autem

prorsus omnibus, ut nullum omnino bonum desit uel animi uel corporis, beatissima.

38. Porro ipsa uirtus, . . . quid hic agit nisi perpetua bella cum uitiis, nec exterioribus, sed interioribus, nec alienis, sed plane nostris et propriis . . . ?

39. See *Nicomachean Ethics*, bk. VII, chaps. 1–10.

40. Narrabat haec Ponticianus. tu autem, domine, inter verba eius retorquebas me ad me ipsum, auferens me a dorso meo, ubi me posueram, dum nollem me adtendere; et constituebas me ante faciem meam, ut viderem, quam turpis essem, quam distortus et sordidus, maculosus et ulcerosus. et videbam et horrebam, et quo a me fugerem non erat. et si conabar a me avertere aspectum, narrabat ille quod narrabat; et tu me rursus opponebas mihi, et inpingebas me in oculos meos, ut invenirem iniquitatem et odissem. noveram eam, sed dissimulabam et cohibebam et obliviscebar.

41. Alasdair MacIntyre, "What Has Christianity to Say to the Moral Philosopher?" John Coffin Memorial Lecture in Christian Ethics, delivered in the University of London, May 21, 1998.

42. Et primo volens ostendere mihi, quam resistas superbis, humilibus autem des gratiam, et quanta misericordia tua demonstrata sit hominibus via humilitatis, quod verbum caro factum est et habitavit inter homines: procurasti mihi per quendam hominem, inmanissimo typho turgidum, quosdam Platonicorum libros ex graeca lingua in latinum verso.

43. Iam uero illa uirtus, cuius nomen est fortitudo, in quantacumque sapientia euidentissima testis est humanorum malorum, quae compellitur patientia tolerare.

44. Respondeo dicendum quod per iustitiam originalem perfecte ratio continebat inferiores animae vires, et ipsa ratio a Deo perficiebatur ei subiecta. Haec autem originalis iustitia subtracta est per peccatum primi parentis, sicut iam dictum est. Et ideo omnes vires animae remanent quodammodo destitutae proprio ordine, quo naturaliter ordinantur ad virtutem, et ipsa destitutio vulneratio naturae dicitur. Sunt autem quatuor potentiae animae quae possunt esse subiecta virtutum, ut supra dictum est, scilicet ratio, in qua est prudentia; voluntas, in qua est iustitia; irascibilis, in qua est fortitudo; concupiscibilis, in qua est temperantia. Inquantum ergo ratio destituitur suo ordine ad verum, est vulnus ignorantiae; inquantum vero voluntas destituitur ordine ad bonum, est vulnus malitiae; inquantum vero irascibilis destituitur suo ordine ad arduum, est vulnus infirmitatis; inquantum vero concupiscentia destituitur ordine ad delectabile moderatum ratione, est vulnus concupiscentiae.

Sic igitur ita quatuor sunt vulnera inflicta toti humanae naturae ex peccato primi parentis. Sed quia inclinatio ad bonum virtutis in unoquoque diminuitur per peccatum actuale, ut ex dictis patet, et ista sunt quatuor vulnera ex aliis peccatis consequentia, inquantum scilicet per peccatum et ratio hebetatur, praecipue in agendis; et voluntas induratur ad bonum; et maior difficultas bene agendi accrescit; et concupiscentia magis exardescit.

45. Pax autem nostra propria et hic est cum Deo per fidem et in aeternum erit cum illo per speciem. Sed hic siue illa communis siue nostra propria talis est pax, ut solacium miseriae sit potius quam beatitudinis gaudium. Ipsa quoque nostra iustitia, quamuis uera sit propter uerum boni finem, ad quem refertur, tamen tanta est in hac uita, ut potius remissione peccatorum constet quam perfectione uirtutum. Testis est oratio totius ciuitatis Dei, quae peregrinatur in terris. Per omnia quippe membra sua clamat ad Deum: Dimittc nobis debita nostra, sicut et nos dimittimus debitoribus nostris.

46. For a recent discussion and defense of Aquinas's account of the preambles, see Ralph McInerny, *Praeambula Fidei: Thomism and the God of the Philosophers* (Washington, DC: Catholic University of America Press, 2006).

47. lex vetus manifestabat praecepta legis naturae, et superaddebat quaedam propria praecepta.

48. Dei cognitio, quae homines maxime perfectos et bonos facit, non nisi quibusdam paucis, et his etiam post temporis longitudinem proveniret.

49. humanum genus, si sola rationis via ad Deum cognoscendum pateret, in maximis ignorantiae tenebris.

50. tunc maxime populo necessarium fuit, quando lex naturalis obscurari incipiebat propter exuberantiam peccatorum.

51. Oportebat autem huiusmodi auxilium quodam ordine dari, ut per imperfecta ad perfectionem manuducerentur. Et ideo inter legem naturae et legem gratiae, oportuit legem veterem dari.

52. Et ideo post haec tempora fuit necessarium legem scriptam dari in remedium humanae ignorantiae, quia per legem est cognitio peccati, ut dicitur Rom. III.

53. Aquinas's emphasis on law as accusation might seem to anticipate Luther; there is a common source, of course, namely, St. Paul. But Aquinas also holds that the accusation of the law presupposes the universal presence of the law in nature, not just in explicit revelation to the Jewish people. Aquinas is also careful to follow the Pauline understanding of accusation as a subordinate element in the pedagogy of the law whose principal aim is mercy and restoration. For an innovative examination of Paul on these matters, see

Remi Brague, "Jew, Greek, and Christian: Some Reflections on the Pauline Revolution," *Expositions* 1, no. 1 (2007): 15–28. Against the now-dated antinomian reading of Paul, Brague writes that "Paul kept the idea of a set of rules, and even the idea of a divine origin of those rules, but he put the idea of a divine origin of norms at one further remove. Norms are not dictated by God through the mediation of a Prophet at some point in history; they are inscribed in the 'heart' of man (Rom. 2.15)" (p. 23). Concerning the old dispute over whether New Testament authors inappropriately imported Greek concepts into Christianity, Brague writes that " 'secondarity' towards Judaism enabled 'secondarity' towards Hellenism; Greek culture could be included and not digested" (p. 25).

54. Conveniens igitur fuit tali tempore legem veterem dari, ad superbiam hominum convincendam. De duobus enim homo superbiebat, scilicet de scientia, et de potentia. De scientia quidem, quasi ratio naturalis ei posset sufficere ad salutem. Et ideo ut de hoc eius superbia convinceretur permissus est homo regimini suae rationis absque adminiculo legis scriptae, et experimento homo discere potuit quod patiebatur rationis defectum, per hoc quod homines usque ad idololatriam et turpissima vitia circa tempora Abrahae sunt prolapsi. Et ideo post haec tempora fuit necessarium legem scriptam dari in remedium humanae ignorantiae, quia per legem est cognitio peccati, ut dicitur Rom. III. Sed postquam homo est instructus per legem, convicta est eius superbia de infirmitate, dum implere non poterat quod cognoscebat. Et ideo, sicut apostolus concludit, ad Rom. VIII, *quod impossibile erat legi, in qua infirmabatur per carnem, misit Deus filium suum, ut iustificatio legis impleretur in nobis.*

55. Deus aliquando permittit aliquos cadere in peccatum, ut exinde humilientur. Ita etiam voluit talem legem dare quam suis viribus homines implere non possent, ut sic dum homines de se praesumentes peccatores se invenirent, humiliati recurrerent ad auxilium gratiae.

56. Augustinus dicit, in libro de Serm. Dom. in monte, *consilium convenit misericordibus, quia unicum remedium est de tantis malis erui, dimittere aliis et dare.*

57. Although I cannot enter more fully into this topic here, it is important to note that Aquinas's metaphysical account of created being eliminates the possibility of envisioning nature itself as tragic. At the foundation of things, there is not "ontological violence" or "primordial incoherence." On these matters, see John Milbank, *Theology and Social Theory: Beyond Secular Reason* (Oxford: Blackwell, 1990), 278–325; and especially the magisterial work of Paul Ricoeur, *The Symbolism of Evil*, trans. E. Buchanan (New York:

Harper, 1967), 219. Ricoeur notes that overcoming the primacy of the tragic vision requires that "guilt be distinguished from finiteness," and ontology, from the historical origin of evil.

58. caritas dicitur finis aliarum virtutum quia omnes alias virtutes ordinat ad finem suum. Et quia mater est quae in se concipit ex alio, ex hac ratione dicitur mater aliarum virtutum, quia ex appetitu finis ultimi concipit actus aliarum virtutum, imperando ipsos.

59. Augustinus dicit, in III de Doct. Christ., *caritatem voco motum animi ad fruendum Deo propter ipsum.*

60. Cum igitur sit aliqua communicatio hominis ad Deum secundum quod nobis suam beatitudinem communicat, super hac communicatione oportet aliquam amicitiam fundari. De qua quidem communicatione dicitur I ad Cor. I, *fidelis Deus, per quem vocati estis in societatem filii eius.* Amor autem super hac communicatione fundatus est caritas. Unde manifestum est quod caritas amicitia quaedam est hominis ad Deum.

61. Cum autem bonum super quod fundatur quaelibet alia amicitia honesta ordinetur sicut ad finem ad bonum super quod fundatur caritas, consequens est ut caritas imperet actui cuiuslibet alterius amicitiae, sicut ars quae est circa finem imperat arti quae est circa ea quae sunt ad finem.

62. ad virtutem humanam pertinet ut faciat hominem et opus eius secundum rationem esse.

63. Et ideo fortis ex una parte habet unde delectetur, scilicet secundum delectationem animalem, scilicet de ipso actu virtutis et de fine eius, ex alia vero parte habet unde doleat, et animaliter, dum considerat amissionem propriae vitae, et corporaliter.

64. On this issue, see Harry Jaffa's critical comments about Aquinas's interpretation of Aristotle, in *Aristotelianism and Thomism: A Study of the Commentary by Thomas Aquinas on the Nicomachean Ethics* (Westport, CT: Greenwood Press, 1979), 54–56.

65. Ambrosius accipit fortitudinem large, secundum quod importat animi firmitatem respectu quorumcumque impugnantium.

66. Et secundum hoc est generalis virtus, vel potius conditio cuiuslibet virtutis, quia sicut philosophus dicit, in II Ethic., ad virtutem requiritur firmiter et immobiliter operari.

67. fortitudo animi dicatur quae firmiter retinet voluntatem hominis in bono rationis contra maxima mala, quia qui stat firmus contra maiora, consequens est quod stet firmus contra minora, sed non convertitur; et hoc etiam ad rationem virtutis pertinet, ut respiciat ultimum. Maxime autem terribile inter omnia corporalia mala est mors, quae tollit omnia corporalia bona.

68. pericula mortis quae est in bellicis directe imminent homini propter aliquod bonum, inquantum scilicet defendit bonum commune per iustum bellum.

69. Sed et circa pericula cuiuscumque alterius mortis fortis bene se habet, praesertim quia et cuiuslibet mortis homo potest periculum subire propter virtutem; puta cum aliquis non refugit amico infirmanti obsequi propter timorem mortiferae infectionis; vel cum non refugit itinerari ad aliquod pium negotium prosequendum propter timorem naufragii vel latronum.

70. Such tensions are played out dramatically in Shakespeare's *Coriolanus*.

71. sustinere est difficilius quam aggredi, triplici ratione. Primo quidem, quia sustinere videtur aliquis ab aliquo fortiori invadente, qui autem aggreditur invadit per modum fortioris. Difficilius autem est pugnare cum fortiori quam cum debiliori. Secundo, quia ille qui sustinet iam sentit pericula imminentia, ille autem qui aggreditur habet ea ut futura. Difficilius autem est non moveri a praesentibus quam a futuris. Tertio, quia sustinere importat diuturnitatem temporis, sed aggredi potest aliquis ex subito motu. Difficilius autem est diu manere immobilem quam subito motu moveri ad aliquid arduum. Unde philosophus dicit, in III Ethic., quod *quidam sunt praevolantes ante pericula, in ipsis autem discedunt, fortes autem e contrario se habent.*

72. Quia fortitudo non solum sustinet molestias absque perturbatione, quod est patientiae, sed etiam ingerit se eis, cum opus fuerit. Unde quicumque est fortis, est patiens, sed non convertitur, est enim patientia quaedam fortitudinis pars.

73. Et sic timor consiliativos facit. Quia, ut philosophus in III Ethic. dicit, *consiliamur de magnis, in quibus quasi nobis ipsis discredimus.* Ea autem quae timorem incutiunt, non sunt simpliciter mala, sed habent quandam magnitudinem, tum ex eo quod apprehenduntur ut quae difficiliter repelli possunt; tum etiam quia apprehenduntur ut de prope existentia, sicut iam dictum est. Unde homines maxime in timoribus quaerunt consiliari. Alio modo dicitur aliquis consiliativus, a facultate bene consiliandi. Et sic nec timor, nec aliqua passio consiliativos facit. Quia homini affecto secundum aliquam passionem, videtur aliquid vel maius vel minus quam sit secundum rei veritatem, sicut amanti videntur ea quae amat, meliora; et timenti, ea quae timet, terribiliora. Et sic ex defectu rectitudinis iudicii, quaelibet passio, quantum est de se, impedit facultatem bene consiliandi.

74. quanto aliqua passio est fortior, tanto magis homo secundum ipsam affectus, impeditur. Et ideo quando timor fuerit fortis, vult quidem

homo consiliari, sed adeo perturbatur in suis cogitationibus, quod consilium adinvenire non potest.

75. cognoscere Deum esse in aliquo communi, sub quadam confusione, est nobis naturaliter insertum, inquantum scilicet Deus est hominis beatitudo, homo enim naturaliter desiderat beatitudinem, et quod naturaliter desideratur ab homine, naturaliter cognoscitur ab eodem. Sed hoc non est simpliciter cognoscere Deum esse; sicut cognoscere venientem, non est cognoscere Petrum, quamvis sit Petrus veniens, multi enim perfectum hominis bonum, quod est beatitudo, existimant divitias; quidam vero voluptates; quidam autem aliquid aliud.

76. Aquinas's account of courage as endurance brings out the significance of patience for the moral life, even if technically he subordinates patience in the scheme of the virtues and relegates it to the status of a secondary virtue in relation to courage (*ST*, II-II, 136, 4). As noted above, courage is more encompassing than patience.

77. Here is yet another arena in which Aquinas's philosophical account of human action, perhaps prompted by theological examples, is much more supple than that of Aristotle. How so? Of course, death is not something to be actively sought. Indeed, it might seem from the perspective of Aristotle's ethics of human action that martyrdom would be involuntary and thus not subject to moral praise. As Stephen Brock observes, "Aristotle's explanation of what is involuntary" has to do with what is "forced or violent. The violent, he says, is that whose moving principle is outside, with the one who suffers it contributing nothing. Without the notion of consent, it is very difficult to give an accurate statement of what it must mean for the one who suffers to 'contribute' something." See Stephen Brock, *Action and Conduct* (Edinburgh: T & T Clark, 1998), 159–60.

78. Est enim aliquis casus in quo martyrium perferre non est de necessitate salutis, puta cum ex zelo fidei et caritate fraterna multoties leguntur sancti martyres sponte se obtulisse martyrio. (*ST*, II-II, 124, 3 ad 1).

79. Martyrium autem, inter omnes actus virtuosos, maxime demonstrat perfectionem caritatis. Quia tanto magis ostenditur aliquis aliquam rem amare, quanto pro ea rem magis amatam contemnit, et rem magis odiosam eligit pati.

80. Unde Cyprianus dicit, in quodam sermone, *vidit admirans praesentium multitudo caeleste certamen, et in praelio stetisse servos Christi voce libera, mente incorrupta, virtute divina* (ST, II-II, 124, 2).

CHAPTER 10 | From Answers to Questions

A Response to the Responses

Alasdair MacIntyre

In my opening essay I did not invite agreement, but hoped to elicit from others who share the philosophical and theological concerns and commitments of Catholic Christianity both criticism of the theses that I defend and the articulation of alternative perspectives. In these respects I succeeded and have reason to be extraordinarily grateful to all the contributors. They have provided a remarkable range of criticisms and distinctive approaches, adding dimensions to the discussion, deepening our understanding of the issues, and arguing for alternative standpoints. What we are left with, I am going to suggest, is not so much a set of agreements and disagreements as a better defined and more searching set of questions. We have reached a point at which we can say more clearly and sharply just what it is that we and others must do to carry this project forward.

The two essays that advance the most direct and searching criticisms of my own positions are those by Jean Porter and Gerald McKenny. I shall delay my response to McKenny, since in evaluating his criticisms I need to appeal to considerations advanced by some other essayists. So I proceed first to examine Jean Porter's arguments and next to consider how important dimensions are added to the discussion by David A. Clairmont, M. Cathleen Kaveny, and Daniel Philpott. Only then will I address McKenny's powerful case and evaluate it, partly in the light of the essays by Father Kevin L. Flannery, S.J., and by Father John J. Coughlin, O.F.M. The final essay, by Thomas Hibbs, throws badly needed light on how we should proceed further, if we are to move on from the reformulations that result from my engagement with the arguments and insights of the other essayists. Every one of them has insightful points to make on which I will be unable to comment simply for reasons of space. So I hope that I will be forgiven for being selective.

I

Jean Porter begins from the question "Does the natural law provide a universally valid morality?" The answer that she gives is "No." If all that she means by her answer is that the natural law does not provide a morality that all rational agents, whatever their cultural or social background, are able to acknowledge as authoritative, she and I would not be in disagreement. But she means significantly more. For to the contention that adherence to the precepts of the natural law, as characterized by Aquinas, is compatible with a recognition of diversity with respect to "the normative substance of the natural law" (p. 57) she adds the thesis that "even on the most optimistic showing, any attempt to specify the general precepts of the natural law will remain indeterminate and incomplete, apart from the traditions and practices of some specific community." And she adds that "the natural law as we Christians understand and formulate it will inevitably involve some degree of theological specification" (p. 91).

In her impressive book *Nature as Reason: A Thomistic Theory of the Natural Law* (Grand Rapids, MI: William B. Eerdmans, 2005), she made it clear that underlying her view of the indeterminacy of the precepts of the natural law is a thesis about the limitations of practical rationality, no matter how understood. She remarks at one point that "it begins to look as if practical reason alone is not sufficient to generate a moral theory" (p. 244)—or, I take it, the moral judgments that guide our everyday actions—and the tentative character of this remark disappears, as Porter examines and rejects the various claims about the sufficiency of practical rationality advanced by Kantians and utilitarians. So it seems to be her view that the central theses of all the major philosophical standpoints concerning morality and the judgments made in accordance with them, Thomistic, Humean, Kantian, utilitarian, whatever, are either insufficiently supported or underdetermined or both, and that the issues dividing them therefore cannot be settled by rational argument.

For Porter therefore there is no problem about the explanation of moral disagreement. Not all moral disagreement may be explicable by the insufficiency of reason, but the insufficiency of reason makes the occurrence of moral disagreement unsurprising. By contrast on my view—and on the view that, rightly or wrongly, I ascribe to Aquinas—the occurrence of moral disagreement requires a different kind of explanation, since I am committed to holding that, if the requirements of practical reason are rightly understood, then practical rationality provides everything that is required for the moral life, independently of any theological ethics. Practical reason not only provides us with good reason to act in accordance with the precepts of the natural law, but also guides us in how to apply it. To be a rational agent is to be directed towards one's good, and we cannot achieve our individual goods without also directing ourselves towards the achievement of those common goods that we share with others, the common goods of families, of schools, of fishing crews and string quartets, of political societies. To achieve those common goods we must engage in deliberation with the relevant others, as rational agents with other rational agents. To treat those others as rational agents who will in turn deal with us as rational agents is to presuppose that both they and we are bound by the precepts of the natural law. Here Porter and I disagree. She is prepared to allow that it *might* be the case that "mutual deliberation can only take place in a context of mutual equality and security" (p. 74), but she rejects my unqualified assertion that to treat others as rational agents, with whom one, as oneself a rational agent, can either now or at some time in the future deliberate about our common good, requires that one treat them in accordance with the precepts of the natural law, something that I hold to be a conceptual truth. Since however she does not at this point argue for her alternative view, I can do little else than reiterate mine.

If I threaten you with harmful consequences, if you do not arrive at the same conclusion that I do, or if I offer you rewards for arriving at that conclusion, or if I now inflict harm upon you or bribe you, so that you will arrive at that conclusion, I fail to treat you as someone who ought only to agree with my conclusion if you yourself judge, on the basis of your own powers of reasoning, that there are sufficiently good reasons for arriving at that conclusion. Conversely, if I act towards others as a rational agent engaged in, or about to engage in, deliberation with rational agents about our common good, I must understand myself as prohibited from engaging or threatening to engage in such coercive or seductive acts of persuasion or in any other type of act that subverts present or future rational deliberation. And the precepts that prohibit such acts are the precepts of the natural law.

In order to deliberate well about what must be done to achieve some common good in this or that particular situation, I must be disposed to feel, to think, to judge, and to act in ways that direct me towards the achievement of that common good, and beyond it my further and ultimate good, the good that gives me reason to seek that common good. That is, I must have those habits that are the virtues. And reason instructs us as to what habits we need to possess. As Porter notes in *Nature as Reason* (p. 187), Aquinas has often been interpreted as identifying virtuous behavior with rational behavior, and this indeed is how both she and I interpret him. Of course our acquisition of habits is not initially governed by our own reasoning and, when we are young, it may or may not be governed by the reasoning of our parents and other elders. But later, when we have become capable of adequate reflection on ourselves and on the kind of good that our ultimate end must be, then we become able to ask whether our habits are or are not the habits that we need to direct ourselves towards that end, that is, we become able to ask whether our habits are what reason requires them to be. Adequately informed and directed practical reason is all that we need.

This conception of practical reason—and the conception of theoretical reason that is its counterpart—was developed within and gives expression to the presuppositions of a particular social and moral tradition that has been transmitted through the social life of a number of otherwise very different societies: in ancient Greece, in Islamic Baghdad and Egypt and Andalusia, in different times and places in medieval and Renaissance Catholic Europe and in some postmedieval successor cultures. But the claim about natural law made from within that tradition has been not that this is how the requirements of reason appear from the standpoint of that tradition, but that this is what the requirements of reason *are.*

Porter, however, is committed to rejecting this view, and she advances two arguments in support of this rejection. Both direct our attention to important features of the precepts of the natural law. Neither, however, provides sufficient grounds for her rejection. But before I consider them in turn, let me get three less important matters out of the way.

First, what divides us is in part the interpretation of some texts of Aquinas. I will not avoid issues of interpretation altogether, but I deal with them only in the course of considering substantive questions. For, were I to be convinced that Aquinas held some of the views ascribed to him by Porter, I should be as much at odds with him as I am with her. Secondly, Porter's quarrel with me on p. 58, where she says that "the precepts of the Decalogue are *not* included among the primary precepts of the natural law," seems to be due to a misunderstanding. She supposes that I was speaking of the first principles of the natural law when I spoke of its primary precepts. In fact she and I agree that the moral precepts of the Decalogue—identical with what I have, like others, called the primary precepts of the natural law—can be derived from the first principles of practical reason "with only a minimum of reflection." Thirdly, Porter seems to think that, when I say of the precepts of the natural law that they are known noninferentially, I am saying that they are *per se nota*. But some truths can be known noninferentially without being *per se notum* truths. Readers ought to note that Porter's criticisms of my views are grounded in the more extensive arguments that she advanced in her book. But no one should suppose that I take my criticism of particular points that she makes to be anything like an adequate response to the complex and illuminating discussions of her book. That is a larger task for another time.

Porter's first argument concerns what Aquinas calls diversity in respect of rectitude (*Summa Theologiae* Ia-IIae 94, 2). He points out that, in the course of finding application for some precept of the natural law in some particular set of circumstances, we may and often will need to qualify our initial formulation of the precept. So we may conclude in some particular case, that we should not, as we generally should, return a piece of property to its owner, because, for example, he will use it to fight againt his country. Here Aquinas is taking it for granted that in qualifying the application of one precept of the natural law we are guided by another, that which generally prohibits us from taking up arms against our fellow citizens. And Aquinas also takes it for granted that this work of qualification is itself a work of reason and that what any one precept requires in some particular set of circumstances it would also require in any identical set of circumstances. Hence what Aquinas calls diversity in respect of rectitude is not only compatible with, but supportive of the claim that the precepts of the natural law, rightly applied, do provide a universal morality. And, had Aquinas thought otherwise, he would have been mistaken.

How might Porter reply to this? She would, I take it, argue that I have much too narrow and even simpleminded a view of the range of diversity that is possible on Aquinas's account. Imagine there to be some moral tradition in which it is not generally held that there is something wrong in taking up arms against one's fellow citizens. If so, among the adherents of this tradition the set of qualifications of the precept requiring us to return property to its owner will be significantly different. And suppose that such cases are multiplied. Then there may emerge two or more different moralities, each constructed from the same initial set of precepts. So that it would seem right to conclude, as Porter does, that the precepts of the natural law, by themselves, are insufficient to supply a universal morality.

To this my reply can only be a case by case response. In the imaginary example that I have constructed on Porter's behalf it would run as follows. Produce the arguments that allegedly show that it is not true in general that we should not take up arms against our fellow citizens. If they are sufficient to show this, then our original qualification of the precept fails. If they are insufficient, then that qualification stands and the contention of the imagined rival tradition fails. In either case argument will lead to a decisive conclusion. In neither case is there support for Porter's view of possible wide-ranging diversity among equally rational agents. But of course it remains open to Porter to propose a further set of cases in support of her contention.

Her second argument is intended to support the claim that the precepts of the natural law are "not specific enough to guide action" (p. 58). On pp. 71–72 she comments on *ST* Ia-IIae 100, 8 ad 3, and asserts that "the precepts of the Decalogue are always binding, but that does not mean that we can proceed immediately from these to a correct judgment in every instance of moral choice. In many cases, we will be able to do so, but in other cases we will find it necessary to reflect carefully on the meaning of moral concepts such as murder, theft, or adultery." And, according to Porter, as we proceed by rational reflection from the first principles through the primary precepts to judgment in particular cases, the more this process "is subject both to contingency—because general moral concepts can be legitimately applied in more than one way—and to error" (p. 72). Porter seems to believe that what she calls general moral concepts, such as the concepts of murder, are open-textured to such a degree that they are open to development and to application in different and incompatible ways, between which there may be no grounds for rational decision, apart, that is, from the moral and other commitments of some particular community, derived from its particular tradition. So the natural law can function adequately only from the standpoint of some such tradition. Yet, if we examine, for example, how the concept of murder has in fact been developed and applied through a series of arguments within more than one social and moral tradition, this seems to be false. For we are able to arrive at sound conclusions that are as tradition-independent as the primary precepts. The action of killing someone else is a paradigmatic example of not treating that individual as a rational agent, as someone with whom one needs to be able to deliberate about our common good. But, if I can only preserve my own life or the life of someone else, by killing that other individual, because she or he is attacking me or that someone else, then it is not I but the other who has ruled out this possibility. The life that I take is not innocent and my action is not to be accounted murder. Or suppose that my action results in someone's death, but not only was this unintentional, nothing that I could have done could have prevented this outcome. Then my action, whatever it was, was not the action of taking that life. So my action was not murder. Or imagine a case in which I do not intend to take someone's life, but my gross negligence results in loss of life. Then, although my action is not murder—defined as the intentional taking of an innocent life—I am nonetheless guilty of an offence closely related to murder. And so on.

As the concept of murder was in this way better and better defined—and at each stage we have a sound and, I believe, in the end incontrovertible argument for proceeding as we do—so room for rational disagreement about what is and what is not murder is removed. "Murder" is not open-textured in the way and to the extent that Porter suggests. And we should note that in *Nature as Reason* Porter herself provides an account of "justice," taken from Aquinas, that is remarkably parallel to my treatment of "murder." Porter does of course allow that "in many cases" we can proceed without difficulty from a precept of the natural law or the Decalogue to its application in a particular situation (p. 72), but she nowhere tells us how we are to draw the line between cases in which we can and cases in which we cannot do this.

To this Porter might respond by denying that the articulation of the concept of murder—or of kindred concepts—always has to proceed in the way that I have outlined, and she has good reason to do so. For there is one obvious case in which the application of the concept "murder" does seem to be indeterminate, that of the abortion of a human embryo within the first three months after conception. Is such an abortion the taking of an innocent life or not? There are clearly alternative and rival answers advanced to this question, and the partisan advocates of those rival answers remain unpersuaded by each other's arguments. The onus is therefore on me to respond to this case. But I delay doing so, in order that certain other types of relevant consideration may first come into view. So neither Porter nor I have as yet had anything like the last word. And, even if my criticism of her arguments were to stand, it does not follow that she is mistaken in her conclusions. Others, as I shall note later, agree with her in denying that the precepts of the natural law provide a universal morality, although on different grounds. I therefore put this issue on one side only temporarily. And I also need to remark on something else. Reading Porter's responses to my theses and arguments has brought home to me the absence from my essay of an adequate sense of the full complexity of practical reasoning, of how much can be involved in knowing how to formulate and to apply the precepts of the natural law, that is, in knowing how to direct oneself towards common goods and one's own good. To this too I will have to return.

II

Three of the essayists, David A. Clairmont, M. Cathleen Kaveny, and Daniel Philpott, identify crucially important dimensions of moral disagreement that are missing from my account. All three have taken care to find common ground with my positions, something for which I am grateful. But what they have to say would lose none of its importance, if there were not such common ground. So Clairmont's starting-point for his discussion of interreligious conversation on moral matters is developed in terms of the account of practices and goods internal to them that I advanced in *After Virtue,* but his discussion of the goods of interreligious conversation is in fact compatible with a range of different conceptions of goods, and someone who rejected my account would still be well advised to attend carefully to Clairmont's essay.

Clairmont begins by considering three types of good that might be achieved by a participant in extended interreligious conversation on moral matters. First, there may be an increase in the depth of understanding of the other and of the other's moral tradition. Secondly, there may be the achievement of greater awareness of discrepancies between moral profession and moral practice that have characterized either oneself and one's own moral and religious tradition, or the moral and religious tradition with which one has entered into dialogue, or both. And thirdly, there may be a "recognition of morally relevant goods" that have been ignored in the past deliberations of one's own tradition. Whether these goods are or are not achieved will depend on how one prepares oneself for and how one conducts oneself in the ongoing conversation. Here Clairmont identifies an important omission in my account.

I laid some emphasis on the need for a certain kind of intellectual and moral asceticism in our thinking and conversation with others, in order to overcome our prejudices and to resist the temptation to use our rhetoric skills to disguise weaknesses in our reasoning (pp. 22–23, quoted by Clairmont, pp. 114–15). But, so Clairmont suggests, I significantly underestimated what is needed and I did so because I failed to recognize the relevance of what the Church teaches us about penitence and reconciliation. And Clairmont invites us to consider what is involved in preparing oneself adequately for the sacrament of penance.

First of all, someone engaged in such preparation has to become aware of her or his lack of and need for self-knowledge and of her or his capacity for illusion and self-deception. This is something that I have written about elsewhere ("What Has Christianity to Say to the Moral Philosopher?" in *The Doctrine of God and Theological Ethics*, ed. A. J. Torrance and M. Banner [London: T & T Clark, 2006], 21–23), and should have written about here, and I am grateful to Clairmont for pointing this out. He is right to assert that penitential self-knowledge is necessary if the goods of interreligious conversation on moral matters are to be achieved, and he could have gone further than he does by emphasizing that without such self-knowledge what we mistakenly take to be our practical rationality may well be no more than a mask for something else.

Clairmont insists on the importance of slowing down the pace of our self-reflection, and he sees an analogy between what is required in our reckoning with ourselves and our moral failures, as we prepare to make an act of contrition, and what is required in our confrontations with others who have different and incompatible moral convictions. I wish that on both these topics he had said more, but even his brief remarks make it clear that we need, both before and while

engaging in controversy—and not only in moral and religious controversy—to ask ourselves in what ways *we* are defective, in what ways we
need to be other than we now are, if we are to move towards, let alone
arrive at, any resolution of the matters that are in dispute.

Clairmont concludes that the fruitful outcome of asking and answering such questions might be to enable us to conduct our conversations at a more appropriate pace, with a greater degree of transparency, and with appropriate suspicion. We fail in the first respect when
we try to move too quickly, because we have failed to recognize how
long it may take for either or both parties to such a conversation to
come to terms with the other, by recognizing the significance that the
contentions of the other should have for them. And, I might add, it
can also on occasion be important not to move too slowly, something
that often signals to the other party a lack of commitment to the conversation. Clairmont takes the significance of the experience of the
practice of penance to be in part that it teaches us how long it may take
for us to come to terms with our own waywardness—with our disagreements with ourselves—and so it should prepare us to be patient
in our conversations with others. And once again, let me add, there are
times when impatience with ourselves is important and times when
impatience with others is salutary.

Why does transparency matter? It is because others must not
only be able to hear what I am saying, but also to perceive *who* is saying
it, to see someone ready to admit when she or he is at a loss, someone
not concealed by what Clairmont calls "the performative and posturing aspects of much dialogue" (p. 118). And we need to be suspicious of
ourselves and aware of the justified suspicion of others. Preparation
for the sacrament of penance teaches us to be "wary of our patterns
of past failure" and to recognize how our attitudes towards future engagement with others are inescapably shaped by those patterns from
the past.

About all of this I take Clairmont to be right. He has added a dimension missing from my discussion, a dimension that is theological,
yet of the first importance for our understanding of moral or philo-

sophical debates that may have nothing to do with religion or theology. For Clairmont forces on us two questions. The first is: How long do we have to be engaged in debate and disagreement with others, before we are entitled to judge that further conversation would be sterile or that our efforts to move beyond disagreement have been a failure? If we have taken seriously what Clairmont has to say, we will have become open to the thought that, where some debates and disagreements are concerned, the answer may have to be: For decades, even perhaps for centuries. It took getting on five hundred years for Catholics and Lutherans to discover that they agreed on the doctrine of justification.

A second inescapable question is: Concerning this or that set of debates and disagreements, what kind of person do I have to become, if I am to be able to contribute as I should to those particular debates and disagreements? If we have taken seriously what Clairmont has to say, we will have become open to the thought that the answer may be: Someone so far removed in self-knowledge from what I am now, that I must withdraw from the conversation for some indefinitely long period and learn how to recognize when it will be right for me to return.

What is theological about these questions and answers is that to take them seriously requires both faith and hope, faith that what one is committing oneself to is not a barren endeavor, hope that the resources that one will need to overcome one's past failures and to become once again a contributor to the conversation will be supplied, faith and hope that go far beyond any confidence that might be derived from the facts about the conversation so far. To live by such faith and hope would be to refuse to concede that the intractability of our deepest moral disagreements cannot somehow be overcome.

III

Clairmont reminds us of something that we can learn only from theologically informed practice. Kaveny warns us against some particular dangers with which theologically informed utterance may threaten us. But her warning is itself in part a theological warning. Kaveny's subject-matter is provided by a particular tradition of American prophetic rhetoric. In raising questions about that tradition she cannot avoid raising questions about rhetoric in general and by so doing points to one more dimension of disagreement missing from my essay. What we communicate to others is never just a matter of what we say, but always and inescapably also a matter of how we say it. And these two are often not independent of each other. How we utter a sentence may alter the sense conveyed by a sentence, as when we speak ironically, sarcastically, tentatively, happily, despairingly. So what can happen to speech when we speak prophetically? This is Kaveny's question.

Her answer draws upon James Darsey's *The Prophetic Tradition and Radical Rhetoric in America*, noting not only the place of such rhetoric in American life, but also how those who speak in this mode address some particular community and presuppose some common good, some shared sense of values to which the speaker can appeal (pp. 135–36). She then examines the political discourse of the biblical prophets and characterizes their rhetoric in four ways. First, just because the prophet speaks as one who is a messenger of God, the only response left open to the prophet's hearers is either obedience or defiance. There is no room left for saying "Yes, but . . . " or "On the other hand . . . " Secondly, just because of this no room is left for further conversation or for compromise. Closely related to these two characteristics is a third. In such discourse there can be no place for the making of complex distinctions. And finally "the use of prophetic indictment generally marks the end of civil discussion" (p. 145). It is impossible to denounce someone in the terms and tone that, for example, Jeremiah employed and to do so courteously. It follows that, if one speaks in the prophetic mode, one had better be right in claiming to be a prophet.

Kaveny then provides a partial history of the use of prophetic discourse in the debates concerning the moral permissibility of abor-

tion during the thirty-five years since the 1973 Supreme Court decision in *Roe v. Wade,* arguing that such discourse has had just those
four characteristics that she has identified and this to very unfortunate
effect: an oversimplified approach to political and electoral choice, a
refusal to entertain, let alone to think through complex distinctions
concerning particular types of case, an alienation of potential allies
arising from an unwillingness to seek out common ground, and, I
should want to add, a hardening in the positions of those who take
themselves to be denounced in such rhetorical displays. Kaveny offers
as an alternative a reading of key paragraphs from *Evangelium Vitae*
and *Lumen Gentium* that focuses on the declaration in paragraph 81 of
Evangelium Vitae that "Not only must human life not be taken, but it
must be protected with loving concern" (p. 156). This summary does
less than justice to Kaveny's account, but it is, I hope, sufficient to enable us to pursue three points further.

I noticed earlier that Kaveny cites James Darsey's assertion that
prophetic rhetoric can only flourish when addressed to a community
with certain shared values. And she notes that Darsey was misled by
this assertion into predicting an end to prophetic rhetoric in America, because of an increasing absence of that kind of agreement in values. Kaveny's later discussion suggests the importance of carrying this
line of thought further. For Darsey was right in seeing that older
agreements on values had been fractured. What he failed to predict
was that the new disagreements, the new conflicts would still presuppose agreements, but of another kind. What kind of agreement do I
have in mind?

What has been notable about the most vociferous recent proponents in the United States of widely different points of view, religious, moral, political, cultural, whether conservative or liberal, is their
shared failure to acknowledge that what they are defending are not just
a set of assertions, but rather a set of answers to questions, questions
that always have some range of alternative answers, questions that
should lead us to be questioning even in our answers. What we get in

consequence are answers without questions, unquestioning answers, answers that resent questioning. And the extent of agreement in this mode of speech and in the presuppositions of its use is at least as remarkable as the disagreements that are voiced in it.

Secondly, we need to ask what it is that recent prophetic rhetoric communicates, whether or not by conscious intention. What is sometimes communicated is aggression, aggression elicited by often unconscious fear, fear that is characteristically of something in oneself. And such aggression is all too apt to be matched by the aggression of those responding to it. Both parties therefore have good reason to question themselves. They will find this the harder to do, if they are misled into thinking in terms of culture wars, as though there is a righteous "us" and an evil "them." "Controversy, at least in this age," said Newman, "does not lie between the hosts of heaven, Michael and his Angels on the one side, and the powers of evil on the other; but it is a sort of night battle, where each fights for himself, and friend and foe stand together" (*Fifteen Sermons Preached before the University of Oxford* [Notre Dame: University of Notre Dame Press, 1997], 201). What Newman said of his age remains true of ours. And, once we have understood this, we will be ready to pose a third question: What kind of rhetoric do we need to participate truthfully in the moral disagreements of the present? Kaveny draws on *Lumen Gentium* in sketching an answer that needs to be spelled out further, both in characterizing the nature of that rhetoric and in explaining how it might function in the peculiar circumstances of American political life. This is a task well worth undertaking.

IV

Daniel Philpott is concerned with how we should think, feel, and act in the wake of violent conflicts, conflicts arising from intractable moral disagreements, in which monstrous wrongs have been done. Sadly, he is not short of examples. He argues for the further development of a

Catholic tradition of peacemaking through forgiveness and reconciliation, and he contrasts a Catholic ethics of political reconciliation, based on biblical texts, with the tenets of liberal peacebuilding. At the core of that Catholic ethics is a conception of restorative justice, of a remaking of fractured human relationships, in which the biblical understanding of mercy plays a key part. "Mercy is the aspect of reconciliation that involves a process of restoration of right relationship" (p. 173). With much the larger part of what Philpott has to say it is not just that I have no quarrel, but that I badly want to learn what he has to teach. What I do have are some further questions.

I am unclear whether he takes the Catholic ethics of political reconciliation—and other religious conceptions of reconciliation—to be superior to or only different from the liberal and secular ethics with which he contrasts it. And, given the way in which, in a number of the situations which he describes, strands from the liberal program are interwoven with strands from the Catholic program, how far are the two programs complementary rather than rivals? There are after all situations in which a wholly secular idiom is going to be more effective in the aftermath of religious conflicts than any religious mode of speech.

In raising these questions I do not think that I am disagreeing with Philpott. But missing from his essay—and given the constraints of space, how could it have been otherwise?—is any consideration of secular conceptions of forgiveness. I think here especially of Charles L. Griswold's recent and justly praised book, *Forgiveness: A Philosophical Exploration* (Cambridge University Press, 2007). Griswold at the opening of his book provides a list of thirteen questions (pp. xx–xxi) that need to be answered by any adequate account of forgiveness. It would be a thoroughly worthwhile enterprise for someone to contrast the answers that Griswold provides as part of a purely secular and philosophical account with the answers to those same questions that are explicit or implicit in Philpott's essay.

Philpott has generous remarks about my work, but he believes himself to be more optimistic than I am as to whether or not certain "ideas can find agreement across traditions, at least in political matters" (p. 170) and more particularly upon whether "members of different traditions can agree upon something very much like the principles of reconciliation that I have derived from the Catholic tradition" (p. 186). Philpott is right in thinking that there is a good deal on which we disagree. I do not for example interpret the consensus that "emerged among the countries of diverse religious and philosophical traditions to sign the Universal Declaration of Human Rights" in 1948 as a "reason for optimism" (pp. 187, 188). Yet there is also much on which we agree, for example, on the possibility of, on occasion, aiming at achieving some overlapping consensus. But what is more important is that Philpott and I are for the most part answering different questions.

My primary concern has been to ask how far certain moral disagreements are intractable, even when parties to a dispute are rational and have goodwill. Philpott's primary concern is with situations in which disagreement has proved intractable, goodwill has been absent, violent conflict has ensued and the problem has become that of how to negotiate and sustain a political settlement that will enable those who continue to disagree to live at peace. Such political settlements are themselves of course subject-matter for moral evaluation. Are they just or unjust, more just or less just? And, if they are not fully just, how should we weigh the unjustice involved in the settlement against the achievement of peaceful coexistence? About the outcomes of continuing disagreements on the answers to such questions I am neither in general optimistic nor pessimistic. Everything depends on the particular cases, on the situation in, say, Northern Ireland or Kosovo or Rwanda. And about particular cases I see no reason why Philpott and I should disagree.

What we do agree about emphatically and enthusiastically is the importance in situations of conflict of arriving at the kind of political settlement that enables those who continue to disagree to treat each other as fully rational agents. And I should want to argue that this is always more important than achieving the kind of political victory that settles disputed moral matters in favor of *our* views, but at the cost of generating such resentment and antagonism in those who have been defeated that rational dialogue with them is no longer possible. Sometimes it is much worse to defeat one's opponents, even by peaceful means, perhaps by an electoral victory, perhaps by winning a lawsuit, while leaving them quite unpersuaded, than to remain in ongoing dialogue, even if it is dialogue that appears to have little prospect of a fruitful outcome. There are sometimes morally worse things than to remain in intractable moral disagreement.

V

Gerald McKenny pays me a large compliment by contrasting my view of moral disagreement with that of Joseph Ratzinger. (McKenny follows Pope Benedict's own lead in distinguishing his utterances as pope from his utterances as a scholar, by referring to the author of the latter as Ratzinger; I shall do the same.) He notes the common ground that Ratzinger and I share in formulating the problem of moral disagreement. And he advances three telling criticisms of my view, although only after providing a remarkably lucid and accurate account it.

His first criticism is that, although my arguments against relativism as a theoretical position may be sound, my position amounts to "a certain kind of relativism in practice" (p. 209). For on my view a number of mutually antagonistic positions may coexist, the adherents of each claiming truly that by their own standards they have vindicated their position, yet none of them able to provide sufficient grounds to convince their opponents. In consequence an external referee—a representative of the liberal state, for example—is free to argue that no particular position should be privileged over any other. So in the arenas of contemporary politics no more authority could be claimed for the precepts of the natural law than for a number of rival and incompatible sets of precepts. His second criticism is of a different kind. My presentation of the precepts of the natural law as specifying the necessary conditions for shared rational deliberation seems to cut short the list of precepts that comprise the natural law: "there is no obvious match between these conditions and the precepts having to do with sexuality and the rearing of children" (p. 211).

Put these two criticisms together and a third emerges. It is that my position cannot differentiate itself from that of a certain kind of liberalism, moreover a kind of liberalism that I have elsewhere rejected and continue to reject. It is a liberalism that affirms that government and other institutions of public life must act on precepts that are neutral between rival and contending moral standpoints, just because none of these standpoints can vindicate its claim to well-founded authority. And the practical effect of my understanding of moral disagreement will be to strengthen such a liberalism. In putting matters in this way I am perhaps going a little further than McKenny does. But I do so because he has, I believe, identified what many perceptive non-Christian critics also take to be a fatal weakness of my position.

McKenny's contrast between my view of moral disagreement and Ratzinger's concerns the genesis of contemporary moral disagreement. On Ratzinger's view, as McKenny describes it, we live in a transitional period, one in which the moral convictions that were Europe's shared Christian heritage are giving way before a new canon of post-Enlightenment values. What is at issue between these two are not the Enlightenment's championing of freedom of thought, equality, and other democratic values, for on these Christian and Enlightenment thinkers are for the most part in agreement. And both are upholders of reason. What divides Catholic Christians from the heirs of the Enlightenment most deeply are their two rival conceptions of reason.

As McKenny characterizes these two conceptions, the first is Augustinian-Platonist, human reason understood as mirroring the Logos, the divine Word, while the second is reason reduced to a set of empirical and technical uses. "With the reduction of reason to empirical and technical rationality, moral values are relegated to the subjective realm, leaving the calculation of the consequences of acts as the sole task of reason in the moral realm" (p. 215). So "Enlightenment reason authorizes and promotes a 'new canon' of values, based on individual liberty, consequentialist moral reasoning, and the idea of progress" (p. 215). How then are the claims of reason, understood in Augustinian-Platonist fashion, to be presented to a culture informed by Enlightenment or post-Enlightenment conceptions of reason?

On Ratzinger's view, although reason can in principle grasp the natural order of the universe and the moral truths that derive from this order, it cannot by itself make those moral truths "fully credible or effectively persuasive." That requires the presentation of moral truth as embodied "in a historical tradition or community. . . . Moral reason is inextricable from the historical tradition or community that is the bearer of moral truth, and to uproot reason from this context is to claim for it a self-sufficiency that it does not possess" (p. 216). We have been brought back by another route to something very close to the claim that Jean Porter made in her essay. And once again I have to defend the powers of reason, while acknowledging that all rational argument is rooted within and is framed from the perspective of some particular historical tradition.

Let me begin from the second criticism that, so McKenny suggests, could be brought against my position, namely, that my account of the precepts of the natural law seems to provide no justification for those precepts that have to do "with sexuality and the rearing of children" (p. 211). Given what I wrote in my opening essay, this criticism has obvious force. For there, after I had initially spoken of the precepts of the natural law as directed towards our common goods, including among them "the good of sexuality and the goods to be achieved by educating and caring for our children" (p. 5), I moved on immediately to a discussion of how precepts of the natural law inform and are presupposed by shared deliberation about our common goods and said nothing further about those goods themselves.

What I would have had to do to make even a beginning at dealing with such goods adequately, would have been to spell out the way in which familial relationships both sustain and are sustained by shared deliberation and how the ends of sexuality have to be integrated into the ends of family life, as in child rearing the parent as rational agent sustains and teaches the child, so that the child gradually develops her or his own potentialities for acting as an independent reasoner. In so doing I would have had to draw upon the experiences of families and individuals in those traditions within which this kind of understanding of sexuality and child rearing has been at home. And I would throughout have been relying on a different conception of the relationship of reason to tradition from that defended by Ratzinger.

On the view that I am taking, the rational justification of moral and other practical claims is an activity that characteristically makes use of concepts and judgments that derive from some particular tradition of rational enquiry. Such traditions of enquiry are generally embedded in the culture of some larger social and moral tradition, yet have at the same time an identity of their own. When they are so embedded, they articulate the moral and other practical commitments of that larger tradition and so make it possible both to criticize those commitments, to revise them, and to ask how far they can be rationally justified. And so it is with that tradition of rational enquiry in which Socrates' initial questioning elicited a succession of enquiries in which the greatest names are those of Plato, Aristotle, Augustine, Ibn Roschd, Solomon Ben Maimon, Albert, and Aquinas, the tradition from which Thomistic Aristotelianism emerges. For that tradition human reasoning is indeed grounded in its participation in the Logos, whether the reasoner is aware of this or that. But sound practical reasoning can proceed without any explicit reference to the Logos. And sound practical reasoning invites the assent of every rational agent. Why does it so often fail to receive such assent, especially when it concerns disputed moral questions?

Ratzinger's answer is that, at least when disputed moral questions are concerned, reasoning as such is bound to be less than credible, less than persuasive, that it is only when and insofar as reasoning is presented as the expression of the commitments of some particular tradition or community that it can expect to receive assent. It would certainly be wrongheaded for me to deny that there may be occasions when the presentation of the conclusions of some piece of sound reasoning as the conclusions of some particular community or tradition induces an assent that would have been withheld if those conclusions had been presented in some other way. But openness to this possibility should not be allowed to distract us from attending to some features of sound practical reasoning that may suggest a different interpretation of continuing moral disagreement, that may suggest that it is more difficult both to engage in and to appreciate sound practical reasoning than we are apt to think. Father Kevin L. Flannery's essay on Aristotle's conception of practical reasoning provides us with an excellent starting-point for identifying some of those features, and I therefore turn to it now, although I have not yet replied fully to McKenny's criticisms.

VI

Picture someone asking herself or himself whether she or he is acting rightly, that is, as they would have to act, if they were to direct themselves towards their final end. Flannery in the course of his elucidation of Aristotle argues that "the inadequacy of bad acts" need not be "immediately apparent to those who perform or contemplate them" (p. 231) and this perhaps because, although their reasoning presupposes some particular conception of their happiness, their final end, that conception has never been made explicit, or perhaps because even when someone has "an erroneous notion of happiness" "it is not necessarily *obvious* that his practical reasoning—or the way he conducts his life—is flawed" (p. 235).

The context for these remarks is an account of the practical syllogism. Flannery begins from a critique of Anthony Kenny's characterization of practical syllogisms and argues that "the ultimate end (happiness, however conceived)" and "its stability as end" are necessary presuppositions "of any piece of practical reasoning" (p. 230), but that it does not follow that a rational agent must always have that ultimate end explicitly in mind, when reflecting on what to do. (As with Aquinas earlier, so here with Aristotle, I shall not pursue issues of interpretation.) If someone is going astray in their practical reasoning, just because they have a mistaken conception of what their ultimate good is, whether implicit or explicit, how might they correct themselves and how might we be able through argument to assist them in correcting themselves? It is at this point that Flannery reminds us that it can be far from obvious that someone is going astray. Why so?

Flannery quotes Aristotle's chiding of the Platonists because they try to argue from their first principle—a first principle established, so they believe, by theoretical reasoning—and so fail to recognize that in our practical reflection we are initially arguing our way not from, but towards some more adequate conception of the first principle, the ultimate end, than any that we as yet possess, beginning instead from judgments about particular goods. For characteristically—and here I am going beyond both Flannery's text and the passages from Aristotle that he cites, but not, I believe, in a way with which either of them would disagree—we fall into error not by mistakenly taking to be goods what are not in fact goods, but by assigning to some goods a kind of importance that they do not have. Pleasure, health, deserved political honors, money, and power are all goods, but none of them is *the* good, the ultimate end. And what importance each of these types of goods should have in my or your life at this or that particular time and place is determined by their relationship to my or your ultimate end. So the agent has to avoid both of two closely related types of mistake: that of misconceiving her or his ultimate end and in consequence attaching too much or too little importance to certain particular goods and that of attaching too much or too little importance to certain particular goods and in consequence misconceiving her or his ultimate end. And there are yet other sources of error.

About misconceptions of our ultimate end, our happiness, Flannery remarks that some may fall into error because they confuse the conditions of happiness with happiness itself. For someone may have judged on the basis of experience "that no one who lives in penury and pain is happy," but has "confused such conditions with what it *means* to be happy" (p. 243), or again someone who has enjoyed some type of activity may, while recognizing correctly that it is good to enjoy this type of activity, conclude incorrectly that it is good *because* it is pleasant, a mistake about the relationship of pleasure to activity that is illuminatingly diagnosed by Aristotle. These mistakes are *philosophical* mistakes, but philosophical mistakes can also be practical mistakes that may and often enough do inform the reasoning of ordinary non-philosophical agents.

A sound mode of practical reasoning is not one that makes it possible for us to avoid mistakes altogether. It is rather one that enables us to identify our mistakes and to learn from them. And practical reasoning, as understood by Aristotle and Aquinas, is just such a method of learning. What Flannery's essay brings out is how difficult it can sometimes be to learn what needs to be learned.

There is another larger implication of his discussion. It is that the enterprise of practical reasoning, thus understood, which has as its goal the achievement of our goods and our good, provides the context within which the point and purpose of our evaluative and prescriptive concepts and precepts become clear. Abstract them from that context and present them in isolation from it, and it will become impossible to render them fully intelligible, let alone defensible and credible. But just such an act of abstraction is characteristic of the vast majority of occasions on which some precept or other of the natural law is invoked in public debate. It is therefore predictable that, when so presented, the precepts of the natural law will generally fail to elicit assent.

If we expect otherwise, it can only be because we have taken for granted some quite other view of the nature of practical reasoning and believe that the justification that practical reasoners give in support of their conclusions ought, if they are genuine justifications, to elicit the assent of anyone whatsoever, no matter what their point of view or their presuppositions. In fact those for whom in Europe and North America today the precepts of the natural law are a good deal less than compelling do in general presuppose from their utilitarian or Kantian or contractarian standpoints a very different view of practical reasoning. So the obstacles to arriving at rational agreement with them are twofold, deriving both from the nature and complexity of practical reasoning, as understood by Thomistic Aristotelians, and from the difficulties that such critics of natural law have in thinking outside the limitations of their own standpoint.

What then is involved in encounters today between those who speak on behalf of the natural law and those who reject its precepts? If we were to spell out the answer to this question in some detail, it might be that the apparent large difference between Ratzinger's view of contemporary moral disagreement and my own might begin to disappear. How so? Consider as an example the apparently unsettlable controversy between defenders of the precepts of the natural law, who believe that the abortion of a human embryo within the first three months after conception is the taking of an innocent life and therefore prohibited, and those who believe that such abortions are morally permissible.

All of those in contention agree that murder, the taking of an innocent human life, is morally prohibited. So it seems at first that Jean Porter must be right and that the concept of murder *is* indeterminate, and that any precept that prohibits murder needs to be supplemented by some further independent principle that is to govern our interpretation and application of the concept of murder. But is this in fact so? We might begin sketching what would, if fully spelled out, be a very long answer from either of two starting-points. One would be the precept of the natural law that forbids the taking of an innocent human life and would attempt to demonstrate, would indeed succeed in demonstrating, that an embryo is an innocent human life. But there is good reason to believe that this line of argument, no matter how well developed, will be unpersuasive except to those already persuaded. So I turn to a second starting-point, that of the nature of the common goods of family life, common goods to the achievement of which the precepts of the natural law are directed. And I begin with the understanding of ourselves that we have as those to whom some of those goods have already been a gift.

As children and adolescents become more and more independent within the family by whom they have been brought up, they generally recognize—to greater or lesser degree—that they owe their increasing independence to those elders, especially their parents, who took responsibility for them when they were wholly dependent. The wrong of infanticide by parents or other family members is not only that it is the taking of an innocent human life, but that those parents and family members have a special responsibility for caring for this particular human individual and ensuring that she or he is able to develop from total dependence to adult independence, just as they have done. This responsibility to care and protect falls especially on the parents. If they cannot discharge it, as might be the case with a too young unmarried mother deserted by the child's father, then someone must be found who will care for and protect the child. So infanticide is a violation of this duty to care for and protect. But the infant three months after birth is the same human individual as the embryo three or six or eight months before birth. So that the very same duty is violated by an abortion.

The peculiar forms that the responsibility to care and protect takes are what they are because those whom we need to care for and protect are potentially independent rational agents, agents with whom we and others will need to deliberate. So that even those precepts of the natural law that are to do with sexuality and the lives of families are precepts that concern the relationships between rational agents.

This bare sketch of an argument needs to be filled out by a more detailed account both of what is involved in the transition from dependence to independence and of what caring for and protecting requires. What should emerge from such an account is an identification of both the common and the individual goods of family life and an explanation of how without familial relationships structured by conformity to the precepts of the natural law those goods cannot be achieved. So a complex argument has to be constructed, one that enables us to understand what practical rationality requires of us in those particular respects. To fail to be persuaded by its conclusion is to fail to be open to what reason requires. And that this argument emerges from the life of a particular community or tradition should of itself add nothing to its persuasive force for rational agents.

By saying this am I putting myself at odds with Ratzinger? Perhaps not so much as might at first appear. For consider what would be involved in advancing this type of argument in some particular situation. Here points made by David Clairmont and Cathleen Kaveny become relevant. Clairmont's emphasis on the need for self-knowledge, especially in respect of our own past and present failures, suggests that, without such self-knowledge the goods of family life may be misidentified and misunderstood. Kaveny's discussion of the effects of different types of rhetoric makes it clear that, if the structure of our reasoning about the goods of family life is to become compelling to those with whom we are in contention, our choice of rhetoric will not be unimportant. Reflection on these points may suggest that the argument against the permissibility of abortion presupposes a conception of the goods of family life that may become fully intelligible to those with whom we are in contention only when presented to them as exemplified in the lives of actual families functioning well within larger communities, of families directed over extended periods of time towards the achievement of their common goods.

If something like this is what Ratzinger means when he argues that it is only in and through some community or tradition that the rational force of moral arguments can become persuasive, then Ratzinger and I are after all not so far apart. And, if Ratzinger is to respond to McKenny's criticism of his position, that "the more Ratzinger emphasizes the de facto dependence of moral truth on its historical vehicle, the more plausibility he lends to the suspicion that the moral values to which he is committed are derived from a historical tradition rather than from a created moral order that is in principle accessible to reason" (p. 219), then he will have to insist, just as I do, that it is the soundness of those moral arguments that he wishes to render persuasive that makes them deserving of assent by rational agents.

It is by so insisting that I respond to McKenny's charge of "practical relativism." What makes my position not relativistic is my commitment to holding that my views on substantive moral questions can be maintained with integrity only for so long as and insofar as I can show that they can be sustained against their rivals by rational argument, so also committing myself not just to continuing disagreement, but to continuing conflict with those who reject the precepts of the natural law and with those who uphold the authority of positive law that is at odds with the natural law. And commitment to this kind of conflict is incompatible with the norms of the liberal state. Notice that nothing in this position requires that my views should in fact become persuasive to those who disagree. That is *in the end* up to them, not up to me or to those who agree with me.

What I am in addition committed to maintaining is the priority of the natural law to human law and to divine law as revealed through the Scriptures. It is not just that the natural law can be known by the exercise of the powers of reason, independently of revelation, but also that the knowledge of divine law afforded by revelation presupposes a prior knowledge of the precepts of the natural law. It is a revealed truth, that is to say, that the truths of the natural law can be known prior to and independently of any revealed truths, including this particular revealed truth. That in holding this I am not being theologically eccentric, a philosopher trespassing in the discipline of theology, a discipline in which he has no professional competence, is confirmed by Father John Coughlin's account of the long history as a result of which in 1983 recognition was accorded to human rights in the Code of Canon Law.

VII

That history is one in which from the late eleventh century onwards the systematization of canon law, indeed the systematization of law, presupposed and was understood as presupposing an anthropological basis for law. Coughlin argues that appeal to this basis of law in human nature has three kinds of importance. First of all, without such a basis for law we would have to treat all law as positive law and positive law— law that is made and unmade at the varying will of sovereign powers— provides no grounds for appeal against such sovereign powers in the name of rights derived from the natural law, a law whose authority is independent of positive law (pp. 251–53).

Secondly, there are those who have claimed that such rights are at home only in Western cultures and that any attempt to judge, say, East Asian practices from the standpoint of the natural law or of any other conception of universal human rights is no more than a project of Western cultural imperialism (p. 253). Against this claim the only adequate reply is an account of how human rights are what they are because human beings—whatever their culture—are what they are. And, thirdly, what such an account lays bare is what is at stake in the debates between those who accept and those who reject the precepts of the natural law. What is in contention are rival conceptions of what it is to be a human being and of how rational agents have to understand both their rationality and their agency, if they are not to misunderstand themselves (pp. 256–58).

That conception of human nature is, according to Coughlin's narrative, already acknowledged in the work of twelfth-century canon lawyers as they proceeded to distinguish divine, natural, and positive law and to identify the place among these of the *ius gentium*. Coughlin gives special attention to the canonists' use of the concept of equity to show how "immutable principles of divine and natural law" can find application in the very different historical circumstances of different communities (pp. 264–65). So far as the treatment of our powers as rational agents is concerned, the canonists' thought is informed by "epistemological optimism" (p. 256) and the aim of the canonist is "to ensure that practical reason rather than power forms the moral basis of the law" (p. 258).

Here Coughlin not only offers support for conclusions that I have reached, but directs our attention to what would follow a denial of those conclusions. If the relationships between communities are not mediated by some shared acceptance of the standards of practical rationality, so that in conflicts between them both have some conception of shared goods and both are constrained by the requirements of practical rationality, then the outcome of conflicts between them will be determined by whichever is the most powerful. The relationships of power to rationality are complex, but, if our discussion is to proceed further, it will become necessary to take account of them and to recognize what needs to be learned from both Marx and Foucault.

The anthropology presupposed by the canonists is of course a theological anthropology, and the biblical narrative at the heart of that theology confirms and illuminates the ascription of fundamental rights to human beings. Cardinal Walter Kasper's work has been seminal in developing that theology and Kasper believes not only "that theological anthropology offers a better foundation for human rights than does that offered by natural law" (p. 260), but also that "since Vatican II the theological foundation has increasingly taken precedence over the natural law argument in the Church" (p. 260). Coughlin agrees with Kasper in recognizing the crucial importance for any adequate understanding of human rights of those biblical and Christological beliefs that give depth and clarity to that understanding. But he insists against Kasper that the theological anthropology does not displace, but complements the rational understanding of human nature and the appeal, based on that understanding, to the precepts of the natural law.

To this very welcome coincidence of views a postscript needs to be added. I said earlier that I take it to be a revealed truth that we can by the exercise of the powers of natural reason recognize the authority of the precepts of the natural law. Now I want to go one step further. It is also a revealed truth that we human beings all of us stand accused before God of our violations of and rebellion against his law. But we could not be rightly held responsible for those violations and that rebellion if we were not aware of God's law, simply *qua* human beings, and not only aware of the precepts that comprise God's law, but aware of the compelling character of their authority. This is the awareness about which Paul wrote in Romans 2:15, when he said of the Gentiles "that the *ergon* of the law is written in their hearts" and that their *suneidēsis* bears witness to it. What Aquinas did was to spell out further this Pauline truth.

VIII

What then is the relationship between the biblical and Christological grounding for human rights, on which Kasper so strongly and rightly insists, and their grounding in the natural law? Although this is not among the questions that Thomas Hibbs addresses directly in his essay, he nonetheless throws important light on how to answer it. His essay achieves a good deal more than this, for it provides a framework within which a number of contentions advanced in the earlier essays can find a place, a framework that also suggests how we might proceed further. Hibbs has no doubts about the powers of practical reasoning. Like Coughlin and myself, he follows Aquinas closely in his conception of those powers. But his self-set task is to emphasize Aquinas's understanding of "the limits to practical reason and the perils for human agency in the course of ordinary human life" (p. 275). And to fully appreciate "the vulnerability of practical reason, its susceptibility to conflict, to the deceptions of evil, and, even, to tragedy" we need "a more refined and more vigilant form of self-knowledge" (p. 275).

Hibbs first focuses attention on the virtue of prudence, the virtue exercised in our choices to act rightly at particular times and places, the virtue through whose exercise general moral truths—the precepts of the natural law—are brought to bear on particulars. For us to act rightly we not only need sound reasoning, but sound reasoning that informs rightly directed desire. And we are always apt to fail, not only because without taking adequate counsel our view of things is one-sided and partial, our relevant memories apt to be defective, our fears and hopes such that we lack the courage to do what prudence enjoys, and our appetites such that we lack the necessary temperateness, but also because we so often deceive ourselves about these things.

Hibbs's account of this vulnerability of the practical reasoner and that reasoner's need for self-knowledge complements what Clairmont wrote in his essay about penitential self-knowledge. And it is not unimportant that the context of Clairmont's discussion was that of interreligious dialogue, dialogue, that is to say, that on the Catholic side of the conversation at least is theologically informed. For, as Hibbs spells out Aquinas's view of what is needed if the exercise of prudence is to be rescued from its vulnerabilities and its proneness to failure, it becomes clear that only a theological account of the virtue of prudence will be adequate. Why is this so? In what way is a purely philosophical account bound to be defective?

It is because a purely philosophical account of the virtues, an Aristotelian account of the virtues, although it may recognize a variety of types of error into which we may fall, is unable to take full account of all those obstacles from within ourselves that have to be overcome in the course of becoming virtuous. It is only from the standpoint of re-vealed truth that the full extent of the complexities and ingenuities of sinful human nature become clear. For his theological account of the relationship between the natural virtues and the gifts of the Holy Spirit Aquinas drew upon Augustine, correcting as well as adding to the Aris-totelian grounding of his philosophical account. And the second part of Hibbs's essay is devoted to a wonderfully lucid exposition of how Aquinas achieves this integration of the Augustinian and Aristotelian.

To put the point more generally: it is only from the standpoint of faith that we are able to delineate the relationship of faith and reason, because it is only from the standpoint of faith that we are able to diagnose the ways in which secular reason misconceives its own powers and underestimates its own vulnerabilities. So, although Kasper is mistaken insofar as he thinks of his biblical and Christological foundation for human rights as an alternative to, as displacing an identification and defence of such rights by appeal to the precepts of the natural law, he is right to insist that our treatment of human rights will be theoretically and practically defective, until and unless we understand them in theological terms.

In the third and fourth parts of his essay Hibbs considers the part played by law, both natural and divine, in educating us, so that we learn how not to be frustrated by the kind of limited understanding and practice of the virtues that is always apt to be transformed into misunderstanding, as, for example, a limited understanding of courage, acquired in the context of the battlefield, may in other contexts lead us to misidentify what is in fact self-assertion as a form of courage. "Precisely that which is necessary to preserve the common good against deadly threats can turn against the common good in an affirmation of the good of one or of a certain class" (p. 296). And Hibbs cites *Coriolanus* for an example of this corruption.

Earlier Hibbs had quoted Aquinas's Augustinian verdict on our pretensions to virtue (*ST* Ia-IIae, 85, 3), that "all the powers of the soul remain destitute of a proper order, by which naturally they are ordained to virtue, and this deprivation itself is called a wound of nature" (p. 289). The wounds of nature are ignorance, afflicting the intellect and undermining its virtue of prudence, malice, afflicting the will and undermining its virtue of justice, infirmity, afflicting the irascible appetites and undermining their virtue of courage, and inordinate desire, afflicting the concupiscible appetites and their virtue of temperateness. By ignorance Aquinas means not just a lack of knowledge and understanding, but a failure to know and understand what we should have recognized that we need to know and understand, together with a failure to be aware of this failure. So Hibbs and Aquinas jointly have strengthened further the case that Clairmont made concerning our need for penitential self-examination before, during, and after our engagement in controversy with those who reject the precepts of the natural law. But beyond this they suggest that we have to understand both the case to be made for and the case made out against the precepts of the natural law in a new light.

IX

At various points I have sketched—no more than sketched—the philosophical case that has to be made in support of the precepts of the natural law. That case has, I hope, been strengthened by the response that Jean Porter's forceful objections to my initial formulations elicited, by Kevin Flannery's insightful discussion of Aristotelian practical reasoning, and by Gerald McKenny's critical commentary. But, of course, were that philosophical case to be spelled out in full detail, it would have to be at very much greater length. And for the point and purpose of that exercise to be fully understood it would have to be framed with an eye to what has been said by David Clairmont, by Cathleen Kaveny, and by Daniel Philpott. Failure to take adequate account of Clairmont's and Kaveny's theses would be damaging, perhaps fatally damaging to the presentation of the argument. Failure to take account of Philpott's thesis would leave us at a loss when our disagreements with others resulted in a breakdown in the conversation. But this is not all that should have been learned and not even perhaps the most important thing that should have been learned.

Philosophers characteristically have presented their arguments in ways that suggest that they are attempting to secure agreement from those with whom they are in controversy. This mode of presentation presupposes a set of underlying agreements on which the contending parties can rely and a set of shared standards about what does and does not amount to an argument sufficient to establish or to refute each of the contending positions. But this kind of underlying agreement and this sharing of standards is now notably absent in much of our philosophical and moral discourse, as I had occasion to remark over eighteen years ago in the introduction to my Gifford Lectures (*Three Rival Versions of Moral Enquiry* [Notre Dame: University of Notre Dame Press, 1990], 1–8). By now there is even less that is agreed and shared and so we must not present our arguments as if we expected to elicit agreement from those with whom we are in contention. We should instead say to them at the outset that, although our arguments are not only the strongest available to us, but should, in our view, be found rationally compelling, we nonetheless also believe that the presuppositions of those with whom we are in controversy will prevent them from recognizing this. In disputes over the authority of the precepts of the natural law those presuppositions are characteristically of two kinds. Some concern the nature of rationality and what it is that makes an argument rationally compelling. And some have to do with the notion of an *end,* as I characterized it in my introductory essay, and therefore with the relationships of desire to practical judgment and to action.

In spelling out the relevant presuppositions our project will be threefold. First, we will be changing the focus of the debate, moving from a consideration of the arguments that we have been advancing to an examination of the presuppositions of those in disagreement with us. Secondly, we will be attempting and hoping to undermine not only our philosophical opponents' confidence in their use of some of their key concepts, but also the confidence that in our post-Enlightenment culture many nonphilosophical individuals have in the everyday counterparts of those same concepts. I have in mind first, the cluster of concepts that have to do with such notions as those of reason, of presuppositionless reason, of the self-knowledge of rational agents, of rational and irrational desire, and, secondly, the cluster of concepts that have to do with such notions as those of happiness, enjoyment, contentment, and the satisfaction of desire, and correspondingly with those of frustration, deprivation, discontent, and anxiety.

What needs to be shown and, I believe, can be shown in each case is that in spelling out these notions, so that they become available for practical use, those who employ them are confronted either with incoherence or with sets of equally unacceptable alternatives. They are confronted with incoherence if what they have to assert in arguing against the precepts of the natural law is at odds with what they find themselves committed to elsewhere in their thought and activity. They are confronted with unacceptable alternatives, if the cost that they would have to pay for the kind and degree of conceptual revision that would remove this inconsistency is such that they would have to choose between *either* continuing in inconsistency and admitting the reality of this incoherence to themselves as well as to others *or* protecting themselves against such incoherence, but leaving themselves practically resourceless in some other key respects. To show that this is so is a program of philosophical work much of which has yet to be done, although it is a program that I envisaged in the closing sections of my introductory essay and earlier, elsewhere.

What that philosophical work has to address is the continuing inability of post-Enlightenment moral philosophy to reconcile its Enlightenment affirmation of the authority of reason with its inability to find sufficient rational grounds for accepting some version of Kantianism rather than some version of utilitarianism or some version of utilitarianism rather than some version of Kantianism or perhaps for rejecting all versions of both. The numerous attempts to do this have in fact failed and failed by the standards of the Enlightenment, even if post-Enlightenment moral philosophers are rarely able to acknowledge this. When they are so able, their only coherent resort is to some version of Nietzsche or some version of Rorty, and the subtext of some of the most interesting recent writing in such moral philosophy is a summons to resistance to both Nietzsche and Rorty.

It is however not only philosophical work that needs to be done. What I had not recognized up till now and have learned from the essays of my colleagues is the need for and importance of a third aspect of our project, that of providing a theological explanation both of why the hostile philosophical critics of the precepts of the natural law are vulnerable to this critique of their presuppositions and of why it is difficult, usually insuperably difficult, for them to acknowledge this.

The kind of theological account that we need will have to draw upon the resources of that theological anthropology, at its foundations biblical and Christological, of which Coughlin, McKenny, and Hibbs all speak, an anthropology that provides a perspective without which we cannot understand the relationship between the powers and the limitations of reason. We badly need, that is, a theology of reason, one that draws upon both Kasper and Ratzinger, one that has at or near its core an account of the kind of self-knowledge needed by the sound practical reasoner, an account that develops part of Clairmont's essay a good deal further. Such an account would be informed by Augustine's understanding of the relationship between a particular reasoner's self-knowledge and her or his knowledge of God. It would be a theology that would, if adequately carried through, illuminate not only those dangers to self-knowledge that are threatened by the Enlightenment's rejection of God and of the natural law, but also those dangers that threaten us, if we become overconfident and complacent in our defence of the precepts of the natural law.

I have made a series of strong assertions about what needs to be done both philosophically and theologically, if we are to carry our shared enterprise any further. But I would be obviously guilty of just the lack of self-knowledge about which I have been speaking, if I did not remark immediately that those assertions should at once be transformed into a series of questions. For we do not know in advance of engaging in the relevant philosophical and theological enquiries what their outcome will be.

We can perhaps derive some limited confidence from the convergence of views that is already evident in quite a number of essays in this book. But even that confidence must be limited by our awareness of the range of rival and alternative standpoints with regard to the natural law which we have simply ignored, at least in these essays.

Notable among them are the kind of account of the natural law that has been developed by Germaine Grisez and John Finnis, the very different views taken by a range of Catholic philosophers from Gabriel Marcel to Jean-Luc Marion, and the critique of Catholic conceptions of natural law by some Reformed and Lutheran thinkers. How far we have been justified in restricting the scope of our discussions turns on what progress we have made so far and what continuing progress we will be able to make in the future. We hope that others will be encouraged to join with us in carrying forward this project.

abortion, 2, 8, 131, 195, 198, 213, 253
and application of "murder," 321,
338–40
and Catholic casuistic tradition,
157, 161n.38
prophetic rhetoric regarding, 134,
137, 146–51, 152, 153, 154, 155,
158, 326–27
public opinion in United States
regarding, 146–47, 150–51, 158,
161n.36
Roe v. Wade, 146, 147, 148–49,
162n.43, 327
and South Dakota, 148–49
Abu-Nimer, Mohammed, 171
adultery, 55, 71–72, 290, 291
Afghanistan, 170
Africa, 182, 188
Ahlstrom, Sidney, 135
Albert the Great, 58, 79
Alito, Samuel, 149
Allan, Donald J., 250n.32
Allen, John L., Jr., 253
Ambrose, St., 295
American Life League, 148
amnesty, 168, 178
angels, 82
anxiety, 282, 283, 294–95
Apel, Karl-Otto, 215–16
Aquinas, Thomas
vs. Aristotle, 132–33, 275, 283, 295,
303n.15, 312n.77
vs. Augustine, 27, 275, 283,
289–90, 292, 293–94, 295

on capital vices, 301n.5
on charity, 83, 293–94, 300
on common good, 69
on conflict and tragedy, 275, 299
on counsel, 275, 280–82, 292, 298,
299
on courage, 275, 276, 289,
294–300, 301n.4, 302n.6,
312n.76, 346
on the Decalogue, 58, 69, 70–72,
74–75, 80, 85–86, 94n.19,
290–93, 308n.53, 319–20
on deliberation, 15–16, 17–18,
247n.8
on dispensation, 70–71
on faith, 300
on fear, 298
on first principle of practical reason, 4–6, 57, 59–63, 67–68, 70,
72–74, 78, 80, 86–87, 92n.5,
94n.19, 95n.24, 112, 290, 318
on God and human reason, 14
on God as *summum bonum*, 284
on God's creation, 293, 309n.57
on God's existence, 290–91
on God's grace, 274, 290, 292, 293
on God's revelation, 81, 291
on habits, 279–80
on hope, 299
on human dignity, 265
on human nature, 83, 86, 90–91,
95n.23, 256, 265
on *intellectus*, 20–21, 278, 303n.15
on the interior sense, 278

Aquinas, Thomas (*cont.*)
on justice, 71, 94n.19, 112, 129n.28,
276, 277, 294, 321, 346
on knowledge of the good,
247n.9
on lawgivers, 75, 88
on martyrdom, 299–300, 312n.77
on memory, 278–79
on the mentally defective
(*amens*), 6
on mercy, 191n.15, 292, 295,
308n.53
on moral blindness, 132
on moral lapses in cultures, 7–8
on natural inclinations, 60–61,
67, 73–74, 75–84, 86, 89, 93n.9,
95nn.23, 24
on penance, 112, 129n.28
on philosophical disagreement,
14, 18
on positive law, 150, 267
on practical reason, 3, 4–6, 11,
15–16, 54–58, 59–63, 67–68, 70,
72–74, 76–78, 80, 82–84, 86–87,
88–89, 92n.5, 94n.19, 95n.24,
112, 210, 228, 230–31, 247nn.8,
9, 258, 274–82, 289, 290–91,
294, 298–99, 317, 318, 337–38,
344
on precepts of natural law, 3, 4–8,
11, 23, 24, 26–27, 39–40, 54–58,
59–63, 67–75, 78, 80, 83, 85–91,
115, 132–33, 210, 267, 278,
290–94, 305n.28, 317–19, 344
on primary substance, 303n.15
on prudence, 94n.21, 132–33,
274–75, 276, 277–82, 289, 293,
294–95, 298, 299–300, 303n.15,
344–45, 346
on repentance, 295
on salvation, 274, 289

on self-knowledge, 275, 276,
291–92
on sexuality, 5, 9, 60, 69, 83,
95n.23
on sin, 27, 56, 115–16, 132, 239, 289,
291–93
on suicide, 83, 95n.23
on temperance, 276, 277, 294,
302n.6, 346
on theoretical reason, 14–15, 59,
75–76, 81, 82, 83–84, 86, 89–90,
280–81, 290–91, 298–99
on truth, 14–15, 20–21, 60, 256,
265, 280–81, 290–91, 298–99
on ultimate human good (*beati-tudo*), 13–15, 18, 39–40, 45–51,
74, 80–82, 83–84, 208, 210, 228,
230–31, 245, 268, 284, 299
on unity of natural law, 63, 67–70,
72–73, 78, 87, 93n.9, 94n.19,
290, 338
on universality of natural law, 3,
6–8, 11, 24, 54–58, 84, 85,
210–11, 290, 318–19, 344
on virtue, 77, 81, 88, 94n.19,
95n.23, 112, 274–82, 289–90,
293–300, 301n.5, 302nn.6, 7,
304n.21, 317, 346–47
on wounds of nature, 289, 291–92
Aquinas's *Commentary on the Meta-physics*: II lect. 2, 290, 15
Aquinas's *De Divinis Nominibus*: X,
1.1, 857, 77
Aquinas's *De Veritate*: I, 1, 20–21
Aquinas's *Summa Contra Gentiles*: I,
4, 291
Aquinas's *Summa Theologiae*
Boyle on, 273–74
Chenu on, 273–74
and *exitus-reditus* scheme in
neo-Platonism, 273–74

I 1.1, 81
I 1.4, 81
I 1.6 ad 3, 247n.9
I 1.8 ad 2, 81
I 2.1 ad 1, 299
I 60.5, 82, 83
I 79.12, 95n.24
I-II 1.1, 81
I-II 1.5, 13
I-II 1.6, 81, 95n.24
I-II 2.1–8, 13
I-II 3.6, 13
I-II 4.6–7, 13
I-II 6.2, 69, 83
I-II 8.1, 95n.24
I-II 9.1, 95n.24
I-II 10.1, 95n.24
I-II 10.2, 95n.24
I-II 14.2, 17
I-II 14.2c, 247n.8
I-II 14.3, 15–16
I-II 14.6 ad 2, 247n.8
I-II 14.6c, 247n.8
I-II 25.7, 95n.24
I-II 44.2, 298
I-II 44.2 ad 2, 298
I-II 64.4 ad 3, 299
I-II 66.4, 302n.6
I-II 66.4 ad 2, 298
I-II 73.2, 27
I-II 77.2, 9
I-II 85.3, 289, 346
I-II 90, 88
I-II 90.4, 69
I-II 91.2, 76–77, 305n.28
I-II 91.3, 49, 58, 59, 75, 88
I-II 92.4, 7–8
I-II 94.2, 5, 57, 58, 59–63, 67–71, 78, 80, 82, 93n.9, 94n.19, 95n.24, 318–19
I-II 94.3, 80

I-II 94.4, 56–57, 72, 87–88
I-II 94.4 ad 2, 87–88
I-II 94.5, 56
I-II 94.6, 56, 290
I-II 95.1, 58, 85
I-II 95.3, 162n.44
I-II 97.3, 88
I-II 98.2 ad 3, 292
I-II 98.5, 291
I-II 98.6, 291
I-II 99.1 ad 1, 68–69
I-II 99.2 ad 1, 290
I-II 99.3 ad 2, 58, 75, 88
I-II 99.4, 58, 75, 88
I-II 100.1, 80, 86, 94n.19
I-II 100.3 ad 1, 58, 80, 85
I-II 100.8 ad 3, 70–72, 319–20
II-II 2.4, 14
II-II 4.2 ad 3, 81
II-II 4.7, 81
II-II 23.1, 293
II-II 23.2, 293
II-II 23.8 ad 3, 293
II-II 26.2, 83
II-II 26.7, 294
II-II 46.2, 6
II-II 47.3, 159n.4
II-II 47.5 ad 2, 278
II-II 47.6, 95n.24
II-II 47.8, 278
II-II 49.1 ad 2, 279
II-II 49.1 ad 3, 278
II-II 49.2 ad 1, 159n.4, 278
II-II 49.3 ad 2, 280
II-II 49.3 ad 3, 280
II-II 49.8, 281
II-II 52.1 ad 3, 282
II-II 52.1 obj. 1, 281
II-II 52.2 ad 1, 282, 305n.24
II-II 52.2 ad 3, 282
II-II 52.2 obj. 1, 282

Aquinas's *Summa Theologiae* (*cont.*)
  II-II 52.4, 292
  II-II 53.3, 277
  II-II 64.5, 83, 95n.23
  II-II 64.7, 83, 95n.23
  II-II 65.1, 95n.23
  II-II 68.5, 293
  II-II 79.1, 94n.19
  II-II 92.4, 6, 7
  II-II 92.5, 6
  II-II 94.4, 159n.3
  II-II 101.4, 70
  II-II 104.5, 95n.23
  II-II 108.1, 95n.23
  II-II 108.2, 77, 95n.23
  II-II 122.1, 94n.19
  II-II 123.1, 294
  II-II 123.2, 295
  II-II 123.2 ad 2, 295
  II-II 123.4, 295
  II-II 123.5, 295, 296
  II-II 123.6 ad 1, 297
  II-II 123.8, 295
  II-II 124.2, 312n.80
  II-II 124.3, 300
  II-II 124.3 ad 1, 312n.78
  II-II 124.5, 300
  II-II 136.4, 312n.76
  II-II 141.6, 95n.23
  II-II 147.1 ad 2, 95n.23
  II-II 152.2, 70
  II-II 154.11, 83, 95n.23
  III 68.12, 6
  III 85.3, 129
Argentina: political reconciliation
  in, 170, 178
Aristotle
  vs. Aquinas, 132–33, 275, 283, 295,
    303n.15, 312n.77
  on the categories, 247n.11
  on courage, 276–77
  on deliberation, 15, 17–18
  on desire, 276–77, 284
  on exposing unwanted infants, 8
  on form and actuality, 241, 243
  on the four causes, 239
  on habits, 279
  on happiness (*eudaimonia*)/
    ultimate human good, 39–40,
    41, 45–51, 228, 230–31, 233–35,
    241–46, 247n.3, 249n.20,
    250n.32, 268, 284, 285–86,
    335–39
  on hierarchy of goods, 283
  on immaterial substances/first
    principles, 239–41, 243,
    250n.27
  on incontinence, 286
  on involuntary action, 312n.77
  on justice, 87, 231, 244, 277
  on philosophical contemplation,
    243, 250n.32
  on Plato's notion of a universal
    good, 232, 234–35, 236–37,
    241–42, 336
  on pleasure and human activities,
    231–33, 248nn.12, 15
  on potentiality and actuality, 241
  on practical reason, 227–31,
    244–45, 268, 275, 276–77, 286,
    335–39, 347
  on the practical syllogism, 227–31,
    238–39, 244–45, 335–36
  on prudence, 132–33, 275, 277
  on temperance, 244, 276–77
  on theoretical enquiry, 15
  on tragedy, 284, 285, 306n.36
  on truth, 15
  on virtue, 236, 244–45, 249n.21,
    268, 275, 276, 283, 284, 285–86,
    297, 345
Aristotle's *De Anima*, 277
Aristotle's *De Motu Animalium*: vii,
  701a17–20, 246n.1

Aristotle's *Eudemian Ethics*
  i,2,1214b6–11, 235–36
  i,2,1214b7–8, 244
  i,2,1214b11–13, 236
  i,2,1214b24–25, 236
  i,2,1214b26–27, 244
  i,3,1214b28–1215a7, 237
  i,4,1215a25–b5, 237–38
  i,6,1216b26–32, 242–43
  i,6,1216b30–32, 250n.31
  i,7,1217a35–40, 250n.32
  i,8,1217b16–35, 247n.11
  i,8,1218a1–15, 247n.11
  i,8,1218a15–24, 236–37, 241–42,
    249n.19
  i,8,1218a28–30, 250n.30
  i,8,1218b10–12, 235
  ii,1,1219b11–16, 247n.10
  vii,2,1235b13–18, 249n.23
  vii,6, 249n.20
  viii,3,1248b16–26, 250n.32
  viii,3,1248b20–25, 244
  viii,3,1249a14–16, 244–45
  viii,3,1249b16–19, 243
  viii,6, 249n.20
  x,8,1178b7–23, 250n.33
Aristotle's *Metaphysics*
  ii,993b20–21, 15
  iii, 239
  iv,2,1003b5–7, 247n.11
  vi,1,1026a27–31, 240
  ix,6,1048a36–b4, 250n.28
  ix,8,1050b20–21, 241
  xii, 239–40
  xii,6,1071b12–22, 250n.27
  xii,7,1072b3–4, 235
  xii,10,1075a10–11, 235
  xii,10,1075a13–15, 235
Aristotle's *Nicomachean Ethics*
  i,4,1095a17–22, 234
  i,6,1096a17–29, 232, 247n.11
  i,6,1096a19–22, 248n.12

i,6,1096a27–28, 234
i,6,1096b25–26, 234
i,6,1096b26–29, 232, 247n.11
i,7,1098a16–17, 233
i,8, 232
i,10,1100b11–17, 249n.21
i,12,1101b25–26, 231
i,12,1102a2–4, 235, 247n.10
ii,6,1106b14–16, 249n.21
iii,3,1112b10–11, 15
iii,3,1112b11–20, 247n.7
iii,3,1112b13–14, 17
iii,3,1112b15–20, 246n.1
iii,4,1113a15–b2, 238
ix,4, 249n.20
ix,12,1172a1–8, 233–34, 244,
  248n.16
x,2,1172b9–11, 238
x,4, 232
x,4,1174b31–33, 248n.14
x,4,1175a18–21, 248n.15
x,5, 238
x,5,1175a21–26, 232
x,5,1175b24–1176a3, 248n.12
x,5,1176a17–19, 247n.9
x,7,1177a12–18, 243
x,7,1177b28–29, 244
x,8,1178b7–23, 244, 250n.33
Aristotle's *Physics,* 36–38, 50, 202
Aristotle's *Poetics,* 306n.36
Aristotle's *Politics*: vii,1335b19–21, 8
Aristotle's *Posterior Analytics,* 281
  i,13,78a22–b4, 250n.26
Aristotle's *Topics,* 242–43
  i,2,101a32–34, 250n.31
  viii,11,161a33–37, 250n.31
Arnold, Matthew, 133, 140, 142
asceticism, intellectual and moral,
  114–15, 256–57, 323
assent of rational agents
  and the Enlightenment, 53–54
  and human nature, 54

assent of rational agents (*cont.*)
 to principles of justice, 203–4
 vs. rational vindication, 1–3, 4, 11,
  32–38, 50–52, 54–55, 90–91,
  200–201, 210–12, 341, 347–50
Athanasius, St., 173
atheism, 111, 128n.25
Augustine, St., 157, 345, 346, 350
 vs. Aquinas, 27, 275, 283, 289–90,
  292, 293–94, 295
 vs. Aristotle, 285–86
 on charity, 293–94, 310n.59
 conversion of, 286–87
 on courage, 288–89
 on happiness, 284–85, 289–90
 on Platonists, 284–85
 on pursuit of the good, 158
 on self-knowledge, 287–88
 on sin, 287–88
 on social relationships, 285, 289
 on Socratic rationalistic optimism, 283
 tragedy and conflict in the good
  life, 275, 276, 285, 289
 on ultimate end of human life,
  284–85, 288–90
 on virtue, 284–86, 289–90, 292
Augustine's *City of God*, 284–86
 bk. XIX, 1, 284–85
 bk. XIX, 3, 285
 bk. XIX, 4, 286, 288–89, 306n.35
 bk. XIX, 5–6, 285
 bk. XIX, 27, 290, 292
 bk. XX, 165n.59
Augustine's *Confessions*, 284
 VII, 9, 288
 VII, 10–17, 286
 VIII, 7, 287, 288
 VIII, 11–12, 286
Australia: native peoples in, 182,
 188

Barnes, Jonathan: "Aristotle and the
 Method of Ethics," 248n.18
Barnes, Michael: *Theology and the
 Dialogue of Religions*, 124n.7
Barth, Karl, 174, 199
Benedict XV, 174
Benedict XVI
 on the Enlightenment, 192n.22
 on forgiveness and reconcili-
  ation, 169, 174, 191n.19
 on human dignity and human
  rights, 252, 266
 on natural law and universal
  morality, 54, 198
 on peacebuilding, 169, 171
 See also Ratzinger, Joseph
  Cardinal
Bentham, Jeremy, 3, 27–28, 45
 on pleasure and happiness, 29, 41,
  42, 44
Bercovitch, Sacvan: *The American
 Jeremiad*, 135
Berman, Harold, 262
Berti, Enrico: *Le Ragioni di
 Aristotele*, 248n.18
Boethius, 66
Bonhoeffer, Dietrich, 174
Bosnia
 civil war in, 186
 political reconciliation in, 170,
  178, 184, 185
Bourdieu, Pierre: on *habitus*,
 124n.7
Bowlin, John, 92n.6, 301n.4
Boyle, Leonard, 273–74
Bradley, Gerard V., 160n.21
Brague, Remi, 308n.53
Brock, Stephen, 247n.8, 312n.77
Buddhism, 120, 122n.2
Bush, George W., 137, 153–54, 162n.43
Butler, John, 135

Calvin, John, 48, 174, 197
Cambodia, 170
canon law
  Code of Canon Law of 1917, 266
  Code of Canon Law of 1983,
    254–55, 266, 341
  equity in, 254, 262, 263–65, 342–43
  Gratian's *Decretum*, 263–64
  and historical consciousness, 254,
    264–65
  and human dignity, 266–67
  and human nature, 255–56, 259,
    265, 267–69
  and human rights, 241, 254–56,
    262, 265–68, 341, 342
  methodology of canonists,
    262–65, 267–68, 269, 342–43
  and practical reason, 258, 261, 343
capital punishment, 2, 152, 253
Catechism of the Catholic Church,
  The
  on penance and reconciliation,
    110
  on reason, 1–2, 197
  on universality of natural law,
    1–2, 197
Catholic casuistic tradition, 157,
  161n.38
charity, 83, 293–94, 300
Chenu, Marie-Dominique, 273–74
Chile: political reconciliation in,
  184
Cicero, Marcus Tullius
  on memory, 279
  on natural law, 63, 67
common good
  Aquinas on, 69
  and canon law, 259
  and courage, 296–97, 300, 346
  and family relationships, 47, 334,
    339–40

and prophetic rhetoric, 145
relationship to political authority,
  174–75
relationship to precepts of natural law, 2, 5, 47, 315–17, 322,
  333–34, 339–40
common ground, 4, 11
communism, 167, 180, 253
comparative religious ethics:
  motivations in, 125n.15
Compendium of the Social Doctrine
  of the Church, 182
Cone, James, 126n.22
confession, 98, 109–10, 121, 127n.24,
  128n.25
consequentialist moral reasoning,
  215, 223, 333
  regarding punishment of human
    rights violators, 171, 181
  in utilitarianism, 28–29, 38–39,
    41–42, 49–50, 54–55
contraception, 2
contractarians, 51, 338
cooperation with evil, 157, 165n.60
Corecco, Eugenio, 259
Counter-Reformation, 40
courage, 19, 284
  Aquinas on, 275, 276, 289,
    294–300, 301n.4, 302n.6,
    312n.76, 346
  Augustine on, 288–89
  and the common good, 296–97,
    300, 346
  as endurance, 297–98, 299–300,
    312n.76
  as instrumental virtue, 276, 296
  and justice, 277, 302n.6
  relationship to honor, 296–97
  relationship to patience, 298,
    299–300, 312n.76
  and temperance, 302n.6

Darsey, James: *The Prophetic Tradition and Radical Rhetoric in
America*, 135–36, 326, 327
death, 283–84, 295–96, 312n.77
Debs, Eugene, 135
deliberation
Aquinas on, 15–16, 17–18, 247n.8
Aristotle on, 15, 17–18
and liberalism, 211–12
precepts of natural law presupposed by, 3, 23–27, 30–32,
51–52, 74–75, 113, 114–15,
210–12, 316–17, 318, 331–32, 333,
339–40
as social activity, 14–17
democracy, 214
broad consensus in, 197
and moral disagreement, 167–68,
195–97
role in peacebuilding, 167–68, 171,
177, 178, 189n.2
value of, 53
Descartes, René, 37
desire
Aristotle on, 276–77, 284
goods vs. objects of, 12–13, 16,
46–47, 201–2, 243, 336
for honor/prestige, 46, 47, 235–36,
238, 239, 243, 245, 336
for love, 238, 239
for money, 16, 22, 25–26, 46, 47,
114, 115–16, 119, 121, 235, 235–36,
236, 243, 245, 256–57, 336
and moral blindness, 7, 132
for pleasure, 16, 22, 25–26, 46, 114,
115–16, 119, 121, 238, 239,
256–57, 276, 336
for power, 16, 22, 25–26, 46, 47, 48,
114, 115–16, 119, 121, 257, 336
relationship to moral rules,
48–49
Diamond, Larry, 189n.2

distributive justice, 27
Donagan, Alan, 74, 94n.21
Douglas, Stephen, 160n.21

East Timor: political reconciliation
in, 170, 177, 180, 182, 184
El Salvador: political reconciliation
in, 170, 184, 185
Enlightenment, the, 106–7, 195
attitudes toward moral norms
during, 40–41, 53–54, 92n.1,
131–32, 200, 201, 204–5, 213,
217–18, 222, 224
human rights during, 192n.22,
214, 254–55, 265
and liberal peace paradigm, 169,
170–71, 173, 178, 188
and mercy, 173
Ratzinger on, 192n.22, 214–15, 216,
217–18, 221, 222–24, 332–33
reason during, 53–54, 131–32, 200,
201, 204–5, 213, 214–15, 216,
217–18, 222, 224, 332–33, 349
Eucharist, the, 164n.54
European Union, 174, 185
euthanasia, 137, 151, 152, 153, 213, 253

faith, 14, 81, 217, 219, 259, 261, 300,
325, 345–46
Fall, the, 199
family relationships
and the common good, 47, 334,
339–40
marriage, 86, 152, 195, 196
rearing and education of
children, 5, 60, 64, 211, 266,
332, 333–34, 338–40
same-sex marriage, 152
fascism, 167
Finnis, John, 61, 94n.21, 162n.39, 351
on natural inclinations, 73–74, 75,
93n.9

on practical reason, 73–74, 80,
    92n.5
forgiveness, 121, 182, 329
    after violent conflicts, 168, 169,
        183–85, 187
Forsythe, P. T., 174
Foucault, Michel, 343
France
    French Revolution, 253
    relations with Israel, 185
Fredericks, James, 124n.12
free markets, 168
free will, 254, 256, 257, 258, 259, 265
friendship, 285, 293–94, 300

Gadamer, Hans-Georg, 125n.14
Galileo Galilei, 36–38
Gauthier, René-Antoine, 247n.10
genetic testing, 195
George, Robert P., 92n.5, 160n.21
Gerardi, Archbishop Juan, 171
Germany
    political reconciliation in, 177,
        182, 184
    relations with Poland, 185
Glendon, Mary Ann: *Abortion and
    Divorce in Western Law,* 150
God
    counsel of, 281, 282
    creation of, 293, 309n.57
    essence of, 282
    existence of, 290–91
    forgiveness by, 182, 184
    goodness of, 83
    grace of, 54, 202, 260, 274, 284,
        290, 292, 293
    kingdom of, 154–55, 156, 157,
        163n.54
    knowledge of, 5, 14, 290–91, 298
    law of, 56, 58, 64, 65–66, 69, 70,
        70–72, 76–77, 88, 258–61, 263,
        290, 305n.28, 341, 342–43, 346

    love for, 94n.19
    in neo-Platonism, 273–74
    providence of, 76–77, 199
    punishment by, 182
    revelation of, 14, 54, 81, 88, 94n.19,
        127n.23, 199, 202, 219, 225,
        258–61, 290–91, 341, 343–44,
        346, 350
    as *summum bonum,* 284
    truth about, 60
    ultimate justice of, 260
    union with, 290
goods
    of animal nature, 5, 60, 67–68
    as internal to practices, 98–99,
        100–106, 112–13, 124nn.7, 8,
        125n.14, 126n.16
    of interreligious conversation, 98,
        100–106, 109, 110–12, 116–18,
        119–20, 121–22, 125nn.14, 15,
        126n.16, 322–23
    vs. objects of desire, 11–13, 16,
        25–26
    of physical nature, 5, 60, 67–68
    of reason, 5, 60–61, 67, 68
    relationship to natural inclina-
        tions, 73–74, 75–84, 93n.9,
        95n.24
    supreme human good/final end,
        13–15, 17–20, 25, 39–40, 45–51,
        80–82, 105, 201–2, 208, 210, 228,
        230–32, 233–35, 241–46,
        249n.20, 250n.32, 256, 257, 268,
        284–85, 335–39, 348
    thematic vs. nonthematic knowl-
        ege of the good, 230–35, 237,
        238, 245, 247n.9
    See also common good
Gopin, Rabbi Marc, 171
Gratian
    Decretum, 63–64, 67, 263
    on natural law, 63–64, 67, 93n.11

Gray, John, 89, 92n.1
greed, 48, 239
Gregory XVI, 265
Griffin, James, 30
Griffiths, Paul, 122n.2
Grisez, Germaine, 61, 63, 94n.21, 351
    on natural inclinations, 73–74, 75
    on practical reason, 73–74, 80,
        92n.5, 93n.9
    on unity of natural law, 93n.9
Griswold, Charles L.: *Forgiveness: A
    Philosophical Exploration*, 329
Grotius, Hugo, 217, 218
Guatemala
    political reconciliation in, 171,
        177, 179–80, 184
    Recovery of Historical Memory
        Project, 179–80
    truth commission in, 171
Gustafson, James, 139–40, 156
Gutiérrez, Gustavo, 124n.7

Habermas, Jürgen, 215–16
habits, 18, 317
Hall, Pamela, 61, 62, 93n.8, 95n.25
happiness
    Aristotle on, 39–40, 41, 45–51, 228,
        230–31, 233–35, 241–46, 247n.3,
        249n.20, 250n.32, 268, 284,
        285–86, 335–39
    Augustine on, 284–85, 289–90
    Bentham on pleasure and, 29, 41,
        42, 44
    Mill on pleasure and, 29, 41–42,
        43, 44
    and pleasure, 29, 41–42, 44, 238
    in utilitarianism, 27, 28, 29–30,
        38–39, 41–44, 45, 49–50, 52,
        208, 268
    See also Aquinas, Thomas, on
        ultimate human good
        (*beatitudo*)

Harte, Colin, 162n.39
Hartley, David, 41
Hebrew Bible/Old Testament,
    154–55, 172, 173, 182
    Book of Wisdom 9:14, 281–82
    the Decalogue, 58, 69, 70–72,
        74–75, 80, 85–86, 94n.19,
        290–93, 308n.53, 319–20
    Elijah, 138
    Elisha, 138
    exploitation of the poor in,
        141–42
    Hosea, 140–41, 144, 148
    Isaiah, 141–42, 144, 148, 173
    Jeremiah, 143–44, 145, 326
    jubilee tradition, 180–81
    prophetic rhetoric in, 133–46, 148,
        157, 326
Hegel, G. W. F., 262
Helmholtz, Richard, 263
Herdt, Jennifer A., 123n.4
Heschel, Abraham Joshua, 139,
    147–48
Hinduism, 122n.2
Hinze, Bradford: *Practices of
    Dialogue in the Roman
    Catholic Church*, 124n.7
historical traditions/communities
    Aquinas on lawgivers, 75, 88
    and equity in canon law, 254, 262,
        263–65, 342–43
    imaginative identification with
        other traditions, 33–36, 37–38,
        50, 106–7, 207
    Ratzinger on moral truth and,
        201, 213–25, 333, 334–35,
        340–41
    relationship to truth, 201, 205,
        206–7, 212–25, 333, 334–35,
        340–41
    See also Kantianism; Thomism;
        utilitarianism

Hobbes, Thomas, 171
  on power, 48
Holy Spirit
  and counsel, 281, 282, 293
  and human dignity, 259–60
homosexuality, 195, 198
honor, 9–10
hope, 299, 325
Hudson, Deal, 137
Hugh of St. Victor, 93n.11
Huguccio of Ferrara: on natural law
  and reason, 65–66, 67, 68,
  93n.16
human dignity
  and human rights, 175, 215, 252,
    254, 259–60, 265, 266–67
  and peacebuilding, 175, 176
  Ratzinger on human rights and,
    215, 252, 266
human embryo research, 195
human equality, 27, 75–76, 91, 131,
  195, 214, 332
human nature, 2, 20, 301n.5
  Aquinas on, 83, 86, 90–91, 95n.23,
    256, 265
  free will as characteristic of, 254,
    256, 257, 258, 259, 265
  and human end (*telos/finis*),
    13–15, 45–51, 81, 256, 257,
    268
  reason as characteristic of, 74,
    254, 256, 258, 259, 265
  relationship to human rights, 91,
    253–54, 255–58, 260–61,
    267–68, 269–70, 342
  relationship to moral principles,
    10–11, 90–91, 201–2
  sinfulness of, 47–48, 155, 345–46
  as social, 257, 258
  and universality of natural law,
    54, 90–91, 257–58, 342, 344
  See also natural inclinations

human rights, 53, 251–70
  and canon law, 254–56, 262,
    265–67, 341, 342
  and Christian theology, 252, 254,
    255, 258–61, 266–67, 269
  during the Enlightenment,
    192n.22, 214, 254–55, 265
  freedom of association and
    assembly, 266
  freedom of religion, 192n.22, 253
  freedom of speech, 266, 267
  freedom of the press, 253
  freedom of thought and belief,
    214, 332
  and historical consciousness, 254,
    255, 261–62, 265–67, 269
  and human dignity, 175, 215, 252,
    254, 259–60, 265, 266–67
  and human nature, 91, 253–54,
    255–58, 260–61, 267–68,
    269–70, 342
  Kasper on, 254, 259–61, 265, 343,
    344, 346, 350
  and natural law, 252, 254, 255–58,
    260–61, 263–68, 266–68, 341,
    342, 344, 346
  and peacebuilding, 171, 178, 188
  punishment of violators of, 168,
    178, 181–82, 185, 188
Hume, David, 49, 315
Huntington, Samuel P., 198n.2

individual liberty, 131, 215, 216, 223,
  333
international law, 174, 175
International Theological Commission: "Memory and
  Reconciliation," 183
interreligious conversation, 97–122,
  124n.12
  between Catholics and Lu-
    therans, 325

interrreligious conversation (*cont.*)
and Christian penitential practice, 98, 99, 108, 109–12, 116–22,
127n.24, 129n.27, 322–25, 345
and Christian reconciliation, 98,
99, 108, 109–11, 112, 116–22,
127n.24
vs. comparative religious ethics,
125n.15
goods internal to, 98, 100–106,
109, 110–12, 116–18, 119–20,
121–22, 125nn.14, 15, 126n.16
and moral consistency, 104–5,
106, 109, 111–12
and moral scope, 104, 105–6, 109,
112
and moral understanding, 104,
106, 109, 110–11, 116–17, 121,
125nn.14, 15
role of self-knowledge in, 98, 99,
109, 110–12, 117, 118, 119
role of the past, 97, 98–99, 105,
113–14, 118–20, 121–22, 122n.2
Iraq, 170
Irenaeus, St., 173
Irwin, Terrence: "Aristotle's Method
of Ethics," 248n.18
Israeli-French relations, 185

Jaffa, Harry, 310n.64
Jansen, Cornelius, 48
Jesus Christ, 125n.13, 165n.58, 199
call to conversion, 110
commandments to love God and
neighbor, 94n.19
death and resurrection, 127n.23,
154–55, 156, 157–58, 164n.54,
173–74
and forgiveness, 184
as fulfillment of Old Testament
prophetic books, 154–55

as Incarnation, 127n.23, 163n.54,
259, 274
as the Logos made flesh, 214–15
John Birch Society, 135
John of Ostian, 264
John Paul II
on anthropological basis of
law, 252
on the Church as mirror of
justice, 255
and Code of Canon Law of 1983,
255
on culture of life vs. culture of
death, 134, 136–37, 151–54, 156
death penalty opposed by, 152
on distribution of resources, 153
Dives in Misericordia, 173, 174
on ecumenical dialogue, 97
Evangelium Vitae, 134, 136–37,
151–54, 155–56, 157, 158,
163nn.51, 52, 54, 164n.55,
165n.60, 327
on forgiveness and reconciliation, 159, 174, 184
on human rights, 255, 266
on mercy, 173
on peacebuilding, 159, 171
on principle of cooperation with
evil, 157, 165n.60
Ut Unum Sint, 97, 122n.1
Veritatis Splendor, 216
on violence, 153
Johnson, Luke Timothy
on atheism and sin, 111, 128n.25
The Creed, 128n.25
John XXIII: *Pacem in Terris,* 265–66
Jolif, Jean Yves, 247n.10
Jubilee Year 2000, 183
justice, 2, 19, 122, 251
Aquinas on, 71, 94n.19, 112,
129n.28, 276, 277, 294, 321, 346

Aristotle on, 87, 231, 244, 277
Church as mirror of, 255, 269–70
and courage, 277, 302n.6
economic justice, 10, 153, 196
just wars, 131, 161
and mercy, 264
Rawls on, 203
as reconciliation, 172–77, 178
restorative justice, 173–74, 329
as virtue, 71, 94n.19, 276, 277, 321, 346
Justinian, 262

Kantianism, 132, 171, 251
and avoidance of lying, 38
and historical tradition, 216, 220
and moral rules as exceptionless, 38–39
and prudence, 277
and reason, 2–3, 38, 39, 49, 74, 80, 169, 315, 338, 349
and retributivism, 171
vs. Thomism, 2–3, 9, 51, 74, 80, 94n.21, 168–69, 188–89, 315, 338
vs. utilitarianism, 2–3, 38–39, 49, 315
Kasper, Walter Cardinal: on human rights, 254, 259–61, 265, 343, 344, 346, 350
Kenny, Anthony: on practical syllogisms, 227–31, 238–39, 335–36
Kerry, John, 137, 160n.21
King, Martin Luther, Jr.: "I Have a Dream" speech, 136, 159n.17
Kosovo: political reconciliation in, 170, 178, 330
Kuhn, Thomas
on incommensurability of paradigms, 37
on paradigm shifts, 170

Lachtermann, David, 303n.13
Lassalle, Ferdinand, 42
Leo XIII: *Rerum Novarum*, 265
liberalism
and moral disagreement, 195–201
and political reconciliation, 329
and principles of justice, 203–4
vs. Thomism, 201–5, 211–12, 331, 341
Lincoln, Abraham, 160n.21
Lochman, Jan Milic, 174
Locke, John, 171
on broad consensus, 197
love
for God, 94n.19
for neighbor, 94n.19, 264
for one's enemies, 264
loyalty, 9–10
Lumen Gentium, 134, 154–55, 165nn.57, 58, 327, 328
Luther, Martin, 48, 197, 308n.53, 351

Machiavelli, Nicolò, 48
MacIntyre, Alasdair
After Virtue, 100, 123n.3, 124n.8, 131, 322–23
on Clairmont, 314, 322–25, 340, 345, 347, 350
Clairmont on, 98, 99–108, 109, 111, 112–19, 123n.3, 126nn.16, 22, 127n.24
on Coughlin, 314, 341, 342–44, 351
Coughlin on, 251, 254, 256–57, 258, 268, 269
on Flannery, 314, 335–38
on goods internal to practices, 98–99, 100–106, 112–13, 124nn.7, 8, 125n.14, 126n.16
on Hibbs, 314, 344–47, 350
Hibbs on, 288
on Kasper, 343, 344, 346, 350

MacIntyre, Alasdair (*cont.*)
  on Kaveny, 314, 322, 325–28, 340,
    347
  Kaveny on, 131, 132
  on McKenny, 314, 331–35, 340–41,
    350
  McKenny on, 197–98, 200–213,
    216, 222–23, 224–25, 331–32
  on Philpott, 314, 322, 328–31, 347
  Philpott on, 168–69, 170, 171, 177,
    185, 188–89, 329–30
  on Porter, 314–22, 333, 338, 347
  Porter on, 54–56, 58, 61, 74–75, 91,
    92n.1
  on Ratzinger, 331, 332, 334–35, 338,
    340–41, 350
  *Three Rival Versions of Moral
    Enquiry,* 123n.4, 348
  "What Has Christianity to Say to
    the Moral Philosopher?," 323
  *Whose Justice? Which Ratio-
    nality?,* 106–8
Mandela, Nelson, 183
Marcel, Gabriel, 351
Marion, Jean-Luc, 351
Maritain, Jacques, 187–88, 221
marriage, 86, 152, 195, 196
Marx, Karl, 343
Massingale, Bryan N., 126n.18
McCarthy, Joseph, 135
McDowell, John, 301n.5
means and ends, 8–9, 247n.10
  deliberation about, 17–18, 247n.8
  practical syllogisms, 227–31,
    238–39, 244–45, 335–36
  in utilitarianism, 38–39, 42, 49–50
"Memory and Reconciliation," 183
Mennonites, 174
mercy, 173, 174, 264, 329
  Aquinas on, 191n.15, 292, 295,
    308n.53

Milbank, John, 309n.57
Mill, John Stuart
  on avoidance of lying, 38
  on pleasure and happiness, 29,
    41–42, 43, 44
  Utilitarianism, 41–42
  on virtue, 42, 49–50
Miller, Perry, 135
Mitchell, Brian, 95n.27
Moltmann, Jürgen, 174
Moore, Michael, 37
moral blindness, 7–8, 132
moral pluralism, 55–56, 84–91, 206,
    213–14
moral relativism, 206, 207–10,
    212–13, 252, 331, 341
moral skepticism, 52, 253–54
Morrow, Maria: "Pornography and
    Penance," 127n.24
murder, 55, 71–72, 290, 291, 320–21,
    338–40

native peoples: reintegration rituals
    of, 182, 188
natural inclinations
  Aquinas on, 60–61, 67, 73–74,
    75–84, 86, 89, 93n.9, 95nn.23, 24
  Finnis on, 73–74, 75, 93n.9
  Grisez on, 73–74, 75
  relationship to goods, 73–74,
    75–84, 93n.9, 95n.24
  relationship to practical reason,
    82–84
  relationship to precepts of natu-
    ral law, 60–61, 73–74, 86
  relationship to virtue, 77
natural sciences, 36–38, 40
  scientific method, 256
Nelson, Daniel, 61–62, 93n.8
neo-Platonism: *exitus-reditus*
    scheme in, 273–74

Neuhaus, Fr. Richard John, 137
Newman, John Henry Cardinal, 328
New Testament, 172, 173
  Col. 3:11, 260
  1 Cor. 9:24–27, 125n.13
  1 Cor. 12:13, 260
  1 Cor. 13:12, 165n.63
  Eph. 5:15, 281
  Gal. 3:28, 260
  Luke 11:23, 165n.62
  Mark 9:40, 165n.63
  Matt. 12:30, 165n.62
  Matt. 22:37–39, 94n.19
  Rom. 2:14–15, 197, 344
  Rom. 2:15, 308n.53
New Zealand: native peoples in, 188
Nietzsche, Friedrich, 349
  Socrates and *Birth of Tragedy,* 283
nihilism, 206, 213
nongovernmental organizations
  (NGOs), 168, 169
North America: native peoples in,
  182, 188
Northern Ireland, 330
  political reconciliation in, 184

O'Donovan, Oliver, 199
O'Neill, Barry, 183
Orthodox Christianity, 188

Pascal, Blaise, 48, 275
Paul, St., 308n.53
  Col. 3:11, 260
  1 Cor. 9:24–27, 125n.13
  1 Cor. 12:13, 260
  1 Cor. 13:12, 165n.64
  Eph. 5:15, 281
  and idolatry, 144, 148
  Rom. 2:14–15, 197, 344
  Rom. 2:15, 308n.53
Paul VI, 178

peacebuilding, 167–89
  liberal peace paradigm, 169,
    170–71, 172, 173, 178, 181, 184,
    185, 188
  and overlapping consensus,
    186–87
  primary vs. secondary wounds,
    175–76, 179
  relationship to natural law, 169
  relationship to Scripture, 169
  restorative political practices,
    176–85
  role of amnesty in, 168, 178, 182
  role of democracy in, 167–68, 171,
    177, 178, 189n.2
  role of reconciliation in, 169,
    171–72, 174–85, 328–31
  role of truth commissions in, 171,
    174, 179–80
  and victims, 168, 171, 175–76,
    179–80, 184
Peirce, Charles, 206
penance, 180
  Aquinas on, 112, 129n.28
  and interreligious conversation,
    98, 99, 108, 109, 110–11, 116–24,
    129n.27, 323–25, 345
  and justice, 112, 129n.28
  and self-knowledge, 98, 99, 109,
    110–12, 117, 323–24, 345, 347
  See also sin
Petersen, David L.: *The Prophetic
  Literature,* 160n.23
Phillips, Wendell, 135
physics
  of Galileo, 36–38
  impetus theory, 36–38, 50
  of Newton, 37
Pieper, Josef, 279
Pius VI, 265
Pius IX, 265

Pius XI: *Quadragesimo Anno,* 265
Plato
  Apology, 283–84
  on the good, 232, 234–35, 236–37,
    241–42, 336
  Laws: v,736D3–4, 250n.31
  Republic, 296
  on tragedy, 306n.36
pleasure
  Aristotle on human activities
    and, 231–33, 248nn.12, 15
  Bentham on happiness and, 29,
    41, 42, 44
  and happiness, 29, 41–42, 44, 238
  quality vs. quantity of, 29, 41–42
  of sexual activity, 9
Poland
  political reconciliation in, 184
  relations with Germany, 185
political authority, 6, 174–75
Pontifical Commission of Justice
    and Peace, 265
Pontifical Council for Interreligious
    Dialogue: *Dialogue and
    Proclamation,* 127n.23
Porter, Jean, 123n.4, 200
positive law
  Aquinas on, 150, 267
  vs. natural law, 56, 64, 88, 150, 252,
    257–58, 261, 263, 267, 341,
    342–43
  relationship to human rights,
    252–53, 257–58
poverty, 2
power, 20, 258
  desire for, 16, 22, 25–26, 46, 47, 48,
    114, 115–16, 119, 121, 257, 336
  of interest groups, 196–97
  of majorities, 196–97
practical reason
  Aquinas on, 3, 4–6, 11, 15–16,
    54–58, 59–63, 67–68, 70, 72–74,

76–78, 80, 82–84, 86–87, 88–89,
  92n.5, 94n.19, 95n.24, 112, 210,
  228, 230–31, 247nn.8, 9, 258,
  274–82, 289, 290–91, 294,
  298–99, 317, 318, 337–38, 344
Aristotle on, 227–31, 244–45, 268,
  275, 276–77, 286, 335–39, 347
as autonomous and self-
  sufficient, 74, 90, 203–4,
  221–22, 223, 225, 315
and canon law, 258, 261, 343
and conflict, 275, 276
limits of, 198–201, 203–25, 275,
  281–82, 289, 301n.4, 350
practical syllogisms, 227–31,
  238–39, 244–45, 335–36
precepts of natural law as first
  principles of, 3, 23–27, 30–32,
  51–52, 57–58, 59–63, 70, 71–75,
  78, 80, 86–87, 88, 92n.5, 94n.19,
  112, 210–11, 318
relationship to natural inclinations, 82–84
role in moral disagreement, 3,
  14–19
and self-knowledge, 275, 276
vs. theoretical reason, 14–15, 16,
  18, 19, 21–22, 25, 57, 58, 59,
  75–76, 81, 82, 83–84, 86, 89–90,
  280–81, 290–91, 298–99, 317
and tragedy, 275, 276
and truth, 20–22, 23
types of moral disagreement,
  8–11, 348
See also deliberation; precepts of
  natural law
precepts of natural law, 349–51
  application to particular situ-
    ations, 6–7, 55–56, 58, 71–72,
    75, 85–89, 91, 112, 132–33, 278,
    290, 292, 303n.15, 314–15,
    319–22, 338–40

Aquinas on, 3, 4–8, 11, 23, 24,
26–27, 39–40, 54–58, 59–63,
67–75, 78, 80, 83, 85–91, 115,
132–33, 210, 267, 278, 290–94,
305n.28, 317–19, 344
regarding child rearing, 5, 60, 64,
332, 333–34, 338–40
as exceptionless, 24, 39–40,
257–58
as first principles of practical
reason, 3, 23–27, 30–32, 51–52,
57–58, 59–63, 70, 71–75, 78, 80,
86–87, 88, 92n.5, 94n.19, 112,
210–11, 318
Golden Rule, 80
Gratian on, 263–64
and human rights, 252, 254,
255–58, 260–61, 263–68, 341,
342, 344, 346
inviability of innocent life, 5, 23,
30, 55, 71, 257, 258, 267, 320–21,
338–40
knowledge of, 6–7
as necessary conditions of shared
rational enquiry, 3, 23–27,
30–32, 51–52, 74–75, 210–12,
316–17, 318, 331–32, 333, 339–40
preservation of human life, 5, 23,
60, 61, 68, 79, 95n.23, 115, 210,
257, 258, 267
primary precepts, 4–8, 11, 23–27,
39–40, 56, 57–58, 59–63, 71–73,
80, 85–87, 94n.19, 112, 210, 318
prohibition against adultery, 55,
71–72, 290, 291
prohibition against lying, 5, 30,
55, 115, 247
prohibition against murder, 55,
71–72, 290, 291, 320–21,
338–40
prohibition against theft, 55,
71–72, 257, 258, 290, 291, 320

relationship to common good, 2,
5, 47, 315–17, 322, 333–34,
339–40
relationship to Decalogue, 58, 69,
70–72, 74–75, 80, 85, 290–93,
318, 319–21
relationship to divine revelation,
341, 343–44, 349–50
relationship to natural inclinations, 60–61, 73–74, 86
relationship to prudence, 62,
93n.8, 274–75, 277–82, 344–45
relationship to supreme human
good, 39–40, 99
respect for liberty of another, 23,
74, 115, 196, 210, 257, 258
respect for property, 5, 7–8, 23, 55,
115, 210, 257, 258, 264
right of self-defense, 83, 95n.23,
163n.51, 264
secondary precepts, 6, 56, 86–87,
112
as self-evident, 59, 80, 85, 86,
92n.5, 94n.19, 290
regarding sexuality, 5, 9, 60, 64,
69, 83, 95n.23, 211, 332, 333,
338–40
specificity of, 6–7, 55–56, 58,
71–72, 75, 78–79, 80, 85–89, 91,
112, 132–33, 314–16, 319–22,
338–40
See also universality of natural
law
pride, 288
principle of cooperation, 157,
165n.60
progress, idea of, 215, 223, 333
prophetic rhetoric, 131–65, 325–28,
340
regarding abortion, 134, 137,
146–51, 152, 153, 154, 155, 158,
326–27

prophetic rhetoric (*cont.*)
  dangers of, 133–34, 142–46, 147–51,
    153, 155, 156, 157–58
  as prophetic indictment, 138–46,
    156, 326
  and Protestantism, 17, 134, 135, 151,
    155, 158, 326
  role of common values in, 135–36,
    138, 140–41, 142
  and Roman Catholicism, 134,
    136–37, 151–58
  in Scripture, 133–46, 148, 157
Protestantism, 40, 188, 199
  Calvin, 48, 174, 197
  Evangelicals, 134, 137
  Luther, 48, 197, 308n.53
  and prophetic rhetoric, 17, 134,
    135, 151, 155, 158, 326
  Puritans, 135
prudence
  Aquinas on, 94n.21, 132–33,
    274–75, 276, 277–82, 289, 293,
    294–95, 298, 299–300, 303n.15,
    344–45, 346
  Aristotle on, 132–33, 275, 277
  and command, 278, 293
  and counsel, 275, 280–82, 298
  and judgment, 278, 293
  and memory, 278–79
  relationship to precepts of natu-
    ral law, 62, 93n.8, 274–75,
    277–82, 344–45
  and temperance, 302n.6
Puritans, 135

Ratzinger, Joseph Cardinal
  on Christian believers, 219,
    220–21
  on the Enlightenment, 214–15,
    216, 217–18, 221, 222–24,
    332–33
  eschatology and politics, 223–24
  on human dignity and human
    rights, 215
  on human flourishing and
    politics, 223
  vs. Kant, 216, 220
  MacIntyre on, 331, 332, 334–35,
    338, 340–41, 350
  on moral truth and historical
    tradition, 201, 213–25, 333,
    334–35, 340–41
  and natural law, 252
  on natural law and universal
    morality, 54, 198
  on nonbelievers, 218, 219–20
  on reason, 214–18, 219–24, 332–33,
    334–35, 340–41
  See also Benedict XVI
Rawls, John
  on broad consensus, 197
  on the good, 202–3
  on overlapping consensus,
    186–87
  on principles of justice, 203
reason
  and Catholicism, 1–2, 197, 199
  as characteristic of human na-
    ture, 74, 254, 256, 258, 259, 265
  during the Enlightenment, 53–54,
    131–32, 200, 201, 204–5, 213,
    214–15, 216, 217–18, 222, 224,
    332–33, 349
  and imaginative identification
    with other traditions, 33–36,
    37–38, 50
  and Kantianism, 2–3, 38, 39, 49,
    74, 80, 169, 315, 338, 349
  as mirroring the Logos/divine
    Word, 214–15, 219, 222, 332–33,
    334
  vs. passion, 276–78
  preconditions of shared rational
    enquiry, 3, 23–27, 30–32, 51–52,

74–75, 210–12, 316–17, 318,
331–32, 333, 339–40
and principles of justice, 203–4
and Protestantism, 197–98, 199
relationship to courage, 296
relationship to faith, 259, 261,
345–46
relationship to historical tradi-
tions/communities, 4, 11, 32,
33–35, 37, 198–201, 203–25, 348
relationship to power, 343
relationship to universality of
natural law, 1–2, 3, 6, 54, 197
technical-calculative reduction
of, 215–16, 332–33
and utilitarianism, 2–4, 38–39,
54–55, 169, 315, 338, 349
See also assent of rational agents;
practical reason; theoretical
reason
reconciliation
after violent conflicts, 169, 171–73,
177–85, 328–31
Christian practice of, 98, 99, 108,
109–11, 112, 116–24, 127n.24, 156
as justice, 172–78, 184
and mercy, 173, 174
and overlapping consensus,
186–89
primary vs. secondary restorations, 176–77, 178, 184
restorative political practices,
176–85
and right relationship, 172, 173,
177–78, 184
role of acknowledgment in,
179–80, 182, 188
role of apology in, 182, 183, 184,
185, 187, 188
role of forgiveness in, 168, 169,
183–85, 187, 188
role of just institutions in, 177–78

role of punishment in, 168, 178,
181–82, 185, 188
role of reparations in, 180–81, 184,
185, 188
Reformed Church, 351
repentance, 156, 182, 183, 184, 295
reproductive technology, 195
retributivism, 171, 181
Ricoeur, Paul, 125n.14, 309n.57
Robert, John, 149
Roland of Cremona: on natural law,
66–67, 68
Roman Catholic bishops, 108, 109,
111, 127nn.23, 24
Rorty, Richard, 349
rule of law, 171, 175, 181
rules and virtues of enquiry, 21–22
Rwanda: political reconciliation in,
170, 177, 180, 182, 184, 330

salvation, 269
Aquinas on, 274, 289
Schiavo, Terri, 162n.46
scholasticism
and definitions of natural law,
63–70, 72, 93n.11
and societal conventions, 84–85
synderesis in, 66–67
Schweiker, William, 125n.14
Scripture
and justice, 172
and mercy, 173, 174
prophetic rhetoric in, 133–46, 148,
157, 326
and reconciliation, 172–73, 174
relationship to natural law,
63–64, 65–66, 69, 197, 198, 341,
350
relationship to peacebuilding, 169
sin of idolatry in, 140–41, 144
See also Hebrew Bible/Old Testament; New Testament

self-interest, 132, 136, 257
self-knowledge, 300, 340, 350
   Aquinas on, 275, 276, 291–92
   Augustine on, 287–88
   and habit, 279
   in neo-Platonism, 287–88
   and penance, 98, 99, 109, 110–12,
      117, 323–24, 345, 347
self-sufficiency and virtue, 281,
   283–84, 289, 295
sexuality, 196
   Albert the Great on, 79
   Aquinas on, 5, 9, 60, 69, 83, 95n.23
   precepts of natural law regarding,
      5, 9, 60, 64, 69, 83, 95n.23, 211,
      332, 333, 338–40
   Stephen of Tournai on, 64
Shakespeare's *Coriolanus*, 311n.70,
   346
Sierra Leone: political reconciliation
   in, 182, 184
sin
   Aquinas on, 27, 56, 115–16, 132,
      239, 289, 291–93
   and atheism, 111, 128n.25
   in human nature, 47–48, 155,
      345–46
   of idolatry, 140–41, 144
   and moral blindness, 132
   original sin, 177, 199, 259, 289
   self-knowledge of, 287–88
   wounds of nature resulting from,
      289
   See also penance
Singer, Peter, 213–14
Smith, Jonathan Z., 123n.4
Socrates, 283–84, 285, 286, 291–92, 294
Sokolowski, Robert, 45
South Africa
   political reconciliation in, 170,
      171, 174, 182, 183, 184

Truth and Reconciliation Commission (TRC), 171, 174
Southern, R. W., 94n.17
speculative reason. *See* theoretical
   reason
stem cell research, 137, 152, 153
Stephen of Tournai: on natural law,
   64, 69
Stoicism, 222, 283, 288
Stout, Jeffrey, 123n.4, 199, 209
Sudan, 170, 186
suicide, 83, 95n.23, 196, 288

Taylor, Charles, 186
temperance, 95n.23, 277, 297, 302n.6,
   345, 346
   as instrumental virtue, 276, 296
theft, 55, 71–72, 290, 291, 320
theoretical reason
   first principles of, 59
   vs. practical reason, 14–15, 16, 18,
      19, 21–22, 25, 57, 58, 59, 75–76,
      81, 82, 83–84, 86, 89–90,
      280–81, 290–91, 298–99, 317
   and truth, 15, 20–22
Theravada Buddhism, 120
Thomism, 109, 126n.18, 251
   and happiness, 40
   vs. Kantianism, 2–3, 9, 51, 74, 80,
      94n.21, 168–69, 188–89, 315,
      338
   vs. liberalism, 201–5, 211–12, 331,
      341
   rational vindication of, 1–3, 4, 11,
      32–38, 50–52, 54–55, 90–91,
      200–201, 210–12, 341, 347–50
   vs. utilitarianism, 2–4, 30–32, 33,
      38–39, 44–52, 54–55, 168–69,
      170, 188–89, 208, 211, 315
Tierney, Brian, 93n.16, 95n.27
torture, 8–9, 253, 259

tragedy, 292–93, 295, 299
  Aristotle on, 284, 285, 306n.36
  Augustine on, 275, 276, 285, 289
Troeltsch, Ernst, 222
truth
  Aquinas on, 14–15, 20–21, 60,
    256, 265, 280–81, 290–91,
    298–99
  goodness of, 20–21, 114
  John Paul II on, 216
  Peirce on, 206
  and practical reason, 20–22, 23
  relationship to historical tradi-
    tions/communities, 201, 205,
    206–7, 212–25, 333, 334–35,
    340–41
  search for, 15, 20–22, 23, 24, 34–36,
    114, 115, 117, 118–19, 120–21,
    122n.2, 126n.22, 127n.24, 257,
    258, 280–81
  and theoretical reason, 15, 20–22
Tutu, Desmond, 171, 174

Ulpian: on natural law, 63, 67
United Nations, 171, 174, 185
  Universal Declaration of Human
    Rights, 187–88, 253, 266, 330
United States
  Bill of Rights, 253, 266
  Catholic bishops in, 174
  Democratic Party, 137, 152
  Medicare and Medicaid pro-
    grams, 154
  Republican Party, 137, 152, 153,
    162n.46
  Revolution, 135
  Roe v. Wade decision, 146, 147,
    148–49, 162n.43, 327
  role in peacebuilding, 171
  slavery in, 160n.21
  2000 presidential election, 136

2004 presidential election, 137,
    152, 160n.21
unity of natural law
  Aquinas on, 63, 67–70, 72–73, 78,
    87, 93n.9, 94n.19, 290, 338
  Grisez on, 93n.19
  and scholasticism, 63–70
universality of natural law
  Aquinas on, 3, 6–8, 11, 24, 54–58,
    84, 85, 210–11, 290, 318–19,
    344
  Catechism of the Catholic Church
    on, 1–2, 197
  relationship to human nature, 54,
    90–91, 257–58, 342, 344
  relationship to reason, 1–2, 3, 6,
    54, 197
utilitarianism, 27–36, 132, 251
  Bentham on pleasure and hap-
    piness, 29, 41, 42, 44
  consequences of actions in,
    28–29, 38–39, 41–42, 49–50,
    54–55
  happiness in, 27, 28, 29–30, 38–39,
    41–44, 45, 49–50, 52, 208, 268
  vs. Kantianism, 2–3, 38–39, 49,
    315
  and lying, 38
  Mill on pleasure and happiness,
    29, 41–42, 43, 44
  and moral rules, 28, 30–32, 38–39,
    41, 44–45
  and pain, 29
  and prudence, 277
  and reason, 2–4, 38–39, 54–55, 169,
    315, 338, 349
  and satisfaction of preferences,
    29–30, 42, 43–44
  vs. Thomism, 2–4, 30–32, 33,
    38–39, 44–52, 54–55, 168–69,
    170, 188–89, 208, 211, 315

Vatican II, 260, 343
  Dignitatis Humanae, 266
  Gaudium et Spes, 259, 266
  Lumen Gentium, 134, 154–55,
    165nn.57, 58, 327, 328
  Nostra Aetate, 188
  and political reconciliation, 175
Virginia Bill of Rights, 253
virtue
  and anxiety, 282, 283, 294–95
  Aquinas on, 77, 81, 88, 94n.19,
    95n.23, 112, 274–82, 289–90,
    293–300, 301n.5, 302nn.6, 7,
    304n.21, 317, 346–47
  Aristotle on, 236, 244–45, 249n.21,
    268, 275, 276, 283, 284, 285–86,
    297, 345
  Augustine on, 284–86, 289–90,
    292
  cardinal virtues, 276, 289,
    302nn.6, 7
  of enquiry, 21–22
  and habit, 279–80, 317
  instrumental virtues, 276, 296
  intellectual virtues, 277–78
  median status of, 297
  Mill on, 42, 49–50
  natural vs. theological, 274
  and self-sufficiency, 281, 283–84,
    289, 295
  and Socrates, 283–84, 285, 286,
    294–95
  and tragedy, 284
  See also charity; courage; faith;
    hope; justice; prudence;
    temperance
Vogler, Candace, 239, 301n.5
Volf, Miroslav, 171

war, 2, 169, 253
  just wars, 131, 161
  See also peacebuilding
Weber, Max, 215
Weigand, Rudolf, 93n.11
Welch, Robert, 135
Westberg, Daniel, 94n.21, 303n.10
White, Stephen, 306n.36
Wittgenstein, Ludwig, 43
Woods, Michael, 247n.11
World Bank, 169, 170, 171
World Day of Peace, 174
World War I, 174

Yearley, Lee, 124n.12
Yoder, John Howard, 199

Zagzebski, Linda, 304n.21
Zingano, Marco, "Aristotle and the
    Problems of Method in
    Ethics," 248n.18